AdvancED Flex 4

Shashank Tiwari

Elad Elrom

AdvancED Flex 4

Copyright © 2010 by Shashank Tiwari and Elad Elrom

Credits

Contents at a Glance

Contents

Foreword

From the outset, Flex was created to make it easy for developers to take advantage of the Flash Player's runtime capabilities, to help them build cross-platform rich Internet applications.

Today, developers use Flex to deliver a wide range of applications—from multimedia-rich consumer experiences to functional line-of-business applications that run behind the firewall. Flex is an essential component of the Flash platform, which includes powerful client runtime technologies, designer and developer tooling, server technologies, and services.

With each release of Flex, Adobe enhanced and extended the framework, enabling developers to create highly expressive, data-intensive applications by building on the new features and capabilities offered by the client runtimes and server technologies within the Flash platform.

Flex 4 is no exception, and, through a brand-new skinning and component architecture called Spark, it supports an increased level of user interface expressiveness and opens up opportunities for designers and developers to collaborate on Flex applications.

Though it's still incredibly quick to get started with Flex, when it comes to building enterprise-scale applications, or applications with highly expressive and customized user interfaces, adopting application-development best practices, leveraging an optimized design/develop workflow, and truly understanding the capabilities of the underlying platform technologies are keys to success.

That's where this book comes in—the authors have focused their attention specifically on topics that let you progress from merely developing in Flex to delivering robust, scalable, yet visually expressive, rich Internet applications.

From understanding how to approach test-driven development with Flex, through to making the best use of data binding for high-performance application use cases, the practical approach and extensive code examples give you the opportunity to apply best practices to your projects.

Keeping abreast of the changes in the latest version of the framework and runtime technologies can undoubtedly be a challenge when you're in the midst of delivering existing projects. You'll find help in the chapters on workflow, themes, and Adobe AIR, which detail some of the most important enhancements to the Flash platform. And you'll gain insight into how Flash Catalyst and Flash Builder can impact application design, as well as in determining how to leverage the capabilities of the latest Adobe runtimes to deliver both browser and out-of-browser experiences.

When it comes to integrating data services with your Flex applications, you'll find an array of options available, each of which has different performance characteristics and subtleties in the implementation details. The section on integrating client and server technologies will help you select the most appropriate integration approach for your application and provide you with examples that help solve real-world challenges relating to security and deployment.

The authors of the book are experienced Flex application developers who have encountered many of the challenges associated with integrating multiple technologies to deliver a solution. Such challenges are not specific to Flex, but are often an intrinsic part of migrating existing applications, integrating with legacy technologies, and leveraging disparate data services; by taking advantage of their experiences, you'll be able to focus on developing a high-quality user experience and spend less time working through such issues.

At Adobe, we continue to be inspired by the applications that are developed with Flex. As you near completion of your Flex application, I encourage you to submit a case study to Flex.org, so that we and others in the Flex community can be inspired by your work.

Andrew Shorten
Senior Product Manager, Flash Builder
Adobe Systems

About the Authors

 **Shashank Tiwari** is a technology entrepreneur, internationally renowned speaker, author, and innovator. He is currently a managing partner & CTO at Treasury of Ideas (http://www.treasuryofideas.com), a technology-driven innovation and value optimization company. He is adept in a multitude of technologies and his contributions to Java, Flex, Python and many open source tools and technologies have been well recognized over the years. He lives with his wife and two sons in New York. More information about him can be accessed at his website: www.shanky.org.

 **Elad Elrom** is an associate development director for Sigma Group, a consultant, technical writer and technical lead. As a technical writer, Elad wrote books covering Flash technologies. He maintains an active blog and has spoken at several conferences regarding the Flash platform. He has helped companies follow the XP and Scrum methodologies to implement popular frameworks, optimize and automate built processors and code review, and follow best practices. Elad has consulted a variety of clients in different fields and sizes, from large corporations such as Viacom, NBC Universal, and Weight Watchers to startups such as MotionBox.com and KickApps.com. Follow Elad on twitter: EladElrom and visit his blog: http://elromdesign.com/blog/.

About the Technical Reviewer

Tom Barker is a software engineer, solutions architect and technical manager with over a decade of experience working with ActionScript, JavaScript, Perl, PHP, and the Microsoft .Net Framework. Currently he is a Web Development Manager at Comcast Interactive Media. He is also an Adjunct Professor at Philadelphia University where he has been teaching undergrad and graduate courses on web development since 2003, as well as a regular contributor to www.insideRIA.com. When not working, teaching or writing, Tom likes to spend time with his two children, read, and play video games until very early in the morning

Acknowledgments

This book represents the efforts of many people, and I sincerely thank them for their contribution.

Thanks to Elad and Charlie for contributing their expertise and time as co-authors of this book. Special thanks to Elad for proactively leading the work on many of the chapters that deal with the content that relates to the new features in Flex 4.

Many thanks to the team at Friends of Ed (Apress). You made this book possible!

Thanks to my wife and sons for encouraging and supporting me through the endeavor of co-authoring this book.

Thanks to all members of the family and friends who have always believed in me.

Thanks to all who have contributed directly or indirectly to this book and who I may have missed unintentionally.

—Shashank Tiwari

This book would not have made it to print without the tremendous effort and dedication of a whole team over at Friends of Ed. As writers, our names are displayed on the cover, however, the team at Friends of Ed deserve just as much credit. In particular, I would like to thank Ben Renow-Clarke, Laurin Becker and Anne Collett. I also want to thank Clay Andres who is always somehow involved in every book I write.

In addition to the Friends of Ed team, I would like to thank Charlie Schulze, who wrote the "Using 3D in Flex" chapter.

Additionally, I would like to thank Juan Sanchez who provided contribution for the "Creating Themes" chapter and the design file.

Special thanks to Brian Riggs from the OSMF team, who helped review the OSMF materials as well as provide his presentation, which helped create the OSMF content for the "Facilitating Audio and Video Streaming" chapter. Additionally, I would like to thank David Hassoun who provided stable OSMF examples while OSMF was moving from 0.9 to version 1.0.

Finally, I would like to thank the team over at Kindisoft: Brian Noll and Ammar Mardawi who helped review the security chapter and provide some insight in regards to security.

—Elad Elrom

Introduction

The idea of this book emerged in tandem with the evolution of the Flex framework. Flex 3 was a big leap ahead of its predecessors, and that is when Advanced Flex 3 was conceptualized and authored. Then came even bigger changes and a whole lot of new features in Flex 4, and so it was time to revise to keep pace with the changes in the framework. Hence you have this book in your hands!

Like the earlier version, this book assumes only a minimal knowledge of the Flex framework. It illustrates and explains many advanced comcepts that are pertinent to practioners. With no intent to be necessarily exhaustive, this books covers a lot of ground by dealing with topics as varied as designer-developer workflow, Java integration, Mashups and 3D.

We have taken a fairly hands-on approach, so you will find plenty of illustrations and examples. Without being pedantic, enough of the theoretical foundations behind each topic are also covered. And we have included references to external online documents, where relevant.

After you read this book, you will be well on the way to confidently building engaging and interactive applications. We hope you enjoy reading it as much as we enjoyed writing it.

Layout conventions

To keep this book as clear and easy to follow as possible, the following text conventions are used throughout.

Important words or concepts are normally highlighted on the first appearance in **bold type**.

Code is presented in `fixed-width` font.

New or changed code is normally presented in **`bold fixed-width font`**.

Pseudo-code and variable input are written in *`italic fixed-width font`*.

Menu commands are written in the form **Menu ➤ Submenu ➤ Submenu**.

Where we want to draw your attention to something, We've highlighted it like this:

> *Ahem, don't say I didn't warn you.*

Sometimes code won't fit on a single line in a book. Where this happens, we use an arrow like this: ➡.

```
This is a very, very long section of code that should be written all on the same ➡
line without a break.
```

Chapter 1

Building Applications Using Test-Driven Development

by Elad Elrom

In Flex 4, one of the focuses is moving into a design-centric application development which consists of separating the presentation layer from the logic layer and delegating more responsibilities to a designer using Flash Catalyst. Removing some of the responsibility from developers will hopefully allow you to concentrate on creating smarter, more dynamic, and more complex Flash applications.

However, as the Flash application becomes more complex and more dynamic and business requirements are changing rapidly, sometimes even during development, it has become challenging to maintain Flash applications or to scale them up. The challenge is significant, and many Flash developers are finding that even using a framework does not make the application easy to maintain and scale. These challenges are common in any type of development: mobile, web, and desktop.

Consider the following: a large application needs changes because of new business requirements. How do you know that any small changes you made did not break other parts of the application? How can you be sure that your code is bulletproof especially if you are not the person that wrote it?

This problem is not new to software engineers; Java and ASP developers are challenged with the same issues everyday and have found Test-Driven Development (TDD) to be a useful way to create applications that can be easily maintained.

Flash has grown from a small animation tool into a "real" programming language, and methodologies common in other programming languages are necessary to build large dynamic applications. In fact, Adobe and many other companies have found that using TDD has solved many of the challenges that developers are having during every day development cycles.

Personally, I have found that many developers have heard of TDD; however, they are reluctant to use TDD becuase they are not sure how to and are afraid that using TDD will increase development time.

From my personal experience, I found that using TDD correctly does not increase development time. In fact, you will reduce the development time and make the application easier to maintain in the long run. I also found that you could implement and use TDD in existing applications as well as apply its methods to many of the frameworks out there, such as Cairngorm or Robotlegs, in some way or another.

TDD is applicable even in environments where there is a Quality Assurance (QA) department since it is preferable to deliver a more solid code that allows QA to focus on the User Interface (UI) and on creating the use cases that they need to test.

In this chapter, you will be given some of the basics you need to know to get started and some more advanced topics such as how to start using TDD in existing applications and how to create unit testing for more complex classes that include service calls and complex logic.

FlexUnit 4 Overview

Before diving into TDD, we would like to give you an overview of FlexUnit 4 because you will be using FlexUnit 4 as the tool for creating the tests.

Let's take a look how it all started. Back in 2003 iteration::two, a consulting firm that was bought by Adobe and later became Adobe consulting, released a product known as AS2Unit. Shortly after that, Adobe released Flex 1 in 2004 and AS2Unit was reborn as FlexUnit.

Up until the release of Flash Builder 4, you would have to download the SWC, create the test case, and test suite manually. With the release of Flash Builder 4, Adobe has added a FlexUnit plug-in as part of the many wizards and plug-ins to make Flash Builder easier to work with. The plug-in automatically performs many of the tasks you used to do manually and simplifies the process of unit testing. The project was previously published as Flex Unit 0.9. It never got its official 1.0 release and never will, but it is known as FlexUnit 1.

The new version, FlexUnit 4 is closer in functionality to the JUnit (http://www.junit.org/) project and supports many of the features JUnit has and more! FlexUnit 4 combines features from the previous FlexUnit 1.0 and Fluint (http://code.google.com/p/fluint/) projects.

Some of the main features of FlexUnit 4 are the following:

- Easier to create test suite and test case classes.
- Easier to create test runners and integrate runners from other frameworks.
- Better usage with continuous integration.
- Better handling of asynchronous tests.
- Better handling of exceptions.
- Framework is metadata-driven.
- Allows user interface testing.
- Ability to create test sequences.

Writing Your First Test Suite

1. Open Flash Builder 4. Select **File ➤ New ➤ Flex Project**. Name the project FlexUnit4 and select **Finish**.

You can download the entire example we will be showing you in this section from http://code.google.com/p/advancedflex4/. See Chapter 1, example: FlexUnit4.

2. Click on the project name so the package will be selected automatically as the default flexUnitTests and select **File ➤ New ➤ Test Suite Class** (see Figure 1-1).

Figure 1-1. Create new Test Suite Class menu

In the next window, you can set the name and include any tests. Name the suite FlexUnit4Suite and hit **Finish**. Notice that you can select the FlexUnit version. Use FlexUnit4, as shown in Figure 1-2.

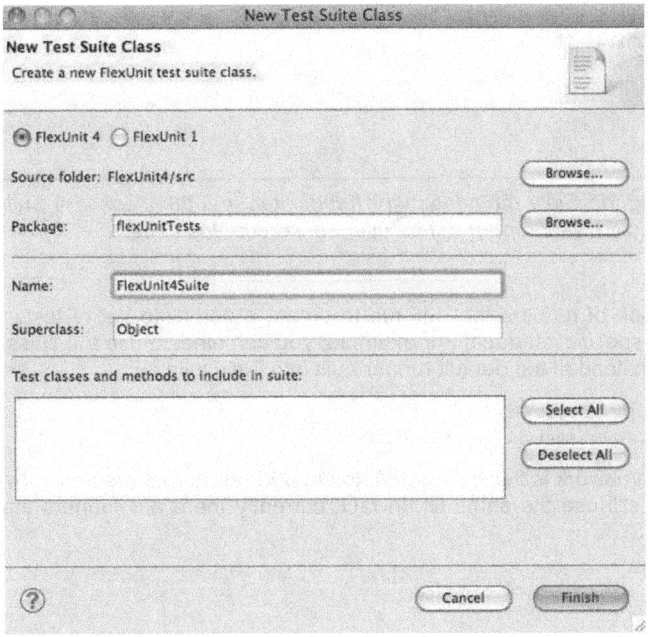

Figure 1-2. New Test Suite Class window

A test suite is a composite of tests. It runs a collection of test cases. During development, you can create a collection of tests packaged into a test suite. Once you are done, you can run the test suite to ensure your code is still working correctly after changes have been made.

The wizard created a flexUnitTests folder and a FlexUnit4Suite.as class (see Figure 1-3).

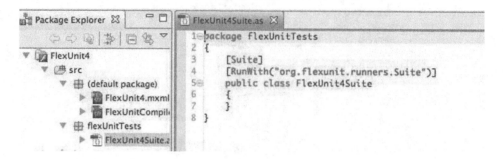

Figure 1-3. Package explorer showing the Test Suite created

Open the FlexUnit4Suite class you created.

```
package flexUnitTests
{
    [Suite]
    [RunWith("org.flexunit.runners.Suite")]
    public class FlexUnit4Suite
    {
    }
}
```

Note that you are using the Suite metadata, which indicates that the class is a Suite. The RunWith tag is using FlexUnit 4 to indicate what runner will be used to execute the code.

FlexUnit 4 is a collection of runners that will run to create a complete set of tests. You can define each runner to implement a specific interface. For example, you can elect to use the class you referenced to run the tests in that class instead of the default runner built into FlexUnit4.

```
[RunWith("org.flexunit.runners.Suite")]
[RunWith("org.flexunit.experimental.theories.Theories")]
```

This means that the framework is flexible enough to support future runners and allow developers to create their own runners but still use the same UI. In fact, currently there are runners that exist for FlexUnit 1, FlexUnit 4, Fluint, and SLT.

Writing Your First Test Case Class

The next step is to create the test case class. A test case is comprised of the conditions you want to assert to verify a business requirement. Each test case in FlexUnit 4 must be connected to a class.

1. Select **File ➤ New ➤ Test Case Class**. For the name choose FlexUnitTester ➤ flexUnitTests. Click **Finish** (see Figure 1-4).

Figure 1-4. New Test Case Class window

The wizard created FlexUnitTester.as automatically, as shown in the following code:

```
package flexUnitTests
{
    public class FlexUnitTester
    {
        [Before]
        public function setUp():void
        {
        }

        [After]
        public function tearDown():void
        {
        }
```

```
    [BeforeClass]
    public static function setUpBeforeClass():void
    {
    }

    [AfterClass]
    public static function tearDownAfterClass():void
    {
    }
    }
}
```

Note that in the test case window you had an option to attach a class to test, as Figure 1-4 illustrates. It is good to have that option available in case you are integrating unit tests to existing code. In case you are not using an existing class, but there may be cases where you want to test existing classes using FlexUnit 4 (which does not go hand in hand with TDD), you can do so by selecting **Next** in the **New TestCase Class** window (instead of **Finish**). On the next page, you can select methods to test, as shown in Figure 1-5.

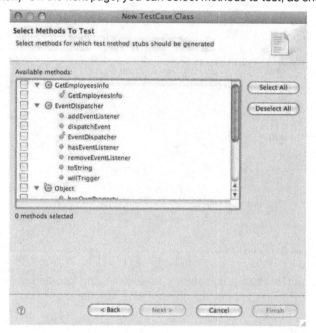

Figure 1-5. New Test Case Class window

You need to attach the Test Case to the Test Suite you created previously. To do so, just add a reference as shown in the following code:

```
package flexUnitTests
{
    [Suite]
    [RunWith("org.flexunit.runners.Suite")]
    public class FlexUnit4Suite
```

```
    {
                public var flexUnitTester:FlexUnitTester;
    }
}
```

You can now run the test. Select the **Run** icon and then select **FlexUnit Tests** from the menu, as shown in Figure 1-6.

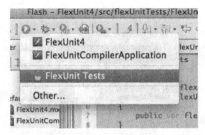

Figure 1-6. Run FlexUnit Tests

In the next window, you can select the Test Suites and Test Cases. In your case, you only have one Test Suite to select and no Test Cases since you have not created any tests in your Test Case class (see Figure 1-7).

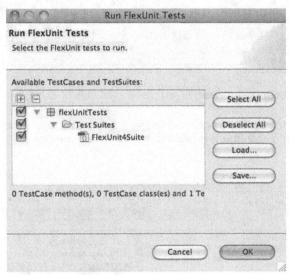

Figure 1-7. Run FlexUnit Tests wizard window

Review the Results

Flash Builder opens a new window where the tests are run and shows the results of your test (see Figure 1-8).

- 1 total test was run.
- 0 were successful.
- 0 was a failure.
- 1 were errors.
- 0 were ignored.

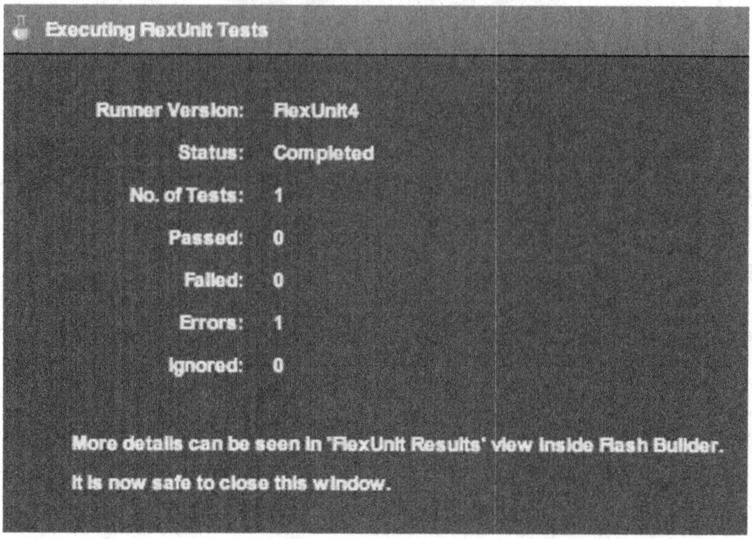

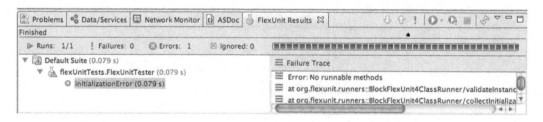

Figure 1-8. FlexUnit Results in the browser

You have one test that ends up in an error. Close the browser and take a look at the FlexUnit Results window in Figure 1-9. The reason the test has failed is that there are not any methods to test since you have not yet created them.

Figure 1-9. FlexUnit Results window

The results view provides several action buttons worth reviewing (see Figure 1-10).

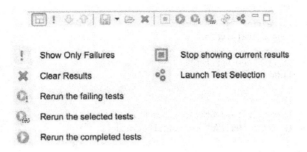

Figure 1-10. Results view action buttons

Replace the existing code in FlexUnitTester.as with the following code. We will explain the code in detail in the next section.

```
package flexUnitTests
{
    import flash.display.Sprite;
    import flexunit.framework.Assert;

    public class FlexUnitTester
    {
        //-------------------------------------------------------------------
        //
        //  Before and After
        //
        //-------------------------------------------------------------------

        [Before]
        public function runBeforeEveryTest():void
        {
            // implement
        }

        [After]
        public function runAfterEveryTest():void
        {
            // implement
        }

        //-------------------------------------------------------------------
        //
        //  Tests
        //
        //-------------------------------------------------------------------

        [Test]
        public function checkMethod():void
        {
            Assert.assertTrue( true );
        }
```

```
[Test(expected="RangeError")]
public function rangeCheck():void
{
    var child:Sprite = new Sprite();
    child.getChildAt(0);
}

[Test(expected="flexunit.framework.AssertionFailedError")]
public function testAssertNullNotEqualsNull():void
{
    Assert.assertEquals( null, "" );
}

[Ignore("Not Ready to Run")]
[Test]
public function methodNotReadyToTest():void
{
    Assert.assertFalse( true );
}
    }
}
```

Run the test again and see results in Figure 1-11. Hooray! You have created your first Test Suite and Test Case, and you received a green light indicating that the test passed correctly.

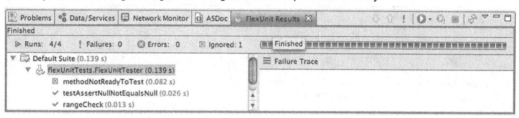

Figure 1-11. FlexUnit Results window

FlexUnit 4 is based on metadata tags. See some of the common tags used in the following:

- [Suite]: Indicates that the class is a `Suite`.
- [Test]: Test metadata replaces the test prefixed in front of each method. Support the `expected`, `async`, `order`, `timeout`, and `ui` attributes.
- [RunWith]: Used to select the runner to be used.
- [Ignore]: Instead of commenting out a method, you can just place the ignore metadata.
- [Before]: Replaces the `setup()` method in FlexUnit 1 and allows using multiple methods. Supports `async`, `timeout`, `order`, and `ui` attributes.
- [After]: Replaces the `teardown()` method in FlexUnit 1 and allows using multiple methods. Supports `async`, `timeout`, `order`, and `ui` attributes.
- [BeforeClass]: Allows running methods before test class. Supports `order` attribute.
- [AfterClass]: Allows running methods after test class. Supports `order` attribute.

As you can see from the example, you have used many tags here, such as the RangeError, AssertionFailedError, and Ignore tag. The usage of the metadata makes writing code easier. We will explain the code in the following section.

Assertion Methods

Back to the example: the `Before` and `After` metadata tags indicate that these methods will run before and after each test method.

```
[Before]
public function runBeforeEveryTest():void
{
    // implement
}

[After]
public function runAfterEveryTest():void
{
        // implement
}
```

The `Test` metadata replaces the prefix in front of each method so you have a method that does not start with test. Notice that unlike the previous version of FlexUnit, you have to indicate the class to assert since your class does not inherit from `TestCase` anymore.

```
[Test]
public function checkMethod():void
{
        Assert.assertTrue( true );
}
```

In FlexUnit 1, you used to comment out methods you do not want to test any more. The `Ignore` metadata tag in FlexUnit 4 allows skipping a method.

```
[Ignore("Not Ready to Run")]
[Test]
public function methodNotReadyToTest():void
{
    Assert.assertFalse( true );
}
```

> *In case you want to create a stack order for the tests or the before and after methods, you can just add the order attribute.*
>
> `[Test(order=1)]`

There are many other assertion methods you can use when creating tests (see Table 1-1).

Table 1-1. Asserts Class Methods and Description

Assert type	Description
assertEquals	Asserts that 2 values are equal.
assertContained	Asserts that the first string is contained in the second one.
assertNoContained	Asserts that the first string is not contained in the second one.
assertFalse	Asserts that a condition is false.
assertTrue	Asserts that a condition is true.
assertMatch	Asserts that a string matches a regexp.
assertNoMatch	Asserts that a string does not match a regexp.
assertNull	Asserts that an object is null.
assertNotNull	Asserts that an object is not null.
assertDefined	Asserts that an object is defined.
assertUndefined	Asserts that an object is undefined.
assertStrictlyEquals	Asserts that two objects are strictly identical.
assertObjectEquals	Asserts that 2 objects are equal.

To use an assertion method, pass a string message and two parameters to compare. The string is the message to be used if the test fails.

```
assertEquals("Error testing the application state", state, 1);
```

If you omit the message string, you'll get the default message. In the editor, type Assert, in order to see code hints for the available assertion methods in FlashBuilder IDE.

Exception Handling

The test metadata allows defining an exception attribute and makes it possible to test exceptions. The way it works is that the test method with the expected attributes points to the error message you expect, and the test will pass when the exception is raised.

The following example demonstrates the expected attribute of the Test metadata. The rangeCheck method creates a new Sprite object. The code will produce a successful test because the child at index 1 does not exist, and thus the code causes an exception during runtime.

```
[Test(expected="RangeError")]
public function rangeCheck():void
{
    var child:Sprite = new Sprite();
    child.getChildAt(0);
}
```

Another example is expecting an assertion error. Take a look at the `testAssertNullNotEqualsNull` method. The method is expecting the `AssertionFailedError` fail error. The `assertEquals` method will succeed since null equals null, so the test will fail. Change the statement to the following:

```
Assert.assertEquals( null, null );
```

Then you will get the test to succeed.

```
[Test(expected="flexunit.framework.AssertionFailedError")]
public function testAssertNullNotEqualsNull():void
{
    Assert.assertEquals( null, null );
}
```

Test Runners

The test runner is similar to FlexUnit1 test runner. See the complete code in the following example.

```xml
<?xml version="1.0" encoding="utf-8"?>
<s:Application xmlns:fx="http://ns.adobe.com/mxml/2009"
    xmlns:s="library://ns.adobe.com/flex/spark"
    xmlns:mx="library://ns.adobe.com/flex/halo"
    xmlns:flexUnitUIRunner="http://www.adobe.com/2009/flexUnitUIRunner"
    minWidth="1024" minHeight="768" creationComplete="creationCompleteHandler(event)">

    <fx:Script>
        <![CDATA[

            import flexUnitTests.FlexUnit4TheorySuite;
            import flexUnitTests.FlexUnit4HamcrestSuite;
            import mx.events.FlexEvent;
            import flexUnitTests.FlexUnit4Suite;

            import org.flexunit.listeners.UIListener;
            import org.flexunit.runner.FlexUnitCore;

            // holds an instance of the <code>FlexUnitCore</code> class
            private var flexUnitCore:FlexUnitCore;

            protected function creationCompleteHandler(event:FlexEvent):void
            {
                flexUnitCore = new FlexUnitCore();

                //Listener for the UI, optional
                flexUnitCore.addListener( new UIListener( testRunner ));

                //This run statements executes the unit tests for the FlexUnit4 framework
                flexUnitCore.run( FlexUnit4Suite, FlexUnit4HamcrestSuite, ←
```

```
FlexUnit4TheorySuite );
            }

        ]]>
    </fx:Script>

    <flexUnitUIRunner:TestRunnerBase id="testRunner" width="100%" height="100%" />

</s:Application>
```

You created an instance of the FlexUnitCore. FlexUnitCore extends EventDispatcher and acts as the facade for running the tests. It mimics the JUnitCore in methods and functionality.

```
// holds an instance of the <code>FlexUnitCore</code> class
private var flexUnitCore:FlexUnitCore;
```

Once the `creationCompleteHandler` handler is called you can add the `UIListener` listener:

```
protected function creationCompleteHandler(event:FlexEvent):void
{
        flexUnitCore = new FlexUnitCore();
```

You have the option to set listener to the UI. What is happening is the `FlexUnitCore` class has an async listener watcher which waits until all listeners are completed before it begins the runner execution.

```
//Listener for the UI, optional
flexUnitCore.addListener( new UIListener( testRunner ));
```

The next line calls the `run` method to start executing the tests. The `run` method accepts `...args` as parameters, so you will be able to list all the suites you want the runner to run.

```
//This run statements executes the unit tests for the FlexUnit4 framework
flexUnitCore.run( FlexUnit4Suite );
}
```

You also need an instance of the `TestRunnerBase` component.

```
<flexUnitUIRunner:TestRunnerBase id="testRunner" width="100%" height="100%" />
```

Compile and run the tests.Then you can see the results.

Hamcrest Assertion Method

In addition to the new standard assertions such as `Assert.assertEquals` or `Assert.assertFalse`, FlexUnit 4 supports new methods thanks to Hamcrest (http://github.com/drewbourne/hamcrest-as3/tree/master). Hamcrest is a library that is based on the idea of matchers. Each matcher can be set to match conditions for your assertions.

Create a new test case and call it `FlexUnitCheckRangeTester`.

```
package flexUnitTests
{
    import org.hamcrest.AbstractMatcherTestCase;
    import org.hamcrest.number.between;

    public class FlexUnitCheckRangeTester extends AbstractMatcherTestCase
```

```
{
    //------------------------------------------------------------------
    //
    //  Before and After
    //
    //------------------------------------------------------------------

    private var numbers:Array;

    [Before]
    public function runBeforeEveryTest():void
    {
        numbers = new Array( 0, 1, 2, 3, 4, 5, 6, 7, 8, 9, 10 );
    }

    [After]
    public function runAfterEveryTest():void
    {
        numbers = null;
    }

    //------------------------------------------------------------------
    //
    //  Tests
    //
    //------------------------------------------------------------------

    [Test]
    public function betweenRangeExclusive():void
    {
        assertMatches("assert inside range", between(numbers[0], numbers[10], true), 5);
        assertDoesNotMatch("assert outside range", between↵
(numbers[0], numbers[10], true), 11);
    }

    [Test]
    public function betweenRangeInclusive():void
    {
        assertMatches("assert inside range", between(numbers[0], numbers[10]), 5);
        assertDoesNotMatch("assert outside range", between(numbers[0], numbers[10]), 11);
    }

    [Test]
    public function betweenReadableDescription():void
    {
        assertDescription("a Number between <0> and <10>", between↵
(numbers[0], numbers[10]));
        assertDescription("a Number between <0> and <10> exclusive", between↵
(numbers[0], numbers[10], true));
    }
  }
}
```

FlexUnit4HamcrestSuite class includes the FlexUnitCheckRangeTester class.

```
package flexUnitTests
{

    [Suite]
    [RunWith("org.flexunit.runners.Suite")]
    public class FlexUnit4HamcrestSuite
    {
        public var flexUnitCheckRangeTester:FlexUnitCheckRangeTester;
    }

}
```

Lastly, do not forget to include the new test suite in FlexUnit4.mxml:

```
flexUnitCore.run( FlexUnit4Suite, FlexUnit4HamcrestSuite );
```

Asynchronous Tests

In case you worked with FlexUnit 1 in the past, you know that it is not always easy to create asynchronous tests and test event driven code. I often found myself modifying existing classes just to accommodate FlexUnit or creating tests in a "hackish" way. One of Fluint's biggest advantages is the ability to accommodate multiple asynchronous events. FlexUnit 4 incorporated Fluint functionality, and it supports enhanced asynchronous testing, including asynchronous setup and teardown.

As an example, create a new Test Case and call it TestAsynchronous.

```
package flexUnitTests
{
    import flash.events.Event;
    import flash.events.EventDispatcher;

    import flexunit.framework.Assert;

    import mx.rpc.events.FaultEvent;
    import mx.rpc.events.ResultEvent;
    import mx.rpc.http.HTTPService;

    import org.flexunit.async.Async;

    public class AsynchronousTester
    {
        private var service:HTTPService;

        //-------------------------------------------------------------------------
        //
        //  Before and After
        //
        //-------------------------------------------------------------------------

        [Before]
        public function runBeforeEveryTest():void
        {
            service = new HTTPService();
            service.resultFormat = "e4x";
        }
```

```actionscript
        [After]
        public function runAfterEveryTest():void
        {
            service = null;
        }

    //-------------------------------------------------------------------------
    //
    //  Tests
    //
    //-------------------------------------------------------------------------

        [Test(async,timeout="500")]
        public function testServiceRequest():void
        {
            service.url = "../assets/file.xml";
            service.addEventListener(ResultEvent.RESULT, Async.asyncHandler↵
( this, onResult, 500 ), false, 0, true );
            service.send();
        }

        [Test(async,timeout="500")]
        public function testeFailedServicRequest():void
        {
            service.url = "file-that-dont-exists";
            service.addEventListener( FaultEvent.FAULT, Async.asyncHandler↵
( this, onFault, 500 ), false, 0, true );
            service.send();
        }

        [Test(async,timeout="500")]
        public function testEvent():void
        {
            var EVENT_TYPE:String = "eventType";
            var eventDispatcher:EventDispatcher = new EventDispatcher();

            eventDispatcher.addEventListener(EVENT_TYPE, Async.asyncHandler↵
( this,  handleAsyncEvnet, 500 ), false, 0, true );
            eventDispatcher.dispatchEvent( new Event(EVENT_TYPE) );
        }

        [Test(async,timeout="500")]
        public function testMultiAsync():void
        {
            testEvent();
            testServiceRequest();
        }

    //-------------------------------------------------------------------------
    //
    //  Asynchronous handlers
    //
```

```
//------------------------------------------------------------------------

private function onResult(event:ResultEvent, passThroughData:Object):void
{
    Assert.assertTrue( event.hasOwnProperty("result") );
}

private function handleAsyncEvnet(event:Event, passThroughData:Object):void
{
    Assert.assertEquals( event.type, "eventType" );
}

private function onFault(event:FaultEvent, passThroughData:Object):void
{
    Assert.assertTrue( event.fault.hasOwnProperty("faultCode") );
}
    }
}
```

The Before and After metadata will be run before each test method. Since you are doing an async test, you can set the service to null once you are done to avoid any memory leaks.

```
[Before]
public function runBeforeEveryTest():void
{
    service = new HTTPService();
    service.resultFormat = "e4x";
}

[After]
public function runAfterEveryTest():void
{
    service = null;
}
```

You can set the test with the async metadata to perform an async test and set the timeout to 500 milliseconds. Once you send the request to retrieve an XML file, the result request will go to onResult method.

```
[Test(async,timeout="500")]
public function testServiceRequest():void
{
    service.url = "../assets/file.xml";
    service.addEventListener(ResultEvent.RESULT, Async.asyncHandler←
( this, onResult, 500 ), false, 0, true );
    service.send();
}
```

The result handler for the `testServiceRequest` test stub uses the `Assert.assertTrue` to ensure there are results in the request you set. Event has a property of `"result"`, so the expression will result in a true Boolean value.

```
private function onResult(event:ResultEvent, passThroughData:Object):void
{
    Assert.assertTrue( event.hasOwnProperty("result") );
```

```
        }
```

The second test will test failed requests. We are purposely setting a URL that does not exist "file-that-dont-exists", which will result in a failed service call. The result method onFault expects that the event object will have faultCode param.

```
        [Test(async,timeout="500")]
        public function testeFailedServicRequest():void
        {
            service.url = "file-that-dont-exists";
            service.addEventListener( FaultEvent.FAULT, Async.asyncHandler↵
( this, onFault, 500 ), false, 0, true );
            service.send();
        }


        private function onFault(event:FaultEvent, passThroughData:Object):void
        {
            Assert.assertTrue( event.fault.hasOwnProperty("faultCode") );
        }
```

In the testEvent test stub, you are testing and dispatching an event and expecting the results after 500 milliseconds. We set the event type to "eventType".

```
        [Test(async,timeout="500")]
        public function testEvent():void
        {
            var EVENT_TYPE:String = "eventType";
            var eventDispatcher:EventDispatcher = new EventDispatcher();

            eventDispatcher.addEventListener(EVENT_TYPE, Async.asyncHandler↵
( this,  handleAsyncEvnet, 500 ), false, 0, true );
            eventDispatcher.dispatchEvent( new Event(EVENT_TYPE) );
        }

        [Test(async,timeout="500")]
        public function testMultiAsync():void
        {
            testEvent();
            testServiceRequest();
        }
```

On the result handler, you ensure that the event type is equal to the event type you set in the request which means this is the correct event.

```
        private function handleAsyncEvnet(event:Event, passThroughData:Object):void
        {
            Assert.assertEquals( event.type, "eventType" );
        }
```

Be sure to remember to adjust the test FlexUnit4Suite.as to include the Test Case class you created before running the test.

```
package flexUnitTests
{
```

```
[Suite]
[RunWith("org.flexunit.runners.Suite")]
public class FlexUnit4Suite
{
    public var flexUnitTester:FlexUnitTester;
    public var asynchronousTester:AsynchronousTester;
}
}
```

ActionScript 3 is an event-driven language, and you often need to test async cases. As you can see from the examples, it is easy to create async tests in FlexUnit 4 and ensure async tests are performed.

Theories

FlexUnit 4 introduces a whole new concept called theories. A theory, as the name suggests, allows you to create a test to check your assumptions in regard to how a test should behave. This type of test is useful when you have a method you would like to test that can have large or even infinite sets of values. The test takes parameters (data points), and these data points can be used in conjunction with the test.

Create a new Test Suite and call it FlexUnit4TheorySuite.

```
package flexUnitTests
{
    import org.flexunit.assertThat;
    import org.flexunit.assumeThat;
    import org.flexunit.experimental.theories.Theories;
    import org.hamcrest.number.greaterThan;
    import org.hamcrest.object.instanceOf;

    [Suite]
    [RunWith("org.flexunit.experimental.theories.Theories")]
    public class FlexUnit4TheorySuite
    {
        private var theory:Theories;

        //---------------------------------------------------------------------
        //
        //  DataPoints
        //
        //---------------------------------------------------------------------

        [DataPoint]
        public static var number:Number = 5;

        //---------------------------------------------------------------------
        //
        //  Theories
        //
        //---------------------------------------------------------------------

          [Theory]
        public function testNumber( number:Number ):void
        {
            assumeThat( number, greaterThan( 0 ) );
```

```
            assertThat( number, instanceOf(Number) );
        }
    }
}
```

The RunWith tag points to a runner that implements a different interface then the default.

```
[Suite]
[RunWith("org.flexunit.experimental.theories.Theories")]
```

We set a data point with a number.

```
[DataPoint]
public static var number:Number = 5;
```

Next, we set the theory test we would like to check. Out test checks that the number is greater than five and is of type Number.

```
[Theory]
public function testNumber( number:Number ):void
{
    assumeThat( number, greaterThan( 0 ) );
    assertThat( number, instanceOf(Number) );
}
```

Add the test suite to the `FlexUnit4.mxml`:

```
flexUnitCore.run( FlexUnit4Suite, FlexUnit4HamcrestSuite, FlexUnit4TheorySuite );
```

Testing User Interfaces

Flex is used to build GUIs and includes visual appearance and behavior. Sometimes there are cases where you want to test the visual and behavior of your application.

In FlexUnit 1, there isn't any ability to test user interfaces, and MXML components were not an options when creating unit tests. FlexUnit 4 includes the concept of sequence, so you can create sequences that include all the operations you would like to perform on the UI.

For instance, let's assume you want to test a user clicking a button in your application. Take a look at the following code:

```
package flexUnitTests
{
    import flash.events.Event;
    import flash.events.MouseEvent;

    import mx.controls.Button;
    import mx.core.UIComponent;
    import mx.events.FlexEvent;

    import org.flexunit.Assert;
    import org.flexunit.async.Async;
    import org.fluint.sequence.SequenceCaller;
    import org.fluint.sequence.SequenceEventDispatcher;
    import org.fluint.sequence.SequenceRunner;
    import org.fluint.sequence.SequenceSetter;
    import org.fluint.sequence.SequenceWaiter;
```

```
import org.fluint.uiImpersonation.UIImpersonator;

public class FlexUnit4CheckUITester
{
    private var component:UIComponent;
    private var btn:Button;

    //--------------------------------------------------------------------------
    //
    //   Before and After
    //
    //--------------------------------------------------------------------------

    [Before(async,ui)]
    public function setUp():void
    {
        component = new UIComponent();
        btn = new Button();
        component.addChild( btn );
        btn.addEventListener( MouseEvent.CLICK, function():void↵
{ component.dispatchEvent( new Event( 'myButtonClicked' ) ); } )

        Async.proceedOnEvent( this, component, FlexEvent.CREATION_COMPLETE, 500 );
        UIImpersonator.addChild( component );
    }

    [After(async,ui)]
    public function tearDown():void
    {
        UIImpersonator.removeChild( component );
        component = null;
    }

    //--------------------------------------------------------------------------
    //
    //   Tests
    //
    //--------------------------------------------------------------------------

    [Test(async,ui)]
    public function testButtonClick():void
    {
        Async.handleEvent( this, component, "myButtonClicked",↵
handleButtonClickEvent, 500 );
        btn.dispatchEvent( new MouseEvent( MouseEvent.CLICK, true, false ) );
    }

    [Test(async,ui)]
    public function testButtonClickSequence():void
    {
        var sequence:SequenceRunner = new SequenceRunner( this );

        var passThroughData:Object = new Object();
```

```
            passThroughData.buttonLable = 'Click button';

            with ( sequence )
            {
                addStep( new SequenceSetter( btn, {label:passThroughData.buttonLable} ) );
                addStep( new SequenceWaiter( component, 'myButtonClicked', 500 ) );
                addAssertHandler( handleButtonClickSqEvent, passThroughData );

                run();
            }

            btn.dispatchEvent( new MouseEvent( MouseEvent.CLICK, true, false ) );
        }

        //-------------------------------------------------------------------------
        //
        //  Handlers
        //
        //-------------------------------------------------------------------------

        private function handleButtonClickEvent( event:Event, passThroughData:Object ):void
        {
            Assert.assertEquals( event.type, "myButtonClicked" );
        }

        private function handleButtonClickSqEvent( event:*, passThroughData:Object ):void
        {
            Assert.assertEquals(passThroughData.buttonLable, btn.label);
        }
    }
}
```

You hold the component and button instances you will be testing. This is just an example, but in real UI tests you will be using the actual MXML component. You can create an instance of an MXML component or application just as you are doing in this example.

```
        private var component:UIComponent;
        private var btn:Button;
```

The Before tag has the async and UI attributes to indicate that you will be waiting for FlexEvent.CREATION_COMPLETE event. Once the event is received, it will add the component you created to the UIImpersonator component. The UIImpersonator extends the Assert class and allows adding components and testing.

In the setUp() method, you add a button and set an event handler once the button is clicked. In your case, you will be dispatching myButtonClicked event.

```
        [Before(async,ui)]
        public function setUp():void
        {
            component = new UIComponent();
            btn = new Button();
            component.addChild( btn );
            btn.addEventListener( MouseEvent.CLICK, function():void
{ component.dispatchEvent( new Event( 'myButtonClicked' ) ); } )
```

```
            Async.proceedOnEvent( this, component, FlexEvent.CREATION_COMPLETE, 500 );
            UIImpersonator.addChild( component );
    }
```

After you complete each test, you will remove the `component` from the `UIImpersonator` and set the `component` to `null`.

```
    [After(async,ui)]
    public function tearDown():void
    {
            UIImpersonator.removeChild( component );
            component = null;
    }
```

The first test you will create is a simple test to check what happens when the button is clicked. As you may recall, we have raised a `myButtonClicked` event. Once the event is dispatched, the handler will call the `handleButtonClickEvent` method.

```
    [Test(async,ui)]
    public function testButtonClick():void
    {
            Async.handleEvent( this, component, "myButtonClicked",↵
handleButtonClickEvent, 500 );
            btn.dispatchEvent( new MouseEvent( MouseEvent.CLICK, true, false ) );
    }
```

In the second test, you will create a sequence. A sequence allows you to try and mimic the user using the component. In our case, we will be setting the label of the button and pressing the button. Notice that you are setting a `passThroughData` object that will hold the label name. You will be passing the label name and compare it once the async test is completed.

```
    [Test(async,ui)]
    public function testButtonClickSequence():void
    {
            var sequence:SequenceRunner = new SequenceRunner( this );

            var passThroughData:Object = new Object();
            passThroughData.buttonLable = 'Click button';

            with ( sequence )
            {
                addStep( new SequenceSetter( btn, {label:passThroughData.buttonLable} ) );
                addStep( new SequenceWaiter( component, 'myButtonClicked', 500 ) );
                addAssertHandler( handleButtonClickSqEvent, passThroughData );

                run();
            }

            btn.dispatchEvent( new MouseEvent( MouseEvent.CLICK, true, false ) );
    }
```

The `handleButtonClickEvent` method is the handler for the `testButtonClick` method. You are just checking that the event dispatched is of type `myButtonClicked`.

```
    private function handleButtonClickEvent( event:Event, passThroughData:Object ):void
```

```
    {
        Assert.assertEquals( event.type, "myButtonClicked" );
    }
```

The second handler will be used by the `testButtonClickSequence` method. Therefore, check that the button label was changed.

```
    private function handleButtonClickSqEvent( event:*, passThroughData:Object ):void
    {
        Assert.assertEquals(passThroughData.buttonLable, btn.label);
    }
}
```

As you can see from the preceding example, you can now test visual appearance as well as visual behavior in FlexUnit 4, which can help greatly when creating GUIs. That said, although you can test a GUI with FlexUnit 4, we recommend an open source tool called FlexMonkey (`http://code.google.com/p/flexmonkey/`) to perform more complex testing.

Test-Driven Development with FlexUnit 4

FlexUnit and TDD go hand in hand. TDD is a software development technique, and we can use FlexUnit 4 to implement the technique. The methodology started by programmers adding a test to their code after writing it. In 1999, Extreme Programming (XP) talked about development of dynamic projects with changing requirements and a development cycle that includes TDD for writing the test before the code itself. Note that TDD is not the complete development cycle, but only part of the XP development paradigm. By preparing the tests before writing the code, it allows you to show the work in small steps rather than have the customer wait for the complete result.

Moving in small increments at a time allows your customers to make changes before writing final code as well as ensuring that things do not go wrong and your code does what it needs to do and nothing more. It is important to mention that the focus of the TDD technique is to produce code and not to create a testing platform. The ability to test is an added benefit.

TDD relies on the concept that anything you build should be tested, and if you are unable to test it, you should think twice about whether you really want to build it.

XP uses the concept of TDD techniques using a short development process every couple of weeks called Iteration Planning which is based on user stories (see the following example). Iteration Planning contains the user stories and consists of the code necessary to pass that test. Once the test is completed, the code gets refactored to remove any extra code and create cleaner code. At the end of iteration planning, the team delivers a working application.

> A user story is a term used to represent a business requirement. The customer explains the requirement to the software engineer, and all those business requirements are user stories which together are part of the specification of requirements. For instance, "once the user logs in, a welcome window pops up."

Let's explore the TDD technique, as shown in Figure 1-12.

1. *Add test*. The first step is to understand the business requirements (which turn into User Stories) and think of all possible scenarios. In case the requirements are not clear enough,

you can raise the questions ahead of time instead of waiting until the software is completed and will require a large level of effort (LOE) to change.

2. *Write failed unit test*. This phase is needed to ensure that the test unit itself is working correctly and does not pass since you did not write any code.

3. *Write code*. During this phase, you write the code in the simplest, most effective way to ensure that the test passes. There is no need to include any design patterns, think about the rest of the application, or to try and clean up the code. Your goal is only to pass the test.

4. *Test passed*. Once you write all the code, the test passes, and you know that your test meets all the business requirements, then you can share the work with the customer or other members of the team.

5. *Refactor*. Now that the test is completed and you confirmed that it meets the business requirements, you can ensure that the code is ready for production by replacing any temporary parameters, adding design patterns, removing duplicates, and creating classes to do the job. Ideally once the refactor phase is completed, the code is given for code review, which is the key to ensure that the code is in good standing and complies with the company's coding standard.

6. *Repeat*. Unit test is completed, and you can move to the next unit test and publish your code to share with the customer or other members of the team.

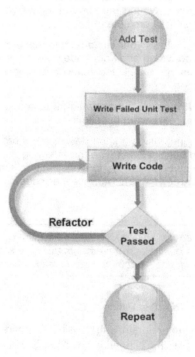

Figure 1-12. Test-Driven Development process diagram

To start working with Flash Builder 4, plug in the following process:

Open Flash Builder 4. Select **File ➤ New ➤ Flex Project**. Call the project FlexUnitExample, and hit ok.

You are now ready to get started. Traditionally, many processors will require you to go to the white board and start creating a diagram such as UML before starting the work; however, creating the diagram first can increase your development time. Consider the following example: You get a task with business requirements, but since you did not do the work yet, you can only assume how things are going to be. Then your diagram can be driven by what you think you need rather than what you really need. TDD turns everything upside down. You start with your business requirements as can be seen in the following.

- You need a utility class that will be able to read an XML file with employee's information.
- Once the employee's information is retrieved, it can be parsed into a value object class.
- The information will then be displayed on a screen.
- With these requirements in mind you can continue.

Creating Test Suite and Test Case

Your next step will be to create the Test Suite and Test Case.

1. Click on the project name so the package will be selected automatically as the default flexUnitTests, and select **File ➤ New ➤ Test Suite Class**.

2. In the next window, you can set the name and include any tests. Name the suite GetEmployeesSuite and hit **Finish**.

3. Next, create the test case class by choosing **File ➤ New ➤ Test Case Class**. For the name choose: GetEmployeesInfoTester and for the **Class to test**. Click Finish.

The generated code looks for Test Suites classes you will be testing. Although the test suite was created automatically for you, the flexUnitTests does not include the Test Suite class.

```
package flexUnitTests
{
    [Suite]
    [RunWith("org.flexunit.runners.Suite")]
    public class GetEmployeesSuite
    {
    }
}
```

Remember to set a reference to all the test cases you will be combining in your Test Suite, so add a reference to the class. See the following code as an example:

```
package flexUnitTests
{
    [Suite]
    [RunWith("org.flexunit.runners.Suite")]
    public class GetEmployeesSuite
    {
        public var getEmployeesInfoTester:GetEmployeesInfoTester;
    }
}
```

FlexUnit 4 Under the Hood

Under the application folder structure you can find the **GetEmployeesInfoTest.as**, **GetEmployeesInfoSuite.as** and **flexUnitCompilerApplication.mxml** (see Figure 1-13).

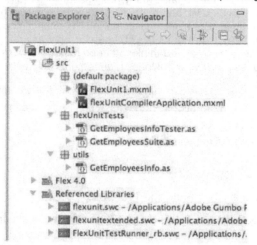

Figure 1-13. Flash Builder 4 package explorer

Under the application folder structure you can find the files GetEmployeesInfoTester.as, GetEmployeesSuite.as, and FlexUnitCompilerApplication.mxml (see Figure 1-14).

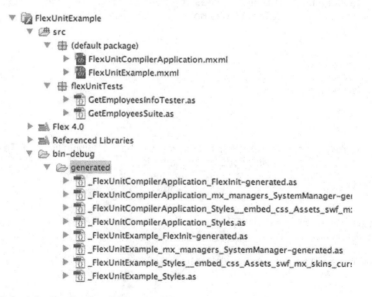

Figure 1-14. The CalculatorApplication folder structure

> *The bin-debug/generated package holds all files that get created by the MXMLC compiler and are normally invisible to you. To see them, select the project, then right-click and select Properties. Under Flex Compiler in Additional Compiler Arguments, add the following option: -keep-generated-actionscript or -keep-generated-actionscript=true.*

Take a look at FlexUnitApplication.mxml.

```
<?xml version="1.0" encoding="utf-8"?>

<!-- This is an auto generated file and is not intended for modification. -->

<s:Application xmlns:fx="http://ns.adobe.com/mxml/2009"
               xmlns:s="library://ns.adobe.com/flex/spark"
               xmlns:mx="library://ns.adobe.com/flex/mx" minWidth="955"
 minHeight="600" xmlns:flexui="flexunit.flexui.*" creationComplete="onCreationComplete()">
    <fx:Script>
        <![CDATA[
            import flexUnitTests.GetEmployeesSuite;

            public function currentRunTestSuite():Array
            {
                var testsToRun:Array = new Array();
                testsToRun.push(flexUnitTests.GetEmployeesSuite);
                return testsToRun;
            }


            private function onCreationComplete():void
            {
                testRunner.runWithFlexUnit4Runner(currentRunTestSuite(),
 "FlexUnitExample");
            }

        ]]>
    </fx:Script>
    <fx:Declarations>
        <!-- Place non-visual elements (e.g., services, value objects) here -->
    </fx:Declarations>
    <flexui:FlexUnitTestRunnerUI id="testRunner">
    </flexui:FlexUnitTestRunnerUI>
</s:Application>
```

As you can see, there is a GUI called FlexUnitTestRunnerUI which is similar in functionality to the FlexUnit TestRunner class in FlexUnit 0.9. Essentially, the application adds the entire test and runs the test in the UI.

In FlexUnitApplication.mxml, you can see that FlexUnit uses the FlexUnit 4 runner:

```
private function onCreationComplete():void
{
    testRunner.runWithFlexUnit4Runner(currentRunTestSuite(), "FlexUnitExample");
}
```

However, the framework is flexible, so you can create and use your own runners but still use the same UI. In fact, there are currently runners for FlexUnit 1, FlexUnit 4, Fluint, and SLT.

The test runner in FlexUnit is a UI component that will create an instance of the test suite and allow you to add all the tests you would like to run. The test runner will also display the test information in your browser.

Write Failed Test Case

Using TDD the next step is to write a failed test. Unlike traditional programming, you write the test before writing the code. This is done by thinking in advance of the class names you will be using, the methods, and what the methods need to do. In this case, let's say you hold a list of employees, and you want to be able to add an employee. The test you will be creating is creating the instance of the utility class you are going to create later: GetEmployeesInfo. Additionally, you are using the [Before] and [After] to set the class instance as well as setting it to null once completed to avoid memory leaks.

```
package flexUnitTests
{
        import org.flexunit.asserts.assertEquals;

        import utils.GetEmployeesInfo;

        public class GetEmployeesInfoTester
        {
                // Reference declaration for class to test
                public var classToTestRef : utils.GetEmployeesInfo;

                [Before]
                public function setUpBeforeClass():void
                {
                        classToTestRef = new GetEmployeesInfo();
                }

                [After]
                public function tearDownAfterClass():void
                {
                        classToTestRef = null;
                }

                [Test]
                public function testAddItem():void
                {
                        classToTestRef.addItem("John Do", "212-222-2222", "25",↵
    "john.do@gmail.com");
                        assertEquals( classToTestRef.employeesCollection.getItemAt(0).name,↵
    "John Do" );
                }
        }
}
```

Object-oriented programming is based on the principles that each method has one purpose, and the goal is to create a test that will assert the purpose of that method.

testAddItem stub uses the utility class to add an item and checks that the first item in the collection was added correctly.

Once you compile the application, you get compile time errors shown in Figure 1-15. That's actually a good thing. The compiler tells you what you need to do next.

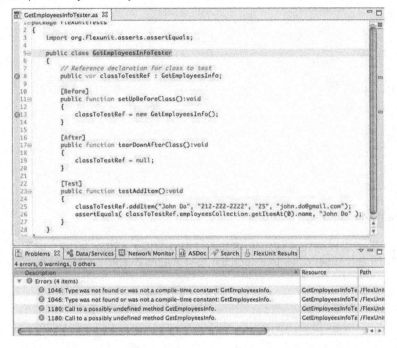

Figure 1-15. FlexUnit Tests shows compile time errors

Write Code

You got the following error messages from the compiler that you need to solve in order to run the application:

- Type was not found GetEmployeesInfo
- Call to a possible undefined method GetEmployeesInfo

The first code is due to the missing utility class. Create the GetEmployeesInfo class and package by selecting **File ➤ New Package**, and set the name to `utils` (see Figure 1-16).

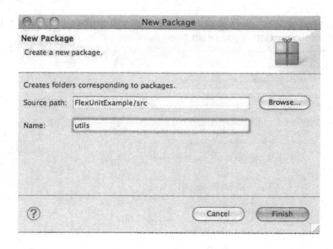

Figure 1-16. Create new package wizard

Next create the class GetEmployeesInfo. **Select File ➤ New ActionScript class**. Set the name to GetEmployeesInfo and super class to extend the flash.events.EventDispatcher class. Select Finish (see Figure 1-17).

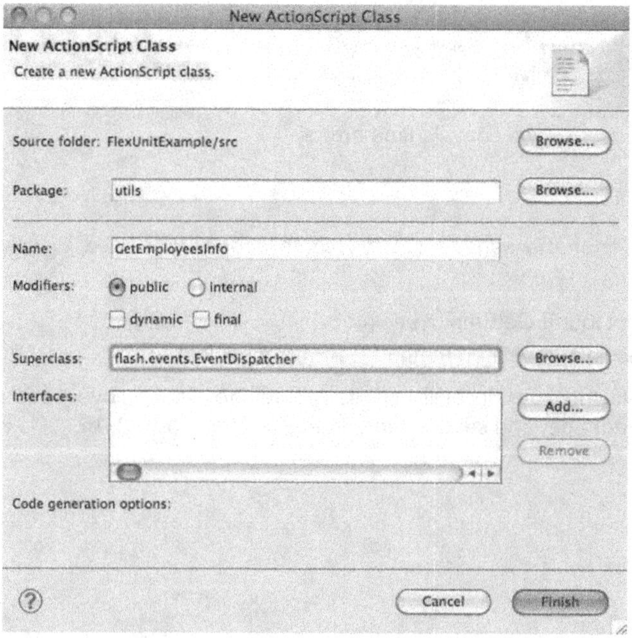

Figure 1-17. Create new Actionscript Class wizard

```
package utils
{
    import flash.events.EventDispatcher;
    import flash.events.IEventDispatcher;
    import mx.collections.ArrayCollection;
    import mx.rpc.events.FaultEvent;
    import mx.rpc.events.ResultEvent;
    import mx.rpc.http.HTTPService;

    public class GetEmployeesInfo extends EventDispatcher
    {
        private var service :HTTPService;
        private var _employeesCollection:ArrayCollection;

        public function GetEmployeesInfo()
        {
            _employeesCollection = new ArrayCollection();
        }

        public function get employeesCollection():ArrayCollection
        {
            return _employeesCollection;
        }

        public function addItem(name:String, phone:String, age:String, email:String):void
        {
            var item:Object = {name: name, phone: phone, age: age, email: email};
            employeesCollection.addItem( item );
        }
    }
}
```

The `testAddItem` method essentially takes an object and adds it to a collection, so you can easily test that by calling the method and passing an employee's information as well as then checking that the collection holds the same value you added.

```
public function testAddItem():void
    {
        classToTestRef.addItem("John Do", "212-222-2222", "25", "john.do@gmail.com");
        assertEquals( classToTestRef.employeesCollection.getItemAt(0).name, ↵
 "John Do" );
    }
```

Also, notice that you have setUp and tearDown methods that just create a new instance of the class you are testing and are setting them to null once you are finished.

So far in `testAddItem` method you used the `assertEquals` assertion which is a method in the Asserts class to which you have access automatically since you are extending `TestCase`. The Asserts class includes many other asserts you can use to test your methods.

Once you compile the application, the compile time error disappears.

Test Passed

To run the FlexUnit tests, Flash builder 4 and SDK added FlexUnit to the menu under the launch and debug icon, as shown in Figure 1-18. Select launch icon ➤ **Execute FlexUnit Tests**.

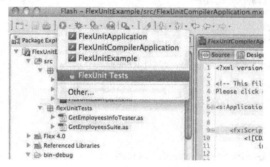

Figure 1-18. Execute FlexUnit Tests plug-in

In the next window, you can select the Suite and Cases or Test Case you would like to run. In this case, you only have one method to test, as shown in Figure 1-19.

We recommend selecting either the Test Suite or the Test Cases but not both, since it will run the test twice.

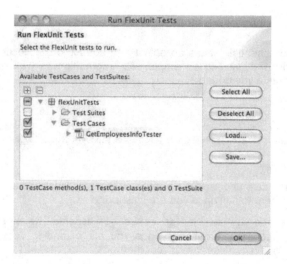

Figure 1-19. Run FlexUnit Test Configuration window

After the compile is completed, the browser opens up and shows the results (see Figure 1-20).

- 1 total test was run.
- 1 were successful.
- 0 was a failure.
- 0 were errors.
- 0 were ignored.

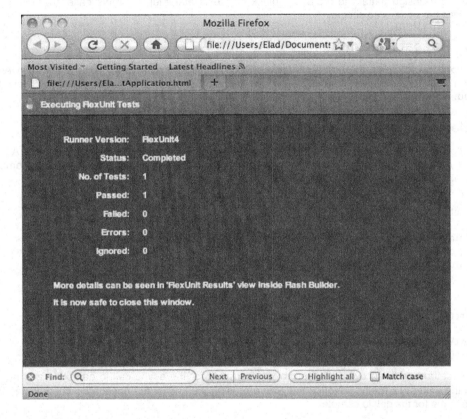

Figure 1-20. FlexUnit Test Run results in browser

Once you close the browser, you can see the results in the FlexUnit Results view (see Figure 1-21). From that view you can see that the test passed and you get a green light.

Figure 1-21. FlexUnit Results view

Once you write all the code and the test passes, you know that your test meets all the business requirements, so you can share the work with the customer or other members of the team.

Refactor code

Now that your test passed, you can refactor the code in order to get it ready for production. For example, you may add a design pattern to replace a block of if..else statements. In this case, there is nothing to refactor since the code is so simple.

Rinse and Repeat If Desired

You can continue to create the unit tests for the Service call and retrieve an XML with employee's data information, then process the information, add all the information to a list, and dispatch an event when completed.

Write Failed Test to Retrieve Employees Information

You can continue and write a test for the service call to retrieve the employee's information. Again, you first start by creating the test. In this case, you can create a custom event that will pass the employee's information. Take a look at the test method:

```
[Test]
public function testLoad():void
{
    classToTestRef.addEventListener( RetrieveInformationEvent.RETRIVE_INFORMATION, ↵
 addAsync( onResult, 500 ) );
    classToTestRef.load("assets/file.xml");
}

[Test]
public function onResult(event:RetrieveInformationEvent):void
{
    assertNotNull( event.employeesCollection );
}
```

testLoad method adds an event listener so you can wait for the async call to complete and handle the results in the onResult method. Notice that you are using the addAsync function which indicates that you will wait 500 ms for the call to complete.

The onResult method checks to ensure you got results. You really don't care what type of results you get in this test. You are just checking that the load method received the results and added the results to the collection. You can also create another test to check the integrity of the data.

Write Code to Retrieve Employee's Information

Here is the complete GetEmployeesInfoTester.as class.

```
package flexUnitTests
{
    import org.flexunit.asserts.assertEquals;
    import org.flexunit.asserts.assertNotNull;
    import org.flexunit.async.Async;
```

```
      import utils.GetEmployeesInfo;
      import utils.events.RetrieveInformationEvent;

      public class GetEmployeesInfoTester
      {
            // Reference declaration for class to test
            public var classToTestRef : GetEmployeesInfo;

            [Before]
            public function setUpBeforeClass():void
            {
                  classToTestRef = new GetEmployeesInfo();
            }

            [After]
            public function tearDownAfterClass():void
            {
                  classToTestRef = null;
            }

            [Test]
            public function testAddItem():void
            {
                  classToTestRef.addItem("John Do", "212-222-2222", "25", "john.do@gmail.com");
                  assertEquals( classToTestRef.employeesCollection.getItemAt(0).name,↵
"John Do" );
            }

            [Test(async,timeout="500")]
            public function testLoad():void
            {
                  classToTestRef.addEventListener( RetrieveInformationEvent↵
.RETRIEVE_INFORMATION, Async.asyncHandler( this,  onResult, 500 ), false, 0, true );
                  classToTestRef.load("assets/file.xml");
            }

            public function onResult(event:RetrieveInformationEvent, passThroughData:Object):void
            {
                  assertNotNull( event.employeesCollection );
            }
      }
}
```

Compile the class and observe the compile time errors. Once again, these errors are your indication of what you need to do next. Go back to the GetEmployeesInfo.as class and add a load method to load the xml. See the complete code in the following:

```
package utils
{
      import flash.events.EventDispatcher;
      import flash.events.IEventDispatcher;
      import mx.collections.ArrayCollection;
      import mx.rpc.events.FaultEvent;
      import mx.rpc.events.ResultEvent;
```

```
import mx.rpc.http.HTTPService;
import utils.events.RetrieveInformationEvent;

public class GetEmployeesInfo extends EventDispatcher
{
    private var service :HTTPService;
    private var _employeesCollection:ArrayCollection;

    public function GetEmployeesInfo()
    {
        _employeesCollection = new ArrayCollection();
    }

    public function get employeesCollection():ArrayCollection
    {
        return _employeesCollection;
    }

    public function load(file:String):void
    {
        service = new HTTPService();
        service.url = file;
        service.resultFormat = "e4x";
        service.addEventListener(ResultEvent.RESULT, onResult);
        service.addEventListener(FaultEvent.FAULT, onFault);

        service.send();
    }

    private function onResult(event:ResultEvent):void
    {
        var employees:XML = new XML( event.result );
        var employee:XML;

        for each (employee in employees.employee)
        {
            this.addItem( employee.name, employee.phone, employee.age,↩
employee.email );
        }

        this.dispatchEvent( new RetrieveInformationEvent( employeesCollection ) );
    }

    private function onFault(event:FaultEvent):void
    {
        trace("errors loading file");
    }

    public function addItem(name:String, phone:String, age:String, email:String):void
    {
        var item:Object = {name: name, phone: phone, age: age, email: email};
        employeesCollection.addItem( item );
    }
```

```
        }
}
```

You have a variable to create an instance of the `HTTPService` service class you will be using to execute the service call.

```
        private var service:HTTPService;
```

The collection is the variable that you will be using to hold the results. You do not want to allow a sub class the ability to change the collection directly, but you still want to leave the ability to access the collection so we can place a setter.

```
        private var _employeesCollection:ArrayCollection;

        public function GetEmployeesInfo()
        {
            _employeesCollection = new ArrayCollection();
        }
```

`GetEmployeesInfo` method is your default constructor, and you just create a new object for the `ArrayCollection`.

```
        public function GetEmployeesInfo()
        {
            employeesCollection = new ArrayCollection();
        }
```

The `load` method will be used to point to the file you will be loading. Add listeners and start the service.

```
        public function load(file:String):void
        {
            service = new HTTPService();
            service.url = file;
            service.resultFormat = "e4x";
            service.addEventListener(ResultEvent.RESULT, onResult);
            service.addEventListener(FaultEvent.FAULT, onFault);

            service.send();
        }
```

The `onResult` method will be called on a successful service call. You iterate through the class and take the data and use the `addItem` method to add the employee into the collection. Once the processing is complete, you use the `dispatchEvent` method to dispatch a `RetrieveInformationEvent` event and pass the `employeesCollection`.

```
        private function onResult(event:ResultEvent):void
        {
            var employees:XML = new XML( event.result );
            var employee:XML;

            for each (employee in employees.employee)
            {
                this.addItem( employee.name, employee.phone, employee.age, employee.email );
            }

            this.dispatchEvent( new RetrieveInformationEvent( employeesCollection ) );
```

```
        }
```

The `onFault` method will be called in cases where you have errors while trying to make the service call, such as calling a file that does not exists or security errors. At this point, you are leaving this method with a trace statement, but feel free to implement with dispatching an error event.

```
        private function onFault(event:FaultEvent):void
        {
            trace("errors loading file");
        }
```

The `addItem` method will be used to take the parameters you are passing and add them as an object to the collection.

```
        public function addItem(name:String, phone:String, age:String, email:String):void
        {
            var item:Object = {name: name, phone: phone, age: age, email: email};
            employeesCollection.addItem( item );
        }
    }
}
```

The `getEmployeesInfo` variable will hold the utility class instance.

```
private var getEmployeesInfo:GetEmployeesInfo;
```

Once the application dispatch the `applicationComplete` event, `applicationCompleteHandler` will be called and can create a new instance of the `GetEmployeesInfo` class and use the `load` method to start the service and pass the location of the XML.

```
protected function applicationCompleteHandler(event:FlexEvent):void
{
    getEmployeesInfo = new GetEmployeesInfo();
    getEmployeesInfo.load("assets/file.xml");

    getEmployeesInfo.addEventListener(RetrieveInformationEvent.RETRIVE_INFORMATION, onInfoRetrieved );
}
```

The XML we will be using is simple. Create a file named `assets/file.xml` and add the following XML into it:

```
<employees>
    <employee>
        <name>John Do</name>
        <phone>212-222-2222</phone>
        <age>20</age>
        <email>john@youremail.com</email>
    </employee>

    <employee>
        <name>Jane Smith</name>
        <phone>212-333-3333</phone>
        <age>21</age>
        <email>jane@youremail.com</email>
    </employee>
</employees>
```

Lastly, once the `RetrieveInformationEvent` event is dispatched we will be handling the event by showing the first item's name attribute.

```
private function onInfoRetrieved(event:RetrieveInformationEvent):void
{
     trace(event.employeesCollection.getItemAt(0).name);
}
```

Create a RetrieveInformationEvent custom event that holds employeesCollection array collection:

```
package utils.events
{
    import flash.events.Event;

    import mx.collections.ArrayCollection;

    public class RetrieveInformationEvent extends Event
    {
        public static const RETRIVE_INFORMATION:String = "RetrieveInformationEvent";

        public var employeesCollection:ArrayCollection;

        public function RetrieveInformationEvent( employeesCollection:ArrayCollection )
        {
            this.employeesCollection = employeesCollection;
            super(RETRIVE_INFORMATION, false, false);
        }
    }
}
```

Compile and run the application. You can see the `trace` statement results in the console window.

Test Passed

Now that we have made your application capable of making a service call and retrieving employee's information. Without modifying `GetEmployeesInfoTester`, you run the test runner and should get a green light, as shown in Figure 1-22.

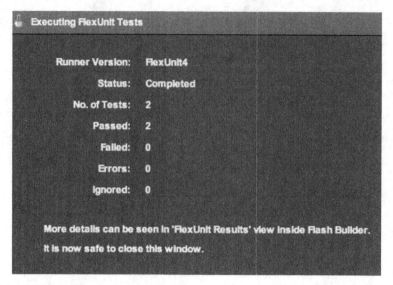

Figure 1-22. Executing FlexUnit tests

Refactor

The only refactoring that you are interested in doing is adding a Metadata to point to the RetrieveInformationEvent event, so you can get code hints when implementing the class in Flex. Add the following code to the beginning of the GetEmployeesInfo class:

```
[Event(name="retriveInformation", type="utils.events.RetrieveInformationEvent")]
```

You can download the complete example from http://code.google.com/p/advancedflex4/. See Chapter 1, example: FlexUnitWithTDDExample.

Summary

In this chapter, we covered FlexUnit 4 and Test Driven Development (TDD). We started by giving you an overview of FlexUnit 4 then we showed you how to create Test Suite, Test Case, and test runner classes. We covered all the assertion methods available in FlexUnit4, asynchronous Tests, and exception handling. We also covered the FlexUnit 4 additional assertion methods such as Hamcrest, theories, tests, and testing User Interfaces.

In the second part of the chapter, we discussed test-driven development with FlexUnit 4. We showed you how to write a failed test case, write code, test passed, and refractor your code. We hope you are inspired to use TDD on your mobile, web, and desktop Flash applications to write better, more scalable, and more reusable code.

Chapter 2

Turbo-Charging Data Binding

by Elad Elrom

Data binding is one of the most used processes when building Flex applications because it allows rapid development of Flex applications. Data binding allows you to pass data between different layers of the application automatically and makes development of Flex applications easy, fast, and enjoyable. Although Data binding contains tremendous value, it also holds some disadvantages for the unwary: without understanding exactly how data binding works and ensuring it is being used correctly and when needed, data binding can create bottlenecks, overheads, and memory leaks, which will cause your application to suffer in term of performance. Although you may not notice these performance differences when building a small Flex application, as your application scales up you may start seeing performance issues and data binding may be responsible for some of these issues, so it is better to build your application correctly from the start and avoid potential issues.

If you have developed Flex applications in the past, I am sure you have already used data binding, so the intention of this chapter is to provide you with basic and advanced techniques to use data binding so you know what's possible, as well as explain in detail what's going on under the hood so you will know how to use data binding correctly without causing any overhead or memory leaks. We are confident that a better understanding of how data binding works, and knowing all the different options that are available to you, while using data binding can help you build a better Flex application and avoid bottlenecks that can be caused by misuse of data binding.

Techniques for Using Data Binding

The Data binding process enables the tying of one object's data with another object. The concept of data binding is that by connecting a source object with a destination object, once the source object changes then the destination object also changes automatically. Additionally, Flex 4 offers two-way data binding, also known as bi-directional data binding, which enables two objects to be tied to each other allowing data to be changed when either object changes.

There are five main techniques for using Data Binding, which we will be covering in this chapter:

- Using braces with MXML tags
- Using the `fx:Binding` tag
- Using the `BindingUtils` class
- Implicit and explicit data binding
- Custom metadata

One and Two-way Data Binding Using Braces in MXML tags

Braces are the most commonly used technique to employ data binding in Flex applications. They allow you to bind properties without writing any actual code other than placing the braces. You set the braces, and once the application is compiled the compiler generates the code that does the binding automatically for you.

Up until Flex 4, you could do a one-way data binding. In Flex 4, you can also do a two-way data binding.

- **One-way Data Binding**: Allows binding of one variable or object property to another object property and any changes in the source will update the destination automatically.
- **Two-way Data Binding**: Allows binding of a pair of object's properties to update each other.

Create a new MXML application and call it OneWayDataBinding.mxml. Take a look at **hello world** minimalist code to use one-way data binding:

```
<?xml version="1.0" encoding="utf-8"?>
<s:Application xmlns:fx="http://ns.adobe.com/mxml/2009"
        xmlns:s="library://ns.adobe.com/flex/spark"
        xmlns:mx="library://ns.adobe.com/flex/halo"
        minWidth="1024" minHeight="768">

    <fx:Script>
        <![CDATA[

        [Bindable]
        public var value:String = "Hello World";

            ]]>
    </fx:Script>

    <s:layout>
            <s:VerticalLayout />
    </s:layout>

    <s:Label text="{value}" />

</s:Application>
```

In the example, you have a Label component to display some text and you tie the `text` property of the component to a `value` variable using data binding. This means the `value` variable is the source and the `text` property is the destination, and you are tying the two together using the braces syntax in the MXML code. Now let's say you change the value of the `bindable` source object during runtime, the text property, which is the destination property, will change as well.

```
Add the following line of code:  <s:TextInput id="textInput" change="{value=textInput.text}" />
```

Once you change the TextInput component, the value variable is changed accordingly. The Label component's text property is binding and you can see the text in the Label component change, as shown in the following code:

```
<?xml version="1.0" encoding="utf-8"?>
<s:Application xmlns:fx="http://ns.adobe.com/mxml/2009"
    xmlns:s="library://ns.adobe.com/flex/spark"
    xmlns:mx="library://ns.adobe.com/flex/halo"
    minWidth="1024" minHeight="768" creationComplete="creationCompleteHandler(event)">

    <fx:Script>
        <![CDATA[
            import mx.events.FlexEvent;

            [Bindable]
            public var value:String = "Hello World";


            protected function creationCompleteHandler(event:FlexEvent):void
            {
                BindingManager.debugBinding("simpleText.text");
            }

        ]]>
    </fx:Script>

    <s:layout>
        <s:VerticalLayout />
    </s:layout>

    <s:TextInput id="textInput" change="{value=textInput.text}" />
    <s:Label id="label" text="{value}" />

</s:Application>
```

So far you saw how to create one-way data binding, however, Flex 4 SDK offers the ability to tie two properties together. Create a new MXML component and call it TwoWayDataBinding.mxml. See the following code:

```
<?xml version="1.0" encoding="utf-8"?>
<s:Application xmlns:fx="http://ns.adobe.com/mxml/2009"
        xmlns:s="library://ns.adobe.com/flex/spark"
        xmlns:mx="library://ns.adobe.com/flex/halo"
        minWidth="1024" minHeight="768">

    <s:layout>
        <s:VerticalLayout />
    </s:layout>

    <s:TextInput id="textInput1" text="@{textInput2.text}" />
    <s:TextInput id="textInput2" text="{textInput1.text}"  />

</s:Application>
```

Two-way data binding works in most cases, however, it does not work with Style or Effect properties nor does it work with arguments for RemoteObject or the request property for HttpService, RemoteObject, or WebService. The reason that the two-way data binding will fail is that both the source and target properties must be bindable as well as readable and writable to allow two-way data binding.

In the example, you added the "@" symbol which creates a two-way binding so a change in the `textInput1` text property will result in a change in `textInput2` text property and vice versa. See Figure 2-1.

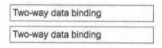

Figure 2-1. Two-way data binding example

Take a look at another example. In the following code, you have a variable and two TextInput components are binding to the same variable.

```
<?xml version="1.0" encoding="utf-8"?>
<s:Application xmlns:fx="http://ns.adobe.com/mxml/2009"
    xmlns:s="library://ns.adobe.com/flex/spark"
    xmlns:mx="library://ns.adobe.com/flex/halo"
    minWidth="1024" minHeight="768"
    viewSourceURL="srcview/index.html">

    <s:layout>
        <s:VerticalLayout />
    </s:layout>

    <fx:Script>
        <![CDATA[

            [Bindable]
            private var text:String = "";

        ]]>
    </fx:Script>
    <s:TextInput id="textInput1" text="@{text}" />
    <s:TextInput id="textInput2" text="@{text}"  />

    <s:Label text="{text}" />

</s:Application>
```

Once you change one text input component, the other changes as well. This type of binding allows two source objects for the same destination. This is useful when you need two properties to be tied together.

Binding an XML Object

Binding using MXML braces and the `fx:Binding` tag also works with XML E4X expressions, and once you bind the XML object all of the properties of the XML bind as well. To see this in action, create a new MXML component and call it BindingE4XExpression.mxml then enter the following code:

```xml
<?xml version="1.0" encoding="utf-8"?>
<s:Application xmlns:fx="http://ns.adobe.com/mxml/2009"
    xmlns:s="library://ns.adobe.com/flex/spark"
    xmlns:mx="library://ns.adobe.com/flex/mx"
    minWidth="1024" minHeight="768">

    <fx:Script>
        <![CDATA[

            [Bindable]
            private var xml:XML = <employees>
                <employee id="1">
                    <name>Tom</name>
                    <address>1st street</address>
                    <phone>212-111-1111</phone>
                </employee>
                <employee id="2">
                    <name>Tim</name>
                    <address>2st street</address>
                    <phone>212-222-2222</phone>
                </employee>
            </employees>;

        ]]>
    </fx:Script>

    <s:Label text="Employee name: {xml.employee.(@id==1).name}" />

</s:Application>
```

In the preceding, you define the XML data type and assign the value of the name to the   Label component. The `xml.employee.(@id==1).name` expression is E4X syntax and works as expected.

Data Binding Using Braces Overhead

You saw how to use MXML tags for data binding and it all appears as if it's magically happening. However, after opening the hood you will realize that there is a lot of overhead associated with this magic. Data binding using the braces works since the Flex compiler and framework adds code on your behalf that the code consists of:

- Generated code
- Event listeners and handlers
- Error catching
- Meta data

To understand how the magic works you need to better understand how the compiler works. The compiler runs the compilation in two steps:

1. *mxmlc*: The mxmlc compiler generates many ActionScript classes.

2. *compc*: The compc compiler compiles the mxmlc-generated classes and your classes to create a swf file.

These steps are not visible to you since these classes are not stored in your project by default. However, you can instruct the compiler to keep these files by adding a compiler argument -keep or -keep-generated-actionscript=true.

To take a closer look at what's happening, create a new project and call it **DataBindingUnderTheHood**. Then, add the following code:

```
<?xml version="1.0" encoding="utf-8"?>
<s:Application xmlns:fx="http://ns.adobe.com/mxml/2009"
    xmlns:s="library://ns.adobe.com/flex/spark"
    xmlns:mx="library://ns.adobe.com/flex/mx"
    minWidth="1024" minHeight="768">

    <fx:Script>
        <![CDATA[

            [Bindable]
            private var text:String;

        ]]>
    </fx:Script>

    <s:layout>
        <s:VerticalLayout />
    </s:layout>

    <s:TextInput id="textInput1" text="@{textInput2.text}" />
    <s:TextInput id="textInput2" text="{text}"  />

</s:Application>
```

In Package explorer, select **DataBindingUnderTheHood project,** then right-click it and select **Properties**. Under **Flex Compiler** in **Additional compiler arguments** add: keep-generated-actionscript=true (see Figure 2-2. Compile and Run the project.

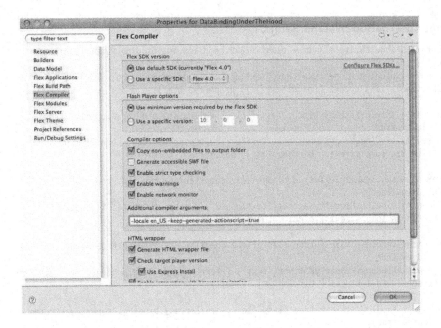

Figure 2-2. Properties for DataBindingUnderTheHood application

Under **src/generated** package, you will find all the files that got created and are normally invisible to you, as shown in Figure 2-3.

Figure 2-3. Package explorer showing files generated by mxmlc

Take a look at some of the code that gets generated to create the binding. This is the **_DataBindingUnderTheHoodWatcherSetupUtil** class.

```
// writeWatcher id=3 shouldWriteSelf=true class=flex2.compiler.as3.binding.PropertyWatcher
  shouldWriteChildren=true
watchers[3] = new mx.binding.PropertyWatcher("textInput1", { propertyChange: true } , //
  writeWatcherListeners id=3 size=1 [ bindings[2] ], propertyGetter);

// writeWatcher id=4 shouldWriteSelf=true class=flex2.compiler.as3.binding.PropertyWatcher
  shouldWriteChildren=true
watchers[4] = new mx.binding.PropertyWatcher("text", { textChanged: true, change: true }, //
  writeWatcherListeners id=4 size=1 [ bindings[2] ], null);

// writeWatcher id=0 shouldWriteSelf=true class=flex2.compiler.as3.binding.PropertyWatcher
  shouldWriteChildren=true
watchers[0] = new mx.binding.PropertyWatcher("textInput2", { propertyChange: true }, //
  writeWatcherListeners id=0 size=1 [ bindings[0] ], propertyGetter);

// writeWatcher id=1 shouldWriteSelf=true class=flex2.compiler.as3.binding.PropertyWatcher
  shouldWriteChildren=true
watchers[1] = new mx.binding.PropertyWatcher("text", { textChanged: true, change: true }, //
  writeWatcherListeners id=1 size=1 [ bindings[0] ], null);

// writeWatcher id=2 shouldWriteSelf=true class=flex2.compiler.as3.binding.PropertyWatcher
  shouldWriteChildren=true
watchers[2] = new mx.binding.PropertyWatcher("text", { propertyChange: true }, //
  writeWatcherListeners id=2 size=1 [ bindings[1] ], propertyGetter);
```

The previous example shows that properties get binding using the `PropertyWatcher` method, which looks for changes in the data.

Additionally, the mxmlc 4.0 compiler creates the **dataBindingUnderTheHood-generated.as** class and using the `IWatcherSetupUtil` interface class it calls the setup method that enable data binding.

```
if (_watcherSetupUtil == null)
{
    var watcherSetupUtilClass:Object =
 getDefinitionByName("_DataBindingUnderTheHoodWatcherSetupUtil");
    watcherSetupUtilClass["init"](null);
}

_watcherSetupUtil.setup(this,
    function(propertyName:String):* { return target[propertyName]; },
    function(propertyName:String):* { return DataBindingUnderTheHood[propertyName]; },
    bindings,
    watchers);

mx_internal::_bindings = mx_internal::_bindings.concat(bindings);
mx_internal::_watchers = mx_internal::_watchers.concat(watchers);
```

dataBindingUnderTheHood-generated.as also sets the binding through the `mx.binding.BindingManager`, which calls the UIComponent `executeBindings` to ensure binding is done through the life cycle of the component.

```
private function _DataBindingUnderTheHood_TextInput1_i() : spark.components.TextInput
```

```
{
    var temp : spark.components.TextInput = new spark.components.TextInput();
    temp.id = "textInput1";
    temp.id = "textInput1";
    if (!temp.document) temp.document = this;
    textInput1 = temp;
    mx.binding.BindingManager.executeBindings(this, "textInput1", textInput1);
    return temp;
}

private function _DataBindingUnderTheHood_TextInput2_i() : spark.components.TextInput
{
    var temp : spark.components.TextInput = new spark.components.TextInput();
    temp.id = "textInput2";
    temp.id = "textInput2";
    if (!temp.document) temp.document = this;
    textInput2 = temp;
    mx.binding.BindingManager.executeBindings(this, "textInput2", textInput2);
    return temp;
}


    //      binding mgmt
    private function _DataBindingUnderTheHood_bindingsSetup():Array
    {
        var result:Array = [];

        result[0] = new mx.binding.Binding(this,
            function():String
            {
                var result:* = textInput2.text;
                return (result == undefined ? null : String(result));
            },
            null,
            "textInput1.text"
            );

        result[1] = new mx.binding.Binding(this,
            function():String
            {
                var result:* = (text);
                return (result == undefined ? null : String(result));
            },
            null,
            "textInput2.text"
            );

        result[2] = new mx.binding.Binding(this,
            function():*
            {

                return textInput1.text;
```

```
            },
            function(_sourceFunctionReturnValue:*):void
            {

                textInput2.text = _sourceFunctionReturnValue;
            },
            "textInput2.text"
            );

        result[2].twoWayCounterpart = result[0];
        result[0].twoWayCounterpart = result[2];

        return result;
    }

    /**
     * @private
     **/
    public static function set watcherSetupUtil(watcherSetupUtil:IWatcherSetupUtil2):void
    {
        (DataBindingUnderTheHood)._watcherSetupUtil = watcherSetupUtil;
    }
```

dataBindingUnderTheHood-binding-generated.as creates a class to behave as a wrapper for the
UIComponent property. We will explain this code in more detail when we cover implicit data binding.

```
import flash.events.Event;
import flash.events.EventDispatcher;
import flash.events.IEventDispatcher;
import mx.core.IPropertyChangeNotifier;
import mx.events.PropertyChangeEvent;
import mx.utils.ObjectProxy;
import mx.utils.UIDUtil;

import spark.components.TextInput;

class BindableProperty
{
    /**
     * generated bindable wrapper for property textInput1 (public)
     * - generated setter
     * - generated getter
     * - original public var 'textInput1' moved to '_1559985460textInput1'
     */

    [Bindable(event="propertyChange")]
    public function get textInput1():spark.components.TextInput
    {
        return this._1559985460textInput1;
    }

    public function set textInput1(value:spark.components.TextInput):void
    {
        var oldValue:Object = this._1559985460textInput1;
```

```
        if (oldValue !== value)
        {
            this._1559985460textInput1 = value;
            this.dispatchEvent(mx.events.PropertyChangeEvent.createUpdateEvent(this,↵
"textInput1", oldValue, value));
        }
    }

    /**
     * generated bindable wrapper for property textInput2 (public)
     * - generated setter
     * - generated getter
     * - original public var 'textInput2' moved to '_1559985461textInput2'
     */

    [Bindable(event="propertyChange")]
    public function get textInput2():spark.components.TextInput
    {
        return this._1559985461textInput2;
    }

    public function set textInput2(value:spark.components.TextInput):void
    {
        var oldValue:Object = this._1559985461textInput2;
        if (oldValue !== value)
        {
            this._1559985461textInput2 = value;
            this.dispatchEvent(mx.events.PropertyChangeEvent.createUpdateEvent(this,↵
"textInput2", oldValue, value));
        }
    }
}
```

As you can see, the magic is actually a lot of code that the mxmlc compiler creates on your behalf. All the code you have seen gets added to your application swf and is an overhead added every time you initialize your application.

Creating one data binding using the curly brace doesn't make any difference, however, when you have many binding tags in an application it can cost you when the user starts the applications. In fact, in tests we created we found out that 10,000 MXML binding tags cost about 0.6 second.

One and Two-ways Data Binding Using Binding tag

In addition to the braces in MXML, the Flex 4 SDK also offers an MXML component that you can use to set binding: the binding tag. The fx:Binding tag is the replacement for the mx:Binding tag in earlier versions of Flex. It generates the same code as using curly braces to make the binding possible, so it makes no difference in terms of performance if you use the MXML braces or the binding tag. Create a new MXML component and call it UsingBindingTag.mxml.

```
<?xml version="1.0" encoding="utf-8"?>
<s:Application xmlns:fx="http://ns.adobe.com/mxml/2009"
    xmlns:s="library://ns.adobe.com/flex/spark"
    xmlns:mx="library://ns.adobe.com/flex/mx"
```

```
    minWidth="1024" minHeight="768">

    <s:layout>
        <s:VerticalLayout />
    </s:layout>

    <s:TextInput id="textInput1" />
    <s:TextInput id="textInput2" />

    <fx:Binding source="textInput1.text"
        destination="textInput2.text"
        twoWay="false" />

</s:Application>
```

The `fx:Binding` tag sets the source and destination of the objects you tie together. Notice that the `twoWay` property is set to `false`. To create two-way data binding set this property to `true`, as you can see in the following code:

```
<fx:Binding source="textInput1.text"
        destination="textInput2.text"
        twoWay="false" />
```

The `binding` tag ties `textInput1.text` with `textInput1.text` object and once you change either one of them you will see the other object change. As mentioned, this works in exactly the same way as using MXML braces and has the same overhead.

Using the BindingUtils Class

The two techniques you have looked at so far: braces in an MXML tag and the `binding` tag work well and are easy to implement. However, there is overhead associated with these methods. Additionally, you cannot "unbind" properties using these techniques. If you are building an application where you care about performance and would like to optimize as much as possible, you can use the `BindingUtils` class to bind your objects. There are two ways to use the `BindingUtils` class, using: `bindProperty` and `bindSetter`.

- `bindProperty()` method: The static method is used to bind a public property.
- `bindSetter()` method: The static method is used to bind a setter function.

> Tip: A weak reference is a reference that doesn't stop the garbage collector from collecting the object.

Take a look at the static `bindProperty` method signature in the following code:

```
public static function bindProperty(
    site:Object, prop:String,
    host:Object, chain:Object,
    commitOnly:Boolean = false,
    useWeakReference:Boolean = false):ChangeWatcher
```

- `site`: Represents the destination object.
- `host`: Represents the source object.

- commitOnly: Set to true in case the handler should be called only on committing change events; set to false in case the handler should be called on both committing and non-committing change events. Default is false.
- useWeakReference: Allows you to decide whether the reference to the host is strong or weak. A strong reference (the default) prevents the host from being garbage collected. A weak reference does not.

The following example holds text input and a simple text component. Once the TextInput is Pre-initialized, it calls the preinitializeHandler, which sets the bindProperty method using the bindingSetter as the setter.

```
<?xml version="1.0" encoding="utf-8"?>
<s:Application xmlns:fx="http://ns.adobe.com/mxml/2009"
    xmlns:s="library://ns.adobe.com/flex/spark"
    xmlns:mx="library://ns.adobe.com/flex/halo"
    minWidth="1024" minHeight="768">
    <fx:Script>
        <![CDATA[
            import mx.binding.utils.BindingUtils;
            import mx.events.FlexEvent;

            protected function preinitializeHandler(event:FlexEvent):void
            {
                BindingUtils.bindProperty(simpleText, "text", textInput, "text");
            }

        ]]>
    </fx:Script>

    <s:layout>
        <s:VerticalLayout />
    </s:layout>

    <s:TextInput id="textInput" preinitialize="preinitializeHandler(event)" />
    <s:SimpleText id="simpleText" />

</s:Application>
```

The second static method is the bindSetter.

```
public static function bindSetter(setter:Function, host:Object,
    chain:Object,
    commitOnly:Boolean = false,
    useWeakReference:Boolean = false):ChangeWatcher
```

- setter: Bind a setter function to a bindable property or chain. Once the ChangeWatcher instance is successfully created, the setter function is invoked with the value or the chain object.
- host: Represents the source object.
- chain: Represents the property name.

- commitOnly : Set to true in case the handler should be called only on committing change events; set to false in case the handler should be called on both committing and non-committing change events. Default is false.
- useWeakReference: Allows you to decide whether the reference to the host is strong or weak. A strong reference (the default) prevents the host from being garbage collected. A weak reference does not.

```xml
<?xml version="1.0" encoding="utf-8"?>
<s:Application xmlns:fx="http://ns.adobe.com/mxml/2009"
    xmlns:s="library://ns.adobe.com/flex/spark"
    xmlns:mx="library://ns.adobe.com/flex/halo"
    minWidth="1024" minHeight="768">

    <fx:Script>
        <![CDATA[
            import mx.binding.utils.BindingUtils;
            import mx.events.FlexEvent;

            protected function preinitializeHandler(event:FlexEvent):void
            {
                    BindingUtils.bindSetter(bindingSetter, textInput, "text");
            }

            private function bindingSetter(str:String):void
            {
                label.text = str;
            }

        ]]>
    </fx:Script>

    <s:layout>
        <s:VerticalLayout />
    </s:layout>

    <s:TextInput id="textInput" preinitialize="preinitializeHandler(event)" />
    <s:Label id="label" />

</s:Application>
```

Behind the scenes, the ChangeWatcher class is used in the BindingUtils class to allow the usage of weak references, which means that you can set the weak reference to true and allow the host to be picked up by the garbage collector. This avoids any potential memory leaks.

Although you can use weak references, as we pointed out, the ChangeWatcher needs to be un-watched once you are complete and it's your responsibility to handle that task which will ensure there are no memory leaks. The best way to handle this is to assign the static method to a ChangeWatcher variable. The static method returns a ChangeWatcher instance, so you can assign it to a variable, and once you don't need to bind the object anymore you can use the unwatch, as you can see in the following code along with Figure 2-4.

```xml
<?xml version="1.0" encoding="utf-8"?>
<s:Application xmlns:fx="http://ns.adobe.com/mxml/2009"
```

```
xmlns:s="library://ns.adobe.com/flex/spark"
xmlns:mx="library://ns.adobe.com/flex/mx"
minWidth="1024" minHeight="768">
<fx:Script>
    <![CDATA[
        import mx.binding.utils.ChangeWatcher;
        import mx.binding.utils.BindingUtils;
        import mx.events.FlexEvent;

        private var change:ChangeWatcher;

        protected function preinitializeHandler(event:FlexEvent):void
        {
            change = BindingUtils.bindProperty( label, "text", textInput, "text");
        }

        protected function clickHandler(event:MouseEvent):void
        {
            change.unwatch();
            change = null;
        }

    ]]>
</fx:Script>

<s:layout>
    <s:VerticalLayout />
</s:layout>

<s:TextInput id="textInput" preinitialize="preinitializeHandler(event)" />
<s:Label id="label" />

<s:Button label="Stop binding" click="clickHandler(event)" />

</s:Application>
```

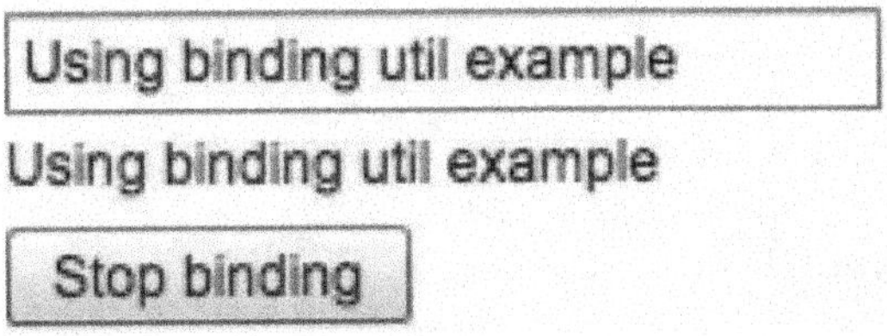

Figure 2-4. Using BindingUtils class and un-binding using a button

The TextInput text property is binding to the Label text property and once you enter text in the TextInput, the data will be copied to the text property in the Label component. When you are ready to unbind, simply press the "Stop binding" button, which will unwatch the properties and set the object to null so it will be picked up by the garbage collection.

If you recall from earlier we showed you how to use XML E4X using the braces. You can do the same thing using the fx:Binding tag. Create a new MXML application and call it BindingE4XExpressionBindingUtils.mxml, see complete code below:

```
<?xml version="1.0" encoding="utf-8"?>
<s:Application xmlns:fx="http://ns.adobe.com/mxml/2009"
    xmlns:s="library://ns.adobe.com/flex/spark"
    xmlns:mx="library://ns.adobe.com/flex/mx"
    minWidth="1024" minHeight="768" creationComplete="onCreationComplete()">

    <fx:Script>
        <![CDATA[
            import mx.events.FlexEvent;

            [Bindable]
            private var xml:XML;


            protected function onCreationComplete():void
            {
                xml = <employees>
                    <employee id="1">
                        <name>Tom</name>
                        <address>1st street</address>
                        <phone>212-111-1111</phone>
                    </employee>
                    <employee id="2">
                        <name>Tim</name>
                        <address>2st street</address>
                        <phone>212-222-2222</phone>
                    </employee>
                </employees>;
            }

        ]]>
    </fx:Script>

    <s:layout>
        <s:BasicLayout/>
    </s:layout>

    <s:Label id="label" text="test" />

    <fx:Binding source="xml.employee.(@id==1).name"
        destination="label.text" />

</s:Application>
```

BindingUtils class methods are quicker than the MXML braces because the class doesn't generate all the additional code that the compiler added.

- There is no need to generate the startup binding logic for the initialize event.
- There is no need for the executeBindings method of the UIComponent class.

In fact, in benchmark tests of 10,000 bindings we got 293 ms instead of 612 ms for MXML braces.

Implicit Data Binding

When building MXML components it's common to use data binding. There are two types of data binding that are used when binding your data: implicit and explicit.

> *The main difference between implicit and explicit data binding is that implicit data binding is done at run time, while explicit data binding is done at compile time.*

Implicit data binding is used in the following cases:

- In functions when values are passed as arguments and when values are returned from functions. Example: `private function SomeMethod(value:Number):String`. In assignment statements.
- In expressions when using some operators and the values are not yet set.

As an example of implicit data binding, you will be using an implicit getter and setter.

You will create a class that holds a variable. Once that variable is changed, you will get a notification, which will allow you to make changes in your application. The example is simple in nature so it will be clear for you to understand how to create an implicit data binding.

First, create a new class and call it `ClassA`. Create the setter and getter and add the `[Bindable]` tag. The `[Bindable]` metadata tag is compiled as `[Bindable(event="propertyChange")]`. The setter dispatches an event that will be added automatically. Although the event string gets set to propertyChange automatically, once you leave it empty you can change it. The mxmlc compiler creates additional code when you don't specify the event string, so it's recommended to add your own name to avoid that.

```
package
{
    import mx.core.UIComponent;

    public class ClassA extends UIComponent
    {
        private var _value:Number;

        [Bindable]
        public function get value():Number
        {
            return _value;
        }

        public function set value(num:Number):void
        {
            _value = num;
        }
    }
}
```

Next, create an MXML entry point and name the application ImplicitDataBinding.mxml. Once the application starts, the init method is called and changes the classA value property to 15. However, since you didn't set the event listener, the event will not be recognized. Next, you set the listener and change the property again to 5, which dispatches the event and calls the handler. The handler displays the message in the console: New value: 5, Old value: 15. See Figure 2-5.

```
<?xml version="1.0" encoding="utf-8"?>
<s:Application xmlns:fx="http://ns.adobe.com/mxml/2009"
    xmlns:s="library://ns.adobe.com/flex/spark"
    xmlns:mx="library://ns.adobe.com/flex/mx"
    minWidth="1024" minHeight="768" initialize="init(15)">

        <fx:Script>
        <![CDATA[

                import mx.events.PropertyChangeEvent;

                private var classA:ClassA = new ClassA();

                private function init(num:Number):void
                {
                    classA.addEventListener("propertyChange", handler);
                    classA.value = num;
                }

                private function handler(event:PropertyChangeEvent):void
                {
                    trace("New value: "+event.newValue + ", Old value: "+event.oldValue);
                }

        ]]>
        </fx:Script>

</s:Application>
```

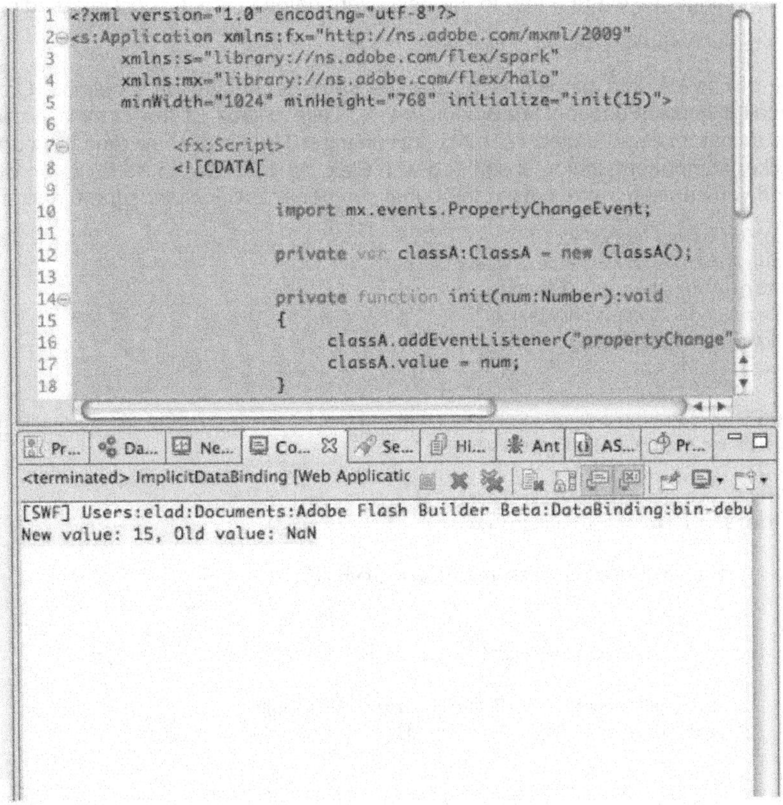

```
1  <?xml version="1.0" encoding="utf-8"?>
2  <s:Application xmlns:fx="http://ns.adobe.com/mxml/2009"
3      xmlns:s="library://ns.adobe.com/flex/spark"
4      xmlns:mx="library://ns.adobe.com/flex/halo"
5      minWidth="1024" minHeight="768" initialize="init(15)">
6
7      <fx:Script>
8          <![CDATA[
9
10             import mx.events.PropertyChangeEvent;
11
12             private var classA:ClassA = new ClassA();
13
14             private function init(num:Number):void
15             {
16                 classA.addEventListener("propertyChange"
17                 classA.value = num;
18             }
```

```
[SWF] Users:elad:Documents:Adobe Flash Builder Beta:DataBinding:bin-debu
New value: 15, Old value: NaN
```

Figure 2-5. Console window showing trace results

To see what's going on behind the scenes, place a line breakpoint where the trace command is located, and you can click the **Step Into** icon in the debugger window options and follow the code. UIComponent is calling dispatchEvent with a PropertyChangeEvent event that includes properties to store the old value and the new value. You can also create your own custom event by changing the ClassA bindable tag to include a specific name, as well as dispatching an event once the setter is called. The following code is exactly the same code you used before for ClassA with the exception that you set the event name.

```
[Bindable(event="valueWasChanged")]
public function get value():Number
{
    return _value;
}
public function set value(num:Number):void
{
    _value = num;
    var eventObj:Event = new Event("valueWasChanged");
    dispatchEvent(eventObj);
}
```

Don't forget to also change the event name to the new event name in the ImplicitDataBinding.mxml:

```
classA.addEventListener("valueWasChanged", handler);
```

Another example of implicit data binding is to use the same technique on functions. Create a new MXML application and call it ImplicitFunctionDataBinding.mxml. Take a look at the complete code \that creates a binding tag with a custom event called colorPickerChange. The function returns the current selected color from the color picker component, which is shipped with Flex. All you have to do is fire an event once the user selects a color and you can see the results in the Label component, which binds the function.

```
<?xml version="1.0" encoding="utf-8"?>
<s:Application xmlns:fx="http://ns.adobe.com/mxml/2009"
    xmlns:s="library://ns.adobe.com/flex/spark"
    xmlns:mx="library://ns.adobe.com/flex/mx"
    minWidth="1024" minHeight="768">

    <fx:Script>
        <![CDATA[
            import mx.events.ColorPickerEvent;

            [Bindable(event="colorPickerChange")]
            private function colorCode():String
            {
                return colorPicker.selectedColor.toString();
            }

            protected function colorPickerChangeHandler(event:ColorPickerEvent):void
            {
                this.dispatchEvent( new Event("colorPickerChange") );
                trace("color selected: "+event.color.toString())
            }

        ]]>
    </fx:Script>

    <s:layout>
        <s:VerticalLayout />
    </s:layout>

    <mx:ColorPicker id="colorPicker"
        change="colorPickerChangeHandler(event)" />
    <s:SimpleText text="{this.colorCode()}" />

</s:Application>
```

Implicit data binding allows you to create an application where your data can change during runtime and your components adjust to the data and perform a certain logic based on changes to properties. This type of architecture promotes the following:

- *Modular design*: Allows the creation of loosely coupled components.
- *Code reusability*: Reuse code on different applications.
- *Team*: Allows multiple developers to work on the same code base.

Explicit Data Binding

In addition to implicit data binding, you can also use explicit data binding, also called casting. Explicit data binding allows you to convert one data type to another data type.

Explicit data binding is often used in the following cases:

- You want to cast an object type with another object type.
- You want to avoid compile-time errors in a mismatch between objects.
- You are dealing with forms where all the properties are of type String, but they need to be converted to another format.

A minimalistic example of explicit data binding is using the trace method with the following statement: `trace(Number("2"));`

In that example, you had the string 2 being converted into the number 2.

Another example is to cast an object to a UIComponent type:

```
var com:UIComponent = object as UIComponent
```

Create a new MXML application and call it ExplicitDataBinding.mxml. In this application, we will show you an example of explicit data binding.

```
<?xml version="1.0" encoding="utf-8"?>
<s:Application xmlns:fx="http://ns.adobe.com/mxml/2009"
      xmlns:s="library://ns.adobe.com/flex/spark"
      xmlns:mx="library://ns.adobe.com/flex/mx"
      minWidth="1024" minHeight="768">

    <fx:Script>
        <![CDATA[

            [Bindable]
            private var num:Number = 5;

            private function init(num:Number):void
            {
                this.num = num;
            }

        ]]>
    </fx:Script>

    <s:Button width="50" label="{num.toString()}"
        click="num++" />

</s:Application>
```

The component assigns a Bindable primitive Number data type; however, the text property expects a primitive value of a String. Once you compile the application, you will get an error message in the console: **Implicit coercion of a value of type Number to an unrelated type String**. The error occurs on compile time since the compiler tried to assign a Number to a String type. What you need to do is cast the Number as a String.

```
<s:SimpleText width="50" text="{num.toString()}" click="num++" />
```

You can also use one of the following methods to cast as a `String`:

```
num as String;
String(num);
```

In addition to the traditional primitive variables, versions of Flex SDK 3.4 and up bring a new data type called `Vector`, which we encourage using when you need to create a collection of a data type. The new type is similar to an array but enforces elements to be of the same type. As you can see, you get compile time errors but you can adjust the code and avoid runtime errors.

> Note: Vectors are similar to Generics in Java and provide compile time type safety since you can specify the array type and ensure you won't get compile time errors.

You can set the size of the array and other features. The `Vector` data type increases performance, efficiency, and error checking of data. Here's an example of how to declare a vector:

```
var vector:Vector.<int> = Vector.<int>([10, 11, 12]);
```

This example generates an array with three numbers. You can enforce and specify the type of the objects.

Using Vectors can help ensure you won't get any compile time errors when using explicit data binding since you won't be able to convert the wrong data type.

Explicit data binding is used often in Flex and it allows you to avoid runtime errors by catching errors during compile time.

Debugging Bindings

There are many places that the binding classes are using the try and catch expressions and the exceptions being thrown are silently captured by the application without generating any errors. There are cases that the binding didn't occur as expected so you would like to debug in order to know what went wrong. To know if an event was dispatched, you can use the `BindingManager` class, which will indicate whether an event was fired, sending a trace message to the console.

Create a new MXML application and call it DebuggingBinding.mxml. The following code is the exact code used to explain one-way data binding with the exception of adding the `BindingManager` class. Once the application fires the `creationComplete` event, you set the object and property you would like to bind. In your case, yoou want to keep track of changes in the `Label` text property.

```
<?xml version="1.0" encoding="utf-8"?>
<s:Application xmlns:fx="http://ns.adobe.com/mxml/2009"
    xmlns:s="library://ns.adobe.com/flex/spark"
    xmlns:mx="library://ns.adobe.com/flex/mx"
    minWidth="1024" minHeight="768" creationComplete="creationCompleteHandler(event)">

    <fx:Script>
        <![CDATA[
            import mx.events.FlexEvent;

            [Bindable]
            public var value:String = "Hello World";
```

```
        protected function creationCompleteHandler(event:FlexEvent):void
        {
            BindingManager.debugBinding("label.text");
        }

    ]]>
</fx:Script>

<s:layout>
    <s:VerticalLayout />
</s:layout>

<s:TextInput id="textInput" change="{value=textInput.text}" />
<s:Label id="label" text="{value}" />

</s:Application>
```

As you compile and run the example, you can see the `trace` statements in the console as you type anything into the input box (see Figure 2-6).

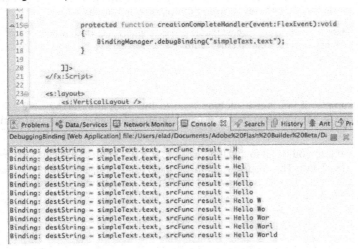

Figure 2-6. Console view for debug binding, typing hello world

TurboBinding Metadata

As mentioned before, data binding is tremendously valuable, but there are also disadvantages. Without understanding exactly how data binding works and ensuring it is being used correctly, it can create overhead and memory leaks, which will cause your application to suffer in terms of performance.

The overhead can cause an application with thousands of `Binding` tags to choke for even half a second. The alternative is to use another method such as `ChangeWatchers` or the `BindingUtils` class, but these require management to avoid memory leaks and are not as easy as using the `[Binding]` metadata tag. A large Flex application needs all the help they can get to get better performance. In our opinion, a half a second delay during initialization is not acceptable.

You can create your own binding metadata and customize the features to your requirements while controlling all the code that will be generated.

As an example we created [TurboBinding], which is a lightweight open source (available from http://github.com/EladElrom/eladlib) binding class with a speed close to the BindingUtils class, but with the ease of setting your binding as a metadata tag, just as you do with the Binding metadata. Here's an example of using the TurboBinding metadata tag:

```
[TurboBinding(destination="simpleText.text")]
```

In addition to performance gain, [TurboBinding] provides additional functionality to help avoid memory leaks. Since you don't need to bind a property anymore, you can set the unwatchCounter property and it will remove the listener and avoid memory leaks. For example, let's say you are making a service call to retrieve customer information but once you receive the information you don't need to bind anymore, you can set the unwatchCounter property to 1 and after the information is retrieved, it will clean up.

```
[TurboBinding(source="textInputOne.text", destination="textInputTwo.text", unwatchCounter=5)]
```

In the [TurboBinding] metadata, you can bind two properties together. Add twoWay="true" to add the same two-way data binding as is built into Flex. Note that once you use the twoWay property with unwatchCounter the binding will be removed from both binding instances.

```
 [TurboBinding(source="textInputOne.text", destination="textInputTwo.text", twoWay="true", unwatchCounter=5)]
public function callBackFunction(newValue:String):void
{
    trace(newValue);
}
```

As you saw in this example, if you set a method next to the [TurboBinding] metadata, it calls back the method once the change is recognized. This is a useful feature for times when you want to do an additional task after binding.

To use the TurboBinding tag, you need to call the setup method, because the code is not generated using the mxmlc as in the [Binding] tag. The following example includes using the unwatchCounter property, which removes the binding after the data changes five times; Simple data binding and two-way binding for two text input is shown in Figure 2-7.

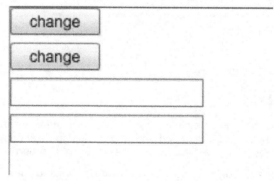

Figure 2-7. Implementation of TurboBinding custom metadata running in the browser

```
<s:Application xmlns:fx="http://ns.adobe.com/mxml/2009"
    xmlns:s="library://ns.adobe.com/flex/spark"
    xmlns:mx="library://ns.adobe.com/flex/mx"
    minWidth="1024" minHeight="768"
    creationComplete="TurboBinding.setup(this);">

    <fx:Script>
        <![CDATA[

            import mx.utils.ObjectProxy;
            import com.elad.framwork.binding.TurboBinding;

            [TurboBinding(destination="btn1.label", unwatchCounter=5,↵
callback="onPropertyChangeHandler")]
            public var customer1:ObjectProxy = new ObjectProxy(new CustomerVO());

            [TurboBinding(destination="btn2.label")]
            public var customer2:ObjectProxy = new ObjectProxy(new CustomerVO());

            [TurboBinding(source="textInputOne.text", destination="textInputTwo.text",↵
twoWay="true", unwatchCounter=5)]
            public function callBackFunction(newValue:String):void
            {
                trace(newValue);
            }

            public function onPropertyChangeHandler(val:String):void
            {
                trace("onPropertyChangeHandler:"+val);
            }

        ]]>
    </fx:Script>

    <s:layout>
        <s:VerticalLayout />
    </s:layout>

    <s:Button id="btn1" label="change" click="customer1.customerID++" />
    <s:Button id="btn2" label="change" click="customer2.customerID++" />

    <mx:TextInput id="textInputOne" width="150" />
    <mx:TextInput id="textInputTwo" width="150" />

</s:Application>
```

We created a benchmark inspired by an open source test class created by Manfred Karrer, (see TestDataBinding.mxml). Once you plugged in the [TurboBinding] tag, you are seeing some major performance gains,as shown in Figure 2-8.

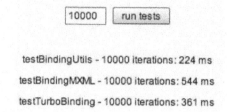

testBindingUtils - 10000 iterations: 224 ms

testBindingMXML - 10000 iterations: 544 ms

testTurboBinding - 10000 iterations: 361 ms

Figure 2-8. Test results to check performance

Data Binding Between Client Side and Server Side

The core of data binding and maintaining client state is the data. When dealing with an application that involves data transfer between a server and a client, it is highly recommended that you separate the data from the UI and keep track of the state. Separation of the data model is common practice in MVC architecture and used often in application development. The view gets updated automatically by binding a property in the view to the model. Once you need to change the view, you change the model and the view gets updated automatically.

Creating Class and Binding All Properties

To achieve separation, it is common practice to use a value object (VO), which contains all the properties of the data. The VO was borrowed from J2EE, which uses an object called a data transfer object (DTO). You will create a data object to store customers' information. Let's translate the object entity into a VO. See the following class, which is a collection of properties that describes the customer:

```
package
{
    [Bindable]
    public class CustomerVO
    {
        public var customerID:int;
        public var fname:String;
        public var lname:String;
        public var address:String;
        public var city:String;
        public var state:String;
        public var zip:String;
        public var phone:String;
        public var email:Date;
        public var updateDate:Date;

        public function CustomerVO(customerID:int, fname:String, lname:String, ↩
address:String,
        city:String, state:String, zip:String, phone:String, email:Date, updateDate:Date)
        {
            this.customerID = customerID;
            this.fname = fname;
            this.lname = lname;
```

```
                this.address = address;
                this.city = city;
                this.state = state;
                this.zip = zip;
                this.phone = phone;
                this.email = email;
                this.updateDate = updateDate;
            }
        }
}
```

Notice that you assigned a [Bindable] tag at the class declaration. The tag makes every property in the customerVO class binding, so there is no need to add the [Bindable] tag to any other property.

Creating an MXML class you can achieve the same functionality and bind all the public properties by placing the [Bindable] tag inside of a Metadata block.

```
<fx:Metadata>
        [Bindable]
</fx:Metadata>
```

The following example binds all the public properties,. Once the application calls the creationComplete event, the fname property is changed and you can see the results on the SimpleText Component.

```
<?xml version="1.0" encoding="utf-8"?>
<s:Application xmlns:fx="http://ns.adobe.com/mxml/2009"
    xmlns:s="library://ns.adobe.com/flex/spark"
    xmlns:mx="library://ns.adobe.com/flex/mx"
    minWidth="1024" minHeight="768"
    creationComplete="creationCompleteHandler()">

    <fx:Metadata>
        [Bindable]
    </fx:Metadata>

    <fx:Script>
        <![CDATA[

            public var customerID:int;
            public var fname:String;
            public var lname:String;
            public var address:String;
            public var city:String;
            public var state:String;
            public var zip:String;
            public var phone:String;
            public var email:Date;
            public var updateDate:Date;

            protected function creationCompleteHandler():void
            {
                fname = "Tom";
            }
```

```
    ]]>
  </fx:Script>

<s:Label text="First name: {fname}" />

</s:Application>
```

Binding Using ObjectProxy

As previously discussed, by using the [Binding] tag the object that you need to watch gets the additional code (setter and getter) that is required, so it can be watched. If you need to bind properties during runtime, then they have to include the IPropertyChangeNotifier interface, otherwise the object cannot be Bindable. However, primitive variables do not implement that interface, so when you need to bind an object during runtime you can use ObjectProxy class, which provides the ability to track changes to an item managed by the proxy. This means objects in your application can "listen" for changes on this object. See ASDOC for more info: http://www.adobe.com/livedocs/flex/3/langref/mx/utils/ObjectProxy.html.

Here's an example of using ObjectProxy. We create a new instance of the ObjectProxy and pass the object you would like to watch, in your case CustomerVO. You can then add an event listener and track changes to an item in CustomerVO.

```
<?xml version="1.0" encoding="utf-8"?>
<s:Application xmlns:fx="http://ns.adobe.com/mxml/2009"
      xmlns:s="library://ns.adobe.com/flex/spark"
      xmlns:mx="library://ns.adobe.com/flex/mx"
      minWidth="1024" minHeight="768"
      creationComplete="setWatcher();">

    <fx:Script>
        <![CDATA[
            import mx.events.PropertyChangeEvent;
            import mx.binding.Watcher;
            import mx.utils.ObjectProxy;

            public var customerVO:CustomerVO = new CustomerVO();
            public var obProxy:ObjectProxy;

            private function setWatcher():void
            {
                obProxy = new ObjectProxy(customerVO);
                obProxy.addEventListener( PropertyChangeEvent.PROPERTY_CHANGE, onChange);

                obProxy.fname = "elad";
            }

            private function onChange(event:*):void
            {
                trace("on change");
            }

        ]]>
```

```
    </fx:Script>

    <s:Label id="simpleText"/>

</s:Application>
```

This technique will come in very handy. You simply created a new instance of your CustomerVO object and are able to listen to changes to all properties in this custom object with very little code.

Flex Data Binding Pitfalls and Common Misuse Mistakes

Data binding is one of the most used processes when building Flex applications, but at the same time, it's a costly process and can delay initialization of an application. It's a good idea to pay attention and ensure it's used correctly and when needed. I compiled a list of five common pitfalls and incorrect misuses that developers do when building a Flex application while using the binding process.

Using Bindable When Binding Is Not Necessary

The use of unnecessary binding tags occurs when you bind a property that can be done easily without the binding tag. In cases where you don't need to bind, and you can do it with direct assignment, then it's best to avoid binding. I have seen this type of mistake many times in many shapes and forms. Take a look at the following code which illustrates one example:

```
<?xml version="1.0" encoding="utf-8"?>
<s:Application xmlns:fx="http://ns.adobe.com/mxml/2009"
    xmlns:s="library://ns.adobe.com/flex/spark"
    xmlns:mx="library://ns.adobe.com/flex/mx"
    minWidth="1024" minHeight="768">

    <fx:Script>
        <![CDATA[

            private var text:String;

        ]]>
    </fx:Script>

    <s:layout>
        <s:VerticalLayout />
    </s:layout>

    <s:TextInput id="textInput2" text="{text}"  />

</s:Application>
```

You have a text input with a text property binding to the text variable. Looks harmless enough, right? I have seen this type of tags often in Flex applications and I must admit that I have placed a few of these in the past myself. The mxmlc generates code to allow the binding. You will find that although you don't need to bind the text String, because this is a one-time assignment, the mxmlc still generates code to accommodate binding of the property.

In this case, you can do direct assignment of the value:

```
<s:TextInput id="textInput2" text="text" />
```

By using direct assignment, you are saving the mxmlc compiler from having to create extra binding code and significantly reducing your overheads.

Using the Wrong Bindable Event Name

Using the wrong event name in the bindable tag can cause your application to refuse binding your property and you won't even know why. When you use the `bindable` tag with a custom name, the following example looks like a good idea.

```
public static const EVENT_CHANGED_CONST:String = "eventChangedConst";

private var _number:Number = 0;

[Bindable(event=EVENT_CHANGED_CONST)]
public function get number():Number
{
        return _number;
}
public function set number(value:Number) : void
{
        _number = value;
        dispatchEvent(new Event(EVENT_CHANGED_CONST));
}
```

You are assigning a static property to the event name so then you can use the same assignment to dispatch the event. However, when the value changes the binding tag doesn't recognize the change. The reason is that the event name will be `EVENT_CHANGED_CONST` and not the value of the variable.

Assuming Execution Order of Binding

A common mistake when binding is assuming that a binding order is in synchronous execution order and will cause your application to generate a warning and not bind your property. Events in ActionScript are executed in an asynchronous manner. Take a look at the following code:

```
<?xml version="1.0" encoding="utf-8"?>
<s:Application xmlns:fx="http://ns.adobe.com/mxml/2009"
    xmlns:s="library://ns.adobe.com/flex/spark"
    xmlns:mx="library://ns.adobe.com/flex/mx"
    minWidth="1024" minHeight="768" creationComplete="creationCompleteHandler(event)">

    <fx:Script>
        <![CDATA[
            import mx.events.FlexEvent;

            [Bindable]
            public var buttonText:String = "Execution order mistake ";

        ]]>
    </fx:Script>
```

```
    <s:layout>
        <s:HorizontalLayout />
    </s:layout>

    <s:Label id="simpleText" text="{buttonText}" />
    <s:Button label="{simpleText.text}" />

</s:Application>
```

Although the code may work, you are assuming that the `simpleText` text property was already set since the value of text is binding and not the actual text property. You also get a compile time warning, as shown in Figure 2-9.

Figure 2-9. Compile time warning showing in Problems window

Here's another example where you assume that the value of the first `TextInput` was already set. Also, this type of assignment generates all the code to create binding from the mxmlc compiler. You have to consider if it's worth it or if direct assignment (`y="35"`) is a better choice.

```
<?xml version="1.0" encoding="utf-8"?>
<s:Application xmlns:fx="http://ns.adobe.com/mxml/2009"
    xmlns:s="library://ns.adobe.com/flex/spark"
    xmlns:mx="library://ns.adobe.com/flex/mx"
    minWidth="1024" minHeight="768">

    <s:TextInput id="textInput1" x="10" y="0" />
    <s:TextInput id="textInput2" x="0" y="{textInput1.x+25}" />

</s:Application>
```

Assigning a Binding Tag When You Don't Need It

There are many cases where you can write your code easily without data binding and use a `ChangeWatcher` or events to assign a value. It's recommended to avoid binding when it's not needed. Consider the following code:

```
<?xml version="1.0" encoding="utf-8"?>
```

```
<s:Application xmlns:fx="http://ns.adobe.com/mxml/2009"
    xmlns:s="library://ns.adobe.com/flex/spark"
    xmlns:mx="library://ns.adobe.com/flex/mx"
    minWidth="1024" minHeight="768">

    <fx:Script>
        <![CDATA[
            import mx.events.FlexEvent;

            [Bindable]
            public var dp:Array = [ { label:"New York", data: "New York" },
                { label:"Miami Beach", data: "Miami Beach" } ];

        ]]>
    </fx:Script>

    <mx:ComboBox id="cb" editable="false" width="100" dataProvider="{dp}" />

</s:Application>
```

Looks like pretty standard code in Flex application, however, this type of binding is not needed. Instead of binding, you can do direct assignment using an event handler as shown in the following code:

```
<s:Application xmlns:fx="http://ns.adobe.com/mxml/2009"
    xmlns:s="library://ns.adobe.com/flex/spark"
    xmlns:mx="library://ns.adobe.com/flex/mx"
    minWidth="1024" minHeight="768" creationComplete="creationCompleteHandler(event)">

    <fx:Script>
        <![CDATA[
            import mx.events.FlexEvent;

            public var dp:Array = [ { label:"New York", data: "New York" },
                { label:"Miami Beach", data: "Miami Beach" } ];

            protected function creationCompleteHandler(event:FlexEvent):void
            {
                cb.dataProvider = dp;
            }

        ]]>
    </fx:Script>

    <mx:ComboBox id="cb" editable="false" width="100" />

</s:Application>
```

Binding Class and Binding Property at the Same Time

Another common mistake is to set a class to be bindable and then assign each property in a class to be bindable as well.

```
package
{
```

```
[Bindable]
public class CustomerVO
{
    [Bindable]
    public var customerID:int;

    public function CustomerVO(customerID:int) {
        this.customerID = customerID;
    }
}
}
```

The reason that the bindable tag is not needed for the `CustomerID` property is because the class is already set to be bindable and every property in the class will be set bindable. This creates compile time errors and is a waste of time writing the extra code. Visit DevNet: `http://www.adobe.com/devnet/flex/articles/databinding_pitfalls.html` to read more about databinding common misuse mistakes.

Summary

Data binding contains tremendous value, but also holds disadvantages. We recommend ensuring it is being used correctly and when needed, because data binding can create overhead and memory leaks, which will cause your application to suffer in terms of performance. In this chapter you learned about techniques for using Data Binding. We covered one and two-way data binding using braces using MXML and binding tag as well as the overhead associated with the process. You learned of using the BindingUtils class as well as implicit and explicit data binding. We continued by showing you how to debug bindings and use a custom TurboBinding Metadata.

We continued by explaining data binding between client side and server side by creating class and binding all properties as well as binding using ObjectProxy class. Lastly, we helped you avoid common Flex data binding pitfalls and common misuse mistakes by given examples.

In the next chapter, you will learn how to tune your applications for superior performance. You will be looking under the hood of Flex and related Flash player features that impact performance.

Chapter 3

Workflow Enhancements with Flash Catalyst

by Elad Elrom

Designer-developer workflow (D-D workflow) in conjunction with Rich Internet Applications (RIA) has become one of the most talked about buzz topics in the Flash community during the last few years. It has created a lot of debate and uncertainty on how designers and developers are going to work together. In this chapter we will talk about how Adobe's Flash Catalyst (FC) should be used to allow designers and developers to work together.

In the last couple of years, we witnessed RIA slowly moving to the mainstream, and the next challenge is to create RIA GUIs and applications that have more animation and interaction and that do not have the traditional Flex "look." In order to achieve this, we need to find a way for designers and developers to work together in parallel while taking into account each other's needs. Do not underestimate the complexity of creating a workflow; it is an important yet complicated problem. How do we combine an artistic vision and story telling with the requirements of productive software development? How do we allow designers to take their ideas and turn them into interfaces that developers can code around? How can we create User Experience that addresses usability and integrates some more complex animation?

Flash Catalyst is a powerful tool that will help in developing applications that look unique and provide more animation between states. Flash Catalyst enables developers and designers to increase their creative productivity and leverage their existing skills to create more interactive and better designed Flex applications. It also facilitates team collaboration when creating Flex applications.

Designers can create the application's visual appearance and interactivity using Adobe Photoshop Illustrator, or Adobe Fireworks, and developers or designers can then convert these graphics into a Flex application by importing the native files into Catalyst while keeping the layers intact.

Catalyst acts as a bridge between Flash Builder and the Creative Suite. This chapter is based on our experience working with Catalyst and is based on creating production grade applications as well as listening and talking to many people in the Flash community. The vision of Catalyst to create a seamless round-trip workflow between Adobe Creative Suite, Flash Catalyst, and Flash Builder may not materialize right away but it is inspiring, and we believe it will change our D-D workflow.

The Flash Catalyst interface was built on top of Eclipse and created to primarily accommodate the designer. The IDE is similar in look and feel to Flash Professional and Photoshop. To some extent, it allows designers to quickly jump in and start using the tool in a familiar environment, without writing ActionScript code. However, parts of Catalyst's capability such as states, transitioning, Heads-Up Display (HUD), and components are not as familiar to the designers as layers and artwork, and they require training as well as experience and a different mind set.

There are different ways to work with Flash Catalyst, and we would like to cover one view on how Flash Catalyst can be used to change the designer and developer workflow. We are aware of the fact that the FC software is still young and is improving, and as new iterations comes out, it will allow better integration between designers and developers; however, we believe that many of the challenges and points we are raising will still be valid and applicable in the next couple of years.

Developers Are from Mars, Designers Are from Venus

You have probably heard about the theory of left-side versus right-side of the brain. The claim is that a person who is "left-brained" is more logical, analytical, and objective while a person who is "right-brained" is more intuitive, thoughtful, and subjective.

The theory was developed from the work Roger Sperry, a Nobel Prize winner, did in regard to medicine back in 1981. Sperry discovered that the human brain has two different ways of thinking. One side, the right brain, is visual and processes information in an intuitive and simultaneous way, looking first at the whole picture then at the details. The other side, the left brain, is verbal and processes information in an analytical and sequential way, looking first at the pieces and then putting them together to get the whole. Although recent research has shown that things are not as black and white or as simple as once thought, it is reasonable to assume that designers usually have a stronger right-brain and developers have a stronger left-brain. This makes a difference in how they process information and in how they work.

In order to create a designer and developer workflow, we need to have the right side of the brain and the left side of the brain working together, and the challenge begins with the current RIA development cycle. Currently, the development is more developer centric, since the designer is only responsible for creating the pixel (visual) discipline and the designer is usually not involved in any of the Flash experience. It becomes challenging to create Flash applications, because the developers need to be able to juggle between all the application disciplines such as converting .psd/.ai files into MXML, handling data, testing, services, coding, transitions, states, and many others responsibilities.

Many developers find it hard to skin a Flex 2 or Flex 3 component, and the level of effort to control every aspect of the component as well as interactivity is high, which leads to many applications using the "out of the box" components making many applications look like "Flex".

Adobe is aware of these challenges and has been working in the last few years to close this gap by creating the Flash Catalyst tool. Flash Catalyst reflects Adobe's continual commitment to the Flash framework and the community, and can help achieve a new design centric workflow, but it will not happen over night.

Utilizing Flash Catalyst As a Developer Tool

Before we start talking about the designer-developer workflow from a developer's point of view, we want you to change your mindset. We are not sure if we should think of Catalyst as a designer's tool. If that is the case, then all of the Flex developers are actually designers.

Wait…before you start arguing, let us explain. Part of creating RIA applications is the need to create the view which includes skinning components, CSS, states, transitions, effects, etc. Although Catalyst is aimed to free developers from controlling the look and the feel of the UI disciplines, I think this is wishful thinking at this point.

Looking at the designer-developer workflow before Flash Player 10 and Catalyst; developers would receive a composition from a designer and convert it into code. To many, that process was a painful process that required creating CSS classes and custom components which took a lot of effort for complex components.

Let's go even further back in time. When Flash was first introduced back in 1996, it was intended to be used mostly by web designers as a basic editing tool with a timeline and other familiar movie editing tools. Flash was slowly adopted by developers as ActionScript 1.0 was introduced, and the ability to add code to drive the animation became possible. Our point is that the tool should serve our needs, and we should avoid putting labels on the product.

Secondly, we believe that although the tool is portrayed as if it allows seamless and effortless round tripping integration between Creative Suite and Flex, in reality, the round trip is not seamless. At the end of the day, if the tool saved you days of work and helped you skin and create interaction of your application while allowing a designer to be more involved, then the product was a success and helped improve the workflow between designers and developers.

Do not assume designers will adopt the technology right away. Designers are just as busy as developers, and many are not thrilled to adopt a new tool that will require them to put in more time and add to their responsibilities, not to mention learning more skills and changing how they think of artwork. There is still a learning curve, and round tripping should be improved for better integration. While that happens, you should enjoy the tool and get designers more involved. We will show you how to do just that.

RIA Designer-Developer Workflow Utilizing Catalyst

By utilizing Flash Catalyst, the experience, such as animation between different states, can be done more quickly instead of handling these tasks in FlashBuilder or importing them into Flash Professional or other techniques that were commonly used up until FlashBuilder 4. Flash Catalyst allows the designer to be more involved with the interaction and choreography of the application in addition to being responsible for the visual appearance.

Once the work is completed, the artwork file can be provided to a developer who can integrate it into the application and add business logic, data, and services. As the project continues, designers can help modify the appearance and interaction and Flash Catalyst can convert these into code.

It is hard to give exact instructions on how a team should behave since it is a matter of the scope of the project, size of the team, back-end technologies, methodologies used to manage the project, and many other factors. However, to give more clarity we will show an example of designer-developer workflow using Flash Catalyst. Figure 3-1 shows an example of a workflow between a designer and a developer building an RIA application. Let's examine these steps.

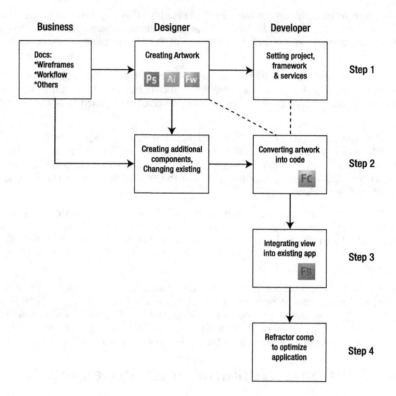

Figure 3-1. Example of a Designer-Developer workflow diagram

Step 1: Preparation

The workflow diagram shows that we have the business side, designer, and developer working in parallel.

The business side needs to provide the business requirements for the project and any other documents such as workflow, iterations, timeline, etc. As an example, we will create an AIR application that connects to twitter showing search results. The business creates a wireframe, as shown in Figure 3-2.

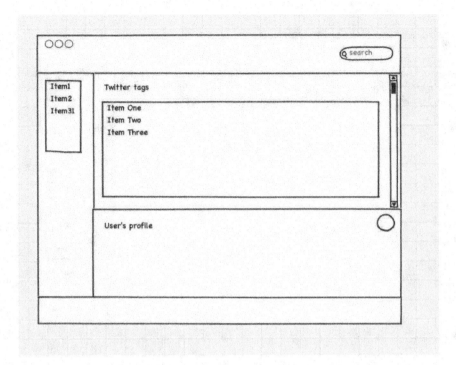

Figure 3-2. Wireframe for Twitter AIR application

These documents can come in very handy. For instance, the wireframe document can be used by the Quality Assurance (QA) team to test the application as well as by the designers and developers to understand the functionality of the application. The business requirements can also be used by the developer to create unit tests and ensure all the business requirements are met in full.

Parallel to the business side team working on the documents, the designer can start creating the artwork. It can be a designer or design team, which can include a graphic designer, art director, UX designer, and other members who can start working on taking the wireframes and bringing them to life. During that process, the designer can consult with the developer and the business side to see what is possible and the level of effort required to find out if it is possible to bring ideas to life under the time constraints. Take a look at Figure 3-3 that shows the artwork that the design team has created in Photoshop CS4.

Figure 3-3. Artwork in Photoshop

While the design team is preparing the artwork, the developer or development team can start by setting version control, continuing integration, unit testing, and so on. The developers can add a micro architecture framework, prepare any documents that are required such as Technical Requirement Document (TRD), UML (Unified Modeling Language) diagrams, and others, start creating Proof Of Concept (POC) to ensure certain parts of the application can be done and find any road block at an early stage. This document depends on the methodology implemented by the team, preference, and other factors.

For your AIR application we will create a project that is based on the Cairngorm micro architecture, which is common in enterprise level development.

Keep in mind we are not trying to tell you what micro framework to use if any, we are just trying to give you a tool to understand a workflow.

---

1. In Flash Builder, create a new AIR project and call it, TwitterTag (see Figure 3-4).

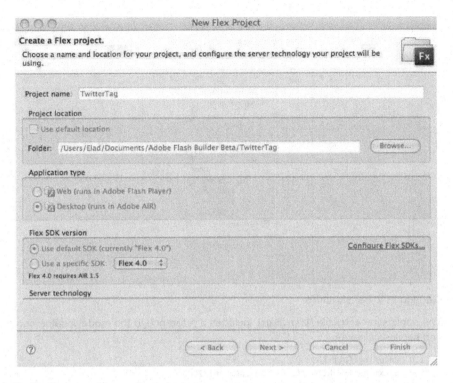

Figure 3-4. TwitterTag new Flex project

We will be using Cairngorm with the presentation model design pattern as an example. However, there are many other micro architectures you can use. We chose this approach in order to show a more realistic project. Cairngorm is not the most popular micro architectures framework out there, however, many corporations still use it because it is the recommended framework to use by Adobe.

2. The next step was to create all the Cairngorm folder structures, plumbing, etc. You created the project folders, Services.mxml, Controller, and Model Locator. See Figure 3-5.

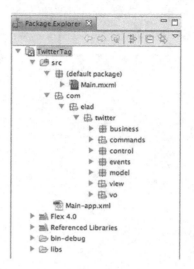

Figure 3-5. Caringorm folder structure

> **3.** The application entry file `Main.mxml` includes a reference to the model locator, controller, and services classes.

```
<?xml version="1.0" encoding="utf-8"?>
<s:WindowedApplication xmlns:fx="http://ns.adobe.com/mxml/2009"
                       xmlns:s="library://ns.adobe.com/flex/spark"
                       xmlns:business="com.elad.twitter.business.*"
                       xmlns:control="com.elad.twitter.control.*"
                       xmlns:view="com.elad.twitter.view.*"
                       initialize="modelLocator.mainPM.initialize()">

    <fx:Script>
        <![CDATA[

            import com.elad.twitter.model.ModelLocator;

            [Bindable]
            private var modelLocator:ModelLocator = ModelLocator.getInstance();

        ]]>
    </fx:Script>

    <fx:Declarations>
        <control:TwitterTagController />
        <business:Services />
    </fx:Declarations>

</s:WindowedApplication>
```

4. For the Model locator you will be taking the approach of using the presentation model, and the Model Locator acts as a locator which references the different Presentation Model classes that hold the data and logic for each component.

```
package com.elad.twitter.model
{
    import com.adobe.cairngorm.model.IModelLocator;
    import com.adobe.cairngorm.CairngormError;
    import com.adobe.cairngorm.CairngormMessageCodes;
    import com.elad.twitter.model.domain.LibraryModel;
    import com.elad.twitter.model.presentation.*;

    [Bindable]
    public final class ModelLocator implements IModelLocator
    {
        // Defines the Singleton instance of the application
        private static var instance:ModelLocator;

        /**
         * The application domain Model. The application Domain Model classes⏎
structures
         * our application data and defines its behavior reducing the role of⏎
the ModelLocator and
         * increase decoupling of the view.
         */
        public var libraryModel:LibraryModel;

        // The application main Presentation Model
        public var mainPM:MainPM;

// Defines the Singleton instance of the Application
        public function ModelLocator(access:Private)
        {
            if ( access == null )
            {
                throw new CairngormError⏎
( CairngormMessageCodes.SINGLETON_EXCEPTION, "ModelLocator" );
            }

            instance = this;
        }

        // Retrieves the Singleton instance of the <code>ModelLocator</code>
        // as well as an instance of <code>LibraryModel</code>⏎
 and <code>mainPM</code>
        public static function getInstance() : ModelLocator
        {
            if ( instance == null )
            {
                instance = new ModelLocator( new Private() );
                instance.libraryModel = new LibraryModel();
                instance.mainPM = new MainPM( instance.libraryModel );
                //todo: add instance
```

```
        }
            return instance;
        }
    }
}

// Inner class which restricts constructor access to Private
class Private {}
```

5. The `LibraryModel` holds the data that will be shared throughout the application.

```
package com.elad.twitter.model.domain
{
    [Bindable]
    // Defines the <code>LibraryModel<code> which contain the application
    // persistence data such as state/model, variables.
    public class LibraryModel
    {
        // place all application data here
    }
}
```

6. The `MainPM` presentation model holds the logic and data for the Main entry point `Main.mxml` of the application. The class extends AbstractPM and includes code to handle pre-initialize, initialize, handle first time application display using the `handleFirstShow` method; handle every other time it starts using `handleSubsequentShows`; and handle once the `initialization` process is completed using `handleCompleted` method. Additionally, we will be using ThunderBolt to log messages.

```
package com.elad.twitter.model.presentation
{
    import com.adobe.cairngorm.control.CairngormEventDispatcher;
    import com.elad.twitter.events.InitializationCommandCompleted;
    import com.elad.twitter.events.PreInitializationCommandCompleted;
    import com.elad.twitter.model.domain.LibraryModel;
    import org.osflash.thunderbolt.ThunderBoltTarget;
    import mx.logging.Log;

    [Bindable]
    // Defines the <code>MainPM<code> Value Object implementation
    public class MainPM extends AbstractPM
    {
        //  Define an instance of ThunderBoltTarget
        private var _target:ThunderBoltTarget = new ThunderBoltTarget();

        public var libraryModel:LibraryModel;

        //  Defualt constructor set the LibraryModel
        public function MainPM(libraryModel:LibraryModel)
        {
            this.libraryModel = libraryModel;
        }
```

```
    //  Method to handle first show of the application
    override protected function handlePreInitialize():void
    {
        // set filter for logging API and inject thunder bolt
        _target.filters = ["com.elad.twitter.commands.*"];
        Log.addTarget(_target);

        // track once pre-initialize completed
        CairngormEventDispatcher.getInstance().addEventListener(↵
PreInitializationCommandCompleted.COMPLETED, preInitializeCompletedHandler );
    }

    //  Method to handle first show of the application
    override protected function handleInitialize():void
    {
        // track once initialize completed
        CairngormEventDispatcher.getInstance().addEventListener(↵
InitializationCommandCompleted.COMPLETED, initializeCompletedHandler );
    }

    //  Method to handle first show of the application
    override protected function handleFirstShow():void
    {
        // implements or leave default
        handleCompleted();
    }

    //  Method to handle dubsequent shows of the application
    override protected function handleSubsequentShows():void
    {
        // implements or leave default
        handleCompleted();
    }

     //  Method to handle the view once preinit and init are completed
    override protected function handleCompleted():void
    {
        // remove event listeners
        CairngormEventDispatcher.getInstance().removeEventListener(↵
  PreInitializationCommandCompleted.COMPLETED, preInitializeCompletedHandler );
        CairngormEventDispatcher.getInstance().removeEventListener(↵
  InitializationCommandCompleted.COMPLETED, initializeCompletedHandler );

        // implements changes in view
    }

}
```

You can download TwitterTag-Step1 to see the process you have made so far.

Step 2: Converting Artwork and Interactions into Code

In the second step, the artwork needs to be converted into code, and any choreography (visual interactivity) should be implemented. We believe that many times the developer, rather than the designer, will end up converting the artwork into code at least until the tool gets adopted by designers fully.

Creating one project file (FXP) will make it very hard to integrate correctly into an existing enterprise application. For instance, think about an RIA application you have built in the past. The approach was not to create one document that holds all the different components but to create custom components and use them all either as one project or create modules to load the ones you need to optimize your application.

Working with Catalyst should not be any different from that approach. In fact, we found that the best approach is to identify the different custom components you would like to break your application into, instead of trying to create one Catalyst application. Additionally, it will be hard, or even impossible, for a team of designers to work on a single Catalyst file. What we mean is that you will figure out how you would like to split your view and create Catalyst projects based on that. For instance take a look at your AIR application in Figure 3-6. You can break the application into the Left navigation, which will hold the navigation, body, header, and footer. You should create two Flash Catalyst projects, and each project can hold the states and the transitions between each state.

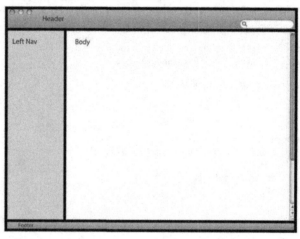

Figure 3-6. Identify components wireframe

Your assumption should be that you will have to change Catalyst's code and adjust it instead of assuming that the code Catalyst will spit out the most optimized code. Another assumption we believe you should make is that it will be impossible or very difficult to port the code back into Catalyst because it is very likely that the code generated by Catalyst will have to be modified.

Another point we would like to discuss is states and transitions. RIAs are known for their richness in media, effects, transitions, and the ability to make changes to the application without refreshing the browser. To create a compelling experience, we need to think about the entire experience rather than the pieces that make the application work. The user gets to the application, and we need to figure out the usability as well as the choreography. Let's think about creating a movie clip in Flash Professional. You can create a timeline and a movie. Although Flash Professional is richer and allows better choreography of animation, Flash Catalyst will enable you to take RIAs one step further by allowingyou to create visual animation for components more easily than was done before.

Although you are showing a workflow where the developer can use Catalyst to convert the artwork into code, a designer that is skillful with Flash Catalyst can take the role of creating the Catalyst project. In any case, he will stay very involved in the process and will provide assistance when states are missing graphics and when elements are being converted into images.

Flash Catalyst uses Flash Player 10's new drawing API and allows the retaining of vector graphics; however, certain things, such as certain drop shadow, will convert the vector into images. It is best practice to avoid vectors being converted into images as much as possible. Using the Flash XML Graphic (FXG), format that Catalyst produces rather than images can give you a much better and crisper look to your applications, not to mention decrease the size of your SWFs (if images are embedded) or increase performance since the FP10 drawing API is faster than loading external images during runtime.

For instance, in your application you will convert the artwork into components.

The first step is to break the artwork into the components you will be creating. In your case, you will have the following components:

- Body
- Footer
- Left Nav
- Header

The next step is to open Flash Catalyst and convert each artwork into a FXP project.

1. Let's start from the first component: Body. Open Flash Catalyst (see Figure 3-7). Select **From Adobe Photoshop PSD File...**

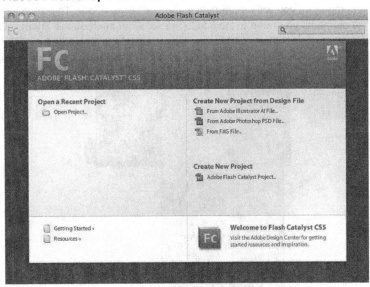

Figure 3-7. Flash Catalyst start page

2. Browse to the directory design directory and select **Body.psd**. Photoshop import options opens up. Keep the defaults and select **Ok**, as shown in Figure 3-8.

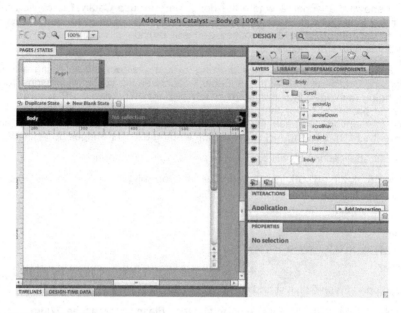

Figure 3-8. Flash Catalyst start page

3. The first component you will be creating is the vertical scrollbar. To create the scrollbar, select the elements you need to include in the scrollbar such as the Thumb, Track, Up, and Down. Once you select these graphic elements, select the **Convert Artwork to Component** in the HUD (Heads Up Display) and select **Vertical Scrollbar**, as shown in Figure 3-9.

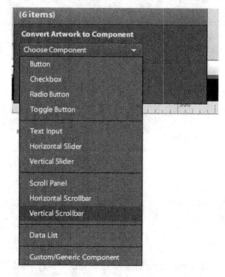

Figure 3-9. HUD convert artwork to component drop down menu

4. Once you have completed the Scrollbar component, you see a new message in the HUD (see Figure 3-10). You need to specify each graphic element as what it is, such as track, thumb, etc.

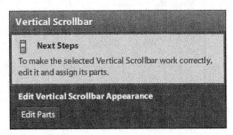

Figure 3-10. Vertical Scrollbar message

5. To do that, click on **Edit Parts** in the HUD. Select each graphic and in the Convert Artwork to Vertical Scrollbar Part drop down menu, select each part (see Figure 3-11).

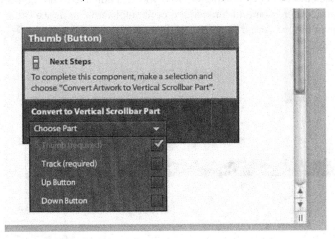

Figure 3-11. Set Thumb in HUD

6. Once you select **File ➤ Run Project** (or command + Return on Mac OS), you will be able to view the scrollbar functioning.

7. Now that you have the scrollbar, you want to assign it to a list component. All the results will be placed in a list, and the user can use the scrollbar with association with that list. From the **WIREFRAME COMPONENTS,** choose the **Data List** and drag and drop it in the stage, as shown in Figure 3-12.

Note In our case we are using the out of the box list component, but we can have a designer mock that component and we can convert it to a list.

91

Figure 3-12. Wireframe components window

8.   Then, select the scrollbar and copy the component (from the top menu select **Edit ➤ Copy**). Double-click the Data List component and you can edit the component's part. Replace the default vertical scrollbar and remove the horizontal scrollbar as well as adjust the size of each item in the list. Add a rectangle that you can replace later with the user's image (see Figure 3-13).

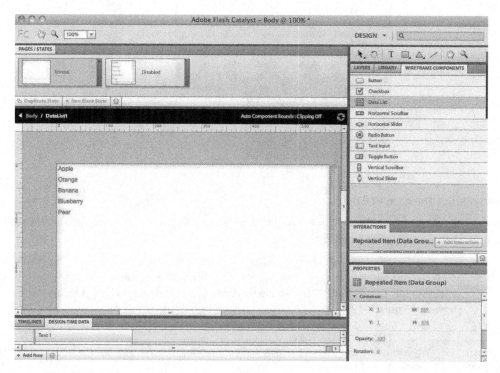

Figure 3-13. Body Flash Catalyst project showing list components

9. We have completed converting the design to FXG code. Save the file as **body.fxp**.

10. Next, create a new Flash Catalyst **Header** project. Select **From Adobe Photoshop PSD File...** and import the **Header.psd**. In the artwork, you have the two states normal and hover. The first step is to convert each of the normal artworks to a button. To select the button artwork, right-click and select **Convert Artwork to Component ➤ Button** or use the HUD menu, as shown in Figure 3-14.

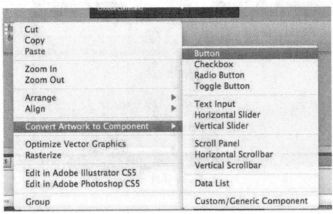

Figure 3-14. Convert artwork to button

11. After you have converted the artwork into **Button,** you can edit the button. Once you select to edit by using the HUD or double-clicking the component, it opens with all the different states. Go back to the main document and copy the hover state. Then, paste it in the button **Over** and **Down** states (see Figure 3-15).

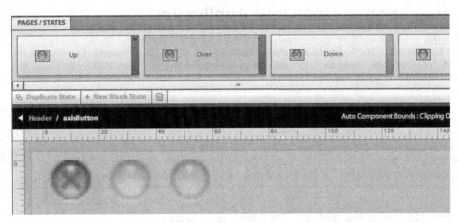

Figure 3-15. Button states

12. To select the search artwork, right-click and select **Convert Artwork to Component** and then **Text Input**, as shown inFigure 3-16. Save the project as **Header.fxp**.

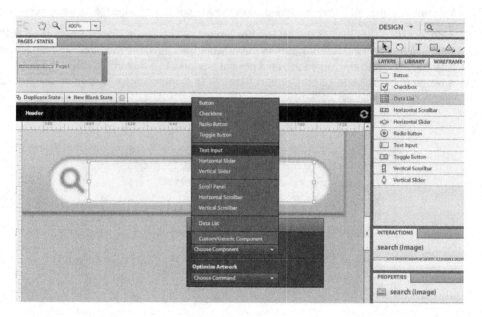

Figure 3-16. Convert artwork into text input component

13. Lastly, open **LeftNav.psd** and **Footer.psd,** and save the Flash Catalyst projects as **LeftNav.fxp** and **Footer.fxp.** At this point, you did not add any navigation or footer components since we wanted to keep the project simple in nature. Therefore, there is no need to convert artwork into components or add any interactivity.

Step 3: Integration of Code into Application

Once the work with Catalyst is completed, the files can be imported. The format is FXP "," which is recognized by Flash Builder 4. There are many ways to use the FXG component such as Inheritance and composition. You can use them as is or use the presentation model. Personally, we found that using the presentation model is a good solution.

> Tip: A Presentation Model is a design pattern where the model represents the behavior and state of a view. It's very similar to the "code behind" that used to be a common implementation in earlier versions of Flex. It's about separating the view from the logic. Once the logic changes, the view updates automatically. There are many implementations of the presentation model such as the view keeping an instance of the presenter and binding properties, or the view being passive and unaware of being changed.

Here are some of the advantages of using the presentation model:

- You can tie it well with unit testing.
- The component is loosely coupled.

- You can replace the view more easily.
- It integrates well with MVC pattern and the new Flex 4 component's architecture.

There are many types of implementations. The idea is to have a "clean" view that does not have any code, which allows you to easily make changes to the view and follow the Flex 4 and Catalyst architecture of separating pixels from the plumbing.

By doing so, you will be able to exchange the components and skins more quickly than having a component that holds code and visual components.

We recommend importing the FXP project as a separate project and slowly copying and pasting the components, skins, and assets into your existing project; then placing them in a namespace that matches your application's frameworkas shown in Figure 3-17.

Figure 3-17. Project folder structure

The next step is to create the presentation model to hold the view and logic of each component.

1. For the Body component, you will create `BodyPM` which will hold the logic:

```
package com.elad.twitter.model.presentation
{
    import com.elad.twitter.model.domain.LibraryModel;

    [Bindable]
    // Defines the TemplatePM Value Object implementation
    public class BodyPM extends AbstractPM
    {

        // Define an instance of the <code>LibraryModel
        public var libraryModel:LibraryModel;
```

```
// Defualt constractor
public function BodyPM(libraryModel:LibraryModel)
{
    this.libraryModel = libraryModel;
}

    }
}
```

2. You also need to modify the model locator to hold an instance of each component presentation model:

```
private var _bodyPM:BodyPM;
    private var _footerPM:FooterPM;
    private var _headerPM:HeaderPM;
    private var _leftnavPM:LeftNavPM;
    private var _mainwindowPM:MainWindowPM;

    public function get mainwindowPM():MainWindowPM
    {
        return _mainwindowPM;
    }

    public function set mainwindowPM(value:MainWindowPM):void
    {
        _mainwindowPM = value;
    }

    public function get leftnavPM():LeftNavPM
    {
        return _leftnavPM;
    }

    public function set leftnavPM(value:LeftNavPM):void
    {
        _leftnavPM = value;
    }

    public function get headerPM():HeaderPM
    {
        return _headerPM;
    }

    public function set headerPM(value:HeaderPM):void
    {
        _headerPM = value;
    }

    public function get footerPM():FooterPM
    {
        return _footerPM;
    }

    public function set footerPM(value:FooterPM):void
    {
        _footerPM = value;
    }
```

```
    public function get bodyPM():BodyPM
    {
        return _bodyPM;
    }

    public function set bodyPM(value:BodyPM):void
    {
        _bodyPM = value;
    }

    public static function getInstance() : ModelLocator
    {
        if ( instance == null )
        {
            instance = new ModelLocator( new Private() );
            instance.libraryModel = new LibraryModel();
            instance.mainPM = new MainPM( instance.libraryModel );
            instance.bodyPM = new BodyPM( instance.libraryModel );
            instance.footerPM = new FooterPM( instance.libraryModel );
            instance.headerPM = new HeaderPM( instance.libraryModel );
            instance.leftnavPM = new LeftNavPM( instance.libraryModel );
            instance.mainwindowPM = new MainWindowPM( instance.libraryModel );
        }
        return instance;
    }
  }
}

/ Inner class which restricts constructor access to Private
class Private {}
```

3. The last part is to add a component to hold the view for each component you imported from Catalyst. See Figure 3-18 for folder structure and files created. An example of BodyView.mxml is shown in the following code:

```
<?xml version="1.0" encoding="utf-8"?>
<s:Group xmlns:fx="http://ns.adobe.com/mxml/2009"
        xmlns:s="library://ns.adobe.com/flex/spark"
        xmlns:mx="library://ns.adobe.com/flex/mx"
        width="400" height="300">

    <fx:Script>
        <![CDATA[

            import com.elad.twitter.model.presentation.BodyPM;

            [Bindable]
            public var body:BodyPM;

        ]]>
    </fx:Script>


    <s:layout>
        <s:BasicLayout/>
```

```
        </s:layout>

</s:Group>
```

4. Next, you need to add references to the `MainWindowView.mxml`, which will hold all the components you imported from Catalyst.

```xml
<?xml version="1.0" encoding="utf-8"?>
<s:Group xmlns:fx="http://ns.adobe.com/mxml/2009"
         xmlns:s="library://ns.adobe.com/flex/spark"
         xmlns:mx="library://ns.adobe.com/flex/mx"
         xmlns:view="com.elad.twitter.view.*"
         width="724" height="553">

    <view:HeaderView />
    <view:BodyView   x="146" y="52" />
    <view:LeftNavView x="0" y="52" />
    <view:FooterView  x="0" y="529" />

</s:Group>
```

```xml
<?xml version="1.0" encoding="utf-8"?>
<s:WindowedApplication xmlns:fx="http://ns.adobe.com/mxml/2009"
                       xmlns:s="library://ns.adobe.com/flex/spark"
                       xmlns:mx="library://ns.adobe.com/flex/halo"
                       xmlns:business="com.elad.twitter.business.*"
                       xmlns:control="com.elad.twitter.control.*"
                       xmlns:view="com.elad.twitter.view.*"
                       width="724" height="553"
                       initialize="modelLocator.mainPM.initialize()">

    <fx:Script>
        <![CDATA[

            import com.elad.twitter.model.ModelLocator;

            [Bindable]
public var modelLocator:ModelLocator = ModelLocator.getInstance();

        ]]>
    </fx:Script>

    <fx:Declarations>
        <control:TwitterTagController />
        <business:Services />
    </fx:Declarations>

    <view:MainWindowView id="mainApp" />

</s:WindowedApplication>
```

Now that you have the scaffolding ready, yu can import the projects you created in Flash Catalyst.

5. To import the project from Flash Catalyst into Flash Builder, open Flash Builder and from the top context menu. Select **File ➤ Import Flex Project (FXP)...** (see Figure 3-18).

Figure 3-18. import project into Flash Builder

6. Follow the same process to import the following projects:

*   Body.fxp
*   Footer.fxp
*   Header.fxp
*   LeftNav.fxp

7. Once you complete the process and import all the projects, you can see the project structure in the package explorer. See Body project import into Flash Builder (Figure 3-19).

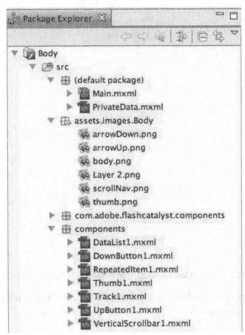

Figure 3-19. Body project imported into Flash Builder

8. Once all the projects are imported it is a good idea to refactor the project to your standards, so it is more readable. Here is an example of refactoring the **DownButton1.mxml** in the **Body.fxp** project.

Refactoring code to be more readable is a matter of personal taste and coding convention. During this process, you will find that you have to make all kind of changes to the code such as the following:

- Refactor code to be more readable
- Rename skins and components to names that make more sense
- Adding id property for components
- Making changes to states and transitions and properties to better fit business requirements

Additionally, you may often find that you need to replace a component to better work with your data. For example, replace DataGrid with List component, add a custom button that was left out, or while integrating the application you may find that pieces that do not make sense may need to be changed. During that process, the designer can help provide any assets necessary. You may also need to get the business side involved in order to adjust documents or get in touch with the client to provide additional information.

Figure 3-20. Folder and files structure after adding presentation model classes into the projects

9. The next step is to copy the code from each FXP project and rename the components. See Table 3-1 for an example.

Table 3-1. Code Copied and Renamed

Project	Component Name	New Name and Namespace
Body	Main.mxml	BodyView.mxml
Footer	Main.mxml	FooterView.mxml
LeftNav	Main.mxml	LeftNavView.mxml
Header	Main.mxml	HeaderView.mxml

10. Flash Catalyst generates names that are generic; changing the names will help in creating a code that is more coherent. See Table 3-2 which shows the original names and new component names.

Table 3-2. Original and New Componet Names

Project name	Original name	New Name
Body.fxp	CustomComponent1.mxml	ListComponent.mxml
Body.fxp	DataList1.mxml	TagsDataList.mxml
Body.fxp	RepeatedItem1.mxml	TagRepeatedItem.mxml
Body.fxp	Thumb1.mxml	TagsListThumb.mxml
Body.fxp	Track1.mxml	TagsListTrack.mxml
Body.fxp	UpButton1.mxml	TagsListUpButton.mxml
Body.fxp	DownButton1.mxml	TagsListDownButton.mxml
Body.fxp	VerticalScrollbar1.mxml	TagsListVerticalScrollbar.mxml
Header.fxp	axisButton1.mxml	AxisButton.mxml
Header.fxp	maxButton1.mxml	MaxButton.mxml
Header.fxp	minButton1.mxml	MinButton.mxml
Header.fxp	searchTextInput1.mxml	SearchTextInput.mxml

11. Adding id properties or renaming id property names should be done on a need to need basis. For example, add an id to the list component in the **Body** project:

```
<s:List x="0" y="0" id="tagsList"↩
 skinClass="com.elad.twitter.view.body.components.TagsDataList">
```

To see the changes you made to the application download **Step2** from `http://code.google.com/p/advancedflex4/` **Chapter 3, TwitterTags-step2**.

Compile and run the AIR application you built so far, as shown in Figure 3-21.

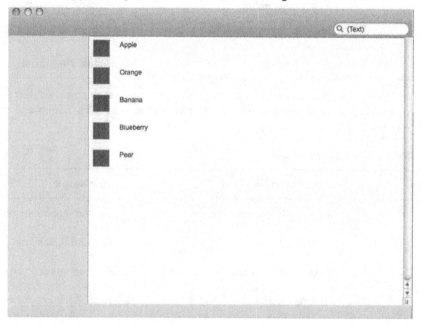

Figure 3-21. The Twitter AIR application screenshot

Step 4: Refactor

As you create different FXP projects, there are cases where you are using very similar components and skins, and you want to avoid that and try to refactor so you take into account reusability, which is one of the building blocks of Object-Oriented programming. For example, because a button label is different you should not have two button skins. You should adjust the skin so it can handle these two instances and remove one skin, which will make your application smaller in size and more optimized.

A good idea is creating a folder named **shared,** which can hold the components you will be sharing as well as components that are tweaked to be used in more than one component.

This example is relatively simple so we don't need to share any skins or components.

Step 5: Develop

At this point, you have a project with separate components and a good structure to build an application that can be scaled. You can now add code so you will be able to search Twitter and display results.

1. In your application, you will be handling moving the application and minimizing, maximizing, and closing the application, so you don't need the default AIR chrome. To remove the AIR application chrome, you first need to open **Main-app.xml** file thenuncomment and set the following line of code:

```
<systemChrome>none</systemChrome>
```

2. The next step is to allow moving, minimizing, and maximizing windows since you removed the chrome. Open **HeaderView.mxml** and add click events.

```
<?xml version="1.0" encoding="utf-8"?>
<s:Group xmlns:d="http://ns.adobe.com/fxg/2008/dt"
         xmlns:fx="http://ns.adobe.com/mxml/2009"
         xmlns:s="library://ns.adobe.com/flex/spark"
         width="723" height="53">

    <fx:Script>
        <![CDATA[
            import flash.events.MouseEvent;

            import com.elad.twitter.model.presentation.HeaderPM;

            [Bindable]
            public var header:HeaderPM;

        ]]>
    </fx:Script>

    <s:Group mouseDown="this.stage.nativeWindow.startMove();">
        <s:BitmapImage smooth="true"↵
 source="@Embed('/assets/images/Header/background.png')"
                        d:userLabel="background" x="0" y="0"/>
        <s:Button skinClass="com.elad.twitter.view.header.components.MinButton"
                    x="25" y="3" click="this.stage.nativeWindow.minimize()"/>
        <s:Button skinClass="com.elad.twitter.view.header.components.MaxButton"
                    x="46" y="3" click="this.stage.nativeWindow.maximize()"/>
        <s:Button skinClass="com.elad.twitter.view.header.components.AxisButton"
                    x="4" y="3" click="this.stage.nativeWindow.close()"/>
        <s:TextInput↵
 skinClass="com.elad.twitter.view.header.components.SearchTextInput"
                        text="" x="602" y="28" />
    </s:Group>

</s:Group>
```

3. Add an event class under the com.elad.twitter.events package and name the event SearchTwitterAPIEvent.as. This event will be used to a user gesture of the user inserts a keyword query. Once the user keys down, the event will be dispatched and pass the keyword result to a command class which will retrieve the results from Twitter.

```
package com.elad.twitter.events
{
    import com.adobe.cairngorm.control.CairngormEvent;
    import flash.events.Event;
```

```
public final class SearchTwitterAPIEvent extends CairngormEvent
{
    public var keyword:String = "";

     public static const SEARCHTWITTERAPI_EVENT:String ~CCC
        = "com.elad.twitter.events.SearchTwitterAPIEvent";

     public function SearchTwitterAPIEvent(keyword:String)
    {
        this.keyword = keyword;

        super( SEARCHTWITTERAPI_EVENT );
    }

     public override function clone() : Event
    {
        var event:SearchTwitterAPIEvent = new SearchTwitterAPIEvent(keyword);
        return event;
    }
  }
}
```

You will set the application so that a keyword search will occur on every user key down.

4. Add a key down event to the `RichEditableText` component in the SearchTextInput.mxml skin:

```
keyDown=" new SearchTwitterAPIEvent(searchInputBox.text).dispatch()"
```

Here's the complete code of SearchTextInput.mxml

```
<?xml version="1.0" encoding="utf-8"?>
<s:Skin xmlns:s="library://ns.adobe.com/flex/spark"↵
 xmlns:fx="http://ns.adobe.com/mxml/2009" xmlns:d="http://ns.adobe.com/fxg/2008/dt">
    <fx:Metadata>[HostComponent("spark.components.TextInput")]</fx:Metadata>

    <fx:Script>
        <![CDATA[
            import com.elad.twitter.events.SearchTwitterAPIEvent;
        ]]>
    </fx:Script>
    <s:states>
        <s:State name="normal"/>
        <s:State name="disabled"/>
    </s:states>
    <s:BitmapImage smooth="true" source="@Embed('/assets/images/Header/search.png')"
                        d:userLabel="search" x="0" y="0"/>
    <s:RichEditableText x="5" y="5" width="97" heightInLines="1"
                            id="searchInputBox" fontFamily="Arial"
                            keyDown="new↵
SearchTwitterAPIEvent(searchInputBox.text).dispatch()"/>
</s:Skin>
```

5. In the `SearchTwitterAPICommand`, you will implement the logic to call the Twitter service

```
package com.elad.twitter.commands.services
{
    import com.adobe.cairngorm.commands.ICommand;
    import com.adobe.cairngorm.control.CairngormEvent;
    import com.adobe.serialization.json.JSON;
    import com.elad.twitter.business.SearchTwitterAPIDelegate;
    import com.elad.twitter.events.SearchTwitterAPIEvent;
    import com.elad.twitter.model.ModelLocator;
    import com.elad.twitter.vo.TweetsCollectionVO;

    import flash.utils.getQualifiedClassName;

    import mx.collections.ArrayCollection;
    import mx.logging.ILogger;
    import mx.logging.Log;
    import mx.rpc.IResponder;
    import mx.rpc.events.FaultEvent;
    import mx.rpc.events.ResultEvent;

    public final class SearchTwitterAPICommand implements ICommand, IResponder
    {
        // Defines a local convenience reference to the application model
        private var model:ModelLocator = ModelLocator.getInstance();

        //  Create variable to point to this class.
        private var logger:ILogger =↵
Log.getLogger(getQualifiedClassName(this).replace("::", "."));

         // Concrete ICommand implementation which handles
         // SearchTwitterAPIEvent.
        public function execute(event:CairngormEvent) : void
        {
            // logging command to logging API
            logger.info("execute");

            var evt:SearchTwitterAPIEvent = event as SearchTwitterAPIEvent;
            var delegate:SearchTwitterAPIDelegate = new SearchTwitterAPIDelegate(↵
this );

            delegate.getSearchResults(evt.keyword);
        }

        // Handles the service result of the <code>SearchTwitterAPIDelegate</code>
        // service invocation.
        public function result(data:Object) : void
        {
            // logging result to logging API
            logger.info("result");

            var result:ResultEvent = data as ResultEvent;
```

```
        var feedsResults:Object;

        try
        {
            var str:String = String(data.result);
            feedsResults = JSON.decode(str);
        }
        catch (err:Error)
        {
            // todo: handle errors messages
            Log.getLogger("There was and Error loading the Feed Manager Data↵
:: ").error("fault");
            return;
        }

        model.bodyPM.tweetCollection = new TweetsCollectionVO(↵
new ArrayCollection( feedsResults.results ) );
    }

    // Handles the service fault of the <code>SearchTwitterAPIDelegate</code>
    // service invocation.
    public function fault(info:Object) : void
    {
        var fault:FaultEvent = info as FaultEvent;

        // logging fault to logging API
        logger.error("fault", fault);
    }
  }
}
```

Notice that you are using a JSON serialization. That class is an open source class provided by Adobe and is part of the AS3CoreLib SWC, see http://code.google.com/p/as3corelib/.

You also need to add the variable to the BodyPM.as to store the collection of tweets received.

```
private var _tweetCollection:TweetsCollectionVO = null;

public function get tweetCollection():TweetsCollectionVO
{
    return _tweetCollection;
}

public function set tweetCollection(value:TweetsCollectionVO):void
{
    _tweetCollection = value;
}
```

6. Once you receive the response from the Twitter API, you will create a collection to hold the results and assign them to the list. Every Tweet will hold the properties you are setting in TweetVO.as.

```
package com.elad.twitter.vo
```

```
{
    import com.adobe.cairngorm.vo.IValueObject;

    [Bindable]
    // Defines the <code>AssetVO<code> Value Object implementation
    public class TweetVO implements IValueObject
    {
        public var created_at:String;
        public var from_user:String;
        public var from_user_id:String;
        public var id:String;
        public var iso_language_code:String;
        public var profile_image_url:String;
        public var source:String;
        public var text:String;
        public var to_user_id:String;

        public function TweetVO(item:Object)
        {
            this.created_at = item.created_at;
            this.from_user = item.from_user;
            this.from_user_id = item.from_user_id;
            this.id = item.id;
            this.iso_language_code = item.iso_language_code;
            this.profile_image_url = item.profile_image_url;
            this.source = item.source;
            this.text = item.text;
            this.to_user_id = item.to_user_id;
        }
    }
}
```

7. To hold the collection of Tweets, you need to create a VO (Value Object) called TweetsCollectionVO.as and add properties to add an item and retrieve an item.

```
package com.elad.twitter.vo
{
    import com.adobe.cairngorm.vo.IValueObject;

    import mx.collections.ArrayCollection;

    [Bindable]
    // Defines the AssetCollectionVO Value Object implementation
    public class TweetsCollectionVO implements IValueObject
    {
        private var _collection:ArrayCollection;

        public function TweetsCollectionVO(collection:ArrayCollection = null)
        {
            if (collection == null)
            {
                _collection = new ArrayCollection();
            }
            else
```

```
        {
            _collection = collection;
        }
    }

    public function addItem(item:TweetVO):void
    {
        _collection.addItem(item);
    }

    public function getItem(index:int):TweetVO
    {
        return _collection.getItemAt(index) as TweetVO;
    }

    public function readAssets(index:Number):TweetVO
    {
        var retVal:TweetVO;
        retVal = _collection.getItemAt(index) as TweetVO;
        return retVal;
    }

    public function get length():Number
    {
        return _collection.length;
    }

    public function get collection():ArrayCollection
    {
        return _collection;
    }
    }
}
```

8. **Services.mxml** component holds all the service components. In your case, you only need a HTTPService component to access the Twitter search API.

```
<?xml version="1.0" encoding="utf-8"?>
<cairngorm:ServiceLocator xmlns:mx="http://www.adobe.com/2006/mxml"
                          xmlns:cairngorm="com.adobe.cairngorm.business.*" >
    <mx:Script>
        <![CDATA[

            public static var GET_TWITTER_SEARCH_RESULTS:String↵
= "getTwitterSearchResults";

        ]]>
    </mx:Script>

    <mx:HTTPService id="getTwitterSearchResults"
                    url="http://search.twitter.com/search.json"
```

```
                    resultFormat="text"/>

</cairngorm:ServiceLocator>
```

9. The delegate class is using the `Services` class to send a request and direct the result back to the command.Ssee `SearchTwitterAPIDelegate.as` class.

```
package com.elad.twitter.business
{
    import com.adobe.cairngorm.business.ServiceLocator;

    import mx.rpc.AsyncToken;
    import mx.rpc.IResponder;
    import mx.rpc.http.HTTPService;

    public final class SearchTwitterAPIDelegate
    {
        // Defines the reference to the <code>SearchTwitterAPICommand<code>
        // instance.
        private var responder:IResponder;

        // Define reference to the service which can be one
        //  of the RPC (HttpService, WebService or RemoteService)
        private var service:HTTPService;

        // Instantiates a new instance of <code>SearchTwitterAPIDelegate</code>
        // and initializes a reference to the <code>IResponder<code> instance.
        public function SearchTwitterAPIDelegate(responder:IResponder)
        {
            service = ServiceLocator.getInstance().getHTTPService ~CCC
                    (Services.GET_TWITTER_SEARCH_RESULTS);
            this.responder = responder;
        }

        public function getSearchResults(keyword:String):void
        {
            var param:Object = new Object();
            param.q = keyword;

            var token:AsyncToken = service.send( param )
            token.addResponder( responder );
        }
    }
}
```

10. In the `BodyView.mxml` component, you need to add a data provider for the list so it points to the collection you created:`.dataProvider="{body.tweetCollection.collection}"`

```
<?xml version="1.0" encoding="utf-8"?>
<s:Group xmlns:s="library://ns.adobe.com/flex/spark"
        xmlns:components="com.elad.twitter.view.header.components.*"
        xmlns:fx="http://ns.adobe.com/mxml/2009"
        xmlns:d="http://ns.adobe.com/fxg/2008/dt"
        xmlns:th="http://ns.adobe.com/thermo/2009"
```

```
                width="576" height="478">

    <fx:Script>
        <![CDATA[

            import com.elad.twitter.model.presentation.BodyPM;

            [Bindable]
            public var body:BodyPM;

        ]]>
    </fx:Script>

    <s:states>
        <s:State name="DetailView" th:color="0x0081cc"/>
    </s:states>

    <fx:DesignLayer d:userLabel="Body">

        <fx:DesignLayer d:userLabel="Scroll">
            <s:BitmapImage source="@Embed('/assets/Body/scrollNav.png')"
                            resizeMode="scale" d:userLabel="scrollNav"
                            x="561" y="464"/>
        </fx:DesignLayer>
        <s:List x="0" y="0"
                skinClass="com.elad.twitter.view.body.components.TagsDataList"
                dataProvider="{body.tweetCollection.collection}"/>
    </fx:DesignLayer>

</s:Group>
```

11. Lastly, you need to add code that will extract the data in `TagRepeatedItem.mxml` and create a renderer that will display the user profile image and the text of the tweet.

```
<s:ItemRenderer xmlns:fx="http://ns.adobe.com/mxml/2009"
                xmlns:s="library://ns.adobe.com/flex/spark"
                creationComplete="creationCompleteHandler(event)"
                xmlns:mx="library://ns.adobe.com/flex/halo">

    <fx:Script>
        <![CDATA[
            import com.elad.twitter.vo.TweetVO;
            import mx.events.FlexEvent;

            protected function creationCompleteHandler(event:FlexEvent):void
            {
                // TODO Auto-generated method stub
                var tweet:TweetVO = new TweetVO(this.data);

                image.source = tweet.profile_image_url;
                text.text = tweet.text;
            }
```

```
        ]]>
    </fx:Script>

    <s:states>
        <s:State name="normal"/>
    </s:states>

    <s:Rect width="547" height="65"
            id="rect1"
            x="0" y="0">

        <s:fill>
            <s:SolidColor color="0xFFFFFF"/>
        </s:fill>
    </s:Rect>

    <s:RichText id="text"
                text="" height="39" width="424"
                x="84" y="9" />

    <mx:Image id="image" x="18" y="6"/>

</s:ItemRenderer>
```

To compare your application with ours see Step3/TwitterTag application. Once you compile, you can see Figure 3-22.

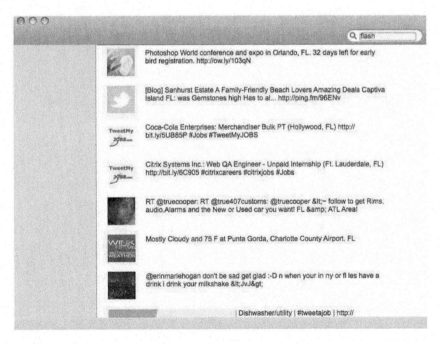

Figure 3-22. AIR application shows search results

Summary

Flash Catalyst is a valuable tool and will change designer-developer workflow. Flash Catalyst will soon be an integrated part of the development cycle and you will find it hard to work without it, mainly because it will save you valuable development time.

The designer can create the artwork and adjust the artwork, as you need to make changes. While the developer may be the one converting the artwork into code, designers and developers can work in parallel to make the changes as required. For example, you may notice that adding a drop-shadow to a vector graphic in Illustrator will convert the graphic into an image in Catalyst. This does not happen all the time except in certain cases. You can work with the designer and have these images adjusted. As you work with the designer, you can show him or her how you are working with Catalyst so the designer can slowly take over some of the Catalyst work when he or she is ready.

Chapter 4

Flex and AIR: Taking Applications to the Desktop

by Elad Elrom

Adobe Integrated Runtime (AIR) technology provides an opportunity for you to bring your Flex application into a whole new domain, the desktop. The API provides access to almost every nook and cranny you could want: the file system, native windows, native menus, and more. It also includes an embedded local database that you can use for offline storage. Plus it's portable between Mac, Windows, and Linux. With these tools in hand and better integration of AIR 2.0 with the OS, it's hard to think of any desktop application that you can't write with AIR.

In this chapter, we'll show several complete examples that push the limits of the AIR API. You are free to use these as templates for your own applications.

AIR Basics

If you haven't built an AIR application before, not to worry, the process is very similar to building a new Flex browser application.

1. It starts with selecting **File ➤ New** and choosing **Flex Project** name the project Tester. See Figure 4-1.

2. From there, you select **Desktop application** instead of **Web application**.

Figure 4-1. Create an AIR application.

Flash Builder then takes care of building the AIR application XML file, the starting MXML application file, and so on. It also takes care of launching your application using the "adl" test launcher.

Flash Builder will also help you put together the shipping version of your AIR application through a special version of the **Export Release Build** dialog under the **Project** menu. This dialog will build the .air file that your customer will download. To create the .air file, you will need to sign the executable by creating a digital certificate and then attaching that to the file. To create the certificate follow these steps:

1. Select **File ➤ Export ➤ Release Build Export To File** text input already includes the air file name (see Figure 4-2).

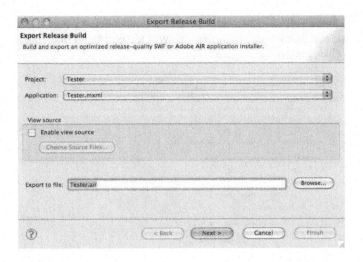

Figure 4-2. Export Release Build

2. Select **Next** and the **Export Release Build** opens up. Click the **Create** button and the wizard displays the **Create Self-Signed Digital Certificate** dialog shown in Figure 4-3. Put the publisher name and password and browse to name and save the file. Click **OK**.

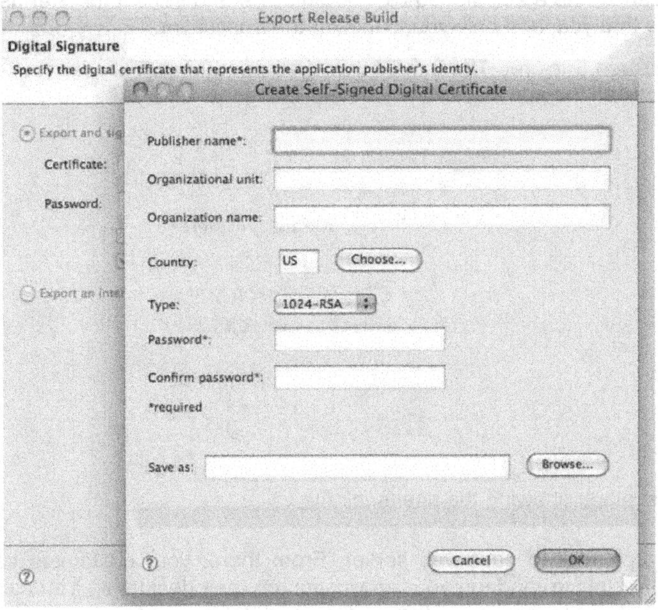

Figure 4-3. The Create Self-Signed Digital Certificate dialog

3. **Export Release Build** dialog is showing up with the certificate file you just created and password. Click **Finish** (see Figure 4-4).

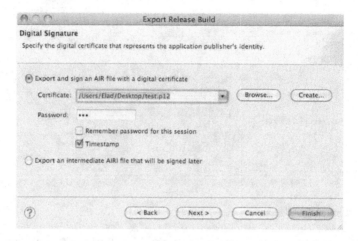

Figure 4-4. Export Release Build complete process

With this dialog, you can create a self-signed digital certificate and store it for later use. It ensures that it is password protected so that you, and only you, can sign the application.

Take a look at the Package Explorer. The .air file was created automatically for you, as shown in Figure 4-5. Therefore, you can install the application by double-clicking the .air file.

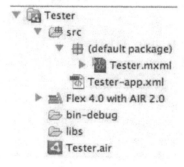

Figure 4-5. Package explorer showing the user's .air file

Additionally, you can upload it to your web server. From there, your customers can download it (after having installed the AIR runtime) and run your application on their desktops. You can also create a badge install similar to what you see on the AIR Marketplace (http://www.adobe.com/cfusion/marketplace/index.cfm) so it can handle installing the runtime, in case it's missing on the user's machine or it needs an upgrade.

Building a Browser

AIR comes with a built-in native web browser that you can use within your Flex application. It works just like any other Flash sprite. Shown here is a simple example AIR application that uses the web browser control to display any web page you wish. Create a new AIR application and call it Browser. The application MXML content is the following code:

```
<?xml version="1.0" encoding="utf-8"?>
<s:WindowedApplication xmlns:fx="http://ns.adobe.com/mxml/2009"
                    xmlns:s="library://ns.adobe.com/flex/spark"
                    xmlns:mx="library://ns.adobe.com/flex/mx"
                    creationComplete="onStartup()" resize="onResize(event)">

    <fx:Script>
        <![CDATA[
            import flash.html.HTMLLoader;
            import mx.core.UIComponent;

            private var htmlPage:HTMLLoader = null;

            private function onStartup() : void
            {
                var ref:UIComponent = new UIComponent();
                ref.setStyle('top', 50);

                htmlPage = new HTMLLoader();
                htmlPage.width = 600;
                htmlPage.height = 600;
                ref.addChild( htmlPage );

                addElement(ref);
            }

            private function onResize(event:Event) : void
            {
                if (htmlPage)
                {
                    htmlPage.height = height - 50;
                    htmlPage.width = width;
                }
            }

            private function onKeyDown(event:KeyboardEvent):void
            {
                if ( event.keyCode == Keyboard.ENTER )
                    htmlPage.load(new URLRequest(txtUrl.text));
            }

        ]]>
    </fx:Script>

    <mx:Form width="100%">
        <mx:FormItem label="Url" width="100%">
```

```
                    <mx:TextInput id="txtUrl" width="100%" text="http://adobe.com"
                                  keyDown="onKeyDown(event)" />
            </mx:FormItem>
        </mx:Form>

</s:WindowedApplication>
```

The code for this example is pretty simple. When the application receives the creation complete event, it builds a new HTMLLoader object. Because the HTMLLoader is based on a sprite, it needs to be wrapped in a Flex UIComponent object. The code then responds to the resize event by resizing the HTML page control to match the new frame size. It also looks at the key-down event on the URL text to see when the user presses the Enter or Return key to start browsing to that location. When you run this AIR application from Flash Builder, you get something that looks like Figure 4-6.

This example shows just a portion of what you can do with the browser control. You can get access to the browsing history as well as inject JavaScript objects into the runtime space of the page.

Another common use case is the viewing of a PDF file within the application. You could use a PDF to store documentation or to present the licensing agreement for the software.

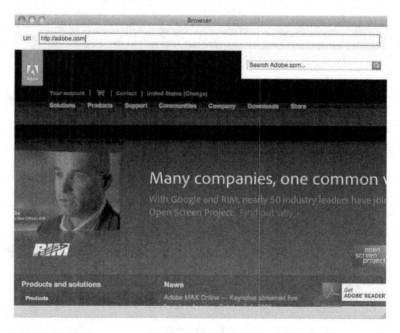

Figure 4-6. The built-in web browser

AIR has special support for PDF built right in. It's just as easy to look at a PDF page as it is any web page. Using the following code, create a new AIR project and call it PDFSupport.

```
<?xml version="1.0" encoding="utf-8"?>
<s:WindowedApplication xmlns:fx="http://ns.adobe.com/mxml/2009"
                       xmlns:s="library://ns.adobe.com/flex/spark"
```

```
            xmlns:mx="library://ns.adobe.com/flex/mx"
            creationComplete="creationCompleteHandler()"
            resize="onResize()">
    <fx:Script>
        <![CDATA[
            import mx.core.UIComponent;

            private var htmlWin:HTMLLoader;

            protected function creationCompleteHandler():void
            {
                var ref:UIComponent = new UIComponent();

                htmlWin = new HTMLLoader();
                htmlWin.width = width;
                htmlWin.height = height;
                ref.addChild( htmlWin );

                addElement( ref );

                htmlWin.load( new URLRequest( '/1.pdf' ) );
            }

            private function onResize():void
            {
                if ( htmlWin )
                {
                    htmlWin.width = width;
                    htmlWin.height = height;
                }
            }

        ]]>
    </fx:Script>

</s:WindowedApplication>
```

In this example, you are loading a local PDF file called 1.pdf, which is in the AIR project locally. Just as with the original HTML reader application, the code watches for the resize event and adjusts the size of the HTML viewer to match the current window size.

Having PDF support (if the reader is installed on the user's computer) can be very helpful when it comes to embedding help support in your application.

Native Menus

Menus are important when it comes to creating a native user experience. Java Swing, for example, puts menus on the window regardless of how the native operating system does it. That makes for an awkward user experience on Macintosh. On the other hand, AIR gives you real native menus and makes them easy to use.

Have a look at the following code, which creates a very simple menu, to see how easy it is to create menus.

```
<?xml version="1.0" encoding="utf-8"?>
<s:WindowedApplication xmlns:fx="http://ns.adobe.com/mxml/2009"
                       xmlns:s="library://ns.adobe.com/flex/spark"
                       xmlns:mx="library://ns.adobe.com/flex/mx"
                       width="650" height="400"
                       creationComplete="creationCompleteHandler()">

    <fx:Script>
        <![CDATA[
            import flash.display.NativeMenu;
            import flash.display.NativeMenuItem;
            import flash.events.Event;
            import flash.filters.BlurFilter;
            import flash.filters.DropShadowFilter;

            private var itemDS:NativeMenuItem = new NativeMenuItem("Drop Shadow" );
            private var itemBlur:NativeMenuItem = new NativeMenuItem( "Blur" );

            protected function creationCompleteHandler():void
            {
                var filterMenu:NativeMenuItem = new NativeMenuItem("Filters");

                if(NativeWindow.supportsMenu)
                {
                    stage.nativeWindow.menu = new NativeMenu();
                    stage.nativeWindow.menu.addItem(filterMenu);
                }

                if(NativeApplication.supportsMenu)
                    NativeApplication.nativeApplication.menu.addItem(filterMenu);

                var filterSubMenu:NativeMenu = new NativeMenu();

                itemBlur.addEventListener(Event.SELECT,onMenuSelect);
                itemDS.addEventListener(Event.SELECT,onMenuSelect);

                filterSubMenu.addItem( itemBlur );
                filterSubMenu.addItem( itemDS );
                filterMenu.submenu = filterSubMenu;
            }

            private function onMenuSelect( event:Event ):void
            {
                var mi:NativeMenuItem = event.target as NativeMenuItem;
                var filters:Array = [];

                mi.checked = !mi.checked;

                if ( itemDS.checked )
```

```
            filters.push( new DropShadowFilter() );

        if ( itemBlur.checked )
            filters.push( new BlurFilter() );

        image.filters = filters;
    }

  ]]>
</fx:Script>

<mx:Image id="image" source="@Embed('max09_640x360_vasava.jpg')" />
```

`</s:WindowedApplication>`

The application starts by creating a new **Filter** menu item. Then, it adds that to the main application or window menu. From there, it adds two submenu items: one for **Blur** and another for **Drop Shadow**. It also adds an event listener to these items to watch for the SELECT message that is sent when the user selects the menu item. From there, the onMenuSelect method applies the selected filters to the image.

When you run this AIR application in Flash Builder 4, you should see an image with no filters.

Then you can switch the filters on and off selectively and have the image instantly updated to match. For example, if you choose **Blur**, you should see the result shown in Figure 4-7.

Figure 4-7. The picture with the Blur filter applied

You can create menu separators, sub-submenus, and so on to give your application all of the menu options that an operating system native application would have.

Building a Photo Browser

Now that you have a sense of how AIR integrates with native operating system elements such as menus, let's have a look at how to do some other things. This next example, a simple photo browser, will use native drag-and-drop, a native sub-window to display the full image, native menus, the native directory chooser, and the native task or dock bar.

We will start by showing the complete source code for the first version of the application, and then dig into each element step by step.

```
<?xml version="1.0" encoding="utf-8"?>
<s:WindowedApplication xmlns:fx="http://ns.adobe.com/mxml/2009"
                        xmlns:s="library://ns.adobe.com/flex/spark"
                        xmlns:mx="library://ns.adobe.com/flex/mx"
                        nativeDragEnter="onNativeDragEnter(event);"
                        nativeDragDrop="onNativeDrop(event);"
                        title="Photo Viewer"
                        creationComplete="creationCompleteHandler()">
    <fx:Script>
        <![CDATA[

            private var images:Array = [];

            protected function creationCompleteHandler():void
            {
                if(NativeApplication.supportsMenu)
                {
                    var fileMenu:NativeMenuItem = ~CC
NativeApplication.nativeApplication.menu.getItemAt(1);
                    fileMenu.submenu.addItemAt(new NativeMenuItem("-",true),0);

                    var openDirectory:NativeMenuItem = new NativeMenuItem⏎
("Open Image Directory..." );
                    openDirectory.addEventListener(Event.SELECT,onOpenDirectory);

                    fileMenu.submenu.addItemAt(openDirectory,0);
                }
            }

            private function onOpenDirectory( event:Event ):void
            {
                var f:File = new flash.filesystem.File();
                f.addEventListener(Event.SELECT,openDirectoryFound);
                f.browseForDirectory( "Open Image Directory" );
            }

            private function openDirectoryFound( event:Event ):void
            {
                var d:File = event.target as File;
                for each ( var img:File in d.getDirectoryListing() )
                {
```

```
            if ( img.hasOwnProperty("extension") && img.extension != null )
            {
                var ext:String = img.extension.toLowerCase();

                if ( ext == 'jpg' )
                    images.push( img );
            }
        }

        dgIimageList.dataProvider = images;
        notifyComplete();

    }

    private  function notifyComplete():void
    {
        if(NativeApplication.supportsDockIcon)
        {
            var dock:DockIcon = NativeApplication.nativeApplication.icon↵
as DockIcon;
            dock.bounce(NotificationType.CRITICAL);
        }
        else if (NativeApplication.supportsSystemTrayIcon)
        {
            stage.nativeWindow.notifyUser(NotificationType.CRITICAL);
        }
    }

    private function onNativeDragEnter( event:NativeDragEvent ):void
    {
        if(event.clipboard.hasFormat(ClipboardFormats.FILE_LIST_FORMAT))
        {
            var files:Array = event.clipboard.getData↵
(ClipboardFormats.FILE_LIST_FORMAT) as Array;

            if( files.length > 0 )
                NativeDragManager.acceptDragDrop(this);

        }
    }

    private function onNativeDrop( event:NativeDragEvent ):void
    {
        for each ( var f:File in event.clipboard.getData↵
(ClipboardFormats.FILE_LIST_FORMAT) as Array )
            images.push(f);

        dgIimageList.dataProvider = images;
        notifyComplete();
    }

    ]]>
</fx:Script>
```

```
<mx:TileList id="dgIimageList"
             width="100%" height="100%"
             itemRenderer="Thumbnail"/>

</s:WindowedApplication>
```

The application handles the startup event by creating a new **Open Image Directory** menu item and adding it to the **File** menu. This new menu item is handled by the onOpenDirectory method. This method launches a native directory chooser by using the browseForDirectory method on the File object. Once the user selects a directory, the openDirectoryFound method is invoked.

The openDirectoryFound method uses the getDirectoryListing method on the File object associated with the directory to get all of the files in the directory. If files are found with the extension .jpg, you add them to the file list. If desired, you could easily do a recursive directory descent here to get all of the images in the directory or any of its subdirectories.

The openDirectoryFound method also uses the notifyComplete method, which bounces the icon on the dock bar, or flashes an icon on the task bar on Windows. This lets the user know when long-running processes are finished.

The application also handles native drag-and-drop by registering the onNativeDragEnter and onNativeDragDrop methods with the WindowedApplication object. The onNativeDragEnter is called when the user first drags a file, or a set of files, over the application window. It's the operating system's way of saying, "Do you want to handle this?" You say yes if the clipboard contains a list of files.

The onNativeDragDrop is called when the user actually drops the files on the application. This method follows a process very similar to the menu item handler's. It goes through each file and adds it to the image list, and then calls the notifyComplete method to tell the user he is done.

The display of the image thumbnails in the main window is handled by the TileList object at the bottom of the application code. This TileList uses an itemRenderer to render each of the thumbnails. The code for the renderer is shown in the following:

```
<?xml version="1.0" encoding="utf-8"?>
<mx:HBox xmlns:mx="http://www.adobe.com/2006/mxml"
         paddingBottom="5" paddingLeft="5"
         paddingRight="5" paddingTop="5">

    <mx:Script>
        <![CDATA[

            private function onPhotoClick( event:Event ):void
            {
                var newWin:Photo = new Photo();
                newWin.data = data;
                newWin.open();
            }
        ]]>
    </mx:Script>

    <mx:Image horizontalAlign="center" verticalAlign="middle"
              source="{data.url}" height="100" width="100"
```

```
                doubleClick="onPhotoClick(event);" doubleClickEnabled="true">

        <mx:rollOverEffect>
            <mx:Glow blurXFrom="0" blurXTo="10" blurYFrom="0" blurYTo="10" />
        </mx:rollOverEffect>

    </mx:Image>

</mx:HBox>
```

This MXML component is based on HBox. It displays the image referenced by the File object, which is given to the component in the data parameter. It also handles a double-click on the image by running the onPhotoClick method, which launches a native sub-window to display the full image.

The code for the native sub-window is as follows:

```
<?xml version="1.0" encoding="utf-8"?>
<mx:Window xmlns:mx="http://www.adobe.com/2006/mxml"
            layout="absolute" width="100" height="100"
            title="{data.name}">

    <mx:Script>
        <![CDATA[
            private function loaded():void
            {
                if ( theImg.content != null && theImg.content.width > 0 )
                {
                    stage.nativeWindow.width = theImg.content.width + 20;
                    stage.nativeWindow.height = theImg.content.height + 40;
                }
            }

        ]]>
    </mx:Script>

    <mx:Image id="theImg" source="{data.url}" httpStatus="loaded();" />

</mx:Window>
```

This MXML component is based on the Window class. This is a new class that comes with the AIR framework. It makes it very easy to build a native window that contains Flex controls.

In this case, the window contains a single image. The code then resizes the window to fit the entire image once the complete image is successfully loaded and the image size is known.

When you first launch this from Flash Builder 4, you should see an empty window. You can then drag a few images over it, as shown in Figure 4-8.

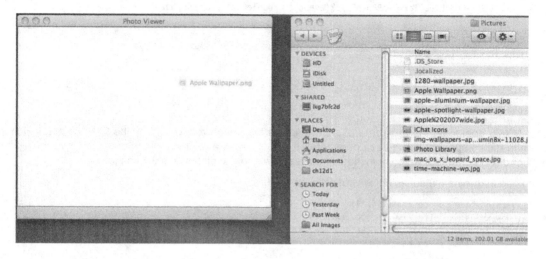

Figure 4-8. The image drag-and-drop in process

If everything is working, the cursor will present a little green plus sign to the user, which indicates that she can drop her files onto this window.

Once you have dropped the files, the list of images is updated and given to the TileList, which then displays the thumbnails, as shown in Figure 4-9.

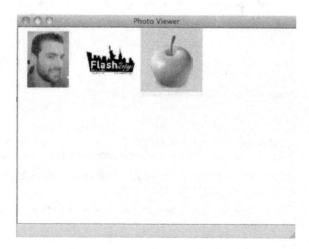

Figure 4-9. The thumbnail images

You can also use the **Open Image Directory** file menu item. That brings up the directory chooser (see Figure 4-10).

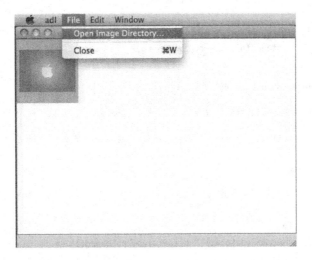

Figure 4-10. The Open Image Directory dialog

This is the best way to bring in masses of images quickly.

Once you have the image list set up, you can get a full-sized version of the image by double-clicking it as shown.

That's fairly cool, but what you really want, especially for photos, is to view the image in a full-screen lightbox. This means that the image comes up in the center of the screen, full size, and that all of the content around the rest of the area is dimmed. You can accomplish this effect by playing around a little with the photo.mxml window component.

The new code for the photo.mxml component is shown in the following:

```
<?xml version="1.0" encoding="utf-8"?>
<mx:Window xmlns:mx="http://www.adobe.com/2006/mxml"
          layout="absolute" title=""
          transparent="true" creationComplete="onStartup()"
          horizontalAlign="center" verticalCenter="middle"
          systemChrome="none" backgroundColor="#000000"
          backgroundAlpha="0.9" click="onClose()">

    <mx:Script>
        <![CDATA[
            import flash.display.StageDisplayState;

            private function onClose() : void
            {
                stage.nativeWindow.close();
            }
            private function onStartup() : void
            {
                stage.displayState = StageDisplayState.FULL_SCREEN_INTERACTIVE;
                x = -10;
                y = -30;
```

```
                width = stage.fullScreenWidth + 20;
                height = stage.fullScreenHeight + 60;
        }

        private function onLoaded() : void
        {
                theImg.setStyle('top', ( stage.fullScreenHeight / 2 ) - ↵
( theImg.content.height / 2 ) );
                theImg.setStyle('left', ( stage.fullScreenWidth / 2 ) - ↵
( theImg.content.width / 2 ) );
        }


    ]]>
  </mx:Script>

  <mx:Image id="theImg" source="{data.url}" httpStatus="onLoaded()" />

</mx:Window>
```

This new version of the code sets the background color of the window to black, and then sets a strong alpha of 0.9. It also sets the transparent attribute to true, and the system chrome to none, which is required to support the transparent attribute. The onLoaded for the image now centers the image within the window. A new startup handler sets the size of the window to the full screen with a little extra and also sets the displayState of the stage to full screen as well.

Now when you double-click the image, you see something like Figure 4-11.

Figure 4-11. The full-screen lightbox effect

The entire screen is turned black with the exception of the image, which is centered in the middle of the frame. To get out of the display, you click anywhere on the screen or press the Esc key.

So far you showed you some of the basics of AIR integration with the native operating system. You created menus elements, you experimented with building a browser, loading PDFs, and building a photo browser. In the next example, you will be connecting to a local SQLite database.

SQLite Database

One of the most significant features of AIR is the ability to work with a SQLite database. Having a local database allows creating offline capabilities for applications that are rich with data as well as opening the door for storing large amounts of data locally.

Creating a complex application using SQLite can be challenging, because an application may use many SQL commands and multiple tables and SQLite doesn't support all these features.

- Different classes in your application may need to use the SQLite database.
- You may want to keep the database connection open and avoid duplicating of code.

You have created a manager class that wraps many of the SQLite classes such as SQLConnection and SQLStatement. The manager also simplifies the complex process. The API is called SQLiteManager, and it allows you to set the database settings and then access the manager from anywhere in your application. It makes the process simpler and integrates very well with micro architecture frameworks.

The SQLiteManager supports the following features:

- Password encryption
- Multiple tables
- Common SQL commands
- Transactions and rollback option
- Better handling of results
- Improved and optimized code
- Save points

The API can be downloaded from here:

```
http://github.com/EladElrom/eladlib/tree/master/EladLibAIR/src/com/elad/framework/
sqlite/
```

The implementation example is here:

```
http://github.com/EladElrom/eladlib/tree/master/EladLibAIR/src/SqliteManager.mxml
```

Let's look at the implementation code. The application will hold two tables, one for users and one for orders. You will be able to insert and read information as well as keep track of transactions and roll back in case there are errors or for any other reasons.

The first step is to set constants with the table names of all the tables you will be running. This way you can identify which request is to what database.

The `creationCompleteHandler` method will be called once the application has completed initialization. You then set the database information and start the connection. Notice that you need to set the array Vector with all of the tables you will have in your application. It works this way in case the application doesn't have the tables created already. They will be generated automatically for the user so you need to specify the SQL command to create these tables and the name of each table. The names can be anything. Just be sure to use unique names.

```
// start database
    protected function creationCompleteHandler():void
    {
        var password:String = null; // leave as null to have the database unsecure or ↵
set a password for secure connection. Example: "Pa55word";
        var sqliteTables:Vector.<SqliteTableVO> = new Vector.<SqliteTableVO>;

        sqliteTables[0] = new SqliteTableVO( "Users", "CREATE TABLE Users↵
(UserId INTEGER PRIMARY KEY, UserName VARCHAR(150)); " );
        sqliteTables[1] = new SqliteTableVO( "Orders", "CREATE TABLE Orders↵
(OrderId INTEGER PRIMARY KEY, UserId VARCHAR(150), OrderTotal DOUBLE);" );

        addListeners();
        this.ordersDataGrid.dataProvider = new Array();

        database.start( "Users.sql3", sqliteTables, password, sqliteTables[0].tableName );
    }
```

You need to call addListeners to set the listeners you will be using. Take a look at this method to see the events you will be listening to.

```
// Set all the listeners
    private function addListeners():void
    {
        database.addEventListener(DatabaseSuccessEvent.DATABASE_CONNECTED↵
_SUCCESSFULLY, function(event:DatabaseSuccessEvent):void
        {
            event.currentTarget.removeEventListener(event.type, arguments.callee);
            database.executeSelectAllCommand( database.sqliteTables[0]↵
.tableName, READ_ALL_USERS_INFO );
        });

        database.addEventListener(DatabaseSuccessEvent.COMMAND_EXEC_SUCCESSFULLY,↵
onSelectResult);

        database.addEventListener(DatabaseSuccessEvent.DATABASE_READY,↵
function(event:DatabaseSuccessEvent):void {
            event.currentTarget.removeEventListener(event.type, arguments.callee);
            trace("database ready!");
        } );
        database.addEventListener(DatabaseFailEvent.COMMAND_EXEC_FAILED,↵
function(event:DatabaseFailEvent):void {
            trace("SQL execution fail: "+event.errorMessage);
        });
        database.addEventListener(DatabaseFailEvent.DATABASE_FAIL,↵
function(event:DatabaseFailEvent):void {
            var message:String = "Database fail: "+event.errorMessage;

            if (event.isRolledBack)
            {
                message += "\nTransaction was rolled back";
            }

            Alert.show(message);
        });
        database.addEventListener(DatabaseSuccessEvent.CREATING_DATABASE,↵
function(event:DatabaseSuccessEvent):void {
            event.currentTarget.removeEventListener(event.type, arguments.callee);
            trace(event.message);
        });
```

```
    }
```

You will be using two methods to generate the insert SQL command for the two tables you have and to make the request.

```
protected function insertDataClickHandler(event:MouseEvent):void
    {
        var SQLStatementText:String = "INSERT INTO Users VALUES('" + userId.text + "','" +
userName.text + "');'";
        database.executeCustomCommand(SQLStatementText, INSERT_USER_INFO);
    }

    protected function insertOrderClickHandler(event:MouseEvent):void
    {
        var SQLStatementText:String = "INSERT INTO Orders VALUES('" +
ordersDataGrid.dataProvider.length+1 + "','" + IdComboBox.selectedItem.label +
"','" + orderTotal.text + "');'";
        database.executeCustomCommand(SQLStatementText, INSERT_ORDER_INFO);
    }
```

Once SQL commands are requested all the results are processed in this implementation with the same handler called onSelectResult. Notice that each request had a unique name so you are able to match the request to the result and update the view as needed.

```
// handles results
    private function onSelectResult(event:StatementCompleteEvent):void
    {
        var result:Array = event.results.data;
        var rowsAffected:int = event.results.rowsAffected;

        switch (event.userGestureName)
        {
            case null:
                break;
            case READ_ALL_USERS_INFO:

                if (result == null)
                    break;

                var len:int = result.length;
                var dp:ArrayCollection = new ArrayCollection();

                for (var i:int; i<len; i++)
                {
                    dp.addItem( { label: result[i].UserId, UserName: result[i]
.UserName } );

                }

                IdComboBox.dataProvider = usersDataGrid.dataProvider = dp;

                database.executeSelectAllCommand( this.database.sqliteTables[1]
.tableName, READ_ALL_ORDERS_INFO );

                break;
            case INSERT_USER_INFO:
                database.executeSelectAllCommand( this.database.sqliteTables[0]
.tableName, READ_ALL_USERS_INFO );
                break;
            case INSERT_ORDER_INFO:
```

```
case READ_ALL_ORDERS_INFO:

                if (result == null)
                    break;

            len = result.length;
            dp = new ArrayCollection();

            for (i = 0; i<len; i++)
            {
                    dp.addItem( { OrderId: result[i].OrderId, OrderTotal:↵
result[i].OrderTotal, UserId: result[i].UserId } );

            }

            ordersDataGrid.dataProvider = dp;

            break;
        }
    }
```

The last part is the view. You have two forms to submit data and data grids to show the results.

```
<!-- Users Form -->
 <mx:Form width="221" y="5">
      <mx:FormItem label="User ID:">
          <s:TextInput id="userId" width="85"/>
      </mx:FormItem>
      <mx:FormItem label="User Name:">
          <s:TextInput id="userName" width="85"/>
      </mx:FormItem>
      <mx:FormItem>
          <s:Button label="Insert User"
                      click="insertDataClickHandler(event)"/>
      </mx:FormItem>
 </mx:Form>

<!-- Orders Form -->
<mx:Form x="239" y="5"
            width="221">
      <mx:FormItem label="User Id">
          <mx:ComboBox id="IdComboBox" editable="true" width="85"></mx:ComboBox>
      </mx:FormItem>
      <mx:FormItem label="Order Total:">
          <s:TextInput id="orderTotal" width="85"/>
      </mx:FormItem>
      <mx:FormItem>
          <s:Button label="Insert Order"
                      click="insertOrderClickHandler(event)"/>
      </mx:FormItem>
</mx:Form>

<!-- Results -->
<mx:DataGrid id="usersDataGrid" x="16" y="123" height="145">
      <mx:columns>
          <mx:DataGridColumn headerText="User Id" dataField="label"/>
          <mx:DataGridColumn headerText="User Name" dataField="UserName"/>
      </mx:columns>
</mx:DataGrid>
```

```
<mx:DataGrid id="ordersDataGrid" x="231" y="123" width="231" height="145">
    <mx:columns>
        <mx:DataGridColumn headerText="Order Id" dataField="OrderId"/>
        <mx:DataGridColumn headerText="User Id" dataField="UserId"/>
        <mx:DataGridColumn headerText="Order Total" dataField="OrderTotal"/>
    </mx:columns>
</mx:DataGrid>
```

You set a button so you can track once you want to roll back a transaction. You set inline logic in the click handler to call the method to roll back and pass a responder (call back) method that will read all the users and orders you have in the SQLite database. Once the user indicates that this is a transaction, he can save a point and roll back to that point. This is very similar to "undo" functionality. All the SQL commands will be rolled back. In the API level, it doesn't commit to the SQL commands before you release the transaction.

Use Case Example

Let's say you have a checkout system but you don't want to insert user information into the database before the user has completed the transaction. You can track that as a transaction and set a save point in case the user wants to re-enter the information.

```
<!-- Transactions -->
<s:Button id="rollbackBtn"
            x="119" y="283"
            label="Rollback"
            enabled="false"
            click="database.rollbackTransaction(new Responder(function(event:SQLEvent):void
            {
                Alert.show( 'Total number of changes being rolled back: ' +↩
database.connection.totalChanges );
            }));
            database.executeSelectAllCommand( this.database.sqliteTables[0]↩
.tableName, READ_ALL_USERS_INFO );
            database.executeSelectAllCommand( this.database.sqliteTables[1]↩
.tableName, READ_ALL_ORDERS_INFO );
            isTransactionCheckBox.selected=false;"/>
```

The checkbox will set and unset a transaction. Once you select the checkbox, the manager will record transaction.

```
<s:CheckBox id="isTransactionCheckBox" x="18" y="284"
            label="isTransaction"
            selected="false"
            change="if ( isTransactionCheckBox.selected )
            {
                database.beginTransaction();
                rollbackBtn.enabled = true;
                setSavePointBtn.enabled = true;
                releaseSavePointBtn.enabled = true;
                rollbackToSavePoint.enabled = true;
            }
            else
            {
                database.stopTransactionAndCommit();
                rollbackBtn.enabled = false;
                setSavePointBtn.enabled = false;
                releaseSavePointBtn.enabled = false;
                rollbackToSavePoint.enabled = false;
            }"
```

```
                    />
```

Additional buttons will set, release, and roll back a saved point. See the following code:

```
<s:Button id="setSavePointBtn"
          x="20" y="312"
          label="setSavePoint"
          enabled="false"
          click="database.setSavepoint('point1');"/>

 <s:Button id="releaseSavePointBtn"
          x="122" y="312"
          label="ReleaseSavePoint"
          enabled="false"
          click="database.releaseSavepoint('point1');"/>

 <s:Button id="rollbackToSavePoint"
          x="249" y="312"
          label="RollbackToSavePoint"
          enabled="false"
          click="database.rollbackToSavepoint('point1', new Responder
(function(event:SQLEvent):void
          {
          Alert.show( 'Total number of transactions: ' + database.connection
.totalChanges );
          }));
          database.executeSelectAllCommand( this.database.sqliteTables[0]
.tableName, READ_ALL_USERS_INFO );
          database.executeSelectAllCommand( this.database.sqliteTables[1]
.tableName, READ_ALL_ORDERS_INFO );
          "/>
```

Launch the application and add users, orders, set transactions, and save points to test functionality (see Figure 4-12).

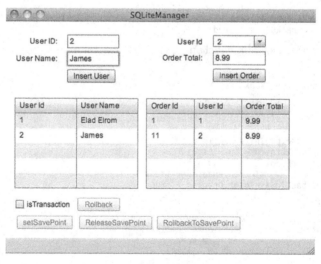

Figure 4-12. SQLiteManager application after entering few users and orders

Click the **isTransaction** checkbox and add new users and orders, as shown in Figure 4-13.

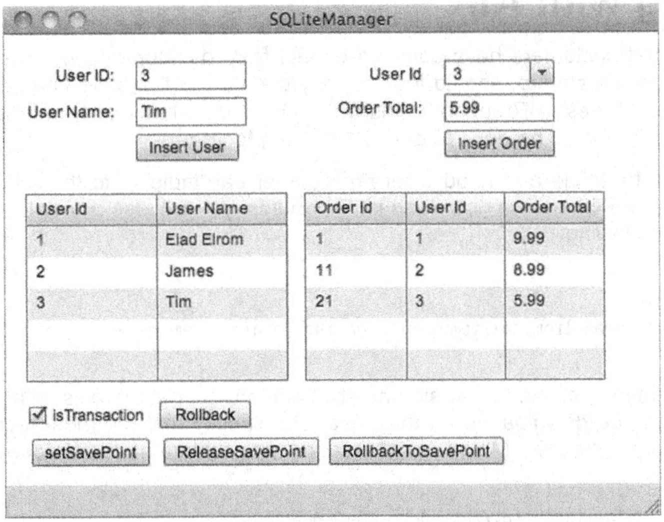

Figure 4-13. SQLiteManager application and isTransaction checkbox is checked.

Once you click the **Rollback** button the transaction will reverse, as shown in Figure 4-14.

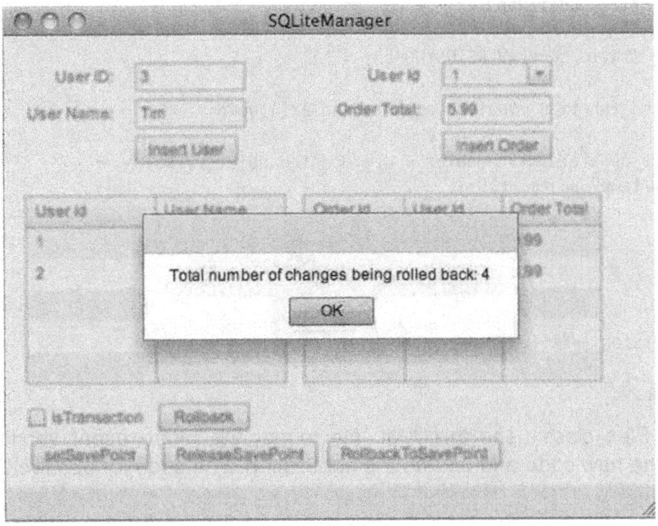

Figure 4-14. SQLiteManager application rollback

Self-Updating with AIR

One of the features that customers have come to expect from desktop applications is the ability to self-update. The application, on startup, should look for any updates to the code and then will download and install them if the user desires. AIR supports this through the `Updater` class, but there is still some user interface and networking work to be done to get it all to hang together.

The first thing to do is to define a method where the server can indicate to the AIR application what the most recent version is and where the download is. To do this, you will use a simple XML file. An example of this is shown in the following:

```
<version>
        <latest>2</latest>
        <download>http://eladelrom.com/temp/SelfUpdatingApp.air</download>
</version>
```

This file contains two key elements: the version number of the most recent revision and the URL where the most recent version can be downloaded. In this case, you specify that the most recent version is 1. You can define your own format for the XML as you please, or use any format you choose for this.

```
<?xml version="1.0" encoding="utf-8"?>
<s:WindowedApplication xmlns:fx="http://ns.adobe.com/mxml/2009"
                        xmlns:s="library://ns.adobe.com/flex/spark"
                        xmlns:mx="library://ns.adobe.com/flex/mx"
                        creationComplete="creationCompleteHandler()">
    <fx:Script>
        <![CDATA[
            import utils.UpdateHandler;

            private static const VERSION:Number = 1;

            protected function creationCompleteHandler():void
            {
                    var update:UpdateHandler = new UpdateHandler( VERSION, ↵
    "http://eladelrom.com/temp/update.xml" );
            }

        ]]>
    </fx:Script>

    <s:Label text="Version {VERSION}" />

</s:WindowedApplication>
```

The `UpdateHandler` Flex class uses this XML file to get the most recent version information and if necessary download the new code and update the application. The code for `UpdateHandler` is as follows:

```
package utils
{
    import flash.desktop.Updater;
    import flash.events.Event;
    import flash.filesystem.*;
    import flash.net.*;
    import flash.utils.ByteArray;
```

```
import mx.controls.Alert;
import mx.events.CloseEvent;
import mx.rpc.events.ResultEvent;
import mx.rpc.http.HTTPService;

public class UpdateHandler
{
     private var _version:Number = 0.0;
     private var _updateUrl:String = null;
     private var _quiet:Boolean = true;
     private var _latestVers:Number;
     private var _downloadUrl:String;

     public function UpdateHandler( version:Number, updateUrl:String, quiet:Boolean =
true )
     {
          _version = version;
          _updateUrl = updateUrl;
          _quiet = quiet;

          var versReq:HTTPService = new HTTPService();
          versReq.addEventListener(ResultEvent.RESULT, onVersionReturn);
          versReq.url = updateUrl;
          versReq.resultFormat = 'object';
          versReq.send();
     }

     private function onVersionReturn( event:ResultEvent ):void
     {
          if ( event.result != null && event.result.version != null &&
event.result.version.latest != null )
          {
               var versionNumber:String = event.result.version.latest;
               _latestVers = parseFloat( versionNumber );
               if ( _latestVers > _version )
               {
                    _downloadUrl = event.result.version.download;
                    Alert.show("Download an update to this application now?",
"Application Update",
                         3, null, onDownloadPromptReturn);
               }
               else
               {
                    if ( _quiet == false )
                         mx.controls.Alert.show( 'You are running the most recent
version' );
               }
          }
     }

     private function onDownloadPromptReturn(event:CloseEvent):void
     {
          if ( event.detail == Alert.YES ) {
               var codeReq:URLRequest = new URLRequest( _downloadUrl );
               var codeStream:URLStream = new URLStream();
               codeStream.addEventListener(Event.COMPLETE,onCodeReturn);
               codeStream.load( codeReq );
          }
     }

     private function onCodeReturn( event:Event ):void
```

```
            {
                var codeStream:URLStream = event.target as URLStream;
                var fileData:ByteArray = new ByteArray();
                codeStream.readBytes(fileData, 0, codeStream.bytesAvailable);

                var fileName:String = _downloadUrl.substr( _downloadUrl.lastIndexOf("/") + 1 );

                var tempDirectory:File = File.createTempDirectory();
                var tempFile:File = new File( tempDirectory.nativePath + File.separator +
    fileName );

                var fileStream:FileStream = new FileStream();
                fileStream.open(tempFile, FileMode.WRITE);
                fileStream.writeBytes(fileData, 0, fileData.length);
                fileStream.close();

                var updater:Updater = new Updater();
                updater.update( tempFile, _latestVers.toString() );
            }
        }
    }
```

The constructor takes two parameters: the current version and the URL of the XML that defines the most recent version. It also takes an optional quiet parameter. If quiet is true, which it is by default, and there is no version, the user isn't notified.

The UpdateHandler constructor makes the request of the server at this URL. The onVersionReturn method is called when the XML is found. This method parses through the objects to find the version number. If the version number is greater, it prompts the user to see if he wants to download the new code. That prompt is handled by the onDownloadPromptReturn method, which starts the download of the new code if the user wants to update the application.

The onCodeReturn method is called when the download of the new code is complete. It starts off by reading all of the data into a binary array. Then it creates a temporary file that will hold all of the code. Once the data is written into the file, the AIR Updater class is called to update the code with the most recent version.

The last part is to update the Descriptor File Template, in this case SelfUpdatingApp-app.xml. Find the following line:

```
<!-- An application version designator (such as "v1", "2.5", or "Alpha 1"). Required. -->
<version>v1</version>
```

You need to build two versions of the code in release mode. The first is version 1, which you keep locally. The second is version 2, which you put on the site. You can then launch the 1 version locally (see Figure 4-15).

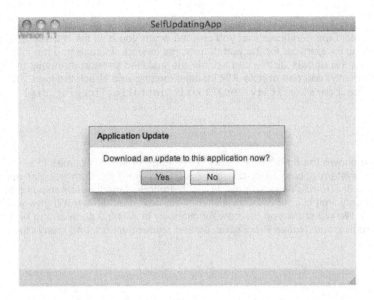

Figure 4-15. The self-updating application version 1.0

If you click **Yes**, then the code is downloaded and the application self-updates, as shown in Figure 4-16. Any local information you had stored could still be accessed by the new version.

Figure 4-16. The updated code

It's not a very complex example, but you get the point.

You should note that this will not work if the application is being run directly from Flash Builder because applications run in the test launcher ("adl") cannot self-update. You need to export the release build and run it from there.

It's important to maintain the certificate that you created when you built the release application, as the two certificates will need to be identical for the update process to work. In case you run into issues when trying to update, check that the update air file can update the installed version manually by trying to install the new version. Additionally, you can enable AIR Installer logging and check the logs. To find out more visit: `http://blogs.adobe.com/simplicity/2007/10/air_installer_logging.html`.

Summary

You have just been shown the tip of the iceberg in this chapter when it comes to what can be done with AIR. With local file system access, you can get directly to the data from popular applications such as Excel, Word, iPhoto, or iTunes. You can provide local storage of media elements like movies or audio for offline access. The only limit is your own creativity. In the next chapter, we will give you a comprehensive overview of AIR 2.0. We will show you the new functionality in AIR 2.0 such as the new Networking class, launching and interacting with Native Processes, screen reader support, and many others.

Chapter 5

AIR 2.0 Enhancements Overview

by Elad Elrom

In the last chapter, we gave you a quick overview of building applications with AIR. AIR 2.0 adds new capabilities that tie in better with the operation systems. The new version of AIR gives your application more control while increasing performance.

The new version will be deployed on Flash Player 10 using Flex 4 SDK (see Figure 5-1). The new features can be split into the following four main categories:

- New functionality
- Additional functionality to existing APIs
- Platform awareness related to APIs
- Optimization

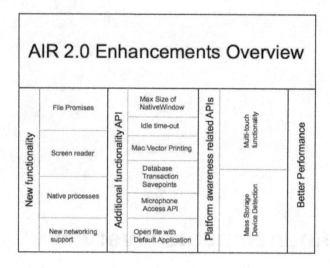

Figure 5-1. AIR 2.0 enhancements overview

We would like to discuss these new features in more detail to give you a better understanding of what is possible with AIR 2.0, and how you can take advantage of these new features in building new applications or integrating these features into existing applications.

New Functionality in AIR 2.0

AIR 2.0 adds new functionality that was not included in previous versions of AIR. They include the following:

- New networking support: New socket class, wired and wireless network interfaces, and DNS records.
- Native processes: API that allows launching and interacting with native processes.
- Screen reader: API that supports a screen reader.
- File promises: API that allows you to drag virtual files to local file systems.

Additional Networking Support

AIR 2.0 provides access to networks. You can now access the low-level network on the user's machine, including IPV6, as well as the user Datagram protocol and DNS records.

User Datagram Protocol

AIR 2.0 adds a new socket class in addition to the existing Socket class. The existing class allows the ability to access Transmission Control Protocol (TCP). In AIR 2.0, you can use a stateless protocol called User Datagram Protocol (UDP) with a new class called DatagramSocket. The DatagramSocket class allows the sending and receiving of UDP packets.

Unlike TCP, UDP uses a transmission method that does not include an implicit handshake and does not guarantee reliability, ordering, or data integrity. The UDP limitations mean that some data may be lost, out of order, duplicated, or missing. The advantage of the UDP protocol is that much of the overhead associated with processing is avoided, and it allows building applications, such as VoIP applications, in which it's acceptable to lose some data. Speed is the key.

Another big advantage UDP has over TCP is that UDP servers can handle more requests from more clients. There are two classes that you can use:

- `flash.net.DatagramSocket`: DatagramSocket is very similar to the Socket class, and provides the ability to send and receive UDP packets.
- `flash.net.ServerSocket`: The ServerSocket class provides the server-side TCP socket methods.

Network Information

The user's machine may have wired and wireless network interfaces. AIR 2.0 allows you to access the low-level network information on the client's machine through a class called `NetworkInfo`. The `NetworkInfo` class can be used to enumerate all the network interfaces on a machine.

The `NetworkInfo` class finds information about the machine's network interfaces, such as the local IP address and wired or wireless networks. The following application finds all the interfaces on the machine and the IP addresses.

Create a new project using **File** ➤ **New** ➤ **Flex Project** and name the project **NetworkInformationExample** (ensure you are using AIR 2.0 with Flex 4.0 SDK). We will create an example of displaying the user's available networks.

```
<?xml version="1.0" encoding="utf-8"?>
<s:WindowedApplication xmlns:fx="http://ns.adobe.com/mxml/2009"
                       xmlns:s="library://ns.adobe.com/flex/spark"
                       xmlns:mx="library://ns.adobe.com/flex/mx"
                       width="700" height="300"
                       initialize="initializeHandler()">
    <fx:Script>
        <![CDATA[
            import flash.net.InterfaceAddress;
            import flash.net.NetworkInfo;
            import flash.net.NetworkInterface;

            import mx.collections.ArrayCollection;

            private var arrayCollection:ArrayCollection = new ArrayCollection();

            protected function initializeHandler():void
            {
                var networkInfo:NetworkInfo = NetworkInfo.networkInfo;
                var networkInterfaces:Vector.<NetworkInterface> =↵
networkInfo.findInterfaces();

                networkInterfaces.forEach( function(networkInterface:NetworkInterface,↵
index:int, vect:Vector.<NetworkInterface>):void
                {
```

```
                        var item:Object = new Object();
                        item.active = networkInterface.active;
                        item.name = networkInterface.name;

                        if ( networkInterface.addresses.length > 0 )
                        {
                                networkInterface.addresses.forEach( function↵
( interfaceAddress:InterfaceAddress, i:int, vect2:Vector.<InterfaceAddress>):void {
                                        item.addresses += networkInterface.addresses[i].↵
ipVersion + ": " + networkInterface.addresses[i].address + ", ";
                                });
                        }
                        else
                        {
                                item.addresses = "";
                        }

                        arrayCollection.addItem( item );

                });

                        dataGrid.dataProvider = new ArrayCollection(arrayCollection.source);
                }

        ]]>
    </fx:Script>

    <mx:DataGrid id="dataGrid" width="700" height="300">
        <mx:columns>
            <mx:DataGridColumn dataField="name" width="40" />
            <mx:DataGridColumn dataField="active" width="80" />
            <mx:DataGridColumn dataField="addresses" />
        </mx:columns>
    </mx:DataGrid>

</s:WindowedApplication>
```

This application will provide a list of wired and wireless networks found on the device (see Figure 5-2).

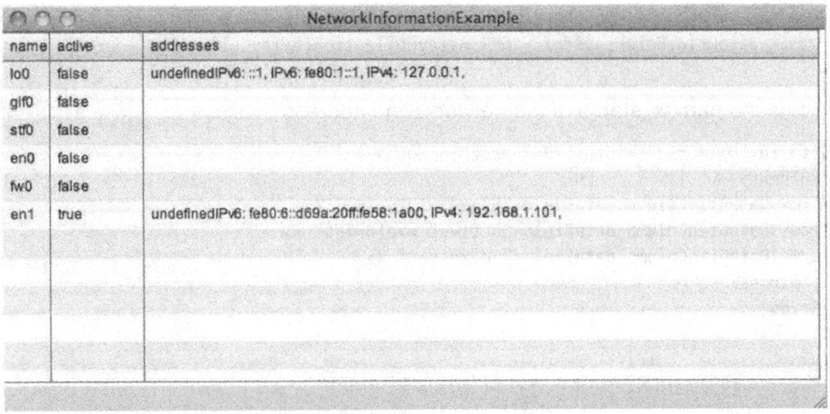

Figure 5-2. NetworkInformationExample application that provides network information

Once the application gets initialized, you call the `initializeHandler` method and iterate through the collection of networks available. Notice that `NetworkInfo` cannot be initialized. You first loop to find all of the `NetworkInterface`, and then iterate through the addresses collection. You then add all that information to an array collection that will be attached to a data grid to show the results.

```
protected function initializeHandler():void
{
        var networkInfo:NetworkInfo = NetworkInfo.networkInfo;
        var networkInterfaces:Vector.<NetworkInterface> =
networkInfo.findInterfaces();

        networkInterfaces.forEach( function(networkInterface:NetworkInterface,
index:int, vect:Vector.<NetworkInterface>):void
        {
                var item:Object = new Object();
                item.active = networkInterface.active;
                item.name = networkInterface.name;

                if ( networkInterface.addresses.length > 0 )
                {
                        networkInterface.addresses.forEach( function
( interfaceAddress:InterfaceAddress, i:int, vect2:Vector.<InterfaceAddress>):void {
                                item.addresses += networkInterface.addresses[i].
ipVersion + ": " + networkInterface.addresses[i].address + ", ";
                        });
                }
                else
                {
                        item.addresses = "";
                }

                arrayCollection.addItem( item );

        });
```

```
        dataGrid.dataProvider = new ArrayCollection(arrayCollection.source);
    }
```

The data grid holds the names, status of the network, and address available.

```
<mx:DataGrid id="dataGrid" width="700" height="300">
    <mx:columns>
        <mx:DataGridColumn dataField="name" width="40" />
        <mx:DataGridColumn dataField="active" width="80" />
        <mx:DataGridColumn dataField="addresses" />
    </mx:columns>
</mx:DataGrid>
```

DNS Records

AIR 2.0 offers an API `flash.net.dns.DNSResolver` that allows the making of queries to find out domain name system (DNS) information. Once information has been found, a `DNSResolverEvent` is dispatched.

To understand how to use the new API, you must first understand what DNS is and how it works. Each domain name on the web is pointing to an IP address. DNS converts domain names into IP addresses. In other words, DNS allows the translation of the information from host name into IP addresses.

The IP address can be of type IPv4 (32-bits) or IPv6 (64-bits). AIR 1.0 supported IPv4, and all the classes in AIR 2.0 now support the IPv6 protocol. There are many record types that are stored in the resource records on DNS, and they include the IPv4 address record, the IPv6 address record, delegation name, DNS key records, and many others.

In this release, AIR supports only the following DNS types:

- flash.net.dns.ARecord: Class that returns 64-bit IPv6 address information. AAAA records (AAAA stands for a resource records code) are usually used to convert hostnames into IP addresses.
- flash.net.dns.AAAARecord: Same as ARecord but used to return a 32-bit IPv4 address.
- flash.net.dns.MXRecord: Class that provides information regarding mapping a domain name to a list of mail exchange (MX) servers for that domain.
- flash.net.dns.SRVRecord: SRV class that returns service location record information about the SRV records. It is used for newer protocols instead of creating protocol-specific records such as MX.
- flash.net.dns.ResourceRecord: Data class for encapsulating the information in a DNS record.
- flash.net.dns.PTRRecord: Class to allow accessing PTR record information. `PTRRecord` is usually used for performing reverse DNS lookups.

Create a new AIR application and call it `DNSRecordExample`. Take a look at the following application, which performs DNS and reverse DNS lookup.

```
<?xml version="1.0" encoding="utf-8"?>
<s:WindowedApplication xmlns:fx="http://ns.adobe.com/mxml/2009"
                       xmlns:s="library://ns.adobe.com/flex/spark"
                       xmlns:mx="library://ns.adobe.com/flex/mx"
                       height="287" width="505">
    <fx:Script>
```

```
<![CDATA[

        import mx.controls.Alert;
        import flash.net.dns.SRVRecord;
        import flash.net.dns.PTRRecord;
        import flash.net.dns.MXRecord;
        import flash.net.dns.ARecord;
        import flash.events.Event;
        import flash.net.dns.AAAARecord;
        import flash.events.DNSResolverEvent;
        import flash.net.dns.DNSResolver;

        private var resolver:DNSResolver;

        public function startLookup( host:String, isARecordSelected:Boolean,↵
isAAAARecordSelected:Boolean, isMXRecordSelected:Boolean, isSRVRecordSelected:Boolean ):void
        {
            if (isARecordSelected) lookup( host + ".", ARecord );
            if (isAAAARecordSelected) lookup( host, AAAARecord );
            if (isMXRecordSelected) lookup( host, MXRecord );
            if (isSRVRecordSelected) lookup( "_sip._tcp." + host + ".", SRVRecord );
        }

        public function lookup( host:String, recordType:Class):void
        {
            resolver = new DNSResolver();
            resolver.addEventListener( DNSResolverEvent.LOOKUP, lookupComplete );
            resolver.addEventListener( ErrorEvent.ERROR, lookupError );

            resolver.lookup( host, recordType );
        }

        private function lookupComplete( event:DNSResolverEvent ):void
        {
            resolver.removeEventListener( DNSResolverEvent.LOOKUP, lookupComplete );
            resolver.removeEventListener( ErrorEvent.ERROR, lookupError );

            setOutput( "Query string: " + event.host );
            setOutput( "Record type: " + flash.utils.getQualifiedClassName↵
( event.resourceRecords[0] ) +
                    ", count: " + event.resourceRecords.length );

            for each( var record:* in event.resourceRecords )
            {
                if( record is ARecord ) setOutput( "ARecord: " + record.name + " :↵
" + record.address );
                if( record is AAAARecord ) setOutput( "AAAARecord: " +↵
record.name + " : " + record.address );
                if( record is MXRecord ) setOutput( "MXRecord: " +↵
record.name + " : " + record.exchange + ", " + record.preference );
                if( record is PTRRecord ) setOutput( "PTRRecord: " +↵
record.name + " : " + record.ptrdName );
                if( record is SRVRecord ) setOutput( "SRVRecord: " +↵
```

```
record.name + " : " + record.target + ", " + record.port +
                        ", " + record.priority + ", " + record.weight );
            }
        }

        private function setOutput(message:String):void
        {
            resolver.removeEventListener( DNSResolverEvent.LOOKUP, lookupComplete );
            resolver.removeEventListener( ErrorEvent.ERROR, lookupError );

            output.text = message + "\n" + output.text;
        }

        private function lookupError( error:ErrorEvent ):void
        {
            Alert.show("Error: " + error.text );
        }

    ]]>
</fx:Script>

<s:TextInput id="DomainTextInput" x="129" y="55" text="yahoo.com"/>

<s:Button x="330" y="55" label="Lookup DNS Information"
            click="startLookup(DomainTextInput.text, checkBoxARecord.↩
selected, checkBoxAAAARecord.selected,
                    checkBoxMXRecord.selected, checkBoxSRVRecord.selected)"/>

<s:CheckBox id="checkBoxARecord" x="28" y="85" label="ARecord" selected="true"/>
<s:CheckBox id="checkBoxAAAARecord" x="101" y="85" label="AAAARecord"/>
<s:CheckBox id="checkBoxMXRecord" x="196" y="85" label="MXRecord"/>
<s:CheckBox id="checkBoxSRVRecord" x="276" y="85" label="SRVRecord"/>

<s:TextInput id="ipAddress" x="129" y="120"/>
<s:Button x="330" y="120" label="Reverse DNS Lookup" width="152"
            click="lookup(ipAddress.text, PTRRecord )"/>

<s:Label x="28" y="21" text="DNS Lookup:"
            fontSize="21"/>

<s:TextArea id="output" x="28" y="158" width="454" height="104" text=""/>
<s:RichText x="28" y="58" text="Host name: " height="15" fontSize="16"/>
<s:RichText x="28" y="123" text="IP Address:" height="15" fontSize="16"/>

</s:WindowedApplication>
```

Once you compile and run the application, you can do a lookup for specific host name record types as well as a reverse lookup (see Figure 5-3).

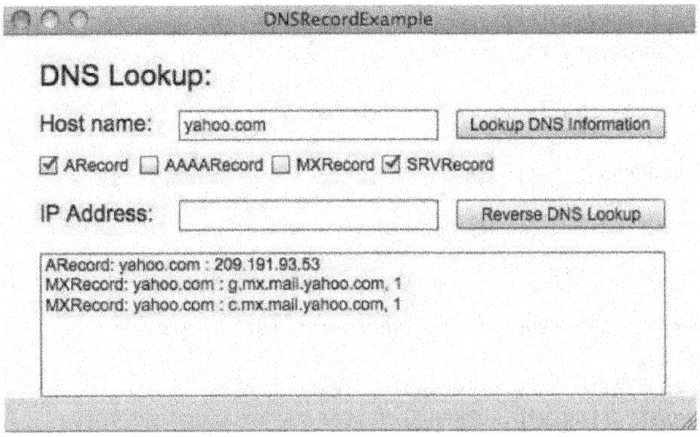

Figure 5-3. DNSRecordExample application for doing DNS lookup

Launching and Interacting with Native Processes

Similar to the operating system opening a file using its default application, AIR 2.0 provides the ability for applications to launch native processes and interact with them. The following classes add support for these capabilities:

- flash.desktop.NativeProcess: Provides command-line integration and general launching capabilities on the host OS. Once a process is launched, the AIR application can monitor the standard input, output, and error of the process.

- flash.desktop.NativeProcessStartupInfo: Provides basic information used to start a process on the host OS.

- flash.events.NativeProcessExitEvent: Event dispatched once a process exits. It is possible that this event will never be dispatched if the child process outlives the AIR application.

Launching and interacting with native processes will be available only for applications that are installed using a native OS installer.

Create a new application and name it `NativeProcessExample`. You need to make sure you have enabled the extended desktop in your descriptor. Then, open `NativeProcessExample-app.xml` and add the following tag:

```
<supportedProfiles>extendedDesktop</supportedProfiles>
```

The following application opens up a text file: `foobar.txt` using the MacOS TextEdit text editor.

```
<?xml version="1.0" encoding="utf-8"?>
<s:WindowedApplication xmlns:fx="http://ns.adobe.com/mxml/2009"
                xmlns:s="library://ns.adobe.com/flex/spark"
                xmlns:mx="library://ns.adobe.com/flex/mx">
    <fx:Script>
        <![CDATA[
            import flash.events.NativeProcessExitEvent;

            public function executeNativeProcess():void
            {
                var executable:File = new
```

```
File("/Applications/TextEdit.app/Contents/MacOS/TextEdit");
            var workingDirectory:File = new File("/");

            var nativeProcess:NativeProcess = new NativeProcess();

            if (NativeProcess.isSupported)
            {
                trace("Native Process Supported");
            }

            var nativeProcessStartupInfo:NativeProcessStartupInfo =↩
new NativeProcessStartupInfo();
            nativeProcessStartupInfo.executable = executable;
            nativeProcessStartupInfo.workingDirectory = workingDirectory;

            var args:Vector.<String> = new Vector.<String>();
            args.push("/Users/Elad/Desktop/foobar.txt"); // open file that was↩
given with the executable application
            nativeProcessStartupInfo.arguments = args;

            nativeProcess.addEventListener( NativeProcessExitEvent.EXIT, onExitError );

            try {
                nativeProcess.start(nativeProcessStartupInfo);
            } catch (error:IllegalOperationError) {
                trace("Illegal Operation: "+error.toString());
            } catch (error:ArgumentError) {
                trace("Argument Error: "+error.toString());
            } catch (error:Error) {
                trace ("Error: "+error.toString());
            }

            if (nativeProcess.running)
            {
                trace ("Native Process Support");
            }
        }

        public function onExitError(event:NativeProcessExitEvent):void
        {
            trace( "Native Process Exit code: "+event.exitCode );
        }

    ]]>
    </fx:Script>

    <s:Button id="button"
            label="Open File foobar.txt with text editor"
            click="executeNativeProcess();"
            width="250" />

</s:WindowedApplication>
```

Once the user clicks the button, the application calls the executeNativeProcess method. That points to the location of the TextEdit native application. Note that to create an application that supports all operating systems, you need to run a test to find out the type of OS the user is using and adjust the app to reflect that.

Set the NativeProcessStartupInfo properties, such as the file to open, using the args property and working directory.

```
        public function executeNativeProcess():void
        {
            var executable:File = new
File("/Applications/TextEdit.app/Contents/MacOS/TextEdit");
            var workingDirectory:File = new File("/");

            var nativeProcess:NativeProcess = new NativeProcess();

            if (NativeProcess.isSupported)
            {
                trace("Native Process Supported");
            }

            var nativeProcessStartupInfo:NativeProcessStartupInfo =
new NativeProcessStartupInfo();
            nativeProcessStartupInfo.executable = executable;
            nativeProcessStartupInfo.workingDirectory = workingDirectory;

            var args:Vector.<String> = new Vector.<String>();
            args.push("/Users/Elad/Desktop/foobar.txt"); // open file that was↩
given with the executable application
            nativeProcessStartupInfo.arguments = args;
```

Next, set the event listener so you can track errors, dispatch the onExitError event, and start the process. Notice that you have placed the code block in try and catch tags to ensure it's working correctly.

```
            nativeProcess.addEventListener( NativeProcessExitEvent.EXIT, onExitError );

            try {
                nativeProcess.start(nativeProcessStartupInfo);
            } catch (error:IllegalOperationError) {
                trace("Illegal Operation: "+error.toString());
            } catch (error:ArgumentError) {
                trace("Argument Error: "+error.toString());
            } catch (error:Error) {
                trace ("Error: "+error.toString());
            }

            if (nativeProcess.running)
            {
                trace ("Native Process Support");
            }
        }

        public function onExitError(event:NativeProcessExitEvent):void
        {
```

```
        trace( "Native Process Exit code: "+event.exitCode );
    }
```

Screen Reader Support

AIR 2.0 allows support for building Flash-based applications that work with screen readers. The functionality is available only on Windows OS at this release. The following support has been added.

- **Runtime dialog boxes**: Dialog boxes are readable by supported screen readers.
- **Flex components and containers**: Flex components and containers are readable by screen readers.

Note that the "Generate accessible SWF file" option in Flex Builder must be turned on in order to enable support for accessibility.

1. Right-click your Flex project (in the Flex Navigator) and select Properties.

2. Select Flex Compiler.

3. Select the "Generate accessible SWF" check box, and then click the OK button (see Figure 5-4).

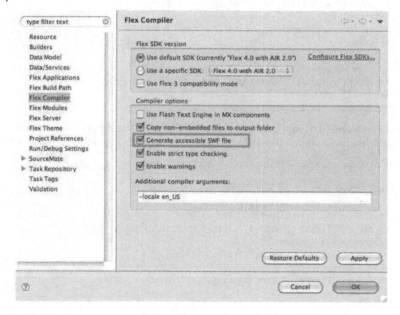

Figure 5-4. Flex Compiler properties showing the Generate accessible SWF File option

File Promise API

File promise is a new API (URLFilePromise) that allows you to access resources at a certain URL and drag them out of the AIR application as a file promise into the local machine. File promise, as the name suggests, is a commitment that the file exists without actually checking. Once the files are dropped, the request will be made to download the file to your local machine.

The `URLFilePromise` class implements the contract of IFilePromise using `URLStream` and `URLRequest` objects as the data source.

To create a URL file promise, you create a `URLFilePromise` object, add the object to an array, and then start the drag, passing the `Clipboard` object the array of file promises.

```
var items:Array = fileData.selectedItems;
var promises:Array = new Array();

for each (var item:Object in items)
{
    var filePromise:URLFilePromise = new URLFilePromise();
    var request:URLRequest = new URLRequest(item.url);

    filePromise.request = request;
    filePromise.relativePath = item.name;
    promises.push(filePromise);
}


clipboard.setData(ClipboardFormats.FILE_PROMISE_LIST_FORMAT, promises);
NativeDragManager.doDrag(fileData, clipboard);
```

When the user completes the drag task and drops the file on the local machine, the runtime downloads the data for each file promise. See Figure 5-5.

Take a look at the following application, which allows the dragging of items from a list into the user's local machine and then the copying of the files.

```
<?xml version="1.0" encoding="utf-8"?>
<s:WindowedApplication xmlns:fx="http://ns.adobe.com/mxml/2009"
                       xmlns:s="library://ns.adobe.com/flex/spark"
                       xmlns:mx="library://ns.adobe.com/flex/mx">
    <fx:Script>
        <![CDATA[
            import air.desktop.URLFilePromise;

            import flash.desktop.Clipboard;
            import flash.desktop.ClipboardFormats;
            import flash.desktop.NativeDragManager;

            private var clipboard:Clipboard = new Clipboard();

            protected function onDragOut(event:MouseEvent):void
            {
                var items:Array = fileData.selectedItems;
                var promises:Array = new Array();

                for each (var item:Object in items)
                {
                    var filePromise:URLFilePromise = new URLFilePromise();
                    var request:URLRequest = new URLRequest(item.url);
```

```
                    filePromise.request = request;
                    filePromise.relativePath = item.name;
                    promises.push(filePromise);
                }

                clipboard.setData(ClipboardFormats.FILE_PROMISE_LIST_FORMAT, promises);
                NativeDragManager.doDrag(fileData, clipboard);
            }

            private function onDragOutComplete(event:NativeDragEvent):void
            {
                trace( "onDragOutComplete" );
            }

        ]]>
    </fx:Script>

    <fx:Declarations>
        <mx:ArrayCollection id="arrColl">
            <mx:source>
                <fx:Array>
                    <fx:Object name="rhall.jpg" url="http://a1.twimg.com/↵
profile_images/57117466/robert_m_hall_bio_photo_big_normal.jpg" />
                    <fx:Object name="bobjim.jpg" url="http://a1.twimg.com/↵
profile_images/51723308/ryancampbell3_normal.jpg"/>
                    <fx:Object name="jenschr.jpg" url="http://a1.twimg.com/↵
profile_images/43222252/jenschr_mugshot3_normal.jpg"/>
                    <fx:Object name="adamflater.jpg" url="http://a1.twimg.com/↵
profile_images/21503622/Photo_8_normal.jpg"/>
                    <fx:Object name="reboog711.jpg" url="http://a1.twimg.com/↵
profile_images/16984682/DSCF0044_normal.jpg"/>
                </fx:Array>
            </mx:source>
        </mx:ArrayCollection>
    </fx:Declarations>

    <mx:DataGrid id="fileData" dragEnabled="true"
                    dataProvider="{arrColl}"
                    mouseMove="onDragOut(event)"
                    nativeDragComplete="onDragOutComplete(event)">
        <mx:columns>
            <mx:DataGridColumn dataField="name" />
            <mx:DataGridColumn dataField="url"/>
        </mx:columns>
    </mx:DataGrid>

</s:WindowedApplication>
```

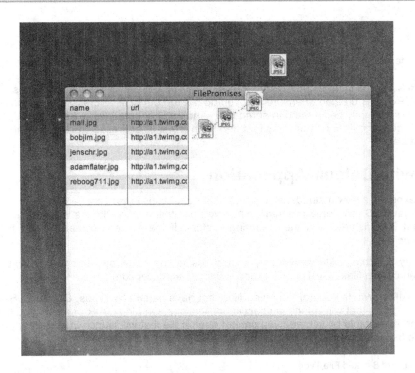

Figure 5-5. File Promises application (dragging an image from the AIR app to the local machine)

Additional Functionality to Existing APIs

In addition to adding new functionality, AIR 2.0 focuses on completing the existing APIs by adding methods to give you better control over the application. Here are some of the additional functionalities that were added to the existing APIs in AIR 2.0:

- **IPv6 support**: AIR 2.0 adds the ability to support IPv6 to all network APIs.
- **Default application**: API that allows opening a file with the OS default application.
- **Microphone byteArray**: AIR 2.0 allows accessing the data in the Microphone API.
- **Transaction savepoints**: New methods for SQLite database and the ability to create savepoints.
- **Vector printing**: In AIR 1.5, you already had the ability to do vector printing, but in AIR 2.0 you can do the same with Mac OS.
- **Idle time-out**: Ability to set the idle time-out settings (Win/Mac only).
- **Increased screen size**: AIR 2.0 supports increasing the maximum size of the AIR windows.

IPv6 Support

AIR 2.0 adds the ability to support IPv6 to all network APIs. Currently, the Internet mostly uses IP version four (IPv4), an address format that is 20 years old. IPv4 uses a 32-bit architecture and is limited in the available address space to 4,294,967,296 or 2^{32} unique IP addresses. Since many devices are consuming IP addresses, IPv6 was created to ensure that you do not run out of IP addresses. IPv6 is not as common as IPv4, and it is currently being used in some tests and early adopter networks. However, it is important to be able to access the IPv6 for networks that are using these IP addresses, and it will only become more common in future.

Open File with Default Application

The File API exposes a new method called openWithDefaultApplication() in AIR 2 to allow opening a file with the default OS registered program. When you use this method the file will open using the default application that is registered with the operating system. If the file is executable, then that executable program is launched.

Due to security concerns, AIR prevents you from using the File.openWithDefaultApplication() method to open certain files (see Table 5-1) and will throw an exception.

On Windows, AIR prevents you from opening files that have certain file types. On Mac OS, AIR prevents you from opening files that will launch in specific applications. On Linux, AIR prevents you from opening a file that has the executable bit set, and you cannot open a file that will launch in certain applications. Take a look at Table 5-1, which shows examples of file types that are blocked.

Table 5-1. Example of Blocked File Types

Type	Windows Application	Mac OS Application	Linux Application
Executable File	exe	executable bit, .app extension	/lib/ld.so
UNIX shell script	sh	Terminal	/bin/bash
UNIX shell script	sh	Terminal	/bin/bash
UNIX ksh shell script	ksh	Terminal	/bin/ksh

The following application allows you to browse for a file in your local system and then open the file with the default application. Notice the try..catch code, which is needed in cases where a failure occurs due to a file that cannot be opened, since there is no default for file type or security reasons.

> Note: You cannot communicate with a launched process after it is opened using the openWithDefaultApplication method.

Create a new AIR application and name it OpenFileDefaultApp using the following code:

```
<?xml version="1.0" encoding="utf-8"?>
```

```
<s:WindowedApplication xmlns:fx="http://ns.adobe.com/mxml/2009"
                       xmlns:s="library://ns.adobe.com/flex/spark"
                       xmlns:mx="library://ns.adobe.com/flex/mx">
    <fx:Script>
        <![CDATA[

            import flash.events.Event;
            import flash.events.MouseEvent;
            import mx.events.FlexEvent;

            private var file:File;

            private function buttonClickHandler(event:MouseEvent):void
            {
                file = new File();
                file.addEventListener(Event.SELECT, onFileSelect);
                file.browseForOpen("Browse for a file:");
            }

            private function onFileSelect(event:Event):void
            {
                richText.text = File(event.currentTarget).nativePath;
                file.load();

                try {
                    file.openWithDefaultApplication();
                }
                catch(error:Error) {
                    trace("The file you selected is prohibited and cannot be opened");
                }
            }

        ]]>
    </fx:Script>

    <s:Button id="button"
              label="Click to browse"
              click="buttonClickHandler(event);"
              width="134" />

    <s:RichText id="richText" x="0" y="29"/>

</s:WindowedApplication>
```

Run the AIR application, browse for a supported file, and watch how the registered application opens the file (see Figure 5-6).

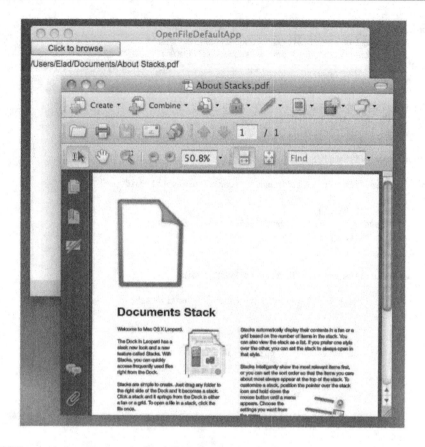

Figure 5-6. PDF selected and opened with default application

AIR 2.0 also adds a property called `downloaded`. Setting that property will instruct the OS that the file was downloaded and may result in a user's notification the first time the file opens in Mac OS X or Windows XP SP2 and later. You can set it as follows:

```
file.downloaded = true;
```

Additionally, you can use the `file.download( request );` method to download the file. In this case, it will be marked as downloaded automatically.

Microphone Access API

AIR 2.0 exposes access to the uncompressed PCM `ByteArray` data on the Microphone API. You can enable or disable the feature by setting or removing the `SampleDataEvent.SAMPLE_DATA` event listener on each `Microphone.getMicrophone()` instance.

We want to point out that the ability to access the `ByteArray` in certain APIs has been a long-standing request to Adobe, and we will not be surprised if this feature is added to Flash Player altogether in a subversion of Flash Player 10 or 11. We hope that Adobe will continue the trend and allow the ability to access `NetStream`'s `ByteArray`.

The following application lets you record from any microphone connected. While you record the audio, you can see a bar that shows the volume of your voice as a graphic. Once you complete recording, you can play back the visualization of your recording and save it as a Wave file.

```
<?xml version="1.0" encoding="utf-8"?>
<s:WindowedApplication xmlns:fx="http://ns.adobe.com/mxml/2009"
                                xmlns:s="library://ns.adobe.com/flex/spark"
                                xmlns:mx="library://ns.adobe.com/flex/mx"
                                xmlns:ui="ui.*"
                                width="470" height="240">
    <fx:Script>
        <![CDATA[
            import com.adobe.audio.format.WAVWriter;

            import flash.events.Event;
            import flash.events.SampleDataEvent;
            import flash.events.StatusEvent;
            import flash.media.Microphone;
            import flash.media.Sound;
            import flash.media.SoundChannel;
            import flash.utils.ByteArray;
            import flash.utils.Endian;

            import ui.AudioVisualization;

            [Bindable]
            private var micNames:Array = Microphone.names;
            private var recordedData:ByteArray;

            private var mic:Microphone;
            private var sound:Sound;
            private var file:File;

            private function onOff():void
            {
                if (recordButton.selected)
                {
                    recordData();
                    recordButton.label = "Stop";
                }
                else
                {
                    stopRecording();
                    recordButton.label = "Record";
                }
            }

            private function recordData():void
            {
                recordedData = new ByteArray();
```

159

```
                    mic = Microphone.getMicrophone( micNamesCombo.selectedIndex );
                    mic.rate = 44;

                    mic.addEventListener(SampleDataEvent.SAMPLE_DATA, dataHandler);
            }

            private function stopRecording():void
            {
                    if (!mic)
                            return;

                    mic.removeEventListener(SampleDataEvent.SAMPLE_DATA, dataHandler);
            }

            private function dataHandler(event:SampleDataEvent):void
            {
                    this.visualization.drawMicBar(mic.activityLevel, 0xFF0000);
recordedData.writeBytes(event.data);
            }

            private function playRecordedData():void
            {
                    recordedData.position = 0;
                    sound = new Sound();
                    sound.addEventListener(SampleDataEvent.SAMPLE_DATA, playSoundHandler);

                    var channel:SoundChannel;
                    channel = sound.play();
                    channel.addEventListener(Event.SOUND_COMPLETE, onPlaybackComplete);

                    visualization.start();
            }

            private function onPlaybackComplete(event:Event):void
            {
                    visualization.stop();
            }

            private function playSoundHandler(event:SampleDataEvent):void
            {
                    if (!recordedData.bytesAvailable > 0)
                            return;

                    var length:int = 8192; // Change between 2048 and 8192
                    for (var i:int = 0; i < length; i++)
                    {
                            var sample:Number = 0;
                            if (recordedData.bytesAvailable > 0)
                                    sample = recordedData.readFloat();

                            event.data.writeFloat(sample);}
            }
```

```
private function save():void
{
        file = new File( );
        file.browseForSave( "Save your wav" );
        file.addEventListener( Event.SELECT, writeWav );
}

private function writeWav(evt:Event):void
{
        var wavWriter:WAVWriter = new WAVWriter();
        var stream:FileStream = new FileStream();

        // Set settings
        recordedData.position = 0;
        wavWriter.numOfChannels = 1;
        wavWriter.sampleBitRate = 16;
        wavWriter.samplingRate = 44100;

        stream.open( file, FileMode.WRITE );

        // convert ByteArray to WAV
        wavWriter.processSamples( stream, recordedData, 44100, 1 );
        stream.close();
}
        ]]>
    </fx:Script>

    <mx:ComboBox id="micNamesCombo" dataProvider="{micNames}" x="283" y="8"/>
    <mx:Button id="recordButton" label="Record" toggle="true" click="onOff()" x="28" y="7"/>
    <s:Button id="playButton" label="Play Recording" click="playRecordedData()"↵
x="102"  y="7"/>
    <s:Button id="saveButton" label="Save" click="save()" x="208" y="7"/>

    <ui:AudioVisualization id="visualization" y="100" />

</s:WindowedApplication>
```

As you can see in Figure 5-7, you can start recording your voice. While you record your voice, you can see a bar that moves with the intensity of your voice. That is possible through the AudioVisualization component.

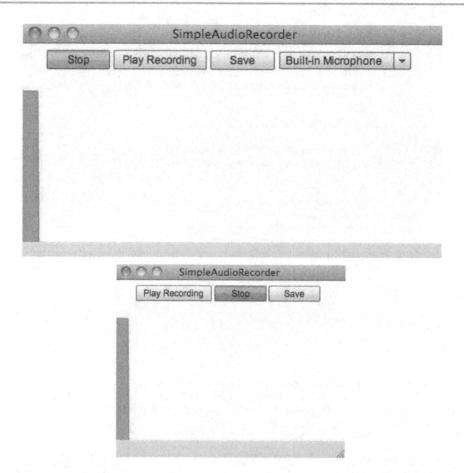

Figure 5-7. SimpleAudioRecorder recording your voice and displaying a bar indicating the intensity

Once the voice is recorded, you can play back, see the equalizer, and save the file as a WAV file (see Figure 5-8).

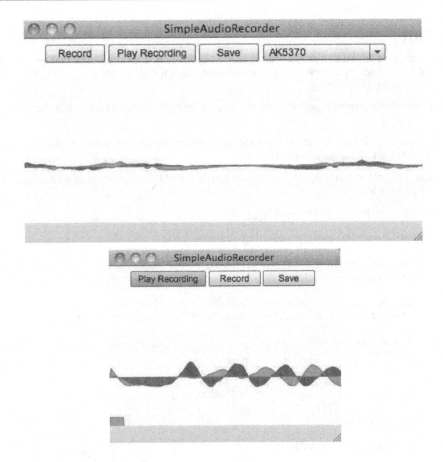

Figure 5-8. SimpleAudioRecorder playback of the recording

Database Transaction Savepoints

The AIR 1.5 SQLConnection class supports transactions. Transactions allow the user to track SQL commands and commit or rollback when needed. AIR 2.0 adds new methods called `savepoints()`, `setSavepoint()`, `releaseSavepoint()`, and `rollbackToSavepoint()`. We show you how to work with the new API in Chapter 7.

Mac Vector Printing Support

AIR 1.5 supports vector-printing for Windows that is done utilizing the `flash.printing.PrintJob` class. AIR 2.0 adds the capability of doing vector printing on a Mac. See the following link for more information on how to use the vector printing in AIR: `http://help.adobe.com/en_US/ActionScript/3.0_ProgrammingAS3/WS5b3ccc516d4fbf351e63e3d118a9b90204-7cc2.html`.

Idle Time-Out

AIR 2.0 adds a method to `URLRequestDefaults`, `HTMLLoader`, and `URLRequest` classes so you can set the idleTimeout (idle) property before the connection gets closed. Having access to the idle timeout opens up options for things like long polling.

Idle means no keystrokes or mouse movements. The acceptable range of values is from 5 (5 seconds) through 86,400 (1 day).

The following application tracks the application idle and present status and sets the idle for `HTMLLoader`. If you set the idle too short, `HTMLLoader` will terminate.

Once the application gets initialized, you can create a new HTMLLoader container and set events to listen to idle and user present events.

```
private function initializeHandler():void
{
    html = new HTMLLoader();

    nativeApp = NativeApplication.nativeApplication;
    nativeApp.idleThreshold = 7;

    nativeApp.addEventListener(Event.USER_IDLE, onUserIdleHandler);
    nativeApp.addEventListener(Event.USER_PRESENT, onUserPresentHandler);

    html.idleTimeout = 7;
    html.width = 800;
    html.height = 800;

    var urlRequest:URLRequest = new URLRequest("http://adobe.com");

    html.load(urlRequest);

    component.addChild(html);
}

private function onUserIdleHandler(evt:Event):void
{
    var lastUserInput:Number =
NativeApplication.nativeApplication.timeSinceLastUserInput;
    console.text = String( lastUserInput )+" sec since last present";
}

private function onUserPresentHandler(event:Event):void
{
    console.text = "Present";
}
```

The GUI holds a `UIComponent` for the HTML container and labels to display the status.

```
<mx:UIComponent id="component" x="0" y="15"/>

<s:Label x="5" y="2" text="Idle status: "/>
```

```
<s:Label id="console" x="74" y="2"/>
```

Increased Maximum Size of NativeWindow

NativeWindow maximum window size has been increased from 2880x2880 pixels in AIR 1.5.2 to 4095x4095 pixels in AIR 2.0. This feature is useful and will allow using AIR on bigger screens. For example, now that AIR is capable of registering multi-touch user gestures, you can create AIR applications that will run on large touchscreens. To test the feature, create a large application and set the width and height to the dimensions. We would like to note that deploying the AIR application on a device that is smaller than the size you provided will set the size to the maximum possible size.

```
<?xml version="1.0" encoding="utf-8"?>
<s:WindowedApplication xmlns:fx="http://ns.adobe.com/mxml/2009"
                       xmlns:s="library://ns.adobe.com/flex/spark"
                       width="4095" height="4095" />
```

Platform Awareness–Related APIs

One of the key elements in AIR 2.0 is moving toward an SDK that better ties into the operation system and gives your application more control. Additionally, the new AIR 2.0 contains platform awareness in which the code base is more adaptable to constant changes in a device. This means that the program knows the user's system capabilities and tracks changes in the user's environment.

- Mass storage: API that allows device detection so you can access networks and storage devices and recognize changes.
- Multi touchscreen: AIR 2.0 adds the ability to recognize multi-touch gestures, one of the most important milestones in building a mobile application.

Mass Storage Device Detection

An element missing from previous versions of AIR was the ability to access and detect mass storage changes. In AIR 2.0, you can detect and access the device's mass storage. There are two classes that enable you to do so:

- flash.filesystem.StorageVolumeInfo: `StorageVolumeInfo` is a singleton manager that keeps track of changes to the mass storage devices. Upon changes, `StorageVolumeChangeEvent` gets dispatched. There are two types of events: `storageVolumeMount` and `storageVolumeUnmount`.
- flash.filesystem.StorageVolume: The `StorageVolume` class holds information regarding the properties of the mass storage volume.

Using the new API, you can query the name, label, root directory, and file system type of a volume. Additionally, it is possible to determine whether a volume is writable or removable. The following application will display the existing storage devices available, as well as add and remove mass storage devices in case you add a new device or remove a device such as a USB key.

```
<?xml version="1.0" encoding="utf-8"?>
<s:WindowedApplication xmlns:fx="http://ns.adobe.com/mxml/2009"
                       xmlns:s="library://ns.adobe.com/flex/spark"
```

```
                        xmlns:mx="library://ns.adobe.com/flex/mx"
                        creationComplete="creationCompleteHandler()">

    <fx:Script>
        <![CDATA[
            import flash.events.StorageVolumeChangeEvent;
            import mx.collections.ArrayCollection;

            [Bindable]
            private var storageCollection:ArrayCollection = new ArrayCollection();

            protected function creationCompleteHandler():void
            {
                var storageVolumes:Vector.<StorageVolume> =↵
StorageVolumeInfo.storageVolumeInfo.getStorageVolumes();
                var length:int = storageVolumes.length;

                addEventListeners();

                for (var i:int = 0; i < length; i++)
                {
                    addItem( storageVolumes[i] );
                }
            }

            private function addEventListeners():void
            {
                StorageVolumeInfo.storageVolumeInfo.addEventListener↵
(StorageVolumeChangeEvent.STORAGE_VOLUME_MOUNT,
                function (event:StorageVolumeChangeEvent):void
                {
                    addItem(event.storageVolume);
                });

                StorageVolumeInfo.storageVolumeInfo.addEventListener↵
(StorageVolumeChangeEvent.STORAGE_VOLUME_UNMOUNT,
                function (event:StorageVolumeChangeEvent):void
                {
                    var nativePath:String = event.rootDirectory.nativePath;
                    removeItemByNativePath( nativePath );
                });
            }

            private function addItem( storageVolume:StorageVolume ):void
            {
                var object:Object = new Object();

                object = new Object();
                object.name = storageVolume.name;
                object.icon = storageVolume.rootDirectory.icon.bitmaps[2];
                object.nativePath = storageVolume.rootDirectory.nativePath;
                object.isWritable = storageVolume.isWritable;
                object.isRemovable = storageVolume.isRemovable;
```

```
                storageCollection.addItem( object );
        }

        private function removeItemByNativePath( nativePath:String ):void
        {
                var len:Number = this.storageCollection.length;
                var object:Object;

                for ( var i:int=0; i<len; i++ )
                {
                    object = this.storageCollection.getItemAt( i );

                    if ( object.nativePath == nativePath )
                    {
                        this.storageCollection.removeItemAt( i );
                        break;
                    }
                }
        }

    ]]>
</fx:Script>

<s:List x="87" y="28"
        skinClass="components.DataList"
        dataProvider="{storageCollection}"/>

</s:WindowedApplication>
```

Once you attach a USB drive, the volume will be added automatically to the list. After you remove the USB drive, it will be removed from the list (see Figure 5-9).

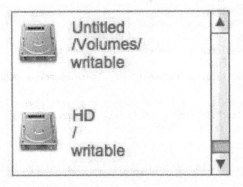

Figure 5-9. Mass Storage Detection Device application

Multi-touch Functionality

Multi-touch is one of the most exciting features in AIR 2. The API is matching the Flash Player 10.1, which will used by mobile devices. Although most of the devices don't support multi-touch user gestures, the excitement is more about the possibilities, since it's clear to many that using a touch screen is becoming very popular. There is a new event called `TouchEvent`, which gets dispatched when the Flash player detects a user gesture.

`MultitouchInputMode` is the enumeration class that holds the three types of multi-touch hardware options.

Flash Player identifies whether the device is capable of touch events with multiple points of contact and specific events for different gestures (such as rotation and pan), only a single point of contact (such as tap), or none at all (contact is handled as a mouse event).

- `GESTURE = "gesture"`: Multiple points of contact and specific events for different gestures (such as rotation and pan).
- `NONE = "none"`: None at all.
- `TOUCH_POINT = "touchPoint"`: Basic single point of contact (such as tap).

First, you need to set the `Multitouch` class to the type of user gesture that the device is capable of capturing. Then, you can start listening to gesture events.

Take a look at the following example. First you switch between the different options, and then you listen to the gesture events that will fire and display the gesture information in the console.

```
<?xml version="1.0" encoding="utf-8"?>
<s:WindowedApplication xmlns:fx="http://ns.adobe.com/mxml/2009"
                       xmlns:s="library://ns.adobe.com/flex/spark"
                       xmlns:mx="library://ns.adobe.com/flex/mx"
                       creationComplete="creationCompleteHandler()">
    <fx:Script>
        <![CDATA[
            import flash.events.TransformGestureEvent;
            import flash.system.Capabilities;
            import flash.system.TouchscreenType;
            import flash.ui.Multitouch;
            import flash.ui.MultitouchInputMode;

            protected function creationCompleteHandler ():void
            {
                if ( Capabilities.touchscreenType == TouchscreenType.NONE )
                {
                    trace("Multitouch is not supported on this device");
                    Multitouch.inputMode = MultitouchInputMode.NONE;
                    return;
                }

                if( Capabilities.touchscreenType == TouchscreenType.FINGER )
                {
                    Multitouch.inputMode = MultitouchInputMode.TOUCH_POINT;
                }
                else if ( Capabilities.touchscreenType == TouchscreenType.STYLUS )
                {
                    Multitouch.inputMode = MultitouchInputMode.GESTURE;
                }

                // Transform Listeners
```

```
                this.addEventListener(TransformGestureEvent.GESTURE_ZOOM, eventHandler);
                this.addEventListener(TransformGestureEvent.GESTURE_SWIPE, eventHandler);
                this.addEventListener(TransformGestureEvent.GESTURE_PAN, eventHandler);
                this.addEventListener(TransformGestureEvent.GESTURE_ROTATE, eventHandler);

                // Touch Listeners
                this.addEventListener(TouchEvent.TOUCH_BEGIN, eventHandler);
                this.addEventListener(TouchEvent.TOUCH_END, eventHandler);
                this.addEventListener(TouchEvent.TOUCH_MOVE, eventHandler);
                this.addEventListener(TouchEvent.TOUCH_OUT, eventHandler);
                this.addEventListener(TouchEvent.TOUCH_OVER, eventHandler);
                this.addEventListener(TouchEvent.TOUCH_ROLL_OUT, eventHandler);
                this.addEventListener(TouchEvent.TOUCH_ROLL_OVER, eventHandler);
                this.addEventListener(TouchEvent.TOUCH_TAP, eventHandler);
            }

            protected function eventHandler(event:TouchEvent) : void
            {
                trace( event.toString() );
            }

        ]]>
    </fx:Script>

</s:WindowedApplication>
```

Better Performance

One of the biggest complaints about AIR applications is that they consume too much CPU memory and have large runtime sizes. It is encouraging to see that in AIR 2.0, Adobe's team put effort into increasing optimization and decreasing resources used by the AIR application:

- File improvement: Smaller runtime size and CPU/memory improvements.
- WebKit upgrade: WebKit HTML-rendering engine was updated to an optimized version.
- Native Linux installed: Linux installer available as native `.deb` and `.rpm` installer. AIR will be available for Linux 64bits.

Decrease in Resources Used

AIR applications have been judged by many to consume too many resources from the machine they are installed on. In AIR 2.0, Adobe put extra effort into decreasing the runtime size and into decreasing the CPU/memory consumed by an AIR application. In fact, you have tested a simple application that includes a text field and noticed a decrease in resources used. Look at the results in Table 5-2 of a sample application you ran as a test.

Table 5-2. Sample Application Results

SDK	CPU	Threads	Real Memory	Virtual Memory
AIR 1.5 & SDK 3.4	2.5	6	30.20 MB	47.80 MB
AIR 2.0 & SDK 4.0	2.5	6	28.6 MB	41.7 MB

WebKit Performance Increase

WebKit (http://webkit.org/) is an open-source browser that has been available since AIR 1.0. The WebKit engine renders HTML and executes JavaScript. WebKit is the engine that drives Safari, claimed by Apple and others to be the fastest browser. Adobe AIR 2.0 uses the same branch of WebKit as the Safari 4 beta: http://trac.webkit.org/browser/releases/Apple/Safari%204%20Public%20Beta. The most significant feature of using this branch of WebKit is the usage of SquirrelFish Extreme (SFX), which has been integrated into the WebKit engine and increases the overall performance of WebKit (see Figure 5-10).

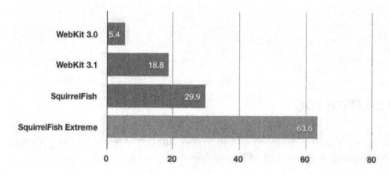

Figure 5-10. WebKit's vs. JavaScript's performance in different versions as provided by WebKit.org

Using a newer branch of WebKit provides faster performance and additional functionality.

- **SquirrelFish Extreme**: The new WebKit engine resulting in faster performance. According to SunSpider, the performance is more than double the speed as compared to the regular SquirrelFish. The reason SFX is faster is mainly due to bytecode optimizations, polymorphic inline caching, a lightweight JIT compiler, and an expression engine that uses the JIT infrastructure. See www.satine.org/archives/2008/09/19/squirrelfish-extreme-fastest-javascript-engine-yet/.
- **CSS transitions**: WebKit added built-in animations using CSS. By describing how to animate from an old value to a new value over time, you can create animations.
- **CSS transformations**: Transformations, via the -webkit-transform property, allows you to scale, rotate, and skew blocks of elements.

- **CSS animations**: Animation that uses the `-webkit-transition` tag and lets you set timings for fades, rotation, expansion, collapses, and others.
- **CSS gradients**: You can create gradients in CSS. There are two types of gradients: linear gradients and radial gradients. The syntax is as follows: `-webkit-gradient(<type>, <point> [, <radius>]?, <point> [, <radius>]? [, <stop>]*)`.
- **WebKit CSS selectors**: You can access the DOM faster and easier using the Selectors API. It allows you to select elements within a document using CSS.

WebKit is embedded into AIR and lets you create HTML/JS/PDF objects and render them as Flash objects. You can then manipulate these objects just like any other object in Flex.

Take a look at a simple application that uses the HTML tag and displays HTML content.

```
<?xml version="1.0" encoding="utf-8"?>
<s:WindowedApplication xmlns:fx="http://ns.adobe.com/mxml/2009"
                        xmlns:s="library://ns.adobe.com/flex/spark"
                        xmlns:mx="library://ns.adobe.com/flex/mx"
                        width="800" height="600">

    <mx:HTML id="htmlObject" location="http://google.com"
                width="400" height="400"
                x="126" y="404" rotation="280"/>


</s:WindowedApplication>
```

Take a look at the following example using the same HTML component, which allows you to test some of the new WebKit functionality:

```
<?xml version="1.0" encoding="utf-8"?>
<s:WindowedApplication xmlns:fx="http://ns.adobe.com/mxml/2009"
                        xmlns:s="library://ns.adobe.com/flex/spark"
                        xmlns:mx="library://ns.adobe.com/flex/mx"
                        width="800" height="600"
                        initialize="initializeHandler(event)">
    <fx:Script>
        <![CDATA[
            import flash.utils.Timer;
            import mx.core.UIComponent;
            import flash.events.Event;
            import mx.controls.HTML;
            import mx.events.FlexEvent;


            private var htmlTransitions:XML =
                <html>
                    <div onmouseover="this.style.opacity = 0;"↵
onmouseout="this.style.opacity=1"
                        style="-webkit-transition: opacity 1s linear; background-color:↵
#efefef; border:5px solid black;">
                        CSS Transitions Example
                    </div>
                </html>;
```

```
            private var html:HTML;

            private var timer:Timer = new Timer(1, 10000);

            protected function initializeHandler(event:FlexEvent):void
            {
                html = new HTML();
                html.width  = 400;
                html.height = 400;
                html.addEventListener( Event.COMPLETE, onComplete );
                component.addChild( html );
            }

            private function loadHTMLCode(htmlText:XML):void
            {
                timer.start();
                html.htmlText = htmlText;
            }

            private function loadHTMLPage(location:String):void
            {
                timer.start();
                html.location = location;
            }

            private function onComplete(event:Event):void
            {
                trace("page loaded after: ");
                label.text = "HTML code executed in " + this.timer.currentCount + " seconds";
                timer = new Timer(1, 10000);
            }

        ]]>
    </fx:Script>
    <fx:Declarations>
        <s:RadioButtonGroup id="radiogroup"/>
    </fx:Declarations>

    <mx:UIComponent id="component" width="400" height="400"  x="10" y="42"/>

    <s:RadioButton x="10" y="10" label="Transitions" groupName="radiogroup"↩
click="loadHTMLCode(htmlTransitions);"/>
    <s:RadioButton x="103" y="10" label="Animations" groupName="radiogroup"↩
click="loadHTMLPage('asset/Animation.html')"/>
    <s:RadioButton x="275" y="10" label="Gradient" groupName="radiogroup"↩
click="loadHTMLPage('asset/Gradient.html')"/>
    <s:RadioButton x="193" y="10" label="Transform" groupName="radiogroup"↩
click="loadHTMLPage('asset/Transform.html')"/>
    <s:RadioButton x="353" y="10" label="Selectors" groupName="radiogroup"↩
click="loadHTMLPage('asset/Selectors.html')"/>

    <mx:Label id="label" x="9" y="450" width="374"/>
```

```
</s:WindowedApplication>
```

There are two methods: `loadHTMLCode` and `loadHTMLPage`. These methods let you load either the HTML as inline code or an HTML page as an object that will be added to the UIComponent.

WebKit Transitions

Since there is not much HTML code for the transition example, you are embedding inline HTML using the HTML component (see Figure 5-11).

Figure 5-11. CSS Transitions example

WebKit Animation

For the HTML implementation, you have used mostly open-source HTML code that you have modified to better fit the presentation. Since the animations are nested inside an object in the Flash VM, the experience of the animation is a bit choppy. We are not sure how much you are really going to use these types of animation, especially when Flash provides much better APIs to handle animations. The following is the code for the `Animation.html` page (see Figure 5-12).

```
<!DOCTYPE HTML PUBLIC "-//W3C//DTD HTML 4.01//EN"
  "http://www.w3.org/TR/html4/strict.dtd">
<html>
  <head>
    <meta http-equiv="Content-type" content="text/html; charset=utf-8">
    <style type="text/css" media="screen">
      @-webkit-keyframes pulse {
      0% {
        background-color: red;
        opacity: 1.0;
        -webkit-transform: scale(1.0) rotate(0deg);
```

```
        }
        33% {
          background-color: blue;
          opacity: 0.75;
          -webkit-transform: scale(1.1) rotate(-5deg);
        }
        67% {
          background-color: green;
          opacity: 0.5;
          -webkit-transform: scale(1.1) rotate(5deg);
        }
        100% {
          background-color: red;
          opacity: 1.0;
          -webkit-transform: scale(1.0) rotate(0deg);
        }
      }

      .pulsedbox {
       -webkit-animation-name: pulse;
       -webkit-animation-duration: 4s;
       -webkit-animation-iteration-count: infinite;
       -webkit-animation-timing-function: ease-in-out;
      }

      div {
        background-color: red;
        width: 40%;
        padding: 0.2em 1em;
        margin: 6em;
      }
    </style>
  </head>

  <body>
    <div class="pulsedbox">
      <p>
        WebKit Animation example
      </p>
    </div>
  </body>

</html>
```

Figure 5-12. WebKit Animation example

WebKit Gradients

AIR's WebKit version supports gradients in CSS. Just as there are in many other design programs, there are two types of gradients: linear and radial.

```
-webkit-gradient(<type>, <point> [, <radius>]?, <point> [, <radius>]? [, <stop>]*)
```

The code for the Gradient.html page is as follows, while Figure 5-13 shows the screenshot.

```
<!DOCTYPE HTML PUBLIC "-//W3C//DTD HTML 4.01//EN"
  "http://www.w3.org/TR/html4/strict.dtd">
<html>

    <head>
        <style>
            div { }
                .radial::after { width:150px; height:150px; border:2px solid black;
                    content: -webkit-gradient(radial, 45 45, 10, 52 50, 30,↵
from(#A7D30C), to(rgba(1,159,98,0)), color-stop(90%, #019F62)),
                            -webkit-gradient(radial, 105 105, 20, 112 120, 50,↵
from(#ff5f98), to(rgba(255,1,136,0)), color-stop(75%, #ff0188)),
                            -webkit-gradient(radial, 95 15, 15, 102 20, 40,↵
from(#00c9ff), to(rgba(0,201,255,0)), color-stop(80%, #00b5e2)),
                            -webkit-gradient(radial, 0 150, 50, 0 140, 90,↵
from(#f4f201), to(rgba(228, 199,0,0)), color-stop(80%, #e4c700));
                    display: block;
            }
            .linear::after { width:130px; height:130px; border:2px solid black;
                content: -webkit-gradient(linear, left top, left bottom, from(#00abeb),↵
```

```
to(#fff), color-stop(0.5, #fff), color-stop(0.5, #66cc00));
                display: block;
            }
        }
    </style>
</head>

<body>
    <div class="radial">WebKit CSS Gradient Radial Example</div>
    <br/>
    <div class="linear">WebKit CSS Gradient Linear Example</div>
</body>
</html>
```

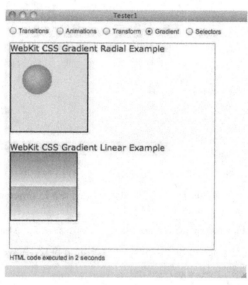

Figure 5-13. WebKit CSS Gradient radial and linear example

WebKit Selectors

The new version of WebKit provides an addition to the traditional DOM. The new API comes in handy when you need to retrieve certain elements or collections of elements. The selectors provide more functionality and the ability to retrieve a list of functions, as well as other features. See the Selectors.html content and Figure 5-14.

```
<!DOCTYPE html>
<html>
    <head>
    </head>

    <body>
        <p id="text1" />
        <p class="text2" />
```

```
<script>
    document.querySelector("p#text1").innerHTML = "Selectors example using Id";
    document.querySelector("p.text2").innerHTML = "Selectors example using class";
</script>

    </body>
</html>
```

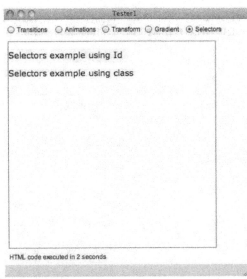

Figure 5-14. Selectors example using Id and class

WebKit Transform

WebKit supports CSS transforms. The syntax is as follows: `-webkit-transform`. Using the WebKit transform, you can set boxes to be scaled, rotated, skewed, or translated. See the `Transform.html` content and Figure 5-15.

```
<!DOCTYPE HTML PUBLIC "-//W3C//DTD HTML 4.01//EN"
  "http://www.w3.org/TR/html4/strict.dtd">

<html>
    <head>
        <style type="text/css">
          .showbox {
            float: left;
            margin: 4em 1em;
            width: 40px;
            height: 20px;
            border: 2px solid green;
            background-color: #fff;
            line-height: 20px;
```

```
            text-align: center;
        }
    </style>
</head>

<body>
    <div class="showbox" style="-webkit-transform: translate(2em,0);">1</div>
    <div class="showbox" style="border-color: red; -webkit-transform:↵
rotate(50deg);">2</div>
        <div class="showbox" style="-webkit-transform: translate(-3em,1em);">3</div>
        <div class="showbox" style="-webkit-transform: scale(2);">4</div>
    </body>

</html>
```

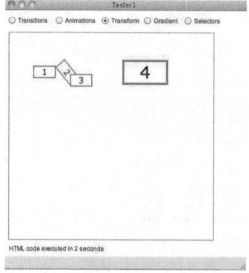

Figure 5-15. WebKit transform

Summary

In this chapter, we gave you a comprehensive overview of AIR 2.0. We showed you the new functionality in AIR 2.0 such as the new Networking class, launching and interacting with Native Processes, and screen reader support. We covered the additional functionality to existing APIs that AIR supports, such as opening files with their default application, access to the ByteArray for the Microphone API, and support for Database Transaction Savepoints. We also showed you how to use APIs that are related to platform awareness, such as mass storage device detection and multi-touch screens. Finally, we discussed the performance improvements in AIR 2.0, such as a decrease in resources used and the new WebKit.

Chapter 6

Creating Themes in Flex 4

by Elad Elrom

Flex 4 SDK has added the Spark skins, which include a complete re-work of the style architecture in Flex 4 components and allow you to easily change CSS or re-skin the components. In this chapter we will give you an overview of the new Spark skins and working with CSS, as well as tutorials for creating themes using Illustrator and Flash Catalyst and mixing Flex 4 with Flex 3 components.

Understanding Spark Style Support

In Flex 3 and Flex 4, SDK supported only Halo skins, but in Flex 4 the default skins used are Spark. Spark is built on top of Halo. We want to give you an overview of the new Spark style support before diving into creating themes.

Flex 4 SDK styles for the Spark skins are designed in a simple, predictable, and more consistent fashion. In fact, you can change the entire appearance of an application with a few global style properties. This is a contrast to styling in Halo, where you have many more knobs to adjust the appearance, and many of these knobs need to be set on individual components or type selectors.

Take a look at an example. The code shown here sets the global inheriting style for the button component to the following (see Figure 6-1):

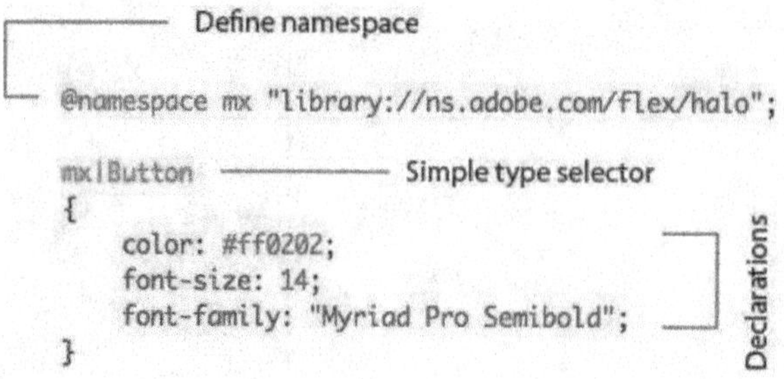

Figure 6-1. Button Halo component skin styled

Notice that in Flex 4 we now have to define the namespaces of the components since many share the same local name as existing MX components, e.g., Button. Defining namespacing will avoid name collisions.

In fact, Halo has created styles purely to style sub-components or states of a component, since you have no access to the states. For instance, to access the sub-component of Accordion you have headerStyleName, or dropDownStyleName on ComboBox.

The advanced CSS features in Spark eliminate the need to use these types of styles. Take a look at a Spark style that gives you more fine-tuning and allows you to access the over state of the button component (see Figure 6-2).

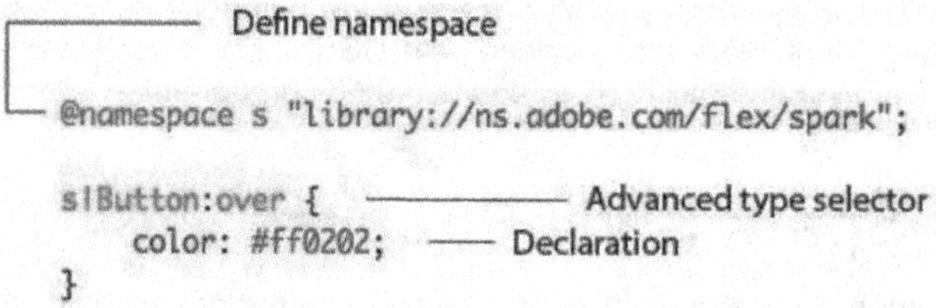

Figure 6-2. Button Spark component skin styled

```
<?xml version="1.0" encoding="utf-8"?>
<s:Application xmlns:fx="http://ns.adobe.com/mxml/2009"
                xmlns:s="library://ns.adobe.com/flex/spark"
                minWidth="1024" minHeight="768">

    <fx:Style source="Main.css" />

    <s:Panel width="400" height="600" title="Panel title goes here">
        <s:TextArea width="200" height="150"  x="22" y="47">
```

```
        <s:text>
                     Lorem ipsum dolor sit amet, consectetuer adipiscing↵ elit, sed diam
nonummy nibh euismod tincidunt ut laoreet dolore magna aliquam erat↵ volutpat. Ut wisi enim ad minim
veniam, quis nostrud exerci tation ullamcorper↵ suscipit lobortis nisl ut aliquip ex ea commodo
consequat. Duis autem vel eum ↵
iriure dolor in hendrerit in vulputate velit esse molestie consequat,
        </s:text>
    </s:TextArea>
    <s:Button width="100" label="test"  x="22" y="10"/>


  </s:Panel>

</s:Application>
```

Here is the content of the style sheet Main.css:

```
@namespace s "library://ns.adobe.com/flex/spark";

s|Panel #titleDisplay {
      fontSize: 20;
      font-style: italic;
}

s|TextArea s|ScrollBar {
      base-color: #DC03FC;
}

s|Button:up {
      color: #0826FF;
}
```

CSS Styling vs. Skins

Flex Developers usually use CSS to customize components; however, there are certain cases where you just cannot achieve the customization you need, and that's where you will use skinning. The decision to use CSS styling or skins has to do with what you are trying to achieve.

The caveat with the new architecture of the component is that simple and common tasks that you used to be able to accomplish with styles in Halo now require a complete re-skinning in Spark.

Each Spark component extends SkinnableComponent, which extends UIComponent SkinnableComponent, the base class for skinnable components. Each skin is a child of the component and has its own life cycle just like any UIComponent.

You can then define each skin in CSS as follows:

```
SomeComponent
{
    skinClass: ClassReference("component.SomeComponentSkin")
}
```

Once you define your own skin, that new skin will be attached to the component instead of the default skin. This type of new architecture allows you to easily replace a skin of a Spark component.

Building a Theme Using Flash Catalyst

1. Open Flash Catalyst CS 5 and select Create "New Project from Design File" ➤ "From Adobe Illustrator AI File…"

2. Browse and select the DarkNight.ai file. You can keep all the default options and click OK. At this point Catalyst opens with the design artwork (see Figure 6-3).

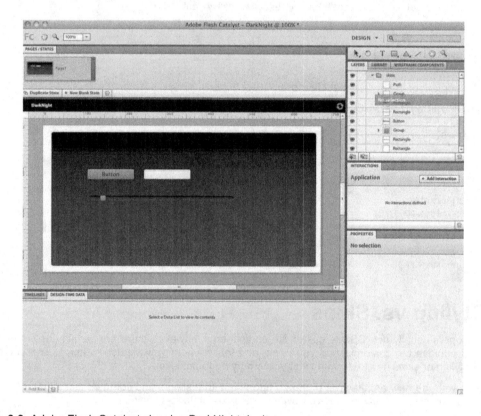

Figure 6-3. Adobe Flash Catalyst showing DarkNight design

Creating a Button Component

1. The next step is to convert the artwork into components. Select all the graphics that are related to the Button, and in the HUD (Heads Up Display) select "Convert Artwork to Component menu" ➤ "Button" (see Figure 6-4).

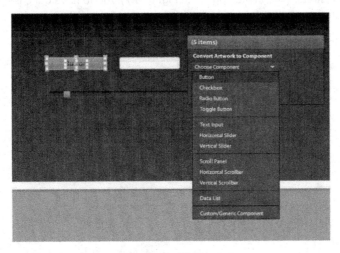

Figure 6-4. Converting artwork to component menu in HUD

2. Double-click the button and you can see the states available (see Figure 6-5).

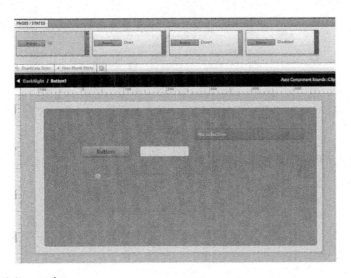

Figure 6-5. Button states mode

3. In the screen where you see all the states, you can make changes to certain properties in Catalyst. Select the Over state, mark the graphics (other than the text), and in the properties files select Appearance ➤ Blend mode: Luminosity (see Figure 6-6). Additionally, you can modify the graphic in Illustrator by selecting the graphic, right-click ➤ Edit in Adobe Illustrator CS5. We will be modifying the document in Illustrator and once we are done, we can select **Done** in Illustrator (see the top option in Figure 6-7). All we have done is change the color of the background so it will be noticeable once you hover over the button.

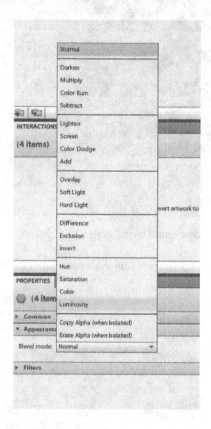

Figure 6-6. Properties window showing Appearance options

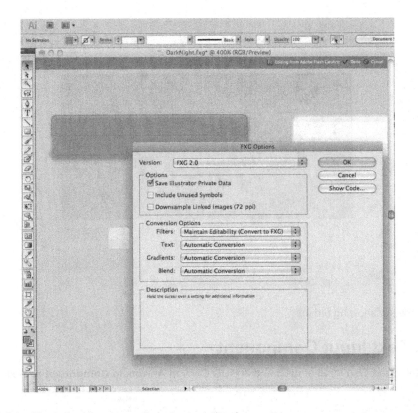

Figure 6-7. Adobe Illustrator showing options to save the document

4. Select the **Down** state, mark the graphics (other than the text), and modify the graphics so the user will be able to notice a difference. At this point you can run the project using File ➤ Run Project. The browser opens and you can see the different states for the button. See Figure 6-8.

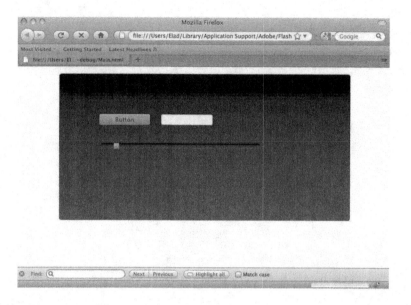

Figure 6-8. Browser showing project

Creating a Text Input Component

1. Select the Text Input graphic and in HUD Convert Artwork to **Component** ➤ Text Input. See Figure 6-9.

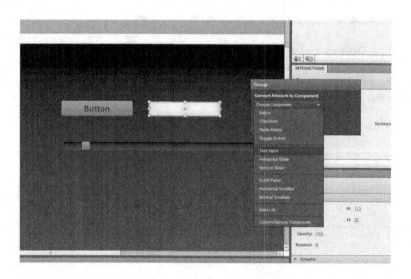

Figure 6-9. Converting artwork to text input

Creating Horizontal Scroll Bar Component

1. Select graphic and in HUD Convert Artwork to Component ➤ Horizontal Scrollbar. See Figure 6-10.

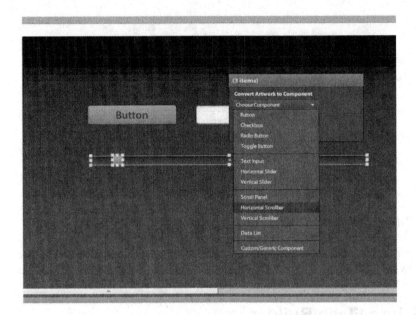

Figure 6-10. Converting artwork to horizontal scrollbar

2. The HUD menu shows the option to edit the appearance of the **Horizontal Scrollbar**. Click **Edit Parts** (see Figure 6-11).

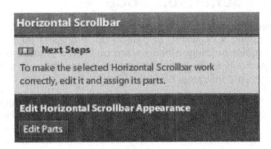

Figure 6-11. HUD menu allowing you to edit the scrollbar appearance

3. The next step is to set the Thumb and Track. In the HUD you can see the **Group** menu (see Figure 6-12) and set the Thumb and Track, which are required, by selecting the graphics that make these components. Then click the check box.

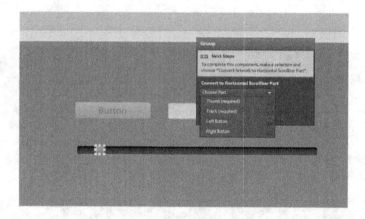

Figure 6-12. HUD menu to convert the horizontal scrollbar part

4. Compile and run the project, and you will be able to see the application we created in the browser and use the components. Save the project by selecting File ➤ Save as DarkNight.fxp.

Import FXP into Flash Builder

The project was saved as FXP, which Flash Builder 4 recognizes, allowing it to import FXP projects. Open Flash Builder 4 and select File ➤ **Import Flex Project** (FXP)... Browse and select DarkNight.fxp, and then select **Finish**.

Adjust Flash Catalyst Generated Code

We often need to do some tweaking before using the Flash Catalyst code. Flash Catalyst generated code places elements with a hard-coded x, y, width, or height, but it doesn't take into account other ways of using the component, which require resizing. Since we are building a theme we need be able to resize the component properly. What we need to do is to find places where there is a hard-coded x, y, width, or height and convert these to use un-constraints based values.

For instance, in our code we need to adjust the button component so it can get resized properly. What we had to do is change the rectangle width from 112 pixels to an un-constraints–based value, in our case 100%. See the following.

Original code:

```
<s:Rect height="24" d:id="4" radiusX="3.00067" radiusY="3.00067" width="112" x="1" y="0">
```

New code:

```
<s:Rect height="24" d:id="4" radiusX="3.00067" radiusY="3.00067" width="100%" x="1" y="0">
```

We also changed the RichText label component from a hard-coded value to be centered. See the following.

Original code:

```
        <s:RichText ai:aa="2" color="#212121" columnCount="1" ↵
fontFamily="Myriad Pro Semibold" fontSize="14" d:id="5" kerning="on" ↵
d:label="ATE Text To TLF Text" text="Button" textAlign="center" ↵
d:userLabel="Button" flm:variant="1" whiteSpaceCollapse="preserve" ↵
x="36" y="6" buttonMode.over="true">
```

New code:

```
        <s:RichText color="#212121"
                    textAlign="center"
                    maxDisplayedLines="1"
                    horizontalCenter="0"
                    left="10" right="10" top="0" bottom="2"
                    fontFamily="Myriad Pro Semibold" fontSize="14"
                    kerning="on" verticalAlign="middle"
                    text="Button"
                    flm:variant="1" whiteSpaceCollapse="preserve"
                    buttonMode.over="true">
```

Create a CSS document

The last step is creating a CSS document that will be used to define the component's skin in Spark or MX. Flash Catalyst already created for us the CSS automatically, Main.css, however, that class is not implemented.

What you should do is define the skinClass and focusColor in the CSS file. Take a look at the implemented code:

```
/*
  Dark Night - Flex 4 Theme by Elad Elrom.
*/

@namespace s "library://ns.adobe.com/flex/spark";
@namespace mx "library://ns.adobe.com/flex/halo";
@namespace d "http://ns.adobe.com/fxg/2008/dt";
@namespace fc "http://ns.adobe.com/flashcatalyst/2009";
@namespace components "components.*";

s|Button
{
        focusColor: #0d103f;
        skinClass: ClassReference("components.Button1");
}

s|HScrollBar
{
        skinClass: ClassReference("components.HorizontalScrollbar1");
}
```

```
s|TextInput
{
        skinClass: ClassReference("components.TextInput1");
}
```

Integrating a Theme into Flash Builder / Flex Plug-In

At this point you have created your first theme and you want to add it to the list of themes in Flash Builder or Eclipse with Flex 4 SDK plug-in. The instructions here work the same way on Flash Builder 4 or Eclipse with Flex 4 plug-in.

1. In Flash Builder 4, switch to Design view, and under Appearance window, click the **Current theme: Spark** link (see Figure 6-13).

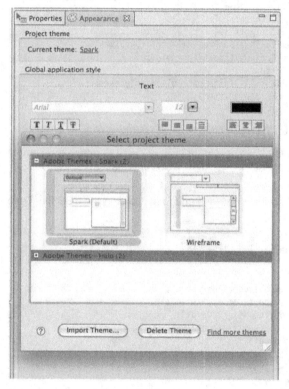

Figure 6-13. Appearance window showing the theme options

2. Click **Import Theme...** ➤ browse to the location of the project and the CSS file, set the theme name, and click OK (see Figure 6-14).

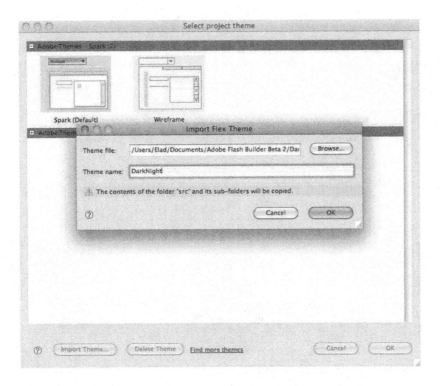

Figure 6-14. Importing Flex theme wizard

3. The new theme is now available for use in your Flex project (see Figure 6-15).

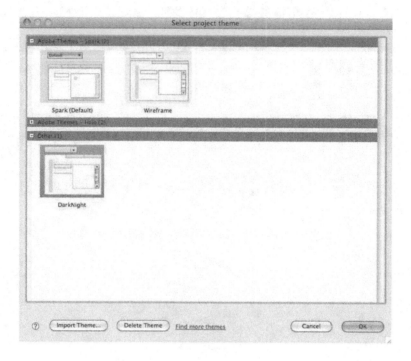

Figure 6-15. Selecting project theme available for use

Once you create a new project you can switch to the theme you just created, and the CSS and components will be copied automatically. You can also delete a theme or share the theme with the community.

Integrating a Theme into Flash Builder 4 / Flex Plug-In

At this point you have created your first theme, and you're ready to add it to the list of themes in Flash Builder 4 or Eclipse with Flex 4 SDK plug-in. The instructions work the same way for Flash Builder 4 and for Eclipse with the Flash Builderex 4 plug-in.

1. In Flash Builder 4 open **Main.mxml** and switch to Design view.

2. Under Select the Appearance window panel, click the **Current theme: Spark** link (see Figure 6-16).

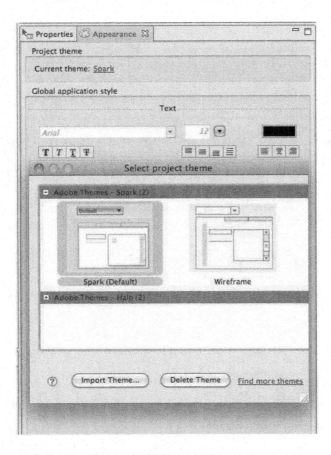

Figure 6-16. Appearance window showing selected project theme options

3. Click **Import Theme....**

4. Browse to the location of the project and the CSS file (**Main.css**), set the type **DarkNight** for the theme name, and click OK (see Figure 6-17).

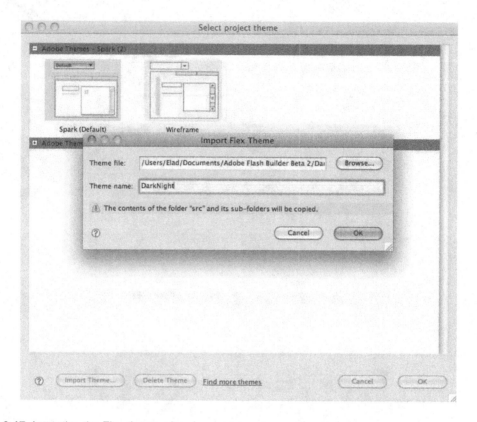

Figure 6-17. Importing the Flex theme wizard

5. The new theme is now available for use in your Flex project (see Figure 6-18). You can also use this dialog box to delete a theme.

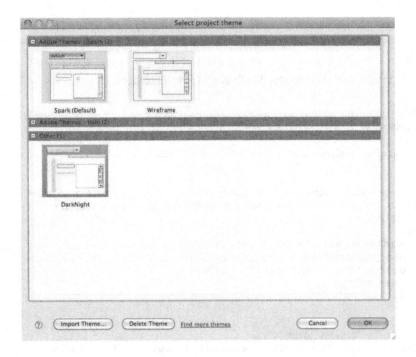

Figure 6-18. DarkNight theme available for use

When you create a new project you can switch to the DarkNight theme you just created, and the CSS components will be copied automatically. You can also delete a theme or share the theme with the community. See `www.adobe.com/cfusion/exchange/index.cfm?s=5&from=1&o=desc&cat=329&l=-1&event=productHome&exc=15`.

Building a Theme Using Adobe Illustrator

Flash Catalyst certainly provides a streamlined way to bring artwork from Creative Suite applications into Flex, but you can also use FXG directly from those applications. This approach might be helpful if you're creating one-off skins or you don't have access to Flash Catalyst. In many ways, going this route is a manual version of what Flash Catalyst does for you however, the code from Illustrator can be used as optimized FXG instead of the MXML Graphics (MXMLG) and will be rendered faster. Let's walk through the steps for creating a single Button skin.

1. Open the **DarkNKnightButton.ai** file in Illustrator CS4. This file contains artwork for another button skin.

2. Select **FileChoose ➤ Save As**. For the Save As Type select FXG, and then click the Save button.

3. A window within the FXG options dialog box will be displayed. Leave the defaults for everything and click the Show Code button.

4. The FXG that represents the skin artwork will be displayed, in addition to markup that is used by Illustrator to translate the FXG. Everything you need for your skin is wrapped in a Group tag.

5. Copy the markup that includes the Group tags to the clipboard:

```
<Group x="106" y="102" d:id="2" d:type="layer" d:userLabel="skins">
    <Group x="3.45605" y="2.54395" ai:knockout="0" d:id="3">
        <filters>
            <DropShadowFilter alpha="0.4" angle="90" blurX="2" blurY="2" distance="1"↵
quality="3"/>
        </filters>
        <Path winding="nonZero" ai:knockout="0" data="M112 21C112 22.6572 110.657 24 109↵
24L3 24C1.34375 24 0 22.6572 0 21L0 3C0 1.34277 1.34375 0 3 0L109 0C110.657 0 112↵
1.34277 112 3L112 21Z" >
            <fill>
                <LinearGradient x="56" y="24" scaleX="24" rotation="-90">
                    <GradientEntry color="#2d6e91" ratio="0"/>
                    <GradientEntry color="#81a8bd" ratio="1"/>
                </LinearGradient>
            </fill>
        </Path>
    </Group>
    <Group x="3.36816" y="2.54395" d:id="4">
        <Path winding="nonZero" ai:knockout="0" data="M112 11.9404L112 3C112 1.34277↵
110.656 0 109 0L3 0C1.34375 0 0 1.34277 0 3L0 11.9404 112 11.9404Z" >
            <fill>
                <LinearGradient x="56" y="11.9404" scaleX="5.57886" rotation="-90">
                    <GradientEntry color="#ffffff" alpha="0.1" ratio="0"/>
                    <GradientEntry color="#ffffff" alpha="0" ratio="1"/>
                </LinearGradient>
            </fill>
        </Path>
    </Group>
    <Path alpha="0.2" winding="nonZero" ai:knockout="0" data="M112 3L7 3C5.34375 3 4↵
4.34277 4 6L4 7C4 5.34277 5.34375 4 7 4L112 4C113.657 4 115 5.34277 115 7L115 6C115↵
4.34277 113.657 3 112 3Z" >
        <fill>
            <SolidColor color="#ffffff"/>
        </fill>
    </Path>
    <Path alpha="0.1" winding="nonZero" ai:knockout="0" data="M7 26L112 26C113.657 26↵
115 24.6572 115 23L115 22C115 23.6572 113.657 25 112 25L7 25C5.34375 25 4 23.6572 4↵
22L4 23C4 24.6572 5.34375 26 7 26Z" >
        <fill>
            <SolidColor/>
        </fill>
    </Path>
    <Group x="38.8467" y="7.19385" ai:knockout="0">
        <filters>
            <DropShadowFilter alpha="0.3" angle="90" blurX="0" blurY="0" color="#ffffff"↵
```

```
distance="1" quality="3"/>
      </filters>
      <TextGraphic textAlign="center" fontFamily="Myriad Pro Light" fontSize="14"↵
fontWeight="bold" lineHeight="120%" color="#212121" whiteSpaceCollapse="preserve"↵
kerning="on" x="0.000244141" y="1.77838" ai:knockout="0">
          <content><p><span>Button</span></p></content>
      </TextGraphic>
   </Group>
</Group>
```

6. Go into Flash Builder 4, create a new MXML file called BlueButtonSkin.mxml, and select Skin as the base class. Select **File ➤ New ➤ MXML Component**. The wizard opens and you can set Based on as spark.components.supportClasses.Skin.

7. Paste the FXG markup you copied in between the s:Skin tags.

8. Since you want the Label of this skin to be dynamic, we need to replace the TextGraphic tag with a RichText tag.

```
<s:RichText color="#212121" columnCount="1" fontFamily="Myriad Pro Semibold" fontSize="14"↵
text="Button" kerning="on" whiteSpaceCollapse="preserve" verticalCenter="0"↵
horizontalCenter="0">
          <s:filters>
              <s:DropShadowFilter alpha="0.3" angle="90" blurX="0" blurY="0" color="#FFFFFF" distance="1"
quality="2"/>
          </s:filters>
      </s:RichText>
```

9. You'll also need to delete any properties prefixed with the d or ai namespace and add an s: in front of every tag, which is better than adding namespaces, since the code will look neater.

10. See the final code here:

```
<?xml version="1.0" encoding="utf-8"?>
<s:Skin xmlns:s="library://ns.adobe.com/flex/spark"
        xmlns:fx="http://ns.adobe.com/mxml/2009"
        xmlns:d="http://ns.adobe.com/fxg/2008/dt"
        xmlns:ai="http://ns.adobe.com/ai/2009"
        xmlns:flm="http://ns.adobe.com/flame/2008">

    <fx:Metadata>[HostComponent("spark.components.Button")]</fx:Metadata>

    <s:states>
        <s:State name="up"/>
        <s:State name="over"/>
        <s:State name="down"/>
        <s:State name="disabled"/>
    </s:states>
```

```
    <s:Rect height="24" d:id="4" radiusX="3.00067" radiusY="3.00067" width="100%"
x="1" y="0">
        <s:filters>
            <s:DropShadowFilter alpha="0.4" angle="90" blurX="2" blurY="2"
distance="1" quality="2"/>
        </s:filters>
        <s:fill.down>
            <s:LinearGradient rotation="270" scaleX="24" x="56" y="24">
                <s:entries>
                    <s:GradientEntry color="#936E91" ratio="0.901841"/>
                    <s:GradientEntry color="#BEA8BD" ratio="1"/>
                </s:entries>
            </s:LinearGradient>
        </s:fill.down>
        <s:fill.disabled>
            <s:LinearGradient rotation="270" scaleX="24" x="56" y="24">
                <s:GradientEntry color="#936E91" ratio="0"/>
                <s:GradientEntry color="#BEA8BD" ratio="1"/>
            </s:LinearGradient>
        </s:fill.disabled>
        <s:fill.up>
            <s:LinearGradient rotation="270" scaleX="24" x="56" y="24">
                <s:GradientEntry color="#936E91" ratio="0"/>
                <s:GradientEntry color="#BEA8BD" ratio="1"/>
            </s:LinearGradient>
        </s:fill.up>
        <s:fill.over>
            <s:SolidColor color="#908FB3"/>
        </s:fill.over>
    </s:Rect>

    <s:Path data="M 112 11.94 L 112 3 C 112 1.343 110.656 0 109 0 L 3 0 C 1.344 0 0
1.343 0 3 L 0 11.94 L 112 11.94 Z" winding="nonZero" x="0.368" y="-0.456" d:id="5"
flm:variant="1">
        <s:fill.down>
            <s:LinearGradient rotation="270" scaleX="5.57886" x="56" y="11.9399">
                <s:entries>
                    <s:GradientEntry alpha="0.1" color="#FFFFFF" ratio="0"/>
                    <s:GradientEntry alpha="0" color="#FFFFFF" ratio="0.773006"/>
                </s:entries>
            </s:LinearGradient>
        </s:fill.down>
        <s:fill.disabled>
            <s:LinearGradient rotation="270" scaleX="5.57886" x="56" y="11.9404">
                <s:GradientEntry alpha="0.1" color="#FFFFFF" ratio="0"/>
                <s:GradientEntry alpha="0" color="#FFFFFF" ratio="1"/>
            </s:LinearGradient>
        </s:fill.disabled>
        <s:fill.up>
            <s:LinearGradient rotation="270" scaleX="5.57886" x="56" y="11.9404">
                <s:GradientEntry alpha="0.1" color="#FFFFFF" ratio="0"/>
                <s:GradientEntry alpha="0" color="#FFFFFF" ratio="1"/>
```

```
                </s:LinearGradient>
            </s:fill.up>
            <s:fill.over>
                <s:SolidColor color="#908FB3"/>
            </s:fill.over>
        </s:Path>
        <s:Path alpha="0.2" data="M 108 0 L 3 0 C 1.344 0 0 1.343 0 3 L 0 4 C 0 2.343↵
1.344 1 3 1 L 108 1 C 109.657 1 111 2.343 111 4 L 111 3 C 111 1.343 109.657 0 108 0 Z"↵
winding="nonZero" x="1" y="0">
            <s:fill>
                <s:SolidColor color="#FFFFFF"/>
            </s:fill>
        </s:Path>
        <s:Path alpha="0.1" data="M 3 4 L 108 4 C 109.657 4 111 2.657 111 1 L 111 0 C 111↵
1.657 109.657 3 108 3 L 3 3 C 1.344 3 0 1.657 0 0 L 0 1 C 0 2.657 1.344 4 3 4 Z"↵
winding="nonZero" x="1" y="19">
            <s:fill>
                <s:SolidColor/>
            </s:fill>
        </s:Path>
        <s:RichText color="#212121"
                    textAlign="center"
                    maxDisplayedLines="1"
                    horizontalCenter="0"
                    left="10" right="10" top="0" bottom="2"
                    fontFamily="Myriad Pro Semibold" fontSize="14"
                    kerning="on" verticalAlign="middle"
                    text="Button"
                    flm:variant="1" whiteSpaceCollapse="preserve"
                    buttonMode.over="true">
            <s:filters>
                <s:DropShadowFilter alpha="0.3" angle="90" blurX="0" blurY="0"↵
color="#FFFFFF" distance="1" quality="2"/>
            </s:filters>
        </s:RichText>

</s:Skin>
```

11. Finally, you just need to create a style definition in your CSS file.

```
s|Button.blueButton
{
    skinClass: ClassReference('components.BlueButtonSkin');
}
```

12. Now, you can apply the blueButton selector to any Button you want, for example:

```
<s:Button skinClass="components.Button1" x="109" y="105"/>
```

As you can see, it's easy to use Illustrator to export FXG to be used as skin artwork. It also allows for the flexibility to create highly-customized user interfaces in Flex. You can take this example further by making more advanced skins and skinning additional Flex components.

Summary

We started by covering the Spark style support and the difference between CSS and Spark skins. We then showed you how to build a theme using Illustrator and Flash Catalyst as well as a theme that includes both Flex 4 and Flex 3 components.

After we created the themes, we showed you how to integrate them into Flash Builder and the Flex 4 plug-in for Eclipse. We hope this chapter will help you create your own Spark skins and integrate them into your project so you can reuse these skins or share them with the Flex community.

Chapter 7

Integrating Flex with Java Using Services

by Shashank Tiwari

Flex and Java are complementary. Flex is a leading technology for building rich, engaging interfaces, while Java is an established player on the server side. Using them together, you can build enterprise-grade applications that are rich, robust, and scalable. Java's ability to serve as a platform for a variety of languages and to integrate with multiple tools and technologies lets Flex make remote calls to multiple languages and to reach out to diverse enterprise systems.

Adobe realized the potential of this synergy and created its data services to support Java. Data services provide a ready-made, robust infrastructure for Flex and Java integration. The concepts behind data services and its API are explained in Chapter 8. Although very beneficial, it isn't necessary to use data services for effective Flex and Java integration. In fact, in some cases, integration is better without it.

This chapter covers those contexts where Flex and Java are loosely coupled without any data services. It illustrates situations where service orientation and server-agnostic user interfaces are very important and form the fundamental tenet of the underlying application architecture.

The integration of Flex and Java can be approached in several ways, depending on the use case and the degree of association. Let's take a look at this in terms of a couple of 2×2 matrices. Figure 7-1 analyzes the integration possibilities using two scales: strong typing requirements and data update frequency. It indicates that if you care about the exact data types and how they are translated between a Java server and a Flex client, and you need frequent data updates, you have a case for tight integration using remote procedure calls and messaging. It also recommends that if the situation is the exact opposite (little need for strong typing and only sporadic need to access or refresh data), you should use simple HTTP-based data interchange. If you are confused and wondering why data typing is important at all, consider the difference between treating a `Person` object as an object with possibly `name`, `id`, and `address` as attributes and `isPolite` as a behavior-introspecting method, versus treating it as a generic collection of name-value pairs.

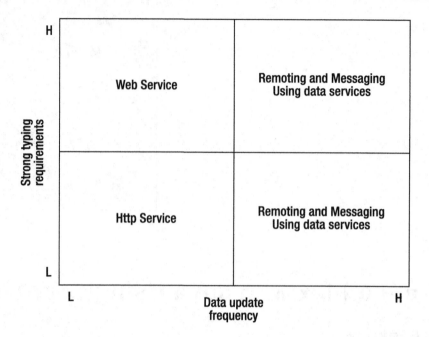

Figure 7-1. Flex and Java integration analyzed via a 2×2 matrix that measures situations on strong typing requirements and data update frequency scales.

Figure 7-2 analyzes the same situation using a different set of scales—payload size and server-side refactoring complexity. Refactoring legacy server-side applications to work with rich clients can be a fairly complicated undertaking. In such cases, it's worthwhile to simply wrap the legacy functionality with a service layer and expose HTTP endpoints to access data. In other instances, the complexity isn't great and refactoring the server-side to work with remoting and messaging destinations is possibly a better choice. When starting from scratch, you always have the choice to design and architect a rich client's server-side counterparts with data services in mind. In most cases of large payload size, tighter coupling helps—unless, of course, the effort in refactoring the server-side is so great that the costs involved outweigh any benefits from the tighter coupling.

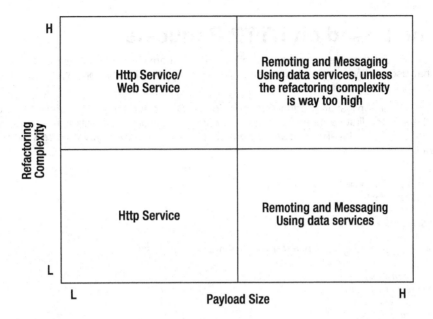

Figure 7-2. Flex and Java integration analyzed via a 2×2 matrix that measures situations on server-side refactoring complexity and payload size scales.

Take a closer look at Figures 7-1 and 7-2. The legends attempt to explain all the possible scenarios. These diagrams should give you a high-level perspective and might prove useful to refer back to when making initial choices.

Some of this may seem new and unfamiliar at first, but we will be getting into the nuts and bolts shortly. As soon as we walk you through the examples, everything should appear lucid and straightforward.

Leveraging HTTP Calls and Web Services

Simple things first! Let's start by integrating Flex and Java using simple HTTP calls and web services. One of the well-known and often talked about benefits of open standards like HTTP and web services is interoperability, with service consumption agnostic to implementation. In other words, you fire up a web site using a URL the same way, irrespective of the language the web site makers use to implement it, and you consume a web service the same way, whether it's written using Java, .NET, or the LAMP stack. Therefore, much of what we say in this chapter is not specific to Java; it is just as applicable to PHP, Python, Ruby, C#/.NET, or any other technology on the server. The only requirement is that the technology that Flex integrates with supports HTTP calls and the standard web services specifications. You'll notice some of this conversation bubbling up again in Chapter 10, which discusses mashups; in Chapter 12, which covers PHP integration; and in Chapter 13, which talks about working with Web 2.0 APIs.

Integration Based on HTTP Requests

HTTP calls are simpler than web services, so let's start with them. Begin by creating a really simple Java application that uses a few simple classes and JSP to generate XML content. We'll consume this XML content from within a Flex application.

This elementary Java application produces a collection of all-time top ten NBA scorers. Each entry in the list includes the scorer's first name and last name, the total score, and his position in the top ten list. Each entry maps to a simple JavaBean class, appropriately called `Scorer.java`. Here's a listing of the `Scorer.java` source:

```
/* Scorer.java */
package org.shanky.flex.examples.nbascorers;
import java.io.Serializable;

public class Scorer implements Serializable {

    private static final long serialVersionUID = 5529587875471400663L;

    private int scorerId;
    private String firstName;
    private String lastName;
    private int totalScore;
    private int position;


        public Scorer() {
                super();
        }

        public Scorer(int scorerId, String firstName, String lastName,
                        int totalScore, int position) {
                super();
                this.scorerId = scorerId;
                this.firstName = firstName;
                this.lastName = lastName;
                this.totalScore = totalScore;
                this.position = position;
        }

        public int getScorerId() {
                return scorerId;
        }
        public void setScorerId(int scorerId) {
                this.scorerId = scorerId;
        }
        public String getFirstName() {
                return firstName;
        }
        public void setFirstName(String firstName) {
                this.firstName = firstName;
        }
...// getters and setters for the lastName, totalScore and position.
```

}

The getter and setter methods for a few attributes are not included in the listing as they are implicitly understood to be similar to the ones included. The complete source code is available in the book's code download bundle.

A collection of the top scorers is returned by a Java service class named `TopScorersService.java`. The `TopScorersService` class has a method, named `getTopScorers`, that returns a collection of top NBA scorers. The simple example here needs to return a list of just the all-time top ten scorers. Therefore, `getTopScorers` ends up calling a private method called `getAllTimeTop10Scorers`, which creates and returns an array list of the top ten scorers. To keep things flexible and allow alternative ways to access and return the top scorers list, the `getTopScorers` method is parameterized, with time interval and collection size as the parameters. Time interval is defined as an enumeration type with `ALL_TIME` and `CURRENT` the two possible values. You can extend this enumeration class to include other time horizons, such as last five years, last twenty years, or any such period. As for the collection size, top ten suffices for now. Ideally, you may want to allow this to be equal to any arbitrary integer, say 20, 100, 350, or 10,000. The implementation of the methods is simple and all the logic resides inline, but the example can be easily extended to include an external data store and a data access intermediation layer. The `TopScorersService.java` class is as follows:

```
/* TopScorersService.java */
package org.shanky.flex.examples.nbascorers;

import java.util.List;
import java.util.ArrayList;


public class TopScorersService {


    public List<Scorer> getTopScorers(TimeInterval timeInterval, int collectionSize) {

        if(timeInterval == TimeInterval.ALL_TIME && collectionSize == 10) {
                return getAllTimeTop10Scorers();
        } else {
                return null;
        }


    }

    private List<Scorer> getAllTimeTop10Scorers() {

    List<Scorer> topScorersList = new ArrayList<Scorer>();

    topScorersList.add(new
            Scorer(1, "Kareem", "Abdul-Jabbar", 38387, 1));
    topScorersList.add (new
            Scorer(2, "Wilt", "Chamberlain", 31419, 2));
    topScorersList.add (new
            Scorer(3, "Karl", "Malone", 30599, 3));
    topScorersList.add (new
            Scorer(4, "Michael", "Jordan", 29277, 4));
```

```
topScorersList.add (new
        Scorer(5, "Moses", "Malone", 27409, 5));
topScorersList.add (new
        Scorer(6, "Elvin", "Hayes", 27313, 6));
topScorersList.add (new
        Scorer(7, "Oscar", "Robertson", 26710, 7));
topScorersList.add (new
        Scorer(8, "Dominique", "Wilkins", 26669, 8));
topScorersList.add (new
        Scorer(9, "John", "Havlicek", 26395, 9));
topScorersList.add (new
        Scorer(10, "Alex", "English", 25613, 10));

return topScorersList;

    }

}
```

The source for the enumeration class, `TimeInterval.java`, is not listed here but is available in the download bundle.

Next we create a really simple JSP that accesses this collection, iterates over it, and prints it out in an XML format. In real-life situations, you may have more complex middleware logic, and JSP generating XML. However, Flex would be unaware of this complexity on the server side. In case it wasn't clear earlier, Flex would interact via HTTP calls in the same manner, irrespective of the server-side technology. That's the benefit of open standards and clean abstractions.

In traditional JSP applications, you often bind these collections to some sort of an HTML view component, like a table, rather than casting it in XML format. When integrating such legacy code with RIA, it may be a good, quick idea to wrap existing JSP(s) to produce XML instead of HTML-rendered output so you can consume it easily in your RIA. Chapter 12 discusses this and other strategies for migrating Web 1.0 applications to RIA. For now, let's stick with this simple example. The code for `topscorers.jsp` follows:

```
<%@page import="org.shanky.flex.examples.nbascorers.*,
                        java.util.List"%>
<?xml version="1.0" encoding="utf-8"?>
<topScorers>
<%
        TopScorersService srv = new TopScorersService();
        List<Scorer> list = null;
        list = srv.getTopScorers(TimeInterval.ALL_TIME, 10);
        Scorer scorer;
        for (int i=0; i<list.size(); i++)
        {
                scorer = (Scorer) list.get(i);
%>
    <scorer scorerId="<%= scorer.getScorerId()%>">
        <firstName><%= scorer.getFirstName() %></firstName>
        <lastName><%= scorer.getLastName() %></lastName>
        <totalScore><%= scorer.getTotalScore() %></totalScore>
        <position><%= scorer.getPosition() %></position>
    </scorer>
<%
```

```
      }
%>
</topScorers>
```

Figure 7-3 shows how the XML output, viewed without any defined XSL, appears in the Eclipse IDE built-in browser. The list in the screenshot is partial and contains only five members.

Figure 7-3. XML output containing the top ten scorers, when viewed without an XSL stylesheet in the Eclipse IDE built-in browser.

This finishes the story on the server side, so let's hop over to the Flex end now. This data is accessible to the Flex client via a URL, so we'll first dig a bit into how Flex interacts with URLs over HTTP in general and then come back to this specific case. The Flex framework has a few different ways it can invoke HTTP URLs and interact with them, three of which we'll discuss here:

- Using the HTTPService component
- Using URLLoader and URLVariables
- Using the Socket class

HTTPService Component

The HTTPService component, which is a part of the mx.rpc.http package, facilitates HTTP request/response communication. It is accessible as an MXML tag and can be imported and invoked as an ActionScript class. Any resource identifiable as a URL and accessible over HTTP or HTTPS can be invoked using this component. The URL to be invoked is bound as the value of the component's url property. A call to our JSP, `topscorers.jsp`, using MXML looks like this:

```
<?xml version="1.0" encoding="utf-8"?>
<s:Application xmlns:fx="http://ns.adobe.com/mxml/2009"
                        xmlns:s="library://ns.adobe.com/flex/spark"
                        xmlns:mx="library://ns.adobe.com/flex/halo" minWidth="1024"⏎
 minHeight="768">
        <fx:Declarations>
                <!-- Place non-visual elements (e.g., services, value objects) here -->
                <mx:HTTPService id="myHTTPService"⏎
url="http://localhost:8080/NBAScorers/topscorers.jsp"/>
        </fx:Declarations>

        <s:SkinnableContainer>
                <s:layout>
                        <s:VerticalLayout horizontalAlign="justify" />
                </s:layout>
                <mx:DataGrid dataProvider="{myHTTPService.lastResult.topScorers.scorer}"⏎
width="100%" height="100%"/>

                <mx:Button label="Invoke HTTPService"
                                click="myHTTPService.send()"/>

        </s:SkinnableContainer>

</s:Application>
```

In Flex 4, the service components—like the `HttpService` class—that facilitate data access are quite the same as in Flex version 3.x. What has changed is how they are referenced and used with both the old component sets (i.e., from Flex 3.x, collectively named "Halo") and the new (i.e., those introduced in Flex 4, referred to as "Spark").

To avoid name collisions when using old and new components, Flex 4 defines four namespaces, as follows:

- *MXML 2006*: The Flex 3 namespace. The URI and default prefix for this namespace are `http://www.adobe.com/2006/mxml` and mx, respectively. This namespace is primarily retained for backward compatibility so that applications written exclusively in Flex 3.x could be compiled using the Flex 4 SDK.

- *MXML 2009*: The new Flex 4 MXML language namespace. Unlike MXML 2006, the new namespace is purely a language namespace and doesn't include any components. The URI and default prefix for this namespace are `http://ns.adobe.com/mxml/2009` and fx, respectively. This namespace is used in the previous MXML code listing.

- *MX/Halo*: The old (Flex 3) components can be used with the new MXML 2009 namespace by referencing them using this namespace, which is identified by the following URI: `library://ns.adobe.com/flex/halo`. The default prefix is mx.

- *Spark*: The new (introduced in Flex 4) components can be used with the new MXML 2009 namespace by referencing them using the Spark namespace. This namespace is identified by the following URI: `library://ns.adobe.com/flex/spark`. The default prefix is s.

If you've been reading this book linearly, you already know about the namespaces and how they are used. However, if you jumped straight to this chapter, it may be beneficial to take another look at the MXML code listing above and notice the use of the MXML 2009, MX/Halo, and the Spark namespaces.

With the namespaces clarified, let's walk through portions of the Flex 4 MXML code behind the elementary example. Unlike previous versions of Flex, Flex 4 mandates that any non-visual component, like `HttpService`, when defined using MXML be declared within the `fx:Declarations` tag. Therefore, the `HttpService` instantiation in the example follows this guideline.

Notice that the `send` method of the `HTTPService` component needs to be called for the invocation to take place. For easy access and user control, we bound the call to this `send` method as an event handler to the `click` event of a button, which we labeled **Invoke HTTPService**. The `send` method could have been called from any other event handler including `creationComplete`, which is triggered when the `creationComplete` system event is fired. Once the application is set up, its child components are all created, laid out, visible, and ready to be used.

This simple example involved the default HTTP `GET` method call. Setting the method property value as `POST` would have allowed `POST` method calls as well. Other HTTP method calls, like `HEAD`, `OPTIONS`, `TRACE`, and `DELETE,` can also be made using the `HTTPService` component, but in that case you'd need to use a proxy. I'll come back to this in a bit.

Once you make a request, the web server will come back with a response. If successful, it returns the desired resource or data; if unsuccessful, it returns an error code, which can help you understand the cause of the failure. In this code, we don't do any of this; we simply bind the returned response referenced through the `lastResult` property of the service component to a data provider attribute. The outcome piped to the data provider of a Halo data grid makes the interface appear, as in Figure 7-4.

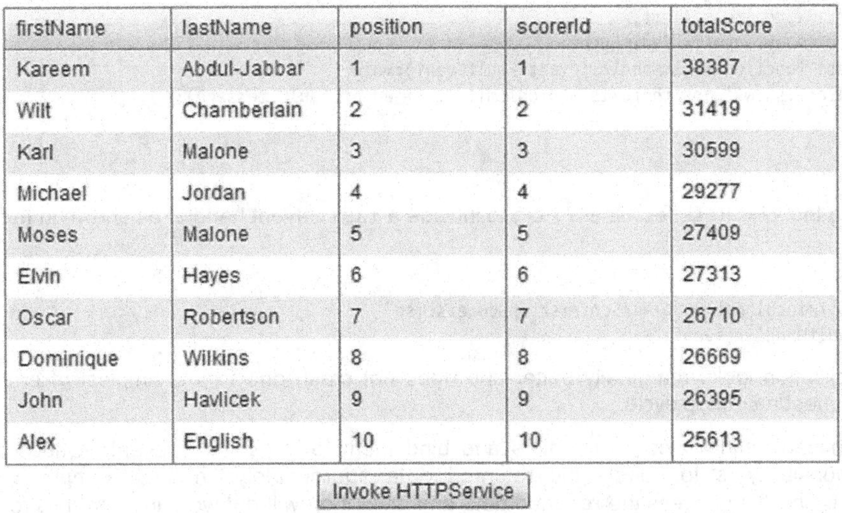

firstName	lastName	position	scorerId	totalScore
Kareem	Abdul-Jabbar	1	1	38387
Wilt	Chamberlain	2	2	31419
Karl	Malone	3	3	30599
Michael	Jordan	4	4	29277
Moses	Malone	5	5	27409
Elvin	Hayes	6	6	27313
Oscar	Robertson	7	7	26710
Dominique	Wilkins	8	8	26669
John	Havlicek	9	9	26395
Alex	English	10	10	25613

Invoke HTTPService

Figure 7-4. HTTP response displayed in a data grid

That was some nice, useful output for the minuscule amount of effort put in so far. Now let's see how this nice example may after all not be that robust.

There's been no error handling in the code so far, not even any budgeting for it. Not handling errors and exceptions is never good. You can experience the pain inflicted by this shortcoming by simply bringing down your web server and invoking the HTTPService one more time. This time there's no nice data grid, but instead complaints from the Flash Player in the form of an error stack trace. Figure 7-5 shows what it looks like.

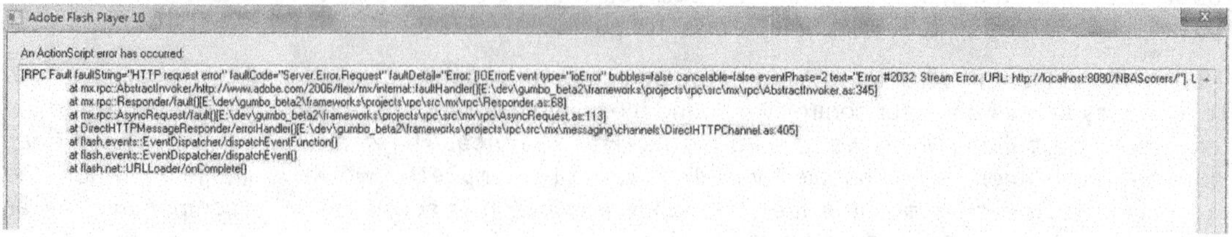

Figure 7-5. Flash player error strack trace

Luckily, HTTPService, like most components and controls in Flex, defines a set of events that are triggered during different stages of its life cycle. In the case of HTTPService, they are result, fault, and invoke, which map to success, failure, and invocation in progress and no failure so far. As with any other event, you can define event handlers to take appropriate action. For instance, alerting the user by printing the error to the screen may be an appropriate way to handle faults. Activating this feature implies adding the following lines to your code:

```
<fx:Script>
    <![CDATA[
        import mx.controls.Alert;
        import mx.rpc.events.FaultEvent;
        private function faultHandler(event:FaultEvent):void {
            Alert.show('Oops there is a problem!....' + event.fault.message);
        }
    ]]>
</fx:Script>
```

and modifying the <mx:HTTPService /> tag to include a fault event handler as shown in the following:

```
<mx:HTTPService
    id="myHTTPService"
    url="http://localhost:8080/NBAScorers/topscorers.jsp"
    fault="faultHandler(event)"/>
```

Now the application looks marginally better and does not crash due to the simplest of errors occurring during the request/response cycle.

Similarly, you can define success handlers and bind them to the result event. A success handler's primary responsibility is to handle the returned data appropriately. In this example, we used the lastResult property to access the returned data and pass it on without worrying about its format. We did nothing special; how did it still work? By default, the result set returned by the HTTP service call is available in the lastResult object and is formatted as a tree of ActionScript objects. The result set is also bindable, which implies that it gets updated as changes to the data set occur. The HTTPService component inherits from the Remote Procedure Call (RPC) executor AbstractInvoker class. The AbstractInvoker object defines the lastResult and the makeObjectsBindable properties. We mentioned a while back that the lastResult property is of type object and holds the result set returned by the service call The `makeObjectsBindable` object is of type `Boolean` and is by default `true`. This flag determines whether the returned object should be bindable or not. In the default case, this property leads to an object type being wrapped in an `ObjectProxy` and an array type being wrapped in an `ArrayCollection`.

In this example, the tree of objects maps to underlying XML. This tree of objects, which is returned as the response of the HTTP request, is assigned as the data provider of the data grid. Such an object structure is the default response data type for HTTP requests made using the Flex `HTTPService` object.

However, you don't always have to rely on defaults and don't have to handle returning data as an object tree. You have ample choices. You can set the `resultFormat` property to `array`, `xml`, `flashvars`, `text`, and `e4x` (ECMAScript for XML) to get data in alternative formats. For example, if you specify the `resultFormat` as `e4x` and use the corresponding syntax and expressions to access the data, the example is marginally modified as follows:

```
<s:Application xmlns:fx="http://ns.adobe.com/mxml/2009"
    xmlns:s="library://ns.adobe.com/flex/spark"
        xmlns:mx="library://ns.adobe.com/flex/halo" minWidth="1024" minHeight="768">
        <fx:Declarations>
                <!-- Place non-visual elements (e.g., services, value objects) here -->
                <mx:HTTPService id="myHTTPService" url="http://localhost:8080/NBAScorers/"↵
resultFormat="e4x"/>
        </fx:Declarations>

        <s:SkinnableContainer>
            <s:layout>
                    <s:VerticalLayout horizontalAlign="center"
                        paddingLeft="40" paddingTop="40" />
            </s:layout>
            <mx:DataGrid dataProvider="{myHTTPService.lastResult.scorer as XMLList}"
                width="100%" height="100%" rowCount="10">
            <mx:columns>
                    <mx:DataGridColumn  headerText="First Name" dataField="firstName"/>
                <mx:DataGridColumn  headerText="Last Name"  dataField="lastName"/>
                <mx:DataGridColumn  headerText="Position" dataField="position"/>
                <mx:DataGridColumn  headerText="Scorer Id" dataField="@scorerId"/>
                <mx:DataGridColumn  headerText="Total Score" dataField="totalScore"/>
            </mx:columns>

        </mx:DataGrid>

            <mx:Button label="Invoke HTTPService" click="myHTTPService.send()"/>

        </s:SkinnableContainer>

</s:Application>
```

When `resultFormat` is set to type `e4x`, the `lastResult` is set to type `XML` and points to the root node of the document. Therefore, you don't need to refer to the collection as `myHTTPService.lastResult.topScorers.scorer`; you can simply access it as `myHTTPService.lastResult.scorer`. In legacy ActionScript, that is, the version prior to ActionScript 3.0 (AS3), the `flash.xml.XMLNode` class represented an XML fragment. This is a bit clumsy considering that an XML fragment contained in a larger XML document is also XML. So the use of this class is now deprecated. However, you may still want to use it for some reason, such as backward compatibility. In such a scenario, you need the `lastResult` object returned as an `XMLNode`, not an XML object. You can achieve this by setting `resultFormat` to `xml` and not `e4x`. Similarly, if you want the result to be in an array or a set of name-value pairs or plain text, you can accomplish this by setting `resultFormat` to `array`, `flashvars`, or `text`, respectively.

So far, we've done almost everything in MXML. Now let's switch gears to ActionScript. This time, let's recode the example using ActionScript only for the `HTTPService` component as follows:

```
/* topscorers_as.mxml */
<?xml version="1.0" encoding="utf-8"?>
<s:Application xmlns:fx="http://ns.adobe.com/mxml/2009"
                    xmlns:s="library://ns.adobe.com/flex/spark"
                    xmlns:mx="library://ns.adobe.com/flex/halo" minWidth="1024"
minHeight="768">
        <fx:Script>
            <![CDATA[
                    import mx.controls.Alert;
                    import mx.rpc.events.FaultEvent;
                    import mx.rpc.events.ResultEvent;
                    import mx.collections.XMLListCollection;
                    import mx.rpc.http.HTTPService;
                    import mx.controls.DataGrid;

                    private var myHTTPService:HTTPService;
                    private var myDataGrid:DataGrid = new DataGrid();

                    public function useHttpService():void {
                            trace("useHttpService invoked");
                            myHTTPService = new HTTPService();
                            myHTTPService.url =
                                    "http://localhost:8080/NBAScorers/topscorers.jsp";
                            myHTTPService.method = "GET";
                            myHTTPService.addEventListener("result", resultHandler);
                            myHTTPService.addEventListener("fault", faultHandler);
                            myHTTPService.send();
                    }
                    public function resultHandler(event:ResultEvent):void {
                            trace("resultHandler invoked");
                            var result:Object = event.result;
                            myDataGrid.dataProvider = result.topScorers.scorer;
                            myDataGrid.percentWidth = 100;
                            myDataGrid.percentHeight = 100;
                            myDataGrid.rowCount = 10;
                            myVBox.addChild(myDataGrid);
                            //Do something with the result.
                    }
                    private function faultHandler(event:FaultEvent):void {
                            trace("faultHandler Invoked");
                            Alert.show('Oops there is a problem!....'
                                    + event.fault.message);
                    }

            ]]>
```

```
        </fx:Script>
        <fx:Declarations>
                <!-- Place non-visual elements (e.g., services, value objects) here -->
        </fx:Declarations>
        <s:SkinnableContainer id="skinnableContainer">
                <s:layout>
                        <s:VerticalLayout horizontalAlign="center"
                                paddingLeft="40" paddingTop="40" />
                </s:layout>
                <mx:VBox id="myVBox" width="100%" height="100%" />

                <mx:Button label="Invoke HTTPService"
                        click="useHttpService()"/>
        </s:SkinnableContainer>
</s:Application>
```

That wasn't too different from what we did using MXML. The example is simple so things remained straightforward, even when we switched over to ActionScript.

In real-life situations, you may want to do a few other things to make your applications work:

- Make POST calls as well as GET calls.
- Send parameters along with the request.
- Invoke URL(s) that are accessible over the secure HTTPS protocol.
- Implement a notion of a user session for purposes like authentication or personalization.
- Invoke URL(s) that originate from domains that define a security policy using crossdomain.xml.
- Invoke URL(s) that originate from domains that don't define a security policy.
- Make HTTP requests that require header manipulation.

The following discussion addresses these points in more detail.

Making POST Calls and GET Calls

Making POST and GET calls is a very simple process. All you have to do is set the method property value to POST or GET, as required, and send the request to the server.

For example, you use the following in MXML:

```
<mx:HTTPService id=" myHTTPService " method="POST" ..../>
```

and here's how you'd do this in ActionScript:

```
myHTTPService.method = "POST";
```

Sending Parameters with the Request

The first step in sending parameters with the request is to create an object of type Object, the root object in ActionScript. The next step is to create variables or attributes in this object. Variable names map to the names in the name-value parameter pairs. Next, assign the value to the corresponding variable values. Finally, pass the object as the send method call argument.

Let's walk through a quick example to see how this plays out.

Say your URL is `myURL` and it takes two parameters, `userName` and `password`, which can be passed to it as a part of the `GET` call query string, like this:

```
http://myHost:myPort/myURL?userName="myName"&password="myPassword"
```

In real life, sending the password over an HTTP `GET` method request poses security risks. To avoid this risk, it's advisable to use either the HTTP `POST` method or the HTTPS secure protocol instead.

In your `HTTPService` request, you do the following:

```
var params:Object = new Object();
params["userName"] = "myName";
params["password"] = "myPassword";
myHTTPService.send(params);
```

If it's a `POST` request, you take the same approach, although it maps to hidden variable passing and is not passed as a part of the query string.

Invoking URL(s) Accessible over the Secure HTTPS Protocol

If a Flex application is served over HTTPS, it can make HTTP and HTTPS requests without making any special provisions. However, if the Flex application is served over HTTP and it needs to make HTTPS requests, a few extra configurations are required.

A security policy needs to be defined so that you don't violate the Flash Player security sandbox model, which restricts HTTPS requests over HTTP without such a security policy definition. Cross-domain security is defined in a file named `crossdomain.xml`. Here's the simplest example of a `crossdomain.xml` file:

```
<cross-domain-policy>
    <allow-access-from domain="*" secure="false" />
</cross-domain-policy>
```

This is because HTTP and HTTPS are served over different ports. HTTPS usually uses port 443 and HTTP uses port 80.

A few more things need to be done beyond this cross-domain file if a server-side proxy is in use. But the focus here is on using `HTTPService` without a server-side proxy, so we'll ignore the entire server-side configuration for now.

Just one quick note before moving to the next topic: you may have read advice to include `https` as the value of the `protocol` attribute in the `HTTPService` (or, for that matter, the `WebService`) tag. However, this isn't applicable when there's no server-side proxy in use. With no server-side proxy, such a setting would throw an exception.

Managing User Sessions

User sessions have two use cases in HTML-based web applications:

- Maintain the conversation between the client (browser) and the server.
- Implement authentication and authorization schemes.

In Flex applications, the first of these is generally not relevant. Maintaining the conversation between the client (browser) and the server is important in HTML-based web applications. HTTP is a stateless protocol, so each request is independent of all others. In order to have continuity between successive requests, you need to have a common token among them. This token or identifier is passed back and forth with each request. Flex is a thick-client technology, because it runs within a Flash Player/VM, which can hold data in memory. Therefore, the use of sessions for the purpose of keeping the conversation going between the client and the server is redundant. However, in data service–driven Flex applications, things can get a bit complicated, and there may be situations where it is still valid.

The second situation is still valid. Flex applications may still need sessions for authentication and authorization. Whatever the purpose, the ways of implementing them are the same. You need to do the following:

1. Pass in the credentials, say username and password, as the part of the first request.

2. Generate a server-side token using the passed-in credentials. This token could be as simple as the original data or as complex as an MD5 signature. Passing the data as is makes it susceptible to hacking and is obviously not recommended.

3. Send the token back to the Flex application as a part of the response.

4. Save this token on the client. For application-wide access, save it in the SharedObject.

5. Pass in the token with all subsequent requests.

You can add a session timeout feature to this process, to avoid the token being alive forever. In that case, set the session timeout when creating the token. Save the session timeout value on the server. On every request that carries the token along, verify whether the session is still valid (i.e., the timeout has not been activated yet). If not, ask the user to pass the credentials one more time or keep extending the timeout with every request so that the user session is kept alive so long as the user is not inactive for the duration of the timeout. These are choices that should be made depending on the application's authentication and authorization needs.

Invoking URLs from Domains That Do and Don't Include crossdomain.xml

If a crossdomain.xml file exists (and defines the required security credentials) at the root of the domain from where the resource is being accessed using a URL, there are no security violations and things work just fine. If crossdomain.xml is missing, the URL request would terminate with a security exception. In general, it's a good idea to understand the crossdomain.xml file, the Flash Player security model, and its significance. It's highly recommended that you read the article "Understanding the security changes in Flash Player 10" by Trevor McCauley, accessible at http://www.adobe.com/devnet/flashplayer/articles/fplayer10_security_changes.html.

Manipulating HTTP Headers with Requests

In short, HTTPService allows custom header settings for HTTP POST method calls, but does not allow them for GET method calls. In Representational State Transfer (REST)-style web services, this can be a problem because things from basic HTTP authentication to content type delivery depend on it. I'll pick the topic up again in the next section when we discuss URLLoader and compare it with HTTPService.

That concludes this discussion of HTTPService. Although HTTPService can utilize server-side proxy with data services, we didn't cover any of that because we haven't started with data services yet. (Data services are covered in Chapter 8) One example of where data services impact HTTPService: HTTP methods other than GET and POST can be used, and access tosites that don't define crossdomain.xml becomes possible under proxied situations.

Let's move on to flash.net.URLLoader and its associated classes.

URLLoader, URLRequest, and URLVariables

HTTPService is the primary class in the Flex framework that enables the making of HTTP requests. HTTPService supports all types of text and XML formats to get and parse text-based data. It supports the popular HTTP GET and POST methods, and it allows parameter passing and provides for event-based handling of call success and failure.

Now let's start exploring alternatives to HTTPService. To begin with, Flex is a framework for creating applications that run in the Flash Player. Such applications are written using ActionScript and MXML, then translated to bytecode and instructions that the Flash VM understands. Before Flex, ActionScript alone could be used successfully to create applications that ran in the Flash Player. It's possible to do that even today. We are not suggesting you avoid the Flex framework, only pointing out that there is more to application-building in the Flash Player than Flex. Also, you can use all the extra good things in your Flex applications.

For example, the classes in the Flash libraries that support HTTP communication provide features available in the Flex framework. URLLoader and its associated classes, URLRequest, URLStream, URLVariables, and URLRequestMethod, can be used instead of the Flex HTTPService class to incorporate HTTP-based requests in an application. URLLoader is positioned as the class that loads networked resources, while HTTPService is the class that fetches remote data, but they do many things in common and can be interchanged in many situations. Sometimes using URLLoader is a more robust option than using HTTPService. One such case is its ability to access binary data. URLLoader is quite capable of accessing any kind of binary data, say an image file. In contrast, HTTPService invocations to access binary data end in an error condition.

To gently get started with URLLoader and its applicability, let's re-implement the HTTPService example using URLLoader. Here is the new code, done up as an MXML application:

```
/* topscorers_urlloader.mxml */
<?xml version="1.0" encoding="utf-8"?>
<s:Application xmlns:fx="http://ns.adobe.com/mxml/2009"
                    xmlns:s="library://ns.adobe.com/flex/spark"
                    xmlns:mx="library://ns.adobe.com/flex/halo" minWidth="1024"↵
  minHeight="768">
      <fx:Script>
            <![CDATA[
                    import XMLDataURLLoader;

                    private function loadXML():void {
                            var xmlDataURLLoader:XMLDataURLLoader =
                                    new XMLDataURLLoader();
                            xmlDataURLLoader.loadXMLData();
                            myVBox.addChild(xmlDataURLLoader.myDataGrid);
                    }

            ]]>
      </fx:Script>
      <s:SkinnableContainer>
            <s:layout>
                    <s:VerticalLayout horizontalAlign="center"
                            paddingLeft="40" paddingTop="40" />
            </s:layout>
```

```
        <mx:VBox id="myVBox" width="100%" height="100%" />
        <mx:Button label="Invoke URLLoader" click="loadXML()"/>
    </s:SkinnableContainer>
</s:Application>

/* XMLDataURLLoader.as */
package
{
        import flash.events.Event;
        import flash.net.URLLoader;
        import flash.net.URLRequest;

        import mx.collections.XMLListCollection;
        import mx.controls.DataGrid;
        import mx.controls.dataGridClasses.DataGridColumn;

        public class XMLDataURLLoader
        {
                private var URL_String:String =
                        "http://localhost:8080/NBAScorers/";
                private var myXMLRequest:URLRequest =
                        new URLRequest(URL_String);
                private var myLoader:URLLoader = new URLLoader();
                [Bindable]
                public var myDataGrid:DataGrid = new DataGrid();

                public function XMLDataURLLoader()
                {
                }

                private function xmlLoad(event:Event):void {
                        var myXML:XML = new XML(event.target.data);
                        trace("Data loaded.");
                        trace(myXML);
                        //trace(myXML.top10ScorersCollection.scorer);

                        /*firstName DataGrid column */
                        var firstNameCol:DataGridColumn = new DataGridColumn();
                        firstNameCol.headerText = "First Name";
                        firstNameCol.dataField = "firstName";

                        /*lastName DataGrid column */
                        var lastNameCol:DataGridColumn = new DataGridColumn();
                        lastNameCol.headerText = "Last Name";
                        lastNameCol.dataField = "lastName";

                        /*totalScore DataGrid column */
                        var totalScoreCol:DataGridColumn = new DataGridColumn();
                        totalScoreCol.headerText = "Total Score";
                        totalScoreCol.dataField = "totalScore";

                        /*position DataGrid column */
```

```
                        var positionCol:DataGridColumn = new DataGridColumn();
                        positionCol.headerText = "Position";
                        positionCol.dataField = "position";

                        var columnArray:Array = new Array();
                        columnArray.push(firstNameCol);
                        columnArray.push(lastNameCol);
                        columnArray.push(totalScoreCol);
                        columnArray.push(positionCol);
                        myDataGrid["columns"] = columnArray;
                        var myXMLListCollection:XMLListCollection =
                                new XMLListCollection(myXML.scorer);
                        trace("XMLListCollection data bound to the Data Grid.");
                        trace("XMLListCollection " + XMLListCollection);
                        myDataGrid.dataProvider = myXMLListCollection;
                        myDataGrid.percentWidth = 100;
                        myDataGrid.percentHeight = 100;
                        myDataGrid.rowCount = 10;
                }

                public function loadXMLData():void {
                        myLoader.addEventListener(Event.COMPLETE, xmlLoad);
                        myLoader.load(myXMLRequest);
                }


        }
}
```

Explaining every single line of the preceding code would be redundant, so here's a quick summary. You create the URLLoader instance and load the XML data from the JSP. The load function of URLLoader uses a URLRequest object, which defines the URL. The returned XML is wrapped in an XMLListCollection and bound to a data grid. The DataGrid is implemented using ActionScript alone. Its columns, corresponding data fields, and header texts are explicitly defined and set on the data grid. There's a button and a VBox component in the MXML application. The data grid is added as a child of the VBox component. The Button click handler indirectly, via an intermediate method, invokes the URLLoader load method. The URLLoader class triggers a set of events as the load activity progresses. In the example, we listen to the COMPLETE event. On completion, an event handler is activated that retrieves the returned data, parses it, and binds it to the data grid. That's about it!

Although URLLoader is quite similar to HTTPService in generating the output in the example, there are a few fundamental differences:

- The events triggered differ and allow for different approaches to interacting with the HTTP request.
- Binary responses are handled differently.
- URL variable and parameter manipulation possibilities vary.
- Support for HTTP methods is not identical.

Life Cycle Events in URLLoader and HTTPService

The URLLoader class defines the following events:

- `complete (flash.events.Event.COMPLETE)`: Dispatched when the data is decoded and assigned to the `data` property of the `URLLoader` object. This is a good time to start using the loaded resource.
- `httpStatus (flash.events.HTTPStatusEvent.HTTP_STATUS)`: Dispatched if the load method invokes a call over HTTP. `URLLoader` is not restricted to making HTTP calls, although it's a popular choice. This event is triggered on an HTTP request, not a response, and it's triggered before the `complete` and error events.
- `ioError (flash.events.IOErrorEvent.IO_ERROR)`: Dispatched if the request encounters a fatal I/O error and terminates the request.
- `open (flash.events.Event.OPEN)`: Dispatched when the request starts on invocation of the `load` method.
- `progress (flash.events.ProgressEvent.PROGRESS)`: Dispatched as the resource gets downloaded. This event is most relevant when the resource is large, say a huge image file, and it downloads incrementally. A progress event is fired on each chunk of bytes getting downloaded.
- `securityError (flash.events.SecurityErrorEvent.SECURITY_ERROR)`: Dispatched if the security sandbox is violated.

Whereas the `HTTPService` class defines the following:

- `result (mx.rpc.events.ResultEvent.RESULT)`: Dispatched when the HTTP call returns.
- `fault (mx.rpc.events.FaultEvent.FAULT)`: Dispatched if the call ends in an error. Interestingly, trying to access a binary resource, say an image file, using `HTTPService` also ends up in an error.
- `invoke (mx.rpc.events.InvokeEvent.INVOKE)`: Dispatched when the call is initiated and no error has shown up yet.

Therefore, there is little event-driven control to monitor progress in `HTTPService`. The assumption is that fetching data is going to be quick and simple, so monitoring progress is not relevant. Error handling and HTTP status propagation is better and more fine-grained in `URLLoader`.

Binary Resource Access

The `HTTPService` class is simply incapable of handling binary resources. Try out the following simple code, which attempts to download an image:

```
<?xml version="1.0" encoding="utf-8"?>
<s:Application xmlns:fx="http://ns.adobe.com/mxml/2009"
                    xmlns:s="library://ns.adobe.com/flex/spark"
                    xmlns:mx="library://ns.adobe.com/flex/halo" minWidth="1024"
minHeight="768">
        <fx:Script>
                <![CDATA[
                        import mx.controls.Image;

                        import mx.controls.Alert;
                        import mx.rpc.events.FaultEvent;
```

```
                    import mx.rpc.events.ResultEvent;
                    import flash.utils.describeType;

                    function faultHandler(event:FaultEvent):void {
                            Alert.show('Oops there is a problem!....'
                                    + event.fault.faultString);
                    }

                    function resultHandler(event:ResultEvent):void {
                            trace(describeType(event.result));
                            var img:Image = new Image();
                            var byteLoader:Loader=new Loader();
                            var byteArray:ByteArray=new ByteArray();
                            byteArray.writeUTFBytes(event.result as String);
                            byteLoader.loadBytes(byteArray);
                            var bitMap:Bitmap=Bitmap(byteLoader.content);
                            img.source = bitMap;
                            myVBox.addChild(img);
                            Alert.show('It Works!....' + event.result);
                    }

            ]]>
        </fx:Script>
        <fx:Declarations>
                <!-- Place non-visual elements (e.g., services, value objects) here -->
                <mx:HTTPService id="myHTTPService"
                                                url="http://localhost:8080/
NBAScorers/treasury_of_ideas_logo.png"
                                                fault="faultHandler(event)"
 result="resultHandler(event)"/>

        </fx:Declarations>

        <s:SkinnableContainer>
                <s:layout>
                        <s:VerticalLayout horizontalAlign="center"
                            paddingLeft="40" paddingTop="40" />
                </s:layout>
        <mx:VBox id="myVBox" width="100%" height="100%" />

        <mx:Button label="Invoke HTTPService" click="myHTTPService.send()"/>
    </s:SkinnableContainer>
</s:Application>
```

Instead of the image coming through, you get an error. In debug mode, you will see this:

```
[SWF] C:\shashank_workfolder\projects\galileo_workspace_default\DownloadImage\
bin-debug\main.swf - 1,179,749 bytes after decompression
<type name="String" base="Object" isDynamic="false" isFinal="true" isStatic="false">
  <extendsClass type="Object"/>
  <constructor>
    <parameter index="1" type="*" optional="true"/>
  </constructor>
  <accessor name="length" access="readonly" type="int" declaredBy="String"/>
```

```
</type>
Error #2044: Unhandled IOErrorEvent:. text=Error #2124: Loaded file is an unknown type.
```

Why does this happen? `HTTPService` is meant to handle text-based data only. Therefore, to include an image using it, your best bet may be one of the following:

- Get the path to the image on the server and then assign it as the source of an image control. This will display the image correctly but will not work for all binary data types. Also, if you need to download the image locally using this technique, you are out of luck.

- Encode the image in Base64 format, transmit it through, decode it, and then consume it. Base64 encoding translates binary data to plain ASCII text and is defined as part of the MIME specification. It reads data in 6 bits and translates it to a character in the 64-character alphabet set. You can readmore about it at `http://en.wikipedia.org/wiki/Base64`. Flex3 has undocumented classes to encode/decode Base64 format: `mx.utils.Base64Encoder` and `mx.utils.Base64Decoder`.

Instead of trying out these workarounds, you could use the `URLLoader` class, which manages binary data loading with ease and elegance. Rewrite the example that failed using `HTTPService` to use `URLLoader`, and this time it works without any problem. Here's what the rewritten code looks like:

```xml
<?xml version="1.0" encoding="utf-8"?>
<s:Application xmlns:fx="http://ns.adobe.com/mxml/2009"
                    xmlns:s="library://ns.adobe.com/flex/spark"
                    xmlns:mx="library://ns.adobe.com/flex/halo" minWidth="1024"↵
minHeight="768">
      <fx:Script>
            <![CDATA[
                  import ImageURLLoader;

                  private function loadImageFunction():void {
                        var imageURLLoader:ImageURLLoader =
                              new ImageURLLoader();
                        imageURLLoader.loadImage();
            ]]>

                        myVBox.addChild(imageURLLoader.myImage);
                  }
      </fx:Script>
      <fx:Declarations>
            <!-- Place non-visual elements (e.g., services, value objects) here -->
      </fx:Declarations>

      <s:SkinnableContainer>
            <s:layout>
                  <s:VerticalLayout horizontalAlign="center"
                                                paddingLeft="40" paddingTop="40" />
            </s:layout>
      <mx:VBox id="myVBox" width="100%" height="100%" />

      <mx:Button label="Invoke URLLoader" click="loadImageFunction()"/>
      </s:SkinnableContainer>
```

```
</s:Application>

/* ImageURLLoader.as */
package
{
        import flash.display.Loader;
        import flash.events.Event;
        import flash.net.URLLoader;
        import flash.net.URLLoaderDataFormat;
        import flash.net.URLRequest;
        import flash.utils.ByteArray;
        import flash.utils.describeType;

        import mx.controls.Image;
        import flash.display.Bitmap;
        import mx.core.FlexLoader;

        public class ImageURLLoader
        {
                private var URL_String:String =
                        "http://localhost:8080/NBAScorers/treasury_of_ideas_logo.png";
                private var myImageRequest:URLRequest =
                        new URLRequest(URL_String);
                private var myLoader:URLLoader = new URLLoader();
                private var loader:FlexLoader = new FlexLoader();

                public var myImage:Image = new Image();


                public function ImageURLLoader()
                {
                }

                private function imageLoad(event:Event):void {
                        trace("Image loaded.");
                        trace(describeType(event.target.data));

                        loader.loadBytes(event.target.data);
                        loader.contentLoaderInfo.addEventListener↵
(Event.COMPLETE,setLoadedBytesToImage);
                }

                public function setLoadedBytesToImage(event:Event):void {
                        myImage.source = loader;
                }

                public function loadImage():void {
                        myLoader.dataFormat = URLLoaderDataFormat.BINARY;
                        myLoader.addEventListener(Event.COMPLETE, imageLoad);
                        myLoader.load(myImageRequest);
                }

        }
```

}

With `URLLoader`, image loading is effortless. The data format can be set to binary and the image data stream read in as an array of bytes. When all the bytes are streamed through, they are bound as the source of an image control. We use a component called `FlexLoader` in this example. `FlexLoader` is part of the BSD-licensed open source Yahoo! ASTRA Flash classes. The documentation is available at `http://developer.yahoo.com/flash/astra-flex/classreference/mx/core/FlexLoader.html`. `FlexLoader` extends `flash.display.Loader` and overrides the `toString` method to show the location of the object in the display objects' hierarchy. Although we used `FlexLoader` here and it's useful to know of the Yahoo! ASTRA classes, you could easily replace `FlexLoader` with `Loader`, and things will still work fine.

The `URLLoader` class can actually load any binary data stream. As long as you have the encoder/decoder in place, you can use this feature without limitations. In Java web applications, a servlet could easily write binary data to an output stream. Such binary data can be consumed with ease using `URLLoader`.

URL Variable and Parameter Manipulation

It's important that URL variables and the HTTP header can be manipulated. It's common to have proprietary object attributes bind as parameters to an HTTP call in both `GET` and `POST` method scenarios. In some cases (for instance, in REST), header manipulation also adds value.

REST is an architectural style that can be loosely defined as a way of transmitting domain-specific information over HTTP without the need for additional protocol layers, as in SOAP. Central to REST is the idea of resources—abstractions that are accessible using URIs and components (clients and servers), which access resource representations using simple interfaces. The REST style can be implemented without HTTP or the Internet, but it has become synonymous with the `GET` style of simple HTTP calls that makes up most of the Web. For more on REST, read Roy Fielding's PhD thesis, "Architectural Styles and the Design of Network-based Software Architectures," which introduced the term REST and defined the way we know it today. You can find Roy's thesis at `http://www.ics.uci.edu/~fielding/pubs/dissertation/top.htm`.

REST defines safe, idempotent services and obligated services. Safe, idempotent services are repeatable and provide a representation of the resource to the client Obligated services lead to the creation of new resources or representations of a resource. Safe services involve `GET` method requests, and obligated services involve `POST` method calls. In either situation, when a representation is negotiated by the client, it is necessary that header values be set appropriately for a request. This means you need to manipulate HTTP headers before sending the request out.

`HTTPService` allows any object to be sent as an argument to its `send` method. A call to the `send` method initiates a request. The passed argument object's attributes and their corresponding values form the name-value pairs, which become arguments for the HTTP methods. Any number of attributes can be defined in the object, and values can be set for these attributes. This works with both `GET` and `POST` calls. In `POST` calls, you can also set the header values. However, things break with `HTTPService` when you try to set the header for a `GET` method call. Sometimes this is necessary, as in the case of REST, and `HTTPService` falls short of the requirements here.

Time to reinforce what you've learned using a simple example! The example integrates fulfillment and checkout functionality in a Flex application using the Google Checkout XML API. This code is available on open source terms on Google Project, which you can access at `http://code.google.com/p/flexcheckout/`. The focus here is exclusively on sending API requests with basic HTTP authentication, which requires that the HTTP request headers are set appropriately. You can read details about what needs to be done at `http://code.google.com/apis/checkout/developer/index.html#https_`

auth_scheme. The part that's relevant here involves the three headers that need to be set for merchant authorization and authentication. Here's an example of the headers as shown in the Google developer manual:

```
Authorization: Basic MTIzNDU2Nzg5MDpIc1lYRm9aZkhBcXlMYONSWWVIOHFR
Content-Type: application/xml;charset=UTF-8
Accept: application/xml;charset=UTF-8
```

To set these values, you create an object, create the attributes, assign the values, and assign the object to the headers property of an HTTPService. You have seen parameter passing before, so skip it this time and focus on the headers alone. Here's a snippet of the header-manipulation code:

```
<! - Call to Google Checkout XML API.
Sending API Request with HTTP Basic Authentication -- >
var headerObject = new Object();
headerObject["Authorization"] =
"Basic MTIzNDU2Nzg5MDpIc1lYRm9aZkhBcXlMYONSWWVIOHFR";
headerObject["Content-Type"] = "application/xml;charset=UTF-8";
headerObject["Accept"] = "application/xml;charset=UTF-8";
<! -- HTTPService that sends Google Checkout API requests -- >
<mx:HTTPService id="myHTTPService"
url=" https://checkout.google.com/api/↵
checkout/v2/request/Merchant/MERCHANT_ID"
/*A merchant on registration with Google
checkout receives a merchant id,
which acts as the primary identifier
for the merchant within the Google checkout application.*/
fault="faultHandler(event)" result="resultHandler(event)"
headers="{headerObject}" method="GET"  />
```

When you send this request, however, it does not go through successfully. HTTPService does not allow header setting for GET method calls, so this fails. Header manipulation works only with POST method calls. This is a limitation, and workarounds like using the Socket class are a way out. The next section has a detailed illustration of this workaround. For now, let's evaluate URLLoader to see if it can stand up to this challenge.

You define a URL request for URLLoader using the URLRequest class. You can define URL headers in a class called URLRequestHeader associated with an URLRequest instance. Then URLLoader could use the instance to send the request. This seems straightforward.

```
var loader:URLLoader = new URLLoader();

//Add event listeners to the loader

//The Base64-encoded part of the string after
the keyword Basic could be dynamically
generated and appended to
Basic before it is assigned to a URLRequestHeader instance

var header1:URLRequestHeader =
new URLRequestHeader("Authorization", "Basic↵
MTIzNDU2Nzg5MDpIc1lYRm9aZkhBcXlMYONSWWVIOHFR");
var header2:URLRequestHeader =
new URLRequestHeader↵
("Content-Type", "application/xml;charset=UTF-8");
```

```
var header3:URLRequestHeader =
new URLRequestHeader("Accept", "application/xml;charset=UTF-8");

var request:URLRequest = new URLRequest("https://checkout.google.com/↩
api/checkout/v2/request/Merchant/MERCHANT_ID");

request.data = new URLVariables("name=value");
request.method = URLRequestMethod.GET;
request.requestHeaders.push(header1);
request.requestHeaders.push(header2);
request.requestHeaders.push(header3);

// Call load() method within a
try-catch block to handle invocation time errors
loader.load(request);
```

With the exception of restricting a few keywords, like get/Get/GET, and not allowing a few header types, like `Accept-Ranges` and `Allow`, the `URLRequestHeader` class lets you set custom headers. Where custom header setting is required, `URLLoader` shines compared with `HTTPService`.

Support for HTTP Methods

By default and in all situations, both `HTTPService` and `URLLoader` allow the HTTP `GET` and `POST` methods. These are the two most popular methods, and so this suffices in most situations. When using a server-side proxy and specifying so by flagging `useProxy="true"`, `HTTPService` is able to send `HEAD`, `OPTIONS`, `PUT`, `TRACE`, and `DELETE` HTTP requests as well. (If you are rusty on where and how to use these additional HTTP methods, refer to the online W3C documentation at `http://www.w3.org/Protocols/rfc2616/rfc2616-sec9.html`.) `URLLoader` can make requests defined in the `URLRequest` class. The `URLRequestMethod` attribute can take only `POST` and `GET` as valued values. These values are defined in `URLRequestMethod`.

This puts you in a fix. You can't do header manipulation in `GET` calls with `HTTPService`, and you can't make any HTTP method calls other than `POST` and `GET` in `URLLoader`. If you needed both simultaneously, you have to look outside of these two options. The last option is writing things from the ground up on top of the `Socket` class, which is what we'll do in the next section. For now, let's look at another issue related to HTTP methods.

WebDAV is an open, community–driven standard to extend HTTP for web authoring, while keeping things interoperable. To quote a line about its goals from the WebDAV charter: "define the HTTP extensions necessary to enable distributed web authoring tools to be broadly interoperable, while supporting user needs." Information about WebDAV is available at `http://www.webdav.org/`. WebDAV defines some additional HTTP methods:

- `PROPFIND` retrieves properties (stored as XML) from a resource.
- `PROPPATCH` modifies multiple properties of a resource at the same time (in a single transaction).
- `MKCOL` creates directory-like collections.
- `COPY` copies a resource between URI(s).
- `MOVE` moves a resource between URI(s).
- `LOCK` locks (shared or exclusive) a resource.
- `UNLOCK` unlocks a resource.

Neither HTTPService nor URLLoader (with URLRequest) allows HTTP method extensions and definition of new ones. Thus they offer no support for WebDAV at the time of writing.

You've seen HTTPService and URLLoader; now let's see how to use the Socket class. In this day and age, spending time on low-level details is typically shunned in the software development world. In that sense, Socket is surely the bad guy in town!

Using Sockets

AS3 defines two types of sockets, one that can be used to transmit XML data and another that can send binary data. You specify a host and a port, and Socket can create a connection on this host and port. The connection will stay alive until explicitly closed. Therefore, a persistent channel is opened up and the client does not need to reconnect between requests if the connection is alive. The server can also send data back to the client on this connection.

Socket implements the IDataInput and IDataOutput interfaces IDataInput and IDataOutput define the different read and write methods, respectively. To get a full list of methods available to read bytes, Boolean, integer, object, float, and double types, take a look at the ASDoc (accessible through Flex 3 LiveDocs). In this manner, Socket is similar to ByteArray and URLStream.

Creating and using a socket in ActionScript is no different in mechanism from creating and using a socket in almost any programming language. The Socket class acts as the socket client. That means you'll need a socket server to listen to the requests your client will make. You can write a socket server in any language you wish. The code for a simple socket server written in Groovy follows. We chose Groovy because this chapter is about integration with Java, and Groovy runs in the JVM. The obvious alternative would be to use Java itself. There's a simpleJava server example in the Flex 3 Live Docs, so re-creating that example, or a similar one, would be a waste of space. Also, we want to reinforce the idea that you can use Groovy, Jython, JRuby, or Scala instead of Java itself in the JVM. This means many Java-specific things discussed in this chapter will hold true for these other JVM languages as well.

```
server = new ServerSocket(8080)
while(true) {
    server.accept() { socket ->
        socket.withStreams { input, output ->
            w = new PrintWriter(output)
            w << "ActionScript Socket Client is Sending Some Through"
            w.flush()
            r = input.readLine()
            System.err.println
"Message received by the the server socket $r"
            w.close()
        }
    }
}
```

That takes care of the server socket; now let's create the socket and send a message to the listening server socket. We could create either Socket or XMLSocket. The choice depends on the type of data transmitted. The example server socket is quite elementary and is not for reading binary data, so we'll create a simple XMLSocket instance. The code for the XMLSocket client could be as follows:

```
package {
    import flash.display.Sprite;
    import flash.events.*;
    import flash.net.XMLSocket;
```

```
public class MyXMLSocket extends Sprite {
    private var hostName:String = "domain.com";
    private var port:uint = 8080;
    private var socket:XMLSocket;

    public function MyXMLSocket() {
        socket = new XMLSocket();
        configureListeners(socket);
        socket.connect(hostName, port);
    }

    public function send(data:Object):void {
        socket.send(data);
    }

    private function configureListeners↵
(dispatcher:IEventDispatcher):void {
        dispatcher.addEventListener(Event.CLOSE, closeHandler);
        dispatcher.addEventListener(Event.CONNECT, connectHandler);
        dispatcher.addEventListener(DataEvent.DATA, dataHandler);
        dispatcher.addEventListener↵
(IOErrorEvent.IO_ERROR, ioErrorHandler);
        dispatcher.addEventListener↵
(ProgressEvent.PROGRESS, progressHandler);
        dispatcher.addEventListener↵
(SecurityErrorEvent.SECURITY_ERROR, securityErrorHandler);
    }

    private function closeHandler(event:Event):void {
        trace("closeHandler: " + event);
    }

    private function connectHandler(event:Event):void {
        trace("connectHandler: " + event);
    }

    private function dataHandler(event:DataEvent):void {
        trace("dataHandler: " + event);
    }

    private function ioErrorHandler(event:IOErrorEvent):void {
        trace("ioErrorHandler: " + event);
    }

    private function progressHandler(event:ProgressEvent):void {
        trace("progressHandler loaded:" ↵
+ event.bytesLoaded + " total: " + event.bytesTotal);
    }

    private function securityErrorHandler↵
(event:SecurityErrorEvent):void {
        trace("securityErrorHandler: " + event);
```

```
        }
    }
}
```

The assumption is that the server socket is running locally. In such an instance, the preceding code works without any extra help. In real-life deployment environments, though, this will rarely be the case. The server socket would run on some domain.com and would listen on some port, say 8080. Like everything else in Flash, the player security restrictions and requirements would kick in and you'd need to define a policy file so that such operations are permitted. You could configure the application in such a way that the policy file is read over the same port, and then the socket connection is established and used for communication.

In this chapter, the primary inspiration is to integrate Flex and Java. Often the remote data published by Java is going to be accessible over standard protocols like HTTP. So classes like `HTTPService` and `URLLoader` would be enough to communicate in most cases. However, as we saw, both these classes have their limitations, and in some cases, it's feasible to use the `Socket` class. In such cases, the requirement may be to connect over port 80, which is usually the default HTTP port. According to the security policy, any port below 1024 when accessed through `Sockets` needs special permission in its policy files. So once more, you'd have to ensure that the policy file has the relevant permissions and is in place.

This ends the peek into the `Socket` classes. However, before wrapping up and moving to the next topic, it is extremely important to mention a few things about `sockets`.

- AS3 does not define any server `socket` class. It is not expecting an application running in the Flash Player to act as one.
- Data could be sent over the persistent `socket` connection, without being asked for. So, data streaming from the server to the client can be achieved quite efficiently. Such arriving data triggers the `DataEvent.DATA` event.
- Data upload onto the socket channel is asynchronous, and as of now, there is no way to measure how much of it has been transmitted to the server until the entire process completes.
- If you are looking to write an HTTP client using `Socket` so that the limitations of `HTTPService` and `URLLoader` are eradicated, you're in luck. Don't reinvent the wheel; just go ahead and use as3httpclientlib (http://code.google.com/p/as3httpclientlib/). This library's API resembles the Apache HTTP client, simple and clean.
- `Sockets` can be used to build real-time systems where the server needs to stream data up to the client, but it wouldn't work if this connection has a firewall to cross.

That finishes our look at `sockets`. Although there's more to the topic than what we cover here, further discussion is outside the scope of this book. Let's jump to the second main topic of this chapter: web services.

Integration through Web Services

A web service, to quote W3C, is "a software system designed to support interoperable machine-to-machine interaction over a network." Rapid adoption in the last few years has taken this standard from obscurity to ubiquity. In general, the idea is simple: service consumers look up a registry, discover a service—which exposes its public operation using a metadata file—and invoke its operations. Service producers create services that are accessible along with the metadata that defines what they are capable of, what they accept, and what they return.

Over the years, there has been much activity and debate over ways to define metadata, expose operations, encode messages, and consume them. SOAP and REST have emerged as the two most popular web service architectural styles. SOAP is a robust choice for building interoperable web services using XML messages. REST uses the basic concepts behind HTTP and the World Wide Web (see the section "URL Variable and Parameter Manipulation" earlier in this chapter). These are not the only two. Following are some other standards linked to web services:

- JSON-RPC
- XINS
- Burlap
- GXA
- Hessian
- XML-RPC
- BEEP

Flex 4 officially has full support only for SOAP web services. You saw in the last section how you could also manage to use REST. JSON-RPC and XML-RPC can be incorporated with the help of a few open libraries. Hessian can be used with Flex quite easily and is well supported as an alternative to sending Action Message Format (AMF) binary data.

Let's start with the stuff that's official: SOAP.

Using SOAP-Based Web Services

SOAP defines the protocol and messaging layer that enables XML messaging between service producers and service consumers. The most common style of interaction involves RPC between one node (the client) and another node (the server). In order to make this happen, SOAP uses a specification called Web Services Description Language (WSDL) to define network services as a set of endpoints. The endpoints are essentially operations that act on messages, which contain document- or procedure-oriented information. WSDL describes the service endpoints in an XML format.

In order to consume a SOAP-based web service in Flex, you first create a WebService object. WebService is the implementation class that abstracts all web service–related features in an object-oriented manner. After that, you access the associated WSDL file. Once WSDL information is read, it is used to initialize the WebService object appropriately, by setting its property values. Now you are ready to call a web service method or operation. A web service component defines a few events that map to the life cycle of a web service interaction and allows for listeners to be added for these events. Two logical outcomes are possible in a method call: success or failure. WebService dispatches events of these two types—they are called result and fault. So, you define event handlers for each of these methods and register them. Finally, you make the web service method call and consume the results.

In Flash Builder 4, there's a nifty little feature to automate the process of web service proxy generation and component binding to web service data sources. It's part of the data management extensions that the IDE provides. You could point to a WSDL file, and it generates the proxy automatically by introspecting the WSDL. You can always manually code the web service proxies and look up the allowed operations by browsing the WSDL port type section, but let's favor productivity here. If you don't use Flash Builder to build Flex applications, you'll have to go back to hand-coding.

To keep the focus on SOAP web services consumption let's look at a simple example. On the XMethods web site (http://www.xmethods.net) is a list of publicly available web services, one of which helps validate 10- and 13-digit ISBNs. An ISBN, short for International Standard Book Number, is a unique way of identifying a published and cataloged item. This web service is provided by a company called Data Access Europe BV (http://www.dataaccess.eu). To get started, you need the WSDL, which you can get from http://webservices.daehosting.com/services/isbnservice.wso?WSDL.

Now create a Flex project in Flash Builder and call it ISBNValidationWebService. Use the following steps to generate the web service proxies on the basis of WSDL:

1. Select **Connect to Web Service...** from the **Data** menu in Flash Builder. The screen looks like the one shown in Figure 7-6. This brings up the wizard.

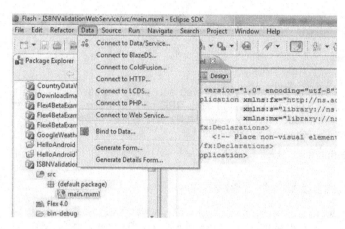

Figure 7-6. Select **Connect to Web Service** from the **Data** menu to start the process of web service proxy generation on the basis of WSDL.

2. Start by specifying the WSDL URI. Figure 7-7 shows how we did it. At this stage, you have two options: direct client access (which requires crossdomain.xml) or proxied access (which implies going through a data service). Because we are focused on integration without the use of data services in this chapter, select **Directly from the client**.

3. You can also specify the service name, service package, and data type package here. Flash Builder populates values for these three parameters on the basis of the WSDL URI and some default configurations. The data type package is set to valueObjects and the service name is usually derived from the service name suggested by the WSDL URI. We will leave these values as such, but you are encouraged to choose appropriate names in line with the rest of your project code structure and naming systems.

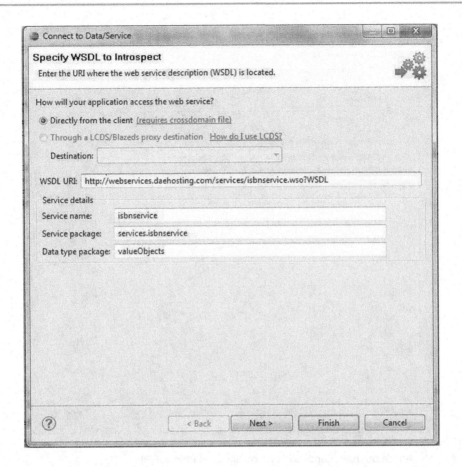

Figure 7-7. Specifying the WSDL URI

4. The tool quickly introspects the WSDL and shows the available operations in the next screen, as you can see in Figure 7-8.

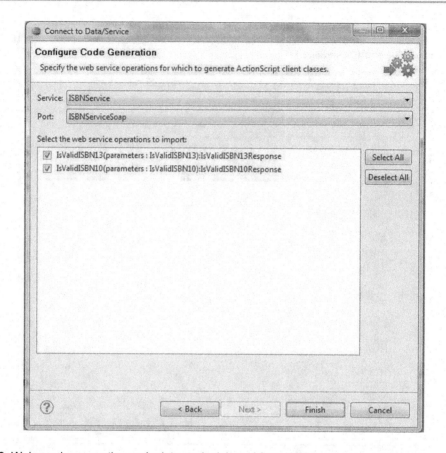

Figure 7-8. Web service operation endpoints as deciphered from WSDL

5.   Next, click **Finish** to generate the required ActionScript classes. Note that you can deselect services for which you don't want to generate stubs. You can also select a different service and port. In this simple example that validates ISBN numbers, there is only one service and port pair to choose from. The service offers two operations and you can include both or just one. We choose to generate stubs for both the operations.

6.   The classes are all generated and are within the specified package structure in the project source folder. Pairs of base and extended classes are generated for the service operations. This allows custom extensions and behavior override in the subclasses, without impacting the generated base classes.

If you need to, you can update the generated classes by adding, deleting, and modifying existing entries.

The automated process generates these classes:

- `_Super_Isbnservice.as`
- `Isbnservice.as`

These classes are now ready to be consumed and bound to user-interface components. When you create the Flex project, an MXML application file is created. We like to name this primary application class `main.mxml`, but that's not required. If you wish to name it something else, you are free to do so.

In `main.mxml`, we first include a set of user interface components and then bind the service to these components. You include a `TextInput` to allow users to enter an ISBN number, a `TextArea` to display the validation result (a Boolean value, either true or false), and a `Button` to invoke a web service call. The components can be included programmatically or by using design mode.

In order to leverage the Flash Player data-binding features, switch to design mode and right-click the `TextArea` to bind it to the result of a web service call. In this small example, we'll validate a 13-digit book ISBN. We'll set the argument value to the ISBN of this book (*AdvancED Flex 4*), which is 9781430224839, entering this value through the `TextInput` component. The application has a button, labeled "Validate ISBN." Clicking the "Validate ISBN" button invokes the web service operation to validate the entered ISBN. The result of the call is bound to the text area, where you can see if the ISBN is valid or not. Things will become clearer as you look through the code:

```
<?xml version="1.0" encoding="utf-8"?>
<s:Application xmlns:fx="http://ns.adobe.com/mxml/2009"
                       xmlns:s="library://ns.adobe.com/flex/spark"
                       xmlns:mx="library://ns.adobe.com/flex/halo" minWidth="1024"
minHeight="768" xmlns:isbnservice="services.isbnservice.*">
        <fx:Script>
                <![CDATA[
                        import mx.controls.Alert;

                        protected function button_clickHandler (event:MouseEvent):void
                        {
                                IsValidISBN13Result.token =
isbnservice.IsValidISBN13(enterIsbnTextInput.text);
                        }

                ]]>
        </fx:Script>
        <fx:Declarations>
                <s:CallResponder id="IsValidISBN13Result"/>
                <isbnservice:Isbnservice id="isbnservice"
fault="Alert.show(event.fault.faultString + '\n' + event.fault.faultDetail)"
showBusyCursor="true"/>
                <!-- Place non-visual elements (e.g., services, value objects) here -->
        </fx:Declarations>
        <s:TextArea x="235" y="120" height="32" id="textArea"
text="{IsValidISBN13Result.lastResult}"/>
        <s:TextInput id="enterIsbnTextInput" x="269" y="56"/>
        <s:Button id="validateIsbnButton" click="button_clickHandler(event)" x="287" y="87"
label="Validate ISBN"/>
</s:Application>
```

Although this is a simple example, you can see that consuming web services using the introspection tool is quite appealing. If you'd like to go the traditional route, you could use the `<mx:WebService />` tag. If you use this tag, you need to know in advance the callable remote methods or procedures, exposed as web service endpoints. This can be done using some means of introspection or by the crude method of browsing the port type definitions in WSDL. If the WSDL exposes very few methods, you can probably physically look it up fairly easily; otherwise, it could be a tedious effort. The rest of the logic, which involves service invocation, and result handling, is hardly different from the previous method. As always in Flex, the service has two events it can dispatch: result and fault. If the call goes through successfully, your result handler populates the text; otherwise it errors out. Let's morph the existing example within this style.

```
<?xml version="1.0" encoding="utf-8"?>
<s:Application xmlns:fx="http://ns.adobe.com/mxml/2009"
                    xmlns:s="library://ns.adobe.com/flex/spark"
                    xmlns:mx="library://ns.adobe.com/flex/halo" minWidth="1024"
 minHeight="768" xmlns:isbnservice="services.isbnservice.*">
      <fx:Script>
            <![CDATA[
                    import mx.controls.Alert;
                    import mx.rpc.events.FaultEvent;
                    import mx.rpc.events.ResultEvent;
                    import mx.rpc.soap.LoadEvent;

                    [Bindable]
                    private var resultString:String;

                    private function loadHandler(event:LoadEvent):void {
                            trace("in loadHanlder: WSDL Loaded");
                            trace("in loadHandler: " + event.wsdl.xml);
                    }

                    private function resultHandler(event:ResultEvent):void {
                            resultString = event.result as String;
                            trace("in resultHandler: passed in argumnent " +
enterIsbnTextInput.text);

                            trace("in resultHandler " + resultString);
                    }

                    private function faultHandler(event:FaultEvent):void {
                            resultString = event.fault.faultString;
                            Alert.show("in faultHandler " + resultString);
                    }


            ]]>
      </fx:Script>
      <fx:Declarations>
            <mx:WebService id="myISBNWebService"
                                wsdl="http://webservices.daehosting.com/services/
isbnservice.wso?WSDL"

                                load="loadHandler(event)"
                                result="resultHandler(event)"
                                fault="faultHandler(event)" />

            <!-- Place non-visual elements (e.g., services, value objects) here -->
      </fx:Declarations>
      <s:TextArea x="235" y="120" height="32" id="textArea" text="{resultString}"/>
      <s:TextInput id="enterIsbnTextInput" x="269" y="56"/>
      <s:Button id="validateIsbnButton" click="myISBNWebService.IsValidISBN13
(enterIsbnTextInput.text)" x="287" y="87" label="Validate ISBN"/>
```

```
</s:Application>
```

In this example, we call a single web service method. You can actually call two or more methods at the same time if you like. If a button's `click` event invokes two methods, say `method1()` and `method2()`, of a web service referenced by the ID `myWebService`, its `click` event looks like the following:

```
click=" myWebService.method1();myWebService.method2()"
```

Doing this without making any other modifications implies that the two methods have a common set of result and fault handlers. This may not be the desired behavior. Different methods would likely need different result handlers because the results will need to be processed appropriately. Sometimes, they may even need different fault handlers. Not to worry, it's easy to define a unique event handler for each of the methods. Just include as many `<mx:operation/>` compiler tags as the number of methods, for which you need unique handlers. The implementation might look like this:

```
<mx:WebService id="myWebService"
wsdl="http://localhost:portNumber/Simple?wsdl"
load=" myWebService.method1(); myWebService.methd2()"
fault="genericFaultHandler(event)">
<mx:operation name="method1" result="method1ResultHandler(event)"/>
<mx:operation name="method2" result="method2ResultHandler(event)"/>
</mx:WebService>
```

Fault and result handlers can be defined for each operation in a web service endpoint. If there are multiple operations and some of these do not have custom fault or result handlers, the default `<mx:operation>` tag-level fault and result handlers are used. The assumption is that the tag-level fault and result handlers are defined.

The information we've discussed so far would get you through most SOAP web services consumption in Flex without any problem. Remember that web services are subject to the same security constraints as `HTTPService` calls. This means that a `crossdomain.xml` file with correct configurations will need to reside in a web service provider domain, if it's different from the one that serves the Flex SWF.

A REST Web Service in Action

We already delved into REST a fair bit in the earlier sections on `HTTPService` and `URLLoader`. Let's walk through a complete simple example to reinforce what you've learned so far.

The example application uses the Yahoo! News Search REST API to fetch news items and then display them on a Flex-built interface. To get started, register with the Yahoo! Developer Network and get an application ID. The application ID is a mandatory part of every request you make to the Yahoo! API. It's easy to get one; just go to `http://developer.yahoo.com/wsregapp/index.php`.

Yahoo! News Search involves simple HTTP REST calls that you can hand-code fairly easily in ActionScript and consume in your Flex application. Essentially, you create a query with all the required parameters and the headers, using `URLRequest`, `URLRequestHeader`, and `URLVariables` to do this. You then pass the URLRequest instance (which contains all the arguments for the REST call) to a `URLLoader` instance and send a request to the service. When the result returns, you consume it and bind it to a view component.

That's exactly what we intended to do here, but then we stumbled upon the excellent client libraries implemented by Yahoo! to do this. Yahoo! has client libraries for the Search API in almost all major languages, including AS3. They package and distribute the AS3 client libraries as a part of the ASTRA Web APIs, which you can download from `http://developer.yahoo.com/flash/astra-webapis/`. These client libraries will save you from reinventing the wheel. If you plan to write a Flex/ActionScript client component for REST web service calls, use this implementation as a guide.

Once we decided to use the Yahoo! AS3 client, all we had to do was consume it in the application.

```xml
<?xml version="1.0" encoding="utf-8"?>
<s:Application xmlns:fx="http://ns.adobe.com/mxml/2009"
               xmlns:s="library://ns.adobe.com/flex/spark"
               xmlns:mx="library://ns.adobe.com/flex/halo"
               xmlns:yahoo="com.yahoo.webapis.search.*"
               minWidth="1024" minHeight="768">
    <fx:Declarations>
        <!-- Place non-visual elements (e.g., services, value objects) here -->
        <!-- The formatter to format the total results with commas -->
        <mx:NumberFormatter id="commaFormatter"/>

        <!-- The Service for all types of searches -->
        <yahoo:SearchService id="searchService"
                             applicationId="YahooDemo"
                             query="{criteriaTextInput.text}"
                             type="web"
                             maximumResults="50"/>

    </fx:Declarations>

    <s:SkinnableContainer>
        <s:layout>
            <s:VerticalLayout horizontalAlign="center"
                              paddingLeft="40" paddingTop="40" />
        </s:layout>



        <s:TextInput id="criteriaTextInput"/>
        <s:Button id="searchButton"
                  label="search"
                  click="searchService.send()"/>


    <s:Label
        text="{commaFormatter.format(searchService.numResultsAvailable)}
        results" visible="{Boolean(searchService.numResultsAvailable)}"/>

    <!-- The results as a List -->
    <mx:List id="resultsList"
             showDataTips="true"
             dataProvider="{searchService.lastResult}"
             variableRowHeight="true" width="100%" height="100%">
    </mx:List>
    </s:SkinnableContainer>
</s:Application>
```

I won't explain the Yahoo! client library itself. For that, you can peruse the ASDoc available in the SDK. Let me assure you it's intuitive and easy to understand.

With that, the REST web service example is complete. Now, let's move on to a few web service protocols beyond SOAP and REST. Aside from the big two, XML-RPC, JSON-RPC, and Hessian (from Caucho Technologies—http://www.caucho.com) seem the best alternatives.

Understanding the Potential of XML-RPC

XML-RPC is a simple set of specifications and software that lets distributed applications talk to each other. It is based on exchanging XML messages over HTTP. You'll find plenty of documentation and information about the vibrant XML-RPC community at http://www.xmlrpc.com/, the official web site for XML-RPC.

XML-RPC is a protocol that makes remote procedure calling possible. It uses the HTTP POST method for this purpose. The XML payload is sent as the body of an HTTP POST request, and responses also come back as XML. XML-RPC supports basic types like strings, numbers, and dates, as well as complex types like lists and records. You can get details about the request-and-response format by reading the specification, available online at http://www.xmlrpc.com/spec.

There are two entities involved in an XML-RPC communication. They play the roles of the client and the server. When you integrate Flex and Java using XML-RPC, you can usually expect Flex to be the client and Java to be the server. Therefore, we present an example application here to illustrate that XML-RPC use assumes the same roles.

Let's start with the server. To get it up and running, do the following:

1. Create a class with a few methods. In this case, create a very simple Java class that joins two strings and reverses a given string, using code that looks like this:

```
package org.shanky.flex.examples.xmlrpc;

    public class StringManipulator {

        public String joinString⏎
(String firstString, String secondString) {
            return firstString + secondString;
        }

        public String reverseString (String sourceString) {
            int i, len = sourceString.length();
            StringBuffer dest = new StringBuffer(len);

            for (i = (len - 1); i >= 0; i--)
                dest.append(sourceString.charAt(i));

            return dest.toString();
        }
    }
```

2. Configure and set up an XML-RPC server. We won't create one here because there are many good ones available already, and it's easy to include them in a Java web application.

3. Expose the methods of your class so that they could be invoked remotely over XML-RPC.

Choose the XML-RPC implementation from Apache, called Apache XML-RPC, for the example application in this chapter. Information and downloads related to the Apache XML-RPC implementation are accessible at `http://ws.apache.org/xmlrpc/index.html`. The Apache XML-RPC server can be effortlessly included in a Java web application (a servlet container or a Java EE application server). You should use Tomcat.

The first thing you do is to download the latest stable release of the software. Get the binary version of the distribution (the file ending with extension `.bin.tar.gz`), unless you intend to modify the source code.

Copy the following files from the `lib` directory of the distribution to your `WEB-INF/lib` folder:

- `commons-logging-1.1.jar`
- `ws-commons-util-1.0.2.jar`
- `xmlrpc-common-3.1.2.jar`
- `xmlrpc-server-3.1.2.jar`
- `xmlrpc-client-3.1.2.jar`

The last one on this list—`xmlrpc-client-3.1.2.jar`—isn't required because your client is going to reside in the Flex application, and you're not going to use a Java client. However, it may be useful to retain it for testing.

The version number we are using is 3.1.2 because it's the latest stable release number. Yours could vary depending on when you download this software.

The server implementation includes an object called `XmlRpcServer`, which receives and executes RPC calls. This server object can be embedded in a servlet container or a web server `XmlRpcServlet`, which is available with the server distribution, contains an embedded instance of `XmlRpcServer`. The example at hand is elementary, so it's best to use `XmlRpcServlet`, which can get you started very quickly.

The object containing the methods that need to be exposed over XML-RPC should be configured with `XmlRpcServlet`. You can do this by making an entry in the `XmlRpcServlet.properties` file. For our example object, the entry looks like this:

`StringManipulator=org.shanky.flex.examples.xmlrpc.StringManipulator`

The last thing you need to do before using `XmlRpcServlet` is to configure it in `web.xml`. Add the following entries to the file:

```
  <servlet>
        <servlet-name>XmlRpcServlet</servlet-name>
        <servlet-class>org.apache.xmlrpc.↩
webserver.XmlRpcServlet</servlet-class>
        <init-param>
          <param-name>enabledForExtensions</param-name>
          <param-value>true</param-value>
          <description>
            Sets, whether the servlet supports
vendor extensions for XML-RPC.
          </description>
        </init-param>
    </servlet>
    <servlet-mapping>
        <servlet-name>XmlRpcServlet</servlet-name>
        <url-pattern>/xmlrpc</url-pattern>
```

```
</servlet-mapping>
```

The XML-RPC server is now ready to be accessed over the following endpoint: `http://127.0.0.1:8080/xmlrpc`.

The assumption is that the server is running locally and Tomcat is listening for HTTP on port 8080.

Next, you do the following:

1. Create a client application able to communicate over XML-RPC.

2. Make the Flex client and the Java server talk to each other over XML-RPC.

To create the Flex client, the idea is again to avoid reinventing the wheel. So an obvious choice is to use an existing open source library such as as3-rpclib (`http://code.google.com/p/as3-rpclib/`), which seems the most robust open source library achieving this functionality for Flex (although at the time of writing it still claims to be in beta). The library implements `HTTPService`-based support for RPC over AMF0 (binary original AMF format), XML-RPC, and JSON-RPC (which is discussed next).

The first step is to download the library and get the SWC file. Next, as with any Flex application (with Flex Builder), you create a Flex project and go with the defaults Then you add the `as3-rpclib.swc` file to the library path as shown in Figure 7-9.

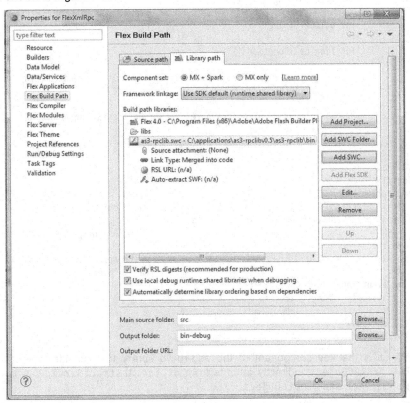

Figure 7-9. Adding as3-rpclib.swc to the Flex project library path

When all of the setup is done, you create the Flex application code that uses XML-RPC to communicate with the server you created a short while back. The server exposes the two string manipulation methods over the channel, and that's what your Flex application invokes. The following is the Flex application code:

```
<?xml version="1.0" encoding="utf-8"?>
<s:Application xmlns:fx="http://ns.adobe.com/mxml/2009"
                        xmlns:s="library://ns.adobe.com/flex/spark"
                        xmlns:mx="library://ns.adobe.com/flex/halo"
                        xmlns:as3rpclib="com.ak33m.rpc.xmlrpc.*"
                        minWidth="1024" minHeight="768">
        <s:creationComplete>
                <![CDATA[
                callFunction();
                ]]>
        </s:creationComplete>
        <fx:Script>
                <![CDATA[
                        import mx.controls.Alert;

                        var firstString:String;
                        var secondString:String;

                        var output:String;

                        function callFunction ()
                        {
                                output = xmlrpctojava.joinString(firstString,secondString);
                                trace(output);

                                output = xmlrpctojava.reverseString(firstString);
                                trace(output);
                        }

                ]]>
        </fx:Script>
        <fx:Declarations>
                <!-- Place non-visual elements (e.g., services, value objects) here -->
                <as3rpclib:XMLRPCObject id="xmlrpctojava"
                                                        endpoint="http://↵
127.0.0.1:8080/xmlrpc"

                                                        destination="xmlrpcendpoint"
                                                        fault="Alert.show(event.↵
fault.faultString,event.fault.faultCode)">
                </as3rpclib:XMLRPCObject >

        </fx:Declarations>
</s:Application>
```

The `XMLRPCObject` is the key component of the as3-rpclib library that provides the XML-RPC client functionality. The `XMLRPCObject` indirectly inherits from `mx.rpc.AbstractService`, which is the base class for both `WebService` and `RemoteObject`.

That's all we'll say here about XML-RPC. To use XML-RPC in real-life situations, you should study as3-rpclib thoroughly and understand how different method invocation types and different data types work with XML-RPC.

Walking Through a JSON-RPC Example

JavaScript Object Notation (JSON) is a lightweight data interchange format. It's based on a subset of the ECMA standard that JavaScript implements but is language-independent and uses a simple text-based format that is easy to parse and generate. The official web site for JSON is http://www.json.org.

AS3 Core Library (http://code.google.com/p/as3corelib/), an open source and well-supported library for AS3, has utility classes to serialize and parse JSON messages. If your remote Java source publishes data in JSON format and is accessible over a URL, you could get the data and consume it with the help of this library. A simple application might look like the following:

```
<?xml version="1.0" encoding="utf-8"?>
<s:Application xmlns:fx="http://ns.adobe.com/mxml/2009"
                 xmlns:s="library://ns.adobe.com/flex/spark"
                 xmlns:mx="library://ns.adobe.com/flex/halo" minWidth="1024"↵
minHeight="768">
      <fx:Script>
            <![CDATA[
                import mx.collections.ArrayCollection;
                import mx.rpc.events.ResultEvent;
                import com.adobe.serialization.json.JSON;

                private function onJSONLoad(event:ResultEvent):void
                {
                        //get the raw JSON data and cast to String
                        var rawData:String = String(event.result);

                        //decode the data to ActionScript using the JSON API
                        //in this case, the JSON data
                        is a serialize Array of Objects.
                        var arr:Array = (JSON.decode(rawData) as Array);

                        //create a new ArrayCollection
                        passing the de-serialized Array
                        //ArrayCollections work better
                        as DataProviders, as they can
                        //be watched for changes.
                        var dp:ArrayCollection = new ArrayCollection(arr);

                        //pass the ArrayCollection to
                        the DataGrid as its dataProvider.
                                grid.dataProvider = dp;


                }

            ]]>
      </fx:Script>
      <fx:Declarations>
            <!-- Place non-visual elements (e.g., services, value objects) here -->
```

```
            <mx:HTTPService id="service" resultFormat="text"
                                url="http://someurl.com/somedata.json"
                                result="onJSONLoad(event)" />

    </fx:Declarations>

    <s:SkinnableContainer>
            <s:layout>
                    <s:VerticalLayout horizontalAlign="center"
                                            paddingLeft="40" paddingTop="40" />
            </s:layout>
            <mx:DataGrid id="grid" right="10" left="10" top="10" bottom="10">
                    <mx:columns>
                            <mx:DataGridColumn
                                    headerText="Service" dataField="src"/>
                            <mx:DataGridColumn
                                    headerText="Title" dataField="title"/>
                    </mx:columns>
            </mx:DataGrid>

    </s:SkinnableContainer>
</s:Application>
```

JSON-RPC is a lightweight Remote Procedure Call specification that uses the simple but powerful JSON message scheme. JSON-RPC defines communication between two peers. The specification does not limit the type of protocol for communication but recommends persistent communication over TCP/IP-based socket connections. JSON-RPC can also use HTTP with a few workarounds. The peers can send two types of messages:

- Requests that must receive a response
- Notifications that are not replied to

A remote method call sends one of these two types of messages. In each case, the message is a single object serialized using JSON.

Request objects have three properties:

- Method: Name of the method to be invoked
- Params: Array of arguments
- Id: Request identifier

Notifications have the same three properties but null for Id, because notifications are not expected to get a response.

Responses to requests have three properties:

- Result: Returned object. Null if error.
- Error: Returned error object. Null of no error.
- Id: Same as the request identifier.

To communicate between a Flex application and a Java server using JSON-RPC, you would need to create JSON-RPC-related gateways/endpoints, serializers, and parsers at both ends.

It's not difficult to set up a Java JSON-RPC server and you can fairly easily set up jabsorb (http://jabsorb.org/), a JSON-RPC implementation for Java, with a web application to act as a JSON-RPC server. We won't include the details of the server setup here, but it is reasonably simple and involves inclusion of jabsorb libraries, a servlet configuration, and registration with web.xml.

Assuming the JSON-RPC endpoint is accessible at http://localhost:8080/jsonrpc, you create a Flex application to consume it. Once again, use the as3-rpclib to create the Flex client. The steps to set that up in a Flex project are identical to those in the section "Understanding the Potential of XML-RPC." Finally, code the application as follows:

```
<?xml version="1.0" encoding="utf-8"?>
<s:Application xmlns:fx="http://ns.adobe.com/mxml/2009"
                      xmlns:s="library://ns.adobe.com/flex/spark"
                      xmlns:mx="library://ns.adobe.com/flex/halo"
                      xmlns:as3rpclib="com.ak33m.rpc.jsonrpc.*"
                      minWidth="1024" minHeight="768">
        <s:creationComplete>
                <![CDATA[
                    callFunction();
                ]]>
        </s:creationComplete>
        <fx:Script>
                <![CDATA[
                        import mx.controls.Alert;

                        var firstString:String;
                        var secondString:String;

                        var output:String;

                        function callFunction ()
                        {
                                output = jsonrpctojava.joinString(firstString,secondString);
                                trace(output);

                                output = jsonrpctojava.reverseString(firstString);
                                trace(output);
                        }

                ]]>
        </fx:Script>
        <fx:Declarations>
                <!-- Place non-visual elements (e.g., services, value objects) here -->
                <as3rpclib:JSONRPCObject id="jsonrpctojava"
                                                    endpoint="http://↵
127.0.0.1:8080/jsonrpc"
                                                    destination="jsonrpcendpoint"
                                                    fault="Alert.show(event.↵
fault.faultString,event.fault.faultCode)">
                </as3rpclib:JSONRPCObject >

        </fx:Declarations>
</s:Application>
```

The example reuses the same string manipulation class used in the XML-RPC example. The only difference is that JSON-RPC is the communication protocol instead of XML-RPC and thus uses a different server infrastructure. `JSONRPCObject` is similar to `XMLRPCObject` and also indirectly extends `mx.rpc.AbstractService`.

XML-RPC and JSON-RPC are both popular protocols for communication between disparate systems. They are based on open standards and offer alternatives to SOAP and REST web services. Although more popular in the JavaScript-driven Ajax world, they have a place in the realm of Flex applications as well. All the communication mechanisms discussed so far involve text-based messaging and have their own limitations related to latency, high volume, and complex structure transmission. Flex brings the efficiency of binary communication with AMF. In the next chapter, which covers remoting to a Java server, we focus on this and show you how the data services infrastructure provides effective integration between Flex and Java. However, before we get to that, let's take a quick look at Hessian, a binary web services protocol developed by Caucho Technologies. Hessian can be used to integrate Flex and Java, and it provides an alternative binary communication to AMF.

Combining Hessian and Flex

Hessian is a binary web services protocol that is open source under the Apache 2.0 license. It has language-specific implementations for many popular languages, including Java, Python, Flash/Flex, Ruby, C# .NET, and PHP. We're interested in the Java and Flash/Flex implementations.

For this discussion, we'll skip over Hessian support and configuration on the Java server side. We will assume it's ready to use. It comes preconfigured in Resin, the application server from Caucho Technologies, the creators of Hessian. In others, it can be configured fairly easily.

The only part we'll discuss (briefly) here are the methods exposed on the remote service. Once again, implement the same mundane yet useful service that exposes two methods, one that joins two strings and the other that reverses a `String`. This time, separate the server-side class into an interface and an implementation. The interface will look like this:

```
package org.shanky.hessian;

    public interface StringManipulator {

        public String↵
joinString(String firstString, String secondString) ;

        public String reverseString (String sourceString) ;
    }
```

The corresponding implementation class would look like this:

```
package org.shanky.hessian;

    public class StringManipulatorImpl
extends HessianServlet implements StringManipulator {

        public String↵
joinString(String firstString, String secondString) {
            return firstString + secondString;
        }

        public String reverseString (String sourceString) {
```

```
        int i, len = sourceString.length();
        StringBuffer dest = new StringBuffer(len);

        for (i = (len - 1); i >= 0; i--)
            dest.append(sourceString.charAt(i));

        return dest.toString();
    }
}
```

To use Hessian to communicate from Flex to Java, you employ the Hessian client-side library for Flash/Flex. You can download the SWC library file from the Hessian home page (http://hessian.caucho.com/). For Flex, you need to get hessian-flex-*version_number*.swc from the binary distribution list. You'll also find links to API documentation and example applications (including server-side push using Comet) on this page.

The Hessian Flash/Flex client library uses mx.rpc.AbstractService and mx.rpc.AbstractOperations like the libraries for XML-RPC, JSON-RPC, WebService, and RemoteService. The service that manages RPC extends AbstractService, and the remote methods map to AbstractOperations. The primary component is abstracted as HessianService, and that's where you configure the remote Hessian destination. In MXML, this tag looks like this:

```
<hessian:HessianService xmlns:hessian="hessian.mxml.*"
    id="hessianService" destination="remoteDestination"/>
```

The destination is what points to the Hessian server endpoint or gateway. By specifying only remoteDestination, you are implying a relative path from the SWF application path. Therefore, a SWF application at a path of the type http://domain:port/approot/MyApp.swf, wanting to access the Hessian endpoint at http://domain:port/approot/remoteDestination, would specify the destination as remoteDestination. Fully qualified URLs can also be assigned as values to the destination property. If the domain of the Hessian endpoint and the SWF are different, the Flash security restrictions apply; don't forget to put a crossdomain.xml file at the remote server root, appropriately configured as necessary.

In your Flex application code, you invoke the remote methods with the configured HessianService handle. So a call to joinString would look somewhat like this:

```
hessianService.joinString.send(firstStringParam, secondStringParam);
```

A call to the Hessian service is asynchronous, where the send method maps to mx.rpc.AbstractOperation.send(), so you need to use the AsyncToken and a callback handler to get the response. The callback handler can be any class that implements the mx.rpc.IResponder interface. The IResponder interface defines two methods, result and fault. On a successful result, the result callback method is invoked, and on error, the fault callback method is invoked.

Very simplistically, you could do this:

```
var token:AsyncToken =
hessianService.joinString(firstStringParam, secondStringParam);
token.addResponder(IResponderImplClass);
```

Now when the response comes back, you'll receive it in the result(event:Object) method. In the IResponderImplClass, you would take event.result and get the response-concatenated string from it.

We've kept this example simple to help you stay focused on understanding the main ideas instead of getting lost in the details.

Summary

We began our examination of Flex and Java integration with a discussion of loose coupling using HTTP, and finished with a look at different styles of web service–based integration. We mentioned that AMF-based integration provides for tighter integration than anything seen so far.

Now let's step back a bit and view the Flex and Java integration options by first illustrating it at a very high level and then progressively drilling down to a detailed perspective.

Using a 30,000-foot analogy, we can view the integration as pull-only vs. pull-and-push, as summarized in Figure 7-10.

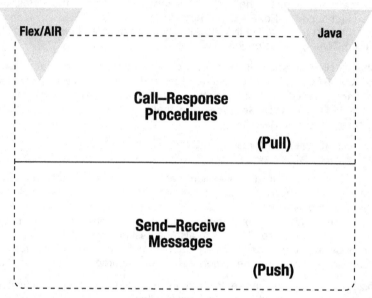

Figure 7-10. A 30,000-foot view of integration between Flex and Java

Drilling down a bit further, and reaching 10,000 feet, the situation seems divided between the ideas and components that facilitate RPCs and those that enable messaging Figure 7-11 shows the 10,000-foot view.

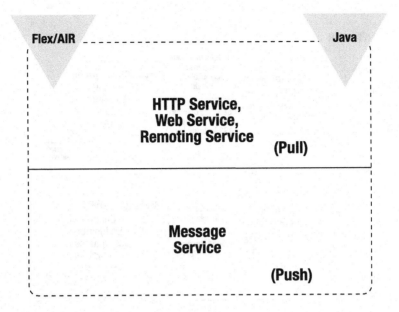

Figure 7-11. 10,000-foot view of integration between Flex and Java

One more level down gets us into the realm of individual components and their roles. Figure 7-12 is a self-explanatory representation of this, which we'll call the 1,000-foot view. The diagram lists a few data services, namely LCDS, BlazeDS, GraniteDS, OpenAMF, and WebORB. Chapter 8 provides more information on these data services.

This chapter has shown a fair bit of these perspectives in practice, and the following chapter builds on them. What you learn from these should be applicable to languages beyond Java and in situations more complex than the ones illustrated. Service-Oriented Architecture (SOA) is transforming legacy applications and driving new applications to create a loosely coupled, scalable, server-side infrastructure. Flex-rich interfaces can be integrated with such an SOA infrastructure using the methodologies discussed in this chapter.

Finally, if we zoom in to a very close range, like 100 feet, the details of the wiring and the interaction model comes to light. Figure 7-13 shows this level.

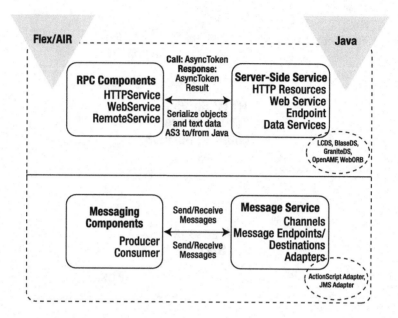

Figure 7-12. 1,000-foot view of integration between Flex and Java

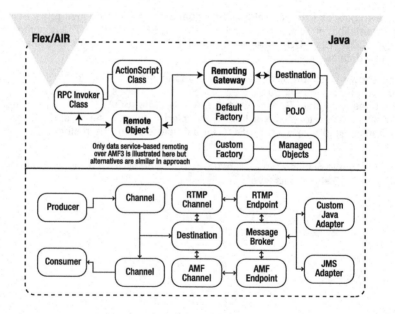

Figure 7-13. 100-foot view of integration between Flex and Java

In the next chapter, we'll focus down even further and move on to the subject of tighter integration between Flex and Java over AMF-based data services and media servers.

Chapter 8

Integrating via Data Services

by Shashank Tiwari

So far, you know how to combine Flex and Java using HTTP and web services. The last chapter surveyed a bunch of alternative mechanisms to achieve this. Most of these mechanisms involve loosely coupled text-based data interchange. Most of them interact by pulling data. Only one of them, Hessian, transmits binary data. Only one, Hessian again (with additional infrastructure powered by the new Java IO), allows data push.

Now, we delve into more tightly coupled scenarios and efficient binary data transmission using AMF (Action Message Format). The AMF specification can be accessed online at `http://opensource.adobe.com`. This chapter looks at both pull- and push-based interactions—using data services and media servers. Adobe offers two alternatives for data services—the commercial LifeCycle Data Services (LCDS) and the open source BlazeDS—and it offers a suite of products for media servers: Flash Media Server (FMS) products. There are a few open source alternatives to these as well.

In this chapter, I will analyze these products in the context of their applicability to rich, engaging enterprise-grade applications. Functionally they can be divided into the following two topics:

- Remoting and RPC
- Messaging and data push

At this point of the book, remoting and RPC should be familiar territory, so let's start there.

Remoting and RPC

Flex applications can access the Java server side using data services. They can access Java objects and invoke remote methods on them. The Flex framework includes a client-side component called

RemoteObject. This object acts as a proxy for a data service destination on the server. When configured properly, this object handle can be used to invoke RPCs. Before we get into the nitty-gritty of this object and destination configuration, let's step back and look at the data services architecture.

Data Services Architecture

Figure 8-1 is a pictorial summary of the data services architecture. The view is biased to highlight the functional elements. It includes technical aspects but skips the internal details in many places. As you look deeper into the nuts and bolts in this chapter, many of these details will emerge.

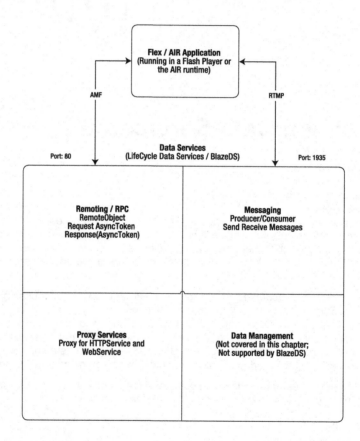

Figure 8-1. Data services architecture: an overview

As Figure 8-1 depicts, data services includes the following:

- Gateway to intercept server-bound calls
- Parser to make sense of AMF messages
- Serializer and deserializer to transform objects between ActionScript 3.0 (AS3) and Java

- Manager to coordinate with and delegate responsibility to server-side objects
- Messaging service provider to send and receive messages

By data services, I mean a class of products that enable remoting and messaging over AMF and protocols like Real Time Messaging Protocol (RTMP). RTMP is a proprietary protocol developed by Adobe Systems for streaming audio, video, and data over the Internet. More information on RTMP can be found on Wikipedia at `http://en.wikipedia.org/wiki/Real_Time_Messaging_Protocol` and at `http://osflash.org/documentation/rtmp`.

As mentioned, there are two data services implementations from Adobe and a few open source alternatives. Following are the most popular ones:

- LifeCycle Data Services (Adobe): `http://www.adobe.com/products/livecycle/dataservices/`
- BlazeDS (open source from Adobe): `http://opensource.adobe.com/wiki/display/blazeds/`
- Granite Data Services (GDS `http://www.graniteds.org/`
- WebORB for Java: `http://www.themidnightcoders.com/weborb/java/`
- OpenAMF `http://sourceforge.net/projects/openamf/`

OpenAMF is not a very active project at the time of writing. The last release dates back to 2006. This project's mission was to port AMFPHP to Java. AMF was a closed specification back then, and AMFPHP was a reverse-engineered open source option for PHP servers. OpenAMF is closer to Flash remoting than data services.

This chapter sticks mostly to LCDS and BlazeDS, but the same concepts apply to the alternatives. LCDS and BlazeDS are quite similar in form and structure and share the same codebase. BlazeDS can be thought of as a marginally scaled-down version of LCDS.

Data services uses AMF3 (Action Message Format version 3) to transmit binary data between Flex and Java. The genesis of this product lies in the Flash remoting server, which used to support AMF0 as the binary protocol. Flash remoting still exists, in many forms, but data services replaces it as a better alternative.

Whichever data service we choose, it is a web application from a Java server perspective. Let's dig a bit deeper to see what this means. (Of course, we are talking only about data services for Java. There are remoting servers for other technologies, but that is beyond the scope of this book.)

It's a Web Application

Web applications are applications built on the technology that powers the Web. The HTTP protocol and the associated programming paradigm are a prominent part of this technology set. In Java, the raw low-level HTTP and related infrastructure is abstracted out as a higher-level API and managed components. At the heart of this abstraction is the Servlet specification, which wraps HTTP methods and HTTP protocol handling in objects. Web applications written in Java are packaged with all assets, associated libraries, class files, and any other resources into a special archive file format: a web application archive (WAR). These WAR files are deployed on a servlet container or an application server (which contains a servlet container).

Most data services, especially LCDS and BlazeDS, are web applications and exist as WAR files. The remoting gateway is a servlet, and data service elements are web components. A little later, in the section

"Downloading and deploying the web application," you will see how deploying LCDS or BlazeDS is identical to deploying any other web application distributed in a WAR file format.

In both BlazeDS and LCDS, the primary communication responsibilities are handled by a message broker, which is created on startup by a servlet called the `MessageBrokerServlet`. The application server's standard class loader loads it like any other servlet. This message broker is extremely flexible, and all types of available services and endpoints can be configured for it fairly easily. All such configurations reside in an XML configuration file, which I talk about later in the section "Configuring data services."

Protocols, Channels, Destinations, and Endpoints

One of the primary advantages of data services is their use of AMF to transmit data between Flex and Java. AMF is a binary protocol, and the Flash Player natively supports it. Therefore, transmission using AMF is fast and efficient. AMF is a high-level (application layer) protocol that uses HTTP for communication. Almost all data services dialog happens over HTTP or its secure alternative, HTTPS. AMF specification is now available under the open source license and is accessible for download at `http://download.macromedia.com/pub/labs/amf/amf3_spec_121207.pdf`. When remoting, AMF is marshaled and unmarshaled at both ends (Java and Flex) for the data interchange to work.

The data services messaging module and media server use RTMP. LCDS and FMS support RTMP, but BlazeDS does not. BlazeDS uses HTTP tunneling and AMF long pooling to achieve a push-based model. Red5 (`http://osflash.org/red5`), an open source alternative to Flash Media Server, partially reverse-engineers RTMP and provides streaming capabilities over this derived protocol.

Apart from AMF over HTTP and RTMP, the Flash Player also supports Transmission Control Protocol (TCP) over Sockets. TCP is a protocol from the Internet protocol suite that facilitates reliable ordered delivery of byte streams. Secure versions of the protocol, such as AMF and HTTP over Secure Sockets Layer (SSL) and RTMP over Transport Layer Security (TLS), can be used as well. Both SSL and TLS are cryptographic protocols that facilitate secure communication over the Internet. TLS is a newer generation protocol compared to SSL. Although similar, SSL and TLS are not interchangeable. TLS 1.0 is a standard that emerged after SSL 3.0. These protocols involve endpoint authentication, message integrity, and key-based encryption. Both protocols support a bunch of cryptographic algorithms including RSA. RSA is a popular cryptographic algorithm for public key cryptography, which involves two different keys, one to encrypt a message and another to decrypt it.

The Flash Player does not support the entire repertoire of protocols and even misses the ubiquitous User Datagram Protocol (UDP), which is very useful for multicasting *Multicasting* is a method of information delivery to multiple destinations simultaneously whereby messages are delivered over each link of the network only once. Copies of the message are created only if the links to the destinations bifurcate.

You will not be able to take advantage of protocols like UDP with data services.

Protocols help make effective and efficient communication possible, but higher-level abstractions increase the usability of these protocols. These higher-level abstractions help you focus on business logic and reduce the burden of dealing with low-level communication handling. One such useful higher-level construct in Flex is called *destination*.

Destinations are one of the key abstractions available in the Flex framework and data services. Server-side entities are mapped to logical names and configured to be invoked using these logical names. These configured server-side elements, or destinations, have a handle (logical name) and expose server-side functionality to remote clients. Many Flex client components, especially those that facilitate remoting—for example `RemoteObject`—map to a destination. The section "Configuring data services," which comes a little later, illustrates the configuration files. In that section, you will learn how to define, configure, and use a destination. Then, in the section "Extending data services for advanced remoting use cases," you will see how to use custom extensions as destinations. In data services, almost all server-side elements that facilitate remoting and messaging are configured as destinations.

HTTPService and WebService, when routed through a data service proxy, also map to a destination.

When you interact with a server-side service via a destination, you use a messaging channel to communicate back and forth A *messaging channel* is a bundle that defines a protocol and an endpoint set. An endpoint set means a URI, a listening port number, and an endpoint type definition. For example, an AMF channel could be established with the help of the AMF channel implementation class (mx.messaging.channels.AMFChannel) and an endpoint definition, which could be a combination of an endpoint type (flex.messaging.endpoints.AmfEndpoint) and its availability via a URI (say /sampleapp/messagebroker/amf) over a certain listening port (which by default for AMF is 8100).

Sometimes, services need special adapters to communicate with server-side elements. These adapters may translate the message and act as the classical conduit that helps different programming interfaces communicate and interact with each other. (An *adapter* by definition is something that modifies an API to make it adapt to the required integration scenario.) Data services define a set of built-in adapters and provide an API to create your own.

That is enough theory; time now to roll our sleeves up and see data services in action. We first install data services and then quickly create a small example application to see how it works.

Installing a Data Service

The last section claimed data services to be a Java web application. You will see that claim reinforced by deploying a data service like any other Java web application in a Java application server (with a servlet container). Once we have deployed it successfully, we will go ahead and configure it so that we are ready to build an example application.

Downloading and Deploying the Web Application

For the purposes of illustration, we will pick BlazeDS as the data service and choose JBoss Application Server (AS) as the Java application server. If the data service is LCDS and the application server is any other, such as Apache Tomcat, BEA WebLogic, IBM WebSphere, Apache Geronimo, Caucho Resin, or GlassFish, the situation is not very different. Each of these application servers has its own directory structure and styles of deployment. Deploying BlazeDS or LCDS involves the same level of complexity as deploying any other Java web application packaged as a WAR. Adobe Labs has published some notes on the specific installation instructions for a few of the popular application servers. These notes are online at http://opensource.adobe.com/wiki/display/blazeds/BlazeDS+3+Release+Notes.

The first step is to get all the required software and to install it.

Getting the software and installing it BlazeDS is available under the open source GNU LGPL license. Go to http://opensource.adobe.com/wiki/display/blazeds/BlazeDS and download the latest stable release build. You will have a choice to download the binary or the source versions. The binary version is what you should choose unless you intend to make modifications to the code. The distribution is available as a ZIP file. When you unzip the archive file, you will find a file called blazeds.war. This is the WAR file that has everything in it needed to use BlazeDS. In addition, you may find the following files:

- blazeds-samples.war: A set of sample applications
- blazeds-console.war: Monitoring application for BlazeDS deployments

If this is the first time you are deploying BlazeDS, it's recommended you deploy `blazeds-samples.war` and verify that the sample applications run without a problem.

The other piece of the puzzle is the Java application server. I will assume that you have downloaded and installed one for your use. In this example, we download the latest stable release of JBoss AS from the community download page accessible at `http://www.jboss.org/projects/download/`. At the time of writing, version 5.1.0.GA is the latest stable release. This may differ depending on when you download it. The JBoss AS download is an archive file that is ready to use as soon as it's expanded in the file system. (It may at most require a few environment variable settings.) On the machine (PC, Mac or Linux/Unix), we just unzip it within a directory on the file system.

The JBoss AS directory server appears as shown in Figure 8-2.

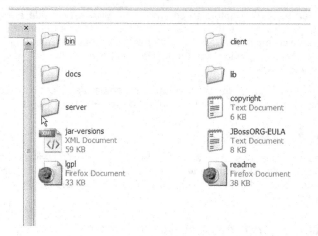

Figure 8-2. JBoss AS directory structured after unzipping it on a Mac

BlazeDS runs with any Java application server that supports JDK 1.4.2+, JDK 5 or higher. Most current versions of application servers support these JDK versions.

Deploying the WAR file Deploying a web application in JBoss is as elementary as traversing down the **server** ➤ **default** ➤ **deploy** folders and copying the WAR files there. Once this is done, start up the server. Go to the `bin` directory and start the server with the "run" script. To verify deployment, fire up your browser and request the samples application. In our case, JBoss is bound to port 8080 for HTTP requests, and so the URL for samples looks like this: `http://localhost:8080/blazeds-samples/`. If you are able to access the samples application, you are ready to move to the next step of configuring data service.

With LCDS, the deployment is no different. The WAR file in LCDS has a different name—`lcds.war` as opposed to `blazeds.war`—and it has a few extra features compared to BlazeDS, but from a deployment standpoint things don't change.

Configuring Data Services

In BlazeDS and LCDS, there is more to configure than code. In both these cases, a message broker servlet is the central manager of all communication and service invocations. Configuring data services is equivalent to configuring this message broker. In the web.xml file where you set up this servlet, you define the configuration file it should read. The portion of web.xml where you define this is as follows:

```
<servlet>
    <servlet-name>MessageBrokerServlet</servlet-name>
    <display-name>MessageBrokerServlet</display-name>
    <servlet-class>flex.messaging.MessageBrokerServlet</servlet-class>
    <init-param>
        <param-name>services.configuration.file</param-name>
        <param-value>/WEB-INF/flex/services-config.xml</param-value>
    </init-param>
    <load-on-startup>1</load-on-startup>
</servlet>
```

You may notice that the value for the services.configuration.file is /WEB-INF/flex/services-config.xml. This is the default configuration, and most often there is no need to change it. However, if you need the configuration file to be at a different location or have a different name, you know where to make the modifications so that the new values are picked up.

All service and endpoint configurations are specified in this configuration file, which by default is called services-config.xml. From a functional standpoint, a data service tries to accomplish the following:

- Facilitate remote procedure calls to Java objects on the server and transmit data between AS3 and Java classes.
- Provide proxy services, especially for HTTPService and WebService, where security restrictions (the lack of a cross-domain definition via crossdomain.xml) disallow these services otherwise.
- Send/Receive messages between Flex and Java and between two different Flex clients.
- Manage data for the application. This topic is not discussed in this book at all. BlazeDS does not provide this off the shelf, but LCDS does.

Therefore, Adobe partitions the configuration file into four different pieces, each corresponding to one of the functional responsibilities just listed. Each of these pieces resides in a separate file, and all are included in the original configuration file by reference. The default names for these four files, in the same order in which they correspond to the functional areas listed previously, are

- remoting-config.xml
- proxy-config.xml
- messaging-config.xml
- data-management-config.xml

The portion of services-config.xml at /flex/WEB-INF from our BlazeDS installation, where three of these four files are included (BlazeDS does not have data management features), is as shown here:

```
<?xml version="1.0" encoding="UTF-8"?>
<services-config>
    <services>
        <service-include file-path="remoting-config.xml" />
        <service-include file-path="proxy-config.xml" />
        <service-include file-path="messaging-config.xml" />
    </services>
```

A few aspects like logging, security, and channel definitions are cross-cutting concerns and are used across services, so these are defined in `services-config.xml` itself. All other service configurations and definitions typically fall in one of the four files (or three if we are using BlazeDS) I spoke about.

In this chapter, there is no intent to cover every single aspect of configuration. Only a few important ones are sampled and explained. For an exhaustive syntax-level account of each allowed configuration, it's advisable to refer to the LiveDocs. For BlazeDS, you could refer specifically to a LiveDocs section titled "About service configuration files," which can be found online at `http://livedocs.adobe.com/blazeds/ 1/blazeds_devguide/help.html?content=services_config_2.html`.

Let's survey a few configuration options to get a flavor of things.

Common configuration Let's start with logging. BlazeDS and LCDS use log4j for logging. Logging-related configurations reside in `services-config.xml` itself. The most important aspect of configuration is the logging level. The permissible values and their respective meanings are as follows:

- `ALL`: Logs every single message.
- `DEBUG`: Includes internal Flex activities. This is an appropriate level during development and troubleshooting, and is an incremental expansion beyond `INFO`. Therefore, all errors, warnings and information messages are included.
- `INFO`: Logs additional information that may be pertinent to developers or administrators. This level builds on top of the `WARN` level.
- `WARN`: Includes warnings as well as errors.
- `ERROR`: Logs only errors that cause service disruption.
- `NONE`: Logs nothing.

If you are familiar with log4j logging levels, then you have seen this before.

Next come channel definitions. In terms of importance, this rates above the logging-level definitions. Channels are the vital protocol and endpoint combination that make communication possible between the Flex client and the server. In BlazeDS, the default AMF channel configurations look like this:

```
<channels>
    <channel-definition id="my-amf" class=
"mx.messaging.channels.AMFChannel">
        <endpoint url="http://{server.name}:{server.port}/
{context.root}/messagebroker/amf"
class="flex.messaging.endpoints.AMFEndpoint"/>
    </channel-definition>

    <channel-definition id="my-secure-amf"
class="mx.messaging.channels.SecureAMFChannel">
        <endpoint url="https://{server.name}:{server.port}/
{context.root}/messagebroker/amfsecure"
class="flex.messaging.endpoints.SecureAMFEndpoint"/>
        <properties>
            <add-no-cache-headers>false</add-no-cache-headers>
        </properties>
    </channel-definition>

    <channel-definition id="my-polling-amf"
```

```
class="mx.messaging.channels.AMFChannel">
        <endpoint url="http://{server.name}:{server.port}/↵
{context.root}/messagebroker/amfpolling"
class="flex.messaging.endpoints.AMFEndpoint"/>
        <properties>
            <polling-enabled>true</polling-enabled>
            <polling-interval-seconds>4</polling-interval-seconds>
        </properties>
    </channel-definition>
</channels>
```

Three different AMF channels are defined using the preceding configuration. In each case, a fully qualified class name specifies the class that implements the channel. The channel is accessible via a configured endpoint. The endpoints include a set of tokens, namely server.name, server.port, and context.root. When a SWF is loaded in a browser, as happens with all Flex applications, these tokens are replaced with the correct values, and the endpoints are configured properly. In AIR and even with RTMP channels (in RTMP, server.port needs a specific port number definition), these tokens are not resolved automatically, and so channels don't work as expected, if configured using tokens.

To test a channel, it may a good idea to try and access the endpoint URL with the browser and see whether you get a success message, such as 200 OK, or not. Where required, channels could accept additional properties. As an example, a polling AMF channel defines the polling interval using properties. An interesting fact is that property settings can create entirely different channels. AMF and polling AMF channels have the same class for implementing the channels, but they have different sets of properties and therefore different behavior.

Using services-config.xml, the channel configurations are done at compile time. It's also possible to configure channels and associate them with destinations at run time. More information about configuration at run time is covered in the section "Configuring at run time" later in this chapter.

The third important common configuration pertains to security. Exhaustive and complex security definitions are possible with data services, but we will go with the defaults for now. We shall deal with security configurations in data services in the section "Additional useful data services tips" later in this chapter.

Although this chapter has not exhaustively covered the configuration options, you know the basics of configuration by now. You will learn more about configuration as you explore the other topics that relate to data services.

Our new focus is to get data services into action. The three configuration files, remoting-config.xml, proxy-config.xml, and messaging-config.xml, configure services, so we will look at these in the next few sections as we implement such services using BlazeDS or LCDS.

Calling Remote Methods and Serializing Objects

You know AMF is an efficient binary protocol and a data service lets you exchange data between Flex and Java. Let's dig deeper so you can see what you need to do to leverage this mechanism in your Flex application. Because "seeing is believing" and, like pictures, working code speaks louder than words, we will first create a simple example application that will establish RPC over AMF using a data service. In this example, our data service is BlazeDS.

A Simple Example in Action

The example application is fairly simple It displays a list of people and the country they come from. A person is identified by an ID, first name, and last name. A country is identified by a name. The initial list is populated from an XML data file that has four names in it. A user is allowed to add names to the list and delete existing ones.

To demonstrate data services and remoting, the list and the methods to manipulate the list are kept on the server. These remote Java objects and their methods are accessed from a Flex client.

We create this example using Flash Builder 4, but we could also do without it and compile directly using `mxmlc`, the command-line compiler, or use Flex Ant tasks, available from within Eclipse. The command-line compiler and the Flex Ant tasks are available free of charge. The command-line compiler comes bundled with the free Flex 4 SDK. The Flex Ant tasks software bundle can be downloaded from `http://labs.adobe.com/wiki/index.php/Flex_Ant_Tasks`.

As a first step, we create a new Flex project, choose **Web application** as the application type and **J2EE** as the server technology. We name this project **VerySimpleRemotingExample**. Figure 8-3 shows these settings in the **New Flex Project** dialog.

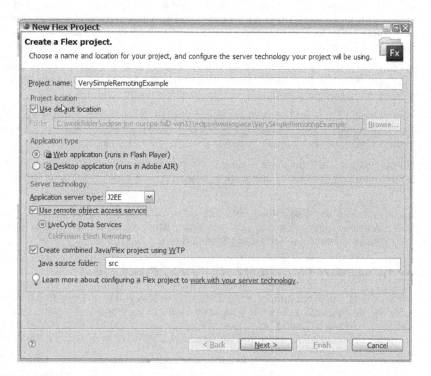

Figure 8-3. The initial screen for new Flex project creation in Flash Builder

You will see that Flash Builder offers only two choices for a data service, namely **LifeCycle Data Services** and **ColdFusion Flash Remoting**. At first, this often causes confusion among developers, when using BlazeDS. Choose **LifeCycle Data Services** as the option in the current dialog box when using BlazeDS. In the next dialog box, you will have an opportunity to point to either the BlazeDS WAR or the BlazeDS directories, deployed on your application server.

In the very first screen, a choice is offered to create a combined Java/Flex project using WTP. WTP, which stands for Web Tools Platform, is the set of tools available within Eclipse to create Java web applications. The WTP project is hosted at `http://www.eclipse.org/webtools/`. You can go to the project page to get more information on WTP.

The "data services" software available for the Flex framework consists of web applications that run in a web container. Any custom logic you write with the data services either will be part of a web application or will be accessed from a web application. Therefore, if you are starting from scratch, choosing to create a joint project is often useful. If your Java-side application already exists, as in the case of integration with existing systems, do not choose this option. Depending on the choice at this stage, the next screen varies.

If you choose the option to create the combined project, the screen lets you define the following:

- **Target runtime**: The application server on which you wish to deploy the data services application. Eclipse allows you to configure the application server run time. A JBoss AS instance is configured for the purpose. The details of JBoss AS configuration are out of the scope of this chapter. However, a quick search on the Web or a look at the JBoss AS documentation (available online at `http://www.jboss.org/jbossas/docs/`) could help you configure a JBoss AS successfully.
- **Context root**: The root of the web application, usually the same as the application name.
- **Content folder**: The folder for the source files.
- **Flex WAR file**: The location of the data services WAR file. The LCDS WAR file is called `flex.war`, and the BlazeDS WAR file is called `blazeds.war`. We are using BlazeDS, so we choose `blazeds.war` from wherever we have locally saved it on our file system. You may recall I said you would get a chance to define BlazeDS-specific files. Here is where you do it.
- **Compilation options**: Options that let you compile the application either locally or on the server when the page is viewed. If you are a servlet or JSP developer, you know that you can either precompile these artifacts or compile them when accessed, initialized, and served based on user request. During development, it's advisable to compile locally in order to catch any errors and warnings as soon as possible.
- **Output folder**: The folder where the compiled and packaged files are saved.

Figure 8-4 shows what this screen looks like.

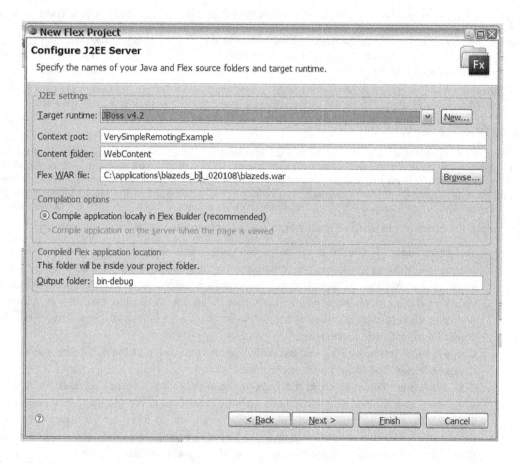

Figure 8-4. The dialog box that appears if you choose to go with the combined Java/Flex project using WTP option

As I said before, it's possible you may be trying to wire up a Flex interface to your existing Java web application or have different teams work on the two pieces fairly independent of each other. In such cases, you do not choose the combined project option. If you reject the combined project option, your next screen will vary from the one in Figure 8-4. This time you are presented with a dialog to specify the following:

- **Root folder**: This is the folder where the existing web application is deployed. Make sure this folder contains a `WEB-INF/flex` folder.
- **Root URL**: This is the URL of the web application. In our case, we configure JBoss AS to listen for HTTP requests on port 8080, and we run it on the same machine from which we access the Flex interface via a browser, so the value is `http://localhost:8080/MyWebApplication`.
- **Context root**: The root of the web application, typically the same as its name.

- **Compilation options**: Already explained, in the context of the joint Java/Flex application.
- **Output folder**: The folder where the compiled and packaged files are saved.

Figure 8-5 shows this alternative screen, which was captured before any choices were made. This is intentional. Flex comes with an integrated JRun Java application server. You can choose to use it or ignore it in favor of any other Java application server. We ignored it and chose JBoss. However, if you decided to choose JRun, you have the advantage of Flash Builder's default configurations coinciding with what JRun wants. In Figure 8-5, you see these choices grayed out because the **Use default location for LifeCycle Data Services server** option is selected.

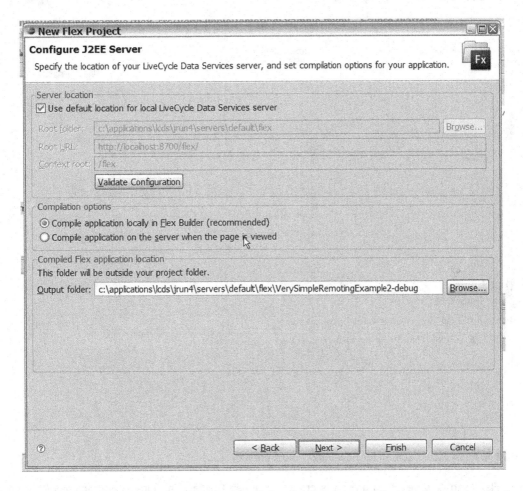

Figure 8-5. The dialog box that appears when an existing Java web application is referenced as the target for the data services application

In either of the two cases, once you make your selections, you move to the next screen, shown in Figure 8-6, which lets you add any external library files to the project and asks you to confirm the project creation. When you click the **Finish** button, the project is created.

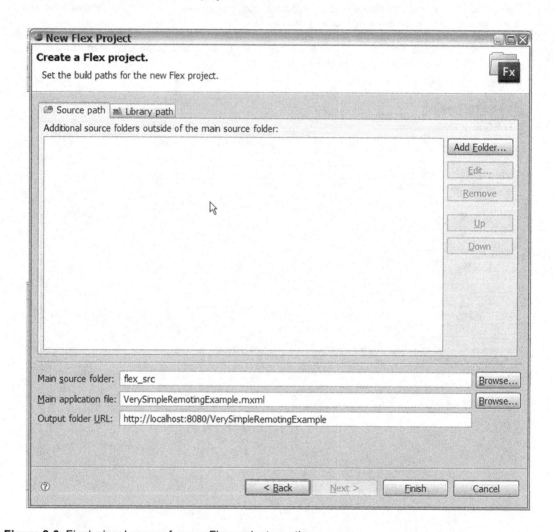

Figure 8-6. Final wizard screen for new Flex project creation

A new Flex (with data services) project is created in Flash Builder. The directory structure of our newly created project looks as illustrated in Figure 8-7. In this figure, notice a WEB-INF folder appears in the WebContent folder. This folder contains most things pertaining to BlazeDS. The flex folder in WEB-INF contains all the configuration files. The lib folder contains all the JARs that implement the BlazeDS functionality.

Now we are set up, and it's time to start building the example application. To represent the data, we define a `Person` class, which has the following attributes:

- `id`
- `firstName`
- `lastName`
- `country`

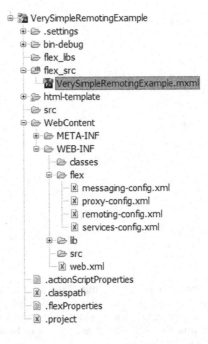

Figure 8-7. The new Flex project, VerySimpleRemotingExample, in Flash Builder

We also define a collection of persons that we call `PeopleCollection`. `PeopleCollection` contains `Person` objects. The object to represent these abstractions is created both in Java and AS3. Here is what the Java class looks like:

```
package advancedflex4.ch08.remoting;
public class Person
{
    private int id;
    private String firstName;
    private String lastName;
    private String country;

    public int getId() {
        return id;
    }
```

```
public void setId(int id) {
    this.id = id;
}

public String getFirstName() {
    return firstName;
}

public void setFirstName(String firstName) {
    this.firstName = firstName;
}

public String getLastName() {
    return lastName;
}

public void setLastName(String lastName) {
    this.lastName = lastName;
}

public String getCountry() {
    return country;
}

public void setCountry(String country) {
    this.country = country;
}
}
```

If you are a Java developer, you will quickly recognize this class as a JavaBean type of class. It has a set of properties and set of accessor methods to get and set the attribute values. We create a similar structure in AS3. Again, we will have a set of attributes and a set of accessors to get/set those attri-butes. The attribute names in the Java class and the AS3 class are identical because that is how the fields are matched. This is what the AS3 class looks like:

```
package advancedflex4.ch08.remoting
{
    [RemoteClass(alias="advancedflex4.ch07.remoting.Person")]
    [Managed]
    public class Person
    {
        public var id:int;
        public var firstName:String;
        public var lastName:String;
        public var country:String;

    }
}
```

Looking at the code, you may wonder where the accessor methods are. In AS3, a class with public variables has implicit accessor methods. Therefore, the lack of explicit get and set method pairs is not a problem in this situation, and things will still work. If the properties (attributes) were private, explicit getters and setters would be required. Also, notice that the RemoteClass metadata links the AS3 class to its Java counterpart by specifying the fully qualified class name of the Java class as a value of the alias parameter. Further, you see this class annotated with another metadata element: Managed. Annotating a class with the Managed metadata tag is another way of implementing the mx.data.IManaged interface. The IManaged interface extends the IPropertyChangeNotifier interface. IPropertyChangeNotifier is a marker interface, which defines a contract such that all implementing classes dispatch a property change event for all properties of the class and any nested class exposed publicly as properties. As a result, as changes occur, the remote server class and the local class are kept in sync.

By explicitly defining a counterpart to our server-side Java class, we establish a typed association. Therefore, on data interchange, the deserialization of the serialized Java class involves mapping of the data elements into this ActionScript class. If we did not define such a class on the ActionScript side, the deserialization would still happen successfully, except that this time the ActionScript class would be dynamically created. From a performance and optimization perspective, typed associations are preferred over dynamic creation.

Next, we create a collection class that holds the set of Person objects on both sides of the wire, and define properties and accessor methods on it. Again, we keep the names and definitions consistent on both sides.

Our collection class on the Java server side is called PeopleCollection.java, and this is how it looks:

```java
package advancedflex4.ch08.remoting;

import java.io.*;
import java.net.URLDecoder;

import javax.xml.parsers.*;
import org.w3c.dom.*;
import java.util.List;
import java.util.ArrayList;

public class PeopleCollection
{
    public PeopleCollection() {

    }

    public List getPersons() {

        List list = new ArrayList();

        try {
            String filePath = URLDecoder.decode(getClass().
getClassLoader().getResource
("advancedflex4/ch07/PeopleCollection.xml").
getFile(), "UTF-8");;
            DocumentBuilderFactory factory =
DocumentBuilderFactory.newInstance();
            factory.setValidating(false);
            Document doc =
factory.newDocumentBuilder().
parse(new File(filePath));
            NodeList personNodes = doc.getElementsByTagName("person");
```

```
            int length = personNodes.getLength();
            Person person;
            Node personNode;
            for (int i=0; i<length; i++) {
                personNode = personNodes.item(i);
                person = new Person();
                person.setId(getIntegerValue(personNode, "id"));
                person.setFirstName(getStringValue↵
(personNode, "firstName"));
                person.setLastName(getStringValue↵
(personNode, "lastName"));
                person.setCountry(getStringValue↵
(personNode, "country"));
            }
        } catch (Exception e) {
            e.printStackTrace();
        }

        return list;
    }

    private String getStringValue(Node node, String name) {
        return ((Element) node).getElementsByTagName↵
(name).item(0).getFirstChild().getNodeValue();
    }

    private int getIntegerValue(Node node, String name) {
        return Integer.parseInt(getStringValue(node, name) );
    }
}
```

You will notice that this class reads the data from an XML file called `PeopleCollection.xml`. This XML file contains four records, each of which corresponds to an attribute of the `Person` class. Here are the entries in that file:

```
<peopleCollection>
    <person>
        <id>1</id>
        <firstName>John</firstName>
        <lastName>Smith</lastName>
        <country>United States</country>
    </person>
    <person>
        <id>2</id>
        <firstName>Amit</firstName>
        <lastName>Sharma</lastName>
        <country>India</country>
    </person>
    <person>
        <id>3</id>
        <firstName>Alex</firstName>
        <lastName>Smirnov</lastName>
        <country>Russia</country>
```

```
        </person>
        <person>
            <id>4</id>
            <firstName>Ying</firstName>
            <lastName>Chen</lastName>
            <country>China</country>
        </person>
</peopleCollection>
```

That takes care of the data on the server side Let's now configure these classes with data services. Once we have done that successfully, we will move on to consuming this remote data by calling remote methods from the Flex client.

We get into the `WEB-INF/flex` directory and open `remoting-config.xml`. You already know that `remoting-config.xml` is one of the constituent files of `services-config.xml`, which configures the message broker servlet and allows data services to deliver the expected functionality.

We configure the `PeopleCollection` object as a remoting destination so that it becomes accessible from the Flex client. Here is the snippet from `remoting-config.xml`:

```
<service id="remoting-service"
    class="flex.messaging.services.RemotingService">
    <adapters>
        <adapter-definition id="java-object"
class="flex.messaging.services.↩
remoting.adapters.JavaAdapter"
default="true"/>
    </adapters>

    <default-channels>
        <channel ref="my-amf"/>
    </default-channels>

    <destination id="peopleCollection">
        <properties>
            <source>advancedflex4.ch07.remoting.↩
PeopleCollection</source>
        </properties>
    </destination>
</service>
```

The adapters and default channels we use here were preconfigured with the BlazeDS distribution. It's possible to configure additional adapters and modify the default channels. The piece we add to this configuration file is the one that defines the destination. That configuration maps a logical name (handle) to the class, identified by the fully qualified class name, which holds the collection of persons. In Flex, the logical name will be referenced from within `RemoteObject` to invoke methods on this class. If you are familiar with any distributed computing technology like web services, EJB, COM, CORBA, or any other RPC-supporting technology, you will find this extremely familiar in approach and style.

A destination allows many more property settings beyond the essential `source` property determination. One of these is the `scope` property, which takes three valid values: `Application`, `Session`, and `Request`. Application-scoped remote objects get bound to the `ServletContext` and are available to the entire web application. Session-scoped objects are bound to a `FlexSession` instance, which abstracts the session of the current conversation. Request-scoped objects are instantiated on each invocation. Other properties commonly used are the `attribute-id` and the `factory` properties. Object instances are bound to the name specified as the value of the `attribute-id` property. The `factory` property specifies the factory that creates the object. In the case of managed components, this property plays a major role. Later in the chapter, in the section "Creating custom factories," you will see this being used.

On the Java server side we are done, except for compiling the code and copying the class files over in the proper directory structure, which maps to the package structure, to `WEB-INF/classes`. This is how BlazeDS would be able to load these classes. It is a standard Java web application requirement to have the compiled Java classes available either in the `WEB-INF/classes` folder or as a packaged archive in the `WEB-INF/lib` folder for it to be available to the web application.

The last part of this example is the Flex application code, which calls the remote methods, gets the data across the wire, and populates a data grid with that data. For now, all of this is put in a single MXML file. The source of that MXML file is as follows:

```
<?xml version="1.0" encoding="utf-8"?>
<s:Application xmlns:fx="http://ns.adobe.com/mxml/2009"
                        xmlns:s="library://ns.adobe.com/flex/spark"
                        xmlns:mx="library://ns.adobe.com/flex/mx" minWidth="955"↵
 minHeight="600"
applicationComplete="initApp()">
        <fx:Declarations>
                <!-- Place non-visual elements (e.g., services, value objects) here -->
<mx: RemoteObject
id="ro"
destination="peopleCollection"
result="resultHandler(event)"/>

        </fx:Declarations>
<fx:Script>
    <![CDATA[
        import advancedflex4.ch07.remoting.Person;
        import mx.rpc.events.ResultEvent;
        import mx.collections.ArrayCollection;
        import mx.controls.Alert;

        [Bindable]
        private var items:ArrayCollection;

        private function initApp():void
        {
            ro.getPersons();

        }

        private function resultHandler(event:ResultEvent):void
        {
            items = event.result as ArrayCollection;
            var length:int = items.length;

        }
    ]]>
```

```
</fx:Script>
      <mx:DataGrid dataProvider="{items}" />
</s:Application>
```

`RemoteObject` maps to the `PeopleCollection` Java class via a destination, which we configured in `remoting-config.xml`. In the preceding MXML file, we could call the `getPersons` method of the `PeopleCollection` class using the remote object handle. If we wanted to manipulate the data further and manipulate the items in this collection, we could do that, because each of the items in the collection is a `Person` object that has a type association in AS3. In the interest of keeping our focus on the basic mechanics of remoting, I will avoid discussing any details of such business logic. However, the code for the application contains an implementation for updating the collection, adding new items and deleting existing ones, and sorting items in the collection. You can peruse the source code to understand how it's implemented.

Now that you have seen a basic remoting example, the next section builds on this knowledge to cover two important related topics:

- Java to/from AS3 serialization/deserialization
- Asynchronous communication

We will start with serialization and deserialization.

Java to Flex Serialization Basics

The simplest of our examples established that objects get serialized and deserialized between Java and AS3, across the wire. To analyze this subject further, it is appropriate to compare and contrast the available data types in the two languages and see how they map to each other Table 8-1 presents this comparison tersely.

Table 8-1. Juxtaposing AS3 and Java Data Types

AS3	Java
int/uint	Integer
Number	Double
Object	Map
String	String
Boolean	Boolean
Date	java.util.Date
Array (dense)	List
Array (sparse)	Map

XML	org.w3c.dom.Document
flash.utils.ByteArray	byte[]
undefined	null

This table is not exhaustive but should serve as an introductory guide. Here are a few notes to help you understand the mappings:

- Java float, long, BigDecimal, and BigInteger convert to AS3 Number.
- Date, Time, and Timestamp (from the java.sql package) and java.util.Calendar map to AS3 Date.
- In AS3, "true" and "false" strings can also represent a Boolean value.
- Dense arrays are those that have no holes. As an example, if an array has four elements and I put the fifth element at position 9, then in a sparse array (the opposite of a dense array) there will be no values, what I call holes, in position 4 to 8. ActionScript sparse arrays tally with java.util.Map to avoid sending null values across.
- Depending on the interface type at the Java end, a dense ActionScript array maps to an implementation type. For example, List and Collection become ArrayList, Set becomes HashSet, and SortedSet becomes TreeSet.
- Typed associations can be established between custom types with the help of corresponding bean type classes on each side and the [RemoteClass] metadata tag. Our simple example uses such a mapping.

In the case of custom type associations, it's possible to include extra properties in the bean type object as far as the existing ones on the source (i.e., the server) match the other properties in the ActionScript type. For example, you may have an object represent an order with a single line item. In such an object, you may want the serializable object to contain the unit price of the item and the quantity of the item, but not the total value (which is essentially a product of the other two properties). You may want the AS3 type to have a third property to hold the total value, which you could calculate by multiplying the other two property values. If you did this and made this AS3 object the associated counterpart of the Java object (which effectively has one property less), nothing would break; everything will still work fine. It's advisable to follow this technique and reduce the serialization overhead, especially when derived and calculated values are involved.

Serialization and deserialization with transmission over AMF is a very efficient process and beats almost all other transmission alternatives.

I mentioned earlier on that I would be covering two more special topics related to remoting. This section dealt with one, and now we will move on to the other—asynchronous communication, the only style that Flex adopts.

Asynchronous Communication

All types of communication in the Flex framework are asynchronous. This has its advantages but also poses some challenges. To list a few, some advantages are as follows:

- Calls are nonblocking and therefore resources are not held up.
- Asynchronous communication and events go well together and help create loosely coupled systems.
- This type of communication allows clean separation of duties: the call invoker and the response receiver could be different entities.
- The sequence in which calls are issued, or their linearity, have little significance, and so there is usually no need to queue calls.

No choice has advantages without disadvantages. The disadvantages of asynchronous communication are often caused by the same things that make it advantageous. A few common challenges of asynchronous communication are as follows:

- Transaction management is not trivial because we are not talking about call and response in the same cycle. To roll back, it's important to have a common token to relate back to the event.
- Flows that need calls in a linear order need to be managed externally.
- In many cases, the invoker has little control over the response, i.e., when it arrives and how it is handled.

A common established way to manage asynchronous communication is to espouse the Asynchronous Completion Token (ACT) pattern, which originated at the Department of Computer Science and Engineering at Washington University in St. Louis. This pattern's universal applicability in the area of asynchronous communication caused it to become popular rather quickly. You can find a description and an explanation of the pattern online at http://www.cs.wustl.edu/~schmidt/PDF/ACT.pdf.

The Flex framework adopts ACT ideas natively in its framework constructs. Almost all asynchronous communication in Flex follows this pattern:

- A call is made and an asynchronous token is returned.
- Every response dispatches events, indicating either success or failure.
- Event listeners are registered with the object that is capable of receiving the response. Sometimes the implementation of a marker interface makes a class eligible to receive responses.
- When a response arrives, events are dispatched. The response comes back with the asynchronous token. Call and response are correlated using this token.
- The appropriate handler gets the response. On receipt, it processes the response.

By default, a call is dispatched as soon as it's made, and there is never any certainty about when the response will come. Let's take a simple example of an editable collection in a data grid, where this behavior could make our life difficult. Say we have a few rows of data. Now we select one of the rows of data and edit the values, and then we do the same with another row. When we are editing the second row, we realize our first row modification wasn't accurate, and so we need to revisit it. Under normal circumstances, the first row modification call has already been dispatched by now, and rolling back the modification is cumbersome. This situation can get more complex if our operation deletes a row and we need to recover it, or if we make two modifications to the same data element and the first modification completes after the second one. In general, to take care of these types of complexities, we need to allow the following:

- Sequencing of calls in some order
- Batching of calls into a logical bundle

- Locking of data elements, where applicable
- Definition of transactional boundaries to facilitate commit and rollback

In LCDS, the data management module takes care of these complicated scenarios, but in most other cases you need to take care of this yourself.

Extending Data Services for Advanced Remoting Use Cases

You have seen the basics of remoting to simple Java classes, which a few years back were given the interesting name of Plain Old Java Objects (POJOs). Now let's look at a couple of advanced use cases.

Supporting Additional Data Types

Although AS3 and Java are strikingly similar in programming style, static type system, and syntax, the mapping between AS3 and Java objects is far from optimal. One of the key reasons for this is the lack of AS3 parallels for many Java data types, a glaring example of which can be seen in the two languages' collection types. Java has many advanced collection data types, whereas AS3 has very few. For example, there is no equivalent of a SortedSet in AS3. Even if such data types were added to AS3, how could they be mapped to the existing Java data types? There is no way of translating automatically between the two. For instance, a strongly typed enumerated type can be created in AS3 to resemble a Java 5 Enum, but it's by no means easy to ensure that serialization and deserialization happen between the two smoothly.

Adding support for additional data types is possible but not trivial. In order to understand the path to this addition, it's important to understand the PropertyProxy interface. PropertyProxy in the flex.messaging.io package allows customized serialization and deserialization of complex objects. It has access to each of the steps in the serialization and the deserialization process. During serialization, a PropertyProxy is asked to provide the class name, its properties, and its peculiarities. During deserialization, a PropertyProxy instantiates an object instance and sets the property values. PropertyProxy is a higher-order interface that has been implemented for many different data types In the BlazeDS Javadocs, you will see the following classes implementing the PropertyProxy interface:

- AbstractProxy
- BeanProxy
- DictionaryProxy
- MapProxy
- PageableRowSetProxy
- SerializationProxy
- StatusInfoProxy
- ThrowableProxy

When adding support for a specific new data type, you could start by either implementing the PropertyProxy for that type or extending one of its available implementations.

Creating Custom Factories

Data services (both LCDS and BlazeDS) can load and instantiate simple Java classes without a problem. However, they don't work without modification if the remote object is a managed object like an EJB or a Spring bean. This is only natural, because these data services cannot automatically instantiate these objects. Managed objects are instantiated, maintained, and garbage collected within the managed environment or container they reside in. If these objects need to be consumed within data services, they warrant a factory mechanism, which can get hold of a managed object instance and make it accessible within a data service namespace.

The custom factory varies depending on how the managed object is accessed. Both LCDS and BlazeDS include a so-called factory mechanism to include objects that reside in other namespaces. Theoretically, the idea is simple and goes like this:

1. Implement a common interface, which defines a method to create a factory.

2. Configure this factory creator so that it can be instantiated and used when needed.

3. Pass the name of this configured factory creator to a destination (which points to the managed object), so that it knows which factory to use to get hold of an object instance.

4. Use the factory to look up an instance of the managed object. Though called a factory, this factory is not really creating anything. It's looking up an instance from a different namespace.

5. Use the object as you would use any other simple Java class. In other words, once bound to a destination and configured, it is ready for RPC.

Practically, most work goes into implementing the lookup method. Start with a custom class and have that custom class implement the `FlexFactory` interface. Implement the three most important methods, namely

- `initialize`: To get the factory instance configured and ready.
- `createFactoryInstance`: To create a `FactoryInstance`
- `lookup`: To return a handle of the object the factory is meant to get hold of

Then configure the factory in `services-config.xml` like this:

```
<factories>
    <factory
id="ejbFactory"
class="flex.samples.factories.EJBFactory"/>
</factories>
```

We configure an EJB factory here. Now we can refer to this factory from within a destination setting. A possible case could be the following:

```
<destination id="MyEJBPoweredService">
    <properties>
        <factory>ejbFactory</factory>
        <source>MyUsefulBean</source>
    </properties>
</destination>
```

We have successfully created a custom factory and it's ready for use. Once again, I show only the logic that helps you learn the topic at hand—namely, creating custom factories.

This chapter has covered a fair bit on remoting, although it has merely scratched the surface. Next, I give you a look at the second most important feature of BlazeDS: messaging.

Messaging and Real-time Updates

Flex reconfirms the supremacy of event-driven systems. It thrives on asynchronous communication, and it defines the loosely coupled robustness that excites all of us to create fascinating applications using it. A concept that goes hand in hand with events and asynchronous communication is message-driven communication. Flex includes it in its repertoire of core features.

Messaging in Flex, with its adapters and channels, makes it possible to push data up from a server or a client to another client. Although today data push can be done in Java using the Java NIO Comet technique, the BlazeDS messaging-based data push provides an easy option to create rich, engaging, real-time event-driven systems. More information on Java NIO and Comet can be obtained from the following links:

- http://en.wikipedia.org/wiki/New_I/O
- http://en.wikipedia.org/wiki/Comet_(programming)

Essential Messaging and Pushing Data

To understand messaging in Flex, we will dive into a sample application first and then explore the different aspects of the model in the light of the application. The application is a collaborative form that is filled in by two users at the same time. Changes on either side are propagated to the other one. A possible use case could be travel booking by a customer in association with an agent, where the agent assists in real time by validating the data and adding expertise to find the best deal.

There are two main roles in the world of messaging: message producer and message consumer. A *message producer*, as the name suggests, produces messages, and a *message consumer* consumes messages. Our collaborative application acts as both a producer and a consumer. As a producer, it sends all updates out as messages. Subscribed consumers receive these messages and process them. The collaborative application is used by two users, although in its current shape the application itself doesn't restrict the number of users collaborating simultaneously. Each instance of the application acts as both consumer and producer, so an instance acting as a consumer receives its own messages, sent in the capacity of a producer. Updates, when applied to the producing instance, have no impact because the data is already present there; after all, it's the source of the updates.

In a real-life situation, you may want to bind these roles to specific parts of the form and have logic to skip and apply updates, but here we adopt the most elementary approach. You can get hold of the code and extend it to include any or all of these features.

Our collaborative application is in a single MXML file, which appears as shown here:

```
<?xml version="1.0" encoding="utf-8"?>
<s:Application xmlns:fx="http://ns.adobe.com/mxml/2009"
                    xmlns:s="library://ns.adobe.com/flex/spark"
                    xmlns:mx="library://ns.adobe.com/flex/mx" minWidth="955"↵
 minHeight="600" applicationComplete="initApp()">
<fx:Script>
        <![CDATA[
            import mx.messaging.messages.*;
            import mx.messaging.events.*;

            private function processUserFormInput↵
```

```
(uName:String, uRequest:String):void {
                /* Set first message parameter to */
/* identify the message sender: a user or an agent */
                sendMessage("user",uName, uRequest);
        }

        private function processAgentFormInput↵
(aName:String, aComments:String):void {
                sendMessage("agent",aName, aComments);
        }

        private function initApp():void {
            consumer.subscribe();
        }

        private function messageHandler(event: MessageEvent):void {
            var paramArray:Array = (event.message.body).split(":");
            if(paramArray[0] == "user") {
                userName = paramArray[1];
                userRequest = paramArray[2];
            }else if(paramArray[0] == "agent") {
                agentName = paramArray[1];
                agentComments = paramArray[2];
            }

        }

        private function sendMessage↵
(param0:String,param1:String, param2:String):void {
                var message: AsyncMessage = new AsyncMessage();
                message.body = param0 + ":" + param1 + ": " + param2;
                producer.send(message);
        }
    ]]>
    </fx:Script>
<fx:Declarations>
            <!-- Place non-visual elements (e.g., services, value objects) here -->
<mx:Producer id="producer" destination="CollaborationTopic"/>
    <mx:Consumer id="consumer"
destination="CollaborationTopic"
message="messageHandler(event)"/>

        </fx:Declarations>

    <mx:Form id="collaborativeForm1" defaultButton="{updateUserInput}">
        <mx:FormItem label="User Name">
            <mx:TextInput id="userName"/>
        </mx:FormItem>
        <mx:FormItem label="User Request">
            <mx:TextInput id="userRequest"/>
        </mx:FormItem>
        <mx:FormItem>
            <mx:Button label="Update User Inputs" id="updateUserInput"
```

```
            click="processUserFormInput↵
(userName.text, userRequest.text);"/>
        </mx:FormItem>
    </mx:Form>
    <mx:Form
id="collaborativeForm2"
defaultButton="{updateAgentInput}">
        <mx:FormItem label="Agent Name">
            <mx:TextInput id="agentName"/>
        </mx:FormItem>
        <mx:FormItem label="Agent Comments">
            <mx:TextInput id="agentComments"/>
        </mx:FormItem>
        <mx:FormItem>
            <mx:Button label="Update Agent Input" id="updateAgentInput"
                click="processAgentFormInput↵
(agentName.text, agentComments.text);"/>
        </mx:FormItem>
    </mx:Form>
</s:Application>
```

The most interesting new controls in the preceding code are those that relate to a producer and a consumer. The `Producer` and the `Consumer` point to a server-side destination, which (as you will have noticed) have the same value. Data services provide messaging services, which are accessible through destinations like the remoting services. Most data services support the two main messaging domains: point-to-point and publish-and-subscribe. Point-to-point messaging is about sending messages from one queue to the other. Publish-and-subscribe messaging is a way of distributing information where topics act as the central conduit. Consumers subscribe to a topic, and producers send messages to it. All subscribed consumers receive all the messages.

Although the concept of messaging domains and the related roles are fairly universal, each programming language or platform has its own set of frameworks and tools to handle them. In Java, messaging is defined by a specification called Java Message Service (JMS). BlazeDS has the ability to plug in adapters to process messages using custom parsers, formatters, and message handlers. By default, it includes adapters for AS3 and JMS. This example does not involve any communication with JMS or Java, but it is restricted to two or more Flex clients, and so utilizes the ActionScript adapter Here is the configuration snippet from `messaging-config.xml`, which may explain things a bit further:

```
<service id="message-service"
    class="flex.messaging.services.MessageService"
    messageTypes="flex.messaging.messages.AsyncMessage">
    <adapters>
        <adapter-definition id="actionscript"
        class="flex.messaging.services.messaging.
            adapters.ActionScriptAdapter" default="true"/>
        <adapter-definition id="jms"
            class="flex.messaging.services.↵
messaging.adapters.JMSAdapter"/>
    </adapters>

    <destination id=" CollaborationTopic">

    <adapter ref="actionscript"/>
```

```
    <properties>
        <server>
            <max-cache-size>1000</max-cache-size>
            <message-time-to-live>0</message-time-to-live>
            <durable>true</durable>
            <durable-store-manager>
                flex.messaging.durability.FileStoreManager
            </durable-store-manager>
        </server>
        <network>
            <session-timeout>0</session-timeout>
            <throttle-inbound policy="ERROR" max-frequency="50"/>
            <throttle-outbound policy="REPLACE" max-frequency="500"/>
        </network>
    </properties>

    <channels>
        <channel ref="samples-rtmp"/>
        <channel ref="samples-amf-polling"/>
    </channels>
    </destination>
</service>
```

This configuration file is divided into three parts to make it easier for you to understand the details part by part and not get consumed in the complexity of a large configuration file. The three parts are as follows:

- Adapters
- Channels
- Destinations

Configuring a message service is not very different from configuring any other service, such as remoting or data management.

Two types of adapters are defined in this configuration. One is for ActionScript and the other is for JMS. The collaborative form destination uses the ActionScript adapter. Destinations use the channels to communicate, and send and receive messages. Channels are abstractions that bundle a protocol and an endpoint. Besides these, a destination can take a few properties to define its behavior. The preceding snippet has settings for the following properties:

- Server: Parameters affecting the storage of messages can be defined here. Maximum cache size, file size, file store root, and durability are typical parameters.
- Network: Timeout and inbound and outbound throttle policies can be set here.

This quick example should have established the elegant message features available with data services. Different data services implement message push differently. Protocols vary. LCDS uses RTMP to stream messages, BlazeDS relies on AMF polling, and GDS uses Java NIO Comet. In all cases, the feature itself is very useful. We built a trivial example, but sophisticated real-time applications can be built on the basis of a reliable message infrastructure.

Before we close this discussion on messaging, we will look at integration with JMS and highlight the performance criteria that may be of paramount importance in production applications. You will also learn how to write a custom message adapter.

Messaging and JMS We will now take our last example the collaborative form, and transform it into a real-time negotiation application. The negotiation involves two parties, a buyer and a seller. A buyer makes a bid and specifies the preferred price and quantity. A seller makes a bid by stating the desired price and the quantity. The matchmaking part of the negotiation is not included here. It's assumed the two parties go back and forth with a few bids and offers and finally close on a price and quantity that is acceptable to both. To keep the negotiation process neutral and unbiased, information about the last price at which somebody else traded is displayed in real time. We assume the system that collates and emits the last trade price is a Java application and is capable of sending these prices out as JMS messages. In the current context, how we consume this external data within our application is the main agenda. The Flex application consumes JMS messages with the help of data services, which rely on the JMS adapter to receive and send messages to JMS.

The application interface is simple and could look like Figure 8-8 on startup. We are assuming the JMS subscription triggers on creation being complete, and so we have fetched some data already.

Figure 8-8. A view of the negotiation application at startup

The code behind this application is equally simple, and its structure is as follows:

```
<?xml version="1.0" encoding="utf-8"?>
<s:Application xmlns:fx="http://ns.adobe.com/mxml/2009"
                    xmlns:s="library://ns.adobe.com/flex/spark"
                    xmlns:mx="library://ns.adobe.com/flex/mx" minWidth="955"↵
 minHeight="600" applicationComplete="init()App">
<fx:Script>
        <![CDATA[
           import mx.messaging.events.MessageEvent;

           private function processBid(zip:String, pn:String):void {
               // Process the Bid ?
               //match it with the average last trade and the ask
           }

           private function processAsk(zip:String, pn:String):void {
               // Process the Ask ?
               //match it with the average last trade and the bid
```

```
        }

        [Bindable]
        var lastTradeValue:String = "USD 99.99";

        private function messageHandler(event:MessageEvent):void {
            // Get the message and process it
            // set the value of lastTradeValue
            //based on the received message
        }

        private function initApp():void {
            //consumer.subscribe();
        }
    ]]>
  </fx:Script>
<fx:Declarations>
            <!-- Place non-visual elements (e.g., services, value objects) here -->
<!-- <mx:Consumer id="consumer"
destination="lastTradePrice"
message="messageHandler(event)" /> -->

    </fx:Declarations>
    <s:Panel
        horizontalCenter="0"
        verticalCenter="0">

<mx:Form id="buyerBid" defaultButton="{submitBid}">
    <mx:FormItem label="Bid Quantity">
        <mx:TextInput id="bidQuantity"/>
    </mx:FormItem>
    <mx:FormItem label="Bid Price">
        <mx:TextInput id="bidPrice"/>
    </mx:FormItem>
    <mx:FormItem>
        <mx:Button label="Submit Bid" id="submitBid"
            click="processBid(bidQuantity.text, bidPrice.text);"/>
    </mx:FormItem>
</mx:Form>

<mx:Form id="sellerAsk" defaultButton="{submitAsk}">
    <mx:FormItem label="Ask Quantity">
        <mx:TextInput id="askQuantity"/>
    </mx:FormItem>
    <mx:FormItem label="Ask Price">
        <mx:TextInput id="askPrice"/>
    </mx:FormItem>
    <mx:FormItem>
        <mx:Button label="Submit Ask" id="submitAsk"
            click="processAsk(askQuantity.text, askPrice.text);"/>
    </mx:FormItem>
</mx:Form>
<mx:Label
```

```
text="Last Trade Price: {lastTradeValue}"
textAlign="center"
fontWeight="bold" />
    </s:Panel>
</s:Application>
```

The highlight of this example isn't the application functionality but the integration with JMS, so we jump to the configuration file to see how that was made to work smoothly Here is the snippet of `messaging-config.xml`:

```
<?xml version="1.0" encoding="UTF-8"?>
<service
id="message-service"
class="flex.messaging.services.MessageService">
    <adapters>
        <adapter-definition
id="actionscript"
class="flex.messaging.services.messaging.↵
adapters.ActionScriptAdapter"
default="true" />
        <adapter-definition
id="jms"
class="flex.messaging.services.↵
messaging.adapters.JMSAdapter"/>

</adapters>
    <default-channels>
<channel ref="my-streaming-amf"/>
<channel ref="my-polling-amf"/>
    </default-channels>
 <destination id="dashboard_chat">
 <properties>
   <server>
<durable>false</durable>
   </server>
   <jms>
     <destination-type>Topic</destination-type>
<message-type>javax.jms.TextMessage</message-type>
<connection-factory>ConnectionFactory</connection-factory>
<destination-jndi-name>topic/testTopic</destination-jndi-name>
<delivery-mode>NON_PERSISTENT</delivery-mode>
<message-priority>DEFAULT_PRIORITY</message-priority>
<acknowledge-mode>AUTO_ACKNOWLEDGE</acknowledge-mode>
<transacted-sessions>false</transacted-sessions>
  </jms>
 </properties>

<channels>
    <channel ref="my-polling-amf"/>
</channels>
 <adapter ref="jms"/>
 </destination>
```

```
</service>
```

JMS defines extensive possibilities for message durability, acknowledgements, and message filtering. Data services extend most of those features to Flex. The default JMS adapter in BlazeDS and LCDS supports these features.

In the preceding example, we send text messages, but it's also possible to send object messages. Data services remoting works in association with messaging to serialize and deserialize between Java and ActionScript.

JMS in Flex started out by supporting only publish-and-subscribe messaging, but point-to-point communication has now been included. The Flex framework also includes filters and subtopics to allow fine-grained and rule-based message filtering. The Consumer control has a selector property to filter messages, which takes a string value. SQL expressions can also be defined to filter messages. For example, to filter messages based on headerProp, a header property, you could have a criterion like this:

```
headerProp > someNumericalValue
```

Message headers are accessible via a message handle. They are stored as an associative array and can be modified as required. It's also possible to add newer members to this hash. For example:

```
var message:AsyncMessage = new AsyncMessage();
message.headers = new Array();
message.headers["newProp"] = newValue;
```

This was just a part of the code but it confirms that arbitrary numbers of header manipulations are possible with messages. Selector tags operate only on the headers and not on the message body.

An alternative to using selectors is to use subtopics. Whereas a selector evaluates every message through an expression, a subtopic creates subcategories within a destination. The subcategories can be created using specific names. Before sending a message out, a producer sets the subtopic. A small code snippet might look like this:

```
var message:AsyncMessage = new AsyncMessage();
producer.subtopic = "subTopicLevel1.subTopicLevel2.subTopicLevel3 ";
producer.send(message);
```

A consumer sets the subtopic at the time of subscription. A subtopic is set before the subscribe method is called. Following is an example code snippet that does this:

```
consumer.destination = "ConfiguredDestination";
consumer.subtopic = " subTopicLevel1.subTopicLevel2.subTopicLevel3";
consumer.subscribe();
```

It's possible to use wildcards with subtopics For example, there may be multiple subtopics at level 2, and you may want to receive messages that fall in all those subcategories. In that case, instead of subscribing to each of them individually, you could subscribe to subTopicLevel1.* and get the same effect.

By now, you know the message service is a useful feature and provides fairly sophisticated ways to build complex applications. You are also familiar with the built-in adapters that work behind the scenes to create robust integration points. Despite these features, the variety of messaging styles and infrastructure requires the ability to write custom adapters to work with scenarios beyond ActionScript and JMS.

The good news is that BlazeDS and LCDS provide a clean and simple API to write custom adapters.

Writing Custom Message Adapters

Writing a custom message adapter involves the following steps:

1. Use the BlazeDS (or LCDS) API to write a custom message adapter.

2. Configure the adapter in `services-config.xml` so that destinations can use it.

3. Refer to this custom adapter in a message destination.

4. Create producers and consumers and send and receive messages using this custom adapter.

I will focus on the first two of these four steps. Also, when I talk about writing the adapter, I will focus on the API and the requirements and not delve into implementation of any specific behavior.

All message adapters in BlazeDS extend directly or indirectly from `flex.messaging.services.ServiceAdapter`. `MessagingAdapter` is the base class for publish-and-subscribe messaging, and it inherits directly from the `ServiceAdapter`. Depending on the desired behavior, and therefore potential reusability of `MessagingAdapter` implementation, you can choose to start with either the `ServiceAdapter` or the `MessagingAdapter`.

All adapters are required to implement the `invoke` method, which is invoked on receipt of a message. The `invoke` method is expected to take a `Message` object and return an `Object` type. It's common to use the `AsyncMessage` class as the class that implements the `Message` interface.

In the ActionScript adapter, the `invoke` method sends the message out to all subscribers by calling the `pushMessageToClients` method. This is the custom behavior that you need to implement depending on what you expect from the adapter.

The `MessagingAdapter` class also defines a few other methods, including those that help initialize it, allow subtopics, and set security constraints. The `initialize` method takes two arguments: a string ID and a `ConfigMap` object. What you define in the `services-config.xml` or its associated configuration files becomes available via the `ConfigMap` object. You have seen JMS adapter–specific property settings in the last example. You can similarly set properties to your custom adapter. For example, you may call your custom adapter `customAdapter` and have its properties within the `<customAdapter>` `</customAdapter>` XML tags. The `initialize` method will be able to get all the properties from such an XML node and will be able to initialize the adapter as you instruct it to.

Writing a custom adapter is a large topic and could fill up an entire chapter, if not a small book; however, I have walked you through the essentials and will stop at that. Before moving on, I would like to mention an open source initiative called dsadapters that I launched a few months back to provide adapters for many common messaging situations and platforms. The project is online at `http://code.google.com/p/dsadapters/`. You might find your desired custom adapter in this project and thus save yourself some time and energy.

Advanced Issues in Messaging

This section picks up an assortment of topics that pertain to advanced messaging concepts. In none of these do I get under the hood. The text only briefly surveys the topics and gives you a preview of some ideas that lie ahead.

Pushing over Sockets

As discussed in the last chapter, it's possible to create socket connections over TCP/IP to an external host and port as long as the security restrictions are satisfied. If the messaging entities (i.e., producers and consumers) are available over a unique network address, creating the connection would be effortless. Socket connections can be of two types: those that transmit text and XML data, and those that transmit binary data. It may be possible to use sockets with binary data to push data efficiently. However, there are drawbacks to this approach, namely the following:

- Non-HTTP ports could have restrictions across a firewall.
- The scalability is seriously suspect, as each logical connection maps to a physical connection.

Therefore, though sockets may be a possibility, it is probably wiser to stick with data services.

Connection Scalability

LCDS uses RTMP to push data, whereas BlazeDS uses AMF polling to send the data through to the client. In AMF polling, data push, though possible, is not scalable. It has limitations because of inefficiencies in the mechanism. BlazeDS does not have RTMP and probably never will, unless RTMP becomes open source.

In the meanwhile, you could use Comet-style persistent connections to push data. The Servlet 3.0 specification is trying to come up with a uniform standard to create HTTP 1.1–style persistent connections for data push using the NIO-based framework Comet. However, even before the specification is ready and accepted, the Apache foundation has already implemented a way to do this in Apache Tomcat. The Jetty team has achieved similar success.

For BlazeDS to use this scalable option, the message broker servlet needs to be modified to listen to Comet events. That way a blocked long-polling connection can be created with no threads being utilized on the server. Such connections can easily scale and have up to 30,000 or more connections on a single 64-bit machine.

Transactions

Message-based systems can support transactions and allow for explicit commit and rollback. With JMS, it's possible to have transactions in a messaging session or have more robust arrangements with the help of the Java Transaction API (JTA). In data services such as LCDS and BlazeDS, it's possible to use a JMS *transacted session*. A transacted session supports transactions within a session. Therefore, a rollback in a transacted session will roll back all the sends and receives in that session. However, it will have no impact on transactions that are outside of the session. In other words, if the JMS messages interacting with Flex also affect a transaction in another enterprise application or the database, a rollback will only impact the JMS session and not these external systems.

Turning this feature on is as simple as setting the `transacted-sessions` value in the configuration file to `true`. This is what it looks like:

```
<jms>
....
    <transacted-sessions>true</transacted-sessions>
....
</jms>
```

Using Server-side Proxies

HTTPService and WebService were covered in enough detail in the last chapter. There we emphasized that these services promote loose coupling and can be used to access data in a Flash Player independent of a server infrastructure. The only mandatory requirement was that the external host provide a cross-domain security policy definition. This requirement was never a concern if the host already had a crossdomain.xml file allowing access or if it was possible to request the host maintainers to put one in place. However, in the vast expanse of the World Wide Web, it's not always possible for such a good arrangement to be in place. In situations where we are unable to access data from an external host due to security restrictions, it's viable to fetch it via data services. In this role, data services provide the proxy service for HTTPService and WebService components.

The server-side configurations for proxy settings are made in the proxy-config.xml file. This file is included by reference in services-config.xml. The HTTPService sends HTTP requests down to the proxy, and the WebService sends SOAP web service calls down to the proxy. In either case, we need a service adapter to take these requests and translate them into the final call. For example, an HTTP request needs to end up with a URL invocation. You saw messaging service adapters in the context of messaging. The service adapters for HTTP and web service proxies implement a similar set of classes to create a service adapter. Default HTTP proxy and SOAP web service proxy adapters are available in BlazeDS.

For HTTPService, you can define a URL for the proxy setting or set up a set of dynamic URL(s) that are resolved to the appropriate URL based on the URL value set in the client-side HTTP call. For web services, you define either the WSDL URL or the SOAP endpoint URL pattern. These URL configurations are done with destination configuration. It's also possible, especially with HTTPService, to define a default destination and have a set of dynamic URLs with it. Then every HTTPService call via data services is routed through this destination to the HTTP proxy adapter.

The proxy service itself can be configured with a number of properties. We present a sample of the configuration file available in the distribution and in the documentation and explain the properties in context. Here is the sample configuration:

```
<service
id="proxy-service"
class="flex.messaging.services.HTTPProxyService">
    <properties>
        <connection-manager>
            <max-total-connections>100</max-total-connections>
            <default-max-connections-per-host>
2</default-max-connections-per-host>
</connection-manager>
<!-- Allow self-signed certificates;
should not be used in production -->
        <allow-lax-ssl>true</allow-lax-ssl>
        <external-proxy>
            <server>10.10.10.10</server>
            <port>3128</port>
            <nt-domain>mycompany</nt-domain>
            <username>flex</username>
            <password>flex</password>
            </external-proxy>
</properties>
</service>
```

The HTTP proxy adapter in BlazeDS uses the Apache `HttpClient` as the user agent. The configuration `max-total-connections` translates to the use of a multithreaded concurrent connections manager for `HttpClient`. `max-connections-per-host` sets the default number of connections if the host supports hardware clustering. The `allow-lax-ssl` true value means self-signed certificates will work. If the connection to the host is made through an external proxy, the external proxy can be specified in the configuration file as well. Authentication credentials like the password can be passed to the external proxy.

Additional Useful Data Services Tips

Data services are useful and extensible pieces of software. You have seen how they can be extended to support additional features with the help of custom factories and custom service adapters. What I discuss next are the interesting features around run-time configuration and application security that data services offer.

Configuring at Run Time

So far, almost all the configurations I have spoken about have related to compile-time configuration, where the entries are made in the configuration files. However, it's also possible to make many of these configurations and settings at run time. Run-time configuration makes systems more flexible and amenable to tweaking at the time of use. At run time, you can define channels, create consumers, set up subscriptions, and affect destination configurations. However, I only show you one of these possibilities here: channel definitions.

Defining channels at run time At run time, channels can be created on the client with the help of a `ChannelSet` object, which may contain one or more `Channel` objects. Essentially, the process is first to create a `ChannelSet` object and then dynamically create channels and add channels to it. After this, the channel set is associated with the `channelSet` property of the `RemoteObject`. This is what a sample piece of code may look like:

```
var cs:ChannelSet = new ChannelSet();
var newChannel:Channel = new AMFChannel("my-amf", endpointUrl);
cs.addChannel(newChannel);
remoteObject.channelSet = cs;
```

The endpoint URL can be defined dynamically at run time. `ChannelSet` has the ability to search among the set of configured channels. Each channel can define a failover URL.

Application Security

In many cases, especially in enterprise scenarios, you may need to restrict access to server-side destinations. It's possible to define a secure destination without much trouble. Data service configurations allow definitions for both authentication and authorization. *Authentication* means confirming one's identity, and *authorization* relates to the server-side resources that an authenticated user can access.

Security is configured using security constraints. These constraints can be defined at multiple levels, namely the following:

- Global: One set of definitions for all destinations. Usually such configuration would reside in the common configuration area: within `services-config.xml` itself.
- Destination specific: Security constraints for a destination. You can define such constraints inline within the destination configuration tags.

- Fine-grained: For remoting destinations, you could create an include list by using multiple `include-method` tags (or using the `exclude-method` tag). Such lists will ensure that only the included methods are callable on the remote destinations. Calling any other method would cause an error.

Authentication mechanisms can be custom or basic. This implies that you could leverage your existing authentication systems using the custom route.

Following is an example of a destination-level configuration that uses custom authentication:

```
<destination id="ro">
    <security>
        <security-constraint>
            <auth-method>Custom</auth-method>
            <roles>
                <role>roUser</role>
            </roles>
        </security-constraint>
    </security>
</destination>
```

`HTTPService`, `WebService`, and `RemoteObject` support passing and invalidation of login credentials using the `setCredentials` and the `logout` methods, respectively. You can also pass credentials to remote services using `setRemoteCredentials`.

A simple example of `setCredentials` with `RemoteObject` is as follows:

```
var myRemoteObject:RemoteObject = new RemoteObject();
myRemoteObject.destination = "SecureDestination";
myRemoteObject.setCredentials("userName", "myPassword");
myRemoteObject.send({param1: 'param1Value'});
```

Implementing custom security and setting up fine-grained access control can be tedious, but with BlazeDS you can utilize such constructs without adding any additional overhead.

Summary

This chapter rapidly covered a fair number of topics related to data services.

The chapter started with an overview of the data services architecture. Then you explored the steps involved in installing data services and configuring it. Subsequently you built an example application and saw data services in action.

The review of the features of data services topics included Java to Flex serialization, asynchronous communication, support for additional data types, custom adapters, connection scalability, data push over sockets, and transactions. Server-side proxy and its usage for HTTP-based calls as well as web services were also illustrated.

Data services positions the Adobe Flex and AIR technologies as viable choices for some serious applications for the present and the future. In the age of event-driven, real-time, responsive rich systems, where the Web is transforming itself into a read-write media network, technologies as these are bound to shine.

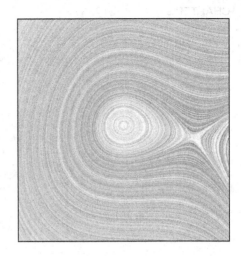

Chapter 9

Talking with JavaScript and HTML: Web Page Integration

by Elad Elrom

There are many cases where you need integration of your Flex applications with JavaScript. For instance, you want to leverage existing JavaScript code in conjunction with your Flex application or you want a better Search Engine Optimization (SEO) by creating part of the page in HTML/JavaScript while integrating a Flex Widget or component.

This chapter will cover JavaScript integration—both in the sense of JavaScript getting called by your Flex application and having the JavaScript on the page call the Flex application code. We will also cover a real life example of a widget using JavaScript integration and leveraging Runtime Shared Libraries (RSL) technology in Flash 9/10 and Flex to build Flash applications small enough to be widgets.

Hacking the Flash Builder Page Template

Since a lot of the work you will be doing in this chapter involves JavaScript, you are going to be messing around with the HTML of the page. Flash Builder 4 maintains an HTML template for your application in the `html-template` directory. This file is shown in Figure 9-1.

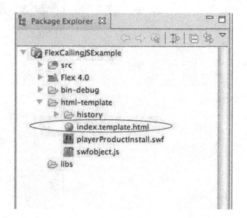

Figure 9-1. The HTML page template

We recommend installing an Eclipse plug-in for JavaScript called JSEclipse.

From the top menu select: **Help ➤ Software updates ➤ Find and install... ➤ New Remote Site...**

Name: **JSEclipse**

URL: `http://download.macromedia.com/pub/labs/jseclipse/autoinstall/`

See Figure 9-2.

Figure 9-2. Add a remote site properties window

After the plug-in is installed, it will take ownership over different file types such as the HTML and JS extensions. Click to open the `index.html` file. Don't edit the `index.html` file in `bin-debug` or `bin-release`. That file is written over each time the application is compiled, so all of your changes will be lost.

Flex Calling JavaScript

The first type of connection between Flex and JavaScript to explore is a Flex application calling out to a JavaScript function. This is handy when you want to integrate some interactive component within the Flex application with another element on the web page. For example, if you use a Flex component to do navigation and you want the JavaScript on the page to use Ajax to dynamically load a section of content, you will want that Flex component to tell you whenever customers have chosen to view some content.

The first example is a fairly arbitrary one. There is a `List` control with a set of values, so when the customer double-clicks a value, the JavaScript function `itemSelected` is called. This code is shown in the following:

```
<?xml version="1.0" encoding="utf-8"?>
<s:Application xmlns:fx="http://ns.adobe.com/mxml/2009"
               xmlns:s="library://ns.adobe.com/flex/spark"
               xmlns:mx="library://ns.adobe.com/flex/mx"
               minWidth="1024" minHeight="768">

    <fx:Script>
        <![CDATA[

            private function onDoubleClick(event:Event):void
            {
                ExternalInterface.call("itemSelected", list.selectedItem );
            }

        ]]>
    </fx:Script>

    <s:List id="list" width="300"
            doubleClick="onDoubleClick(event);"
            doubleClickEnabled="true">

        <s:dataProvider>
            <s:ArrayCollection>
                <fx:String>Apples</fx:String>
                <fx:String>Oranges</fx:String>
                <fx:String>Bananas</fx:String>
            </s:ArrayCollection>
        </s:dataProvider>

    </s:List>

</s:Application>
```

The magic is performed by the Flash Player API's `ExternalInterface` class, which does the work of connecting to JavaScript and registering methods that can be called by JavaScript. In this case, you use the `call` method on the `ExternalInterface` class to call a JavaScript method with the currently selected item's text.

The JavaScript code that responds to this is as follows:

```
<script>
function itemSelected( itemName )
{
    alert( itemName );
}
</script>
```

If you were to stop and run the example at this point, you would get a security violation from the player reading **SecurityError: Error #2060: Security sandbox violation** (see Figure 9-3).

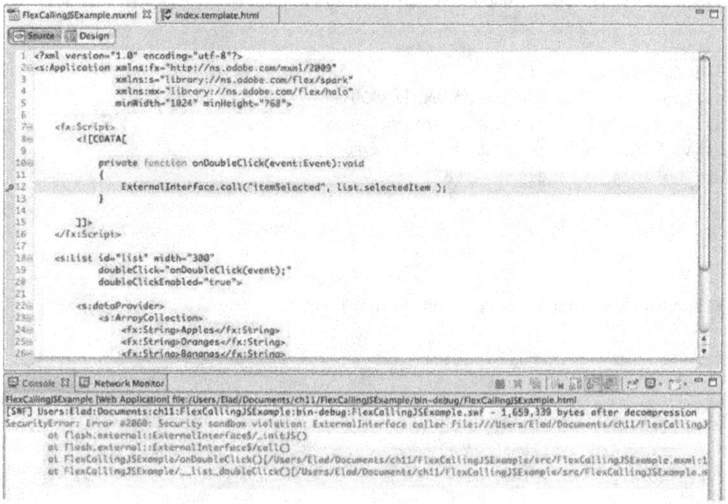

Figure 9-3. Console producing a security sandbox violation error

To get JavaScript and Flash to talk together, you have to change every location in the `index.template.html` file that references `allowScriptAccess` to `always`. The following code is an example portion:

```
            <param name="movie" value="${swf}.swf" />
            <param name="quality" value="high" />

               <param name="bgcolor" value="${bgcolor}" />

             <param name="allowScriptAccess" value="always" />

             <param name="allowFullScreen" value="true" />

         <!--[if !IE]>
            <object type="application/x-shockwave-flash" data="${swf}.swf"↩
width="${width}" height="${height}">
                <param name="quality" value="high" />
```

```
<param name="bgcolor" value="${bgcolor}" />
<param name="allowScriptAccess" value="always" />
<param name="allowFullScreen" value="true" />
```

This means that you are allowing the Flash Player to connect with the JavaScript layer, and vice versa.

Now when you run this from Flash Builder 4, you should see something like Figure 9-4.

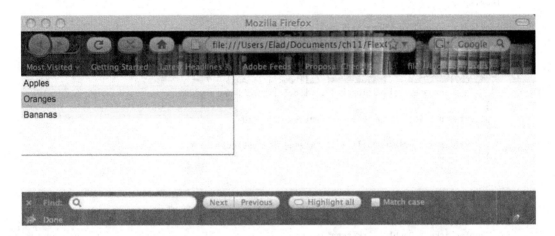

Figure 9-4. The Flex application on the page

Once you double-click an item you will see Figure 9-5.

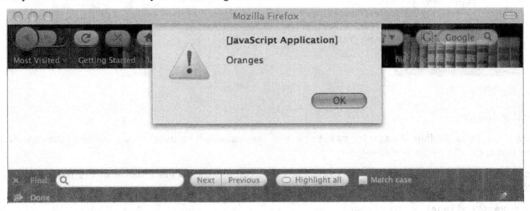

Figure 9-5. The JavaScript callback with the alert

Excellent. Your Flex applications can now talk to the JavaScript layer. But what if you want the JavaScript layer to be able to specify the name of the function to call? Well, in that case, I can specify a parameter to the SWF for the application. That Flex code is shown here:

```
<?xml version="1.0" encoding="utf-8"?>
```

```
<s:Application xmlns:fx="http://ns.adobe.com/mxml/2009"
               xmlns:s="library://ns.adobe.com/flex/spark"
               xmlns:mx="library://ns.adobe.com/flex/mx"
               minWidth="1024" minHeight="768"
               creationComplete="creationCompleteHandler()">

    <fx:Script>
        <![CDATA[

            private var callbackName:String="";

            protected function creationCompleteHandler():void
            {
                callbackName = ( parameters["callback"] != null ) ? ↲
                    parameters["callback"] : "itemSelected";
            }
            private function onDoubleClick(event:Event):void
            {
                ExternalInterface.call(callbackName, list.selectedItem);
            }

        ]]>
    </fx:Script>

    <s:List id="list" width="300"
            doubleClick="onDoubleClick(event);"
            doubleClickEnabled="true">

        <s:dataProvider>
            <s:ArrayCollection>
                <fx:String>Apples</fx:String>
                <fx:String>Oranges</fx:String>
                <fx:String>Bananas</fx:String>
            </s:ArrayCollection>
        </s:dataProvider>

    </s:List>

</s:Application>
```

Now if you pass a different value for `callback`, the new value will be used as the name of the JavaScript function to get the callback message.

You also need to change the `index.template.html` pageto create the Flash with the parameter. This change is shown in Figure 9-6.

```
flashvars.callback = myCallback;
```

```
41
42    <script type="text/javascript" src="swfobject.js"></script>
43    <script type="text/javascript">
44        <!-- For version detection, set to min. required Flash Player version, or 0 (or 0.0.0), for no version detection. -->
45        var swfVersionStr = "${version_major}.${version_minor}.${version_revision}";
46        <!-- To use express install, set to playerProductInstall.swf, otherwise the empty string. -->
47        var xiSwfUrlStr = "${expressInstallSwf}";
48        var flashvars = {};
49        flashvars.callback = myCallback;
50        var params = {};
51        params.quality = "high";
52        params.bgcolor = "${bgcolor}";
53        params.allowscriptaccess = "always";
54        params.allowfullscreen = "true";
55        var attributes = {};
56        attributes.id = "${application}";
57        attributes.name = "${application}";
58        attributes.align = "middle";
59        swfobject.embedSWF(
60            "${swf}.swf", "flashContent",
61            "${width}", "${height}",
62            swfVersionStr, xiSwfUrlStr,
63            flashvars, params, attributes);
64        <!-- JavaScript enabled so display the flashContent div in case it is not replaced with a swf object. -->
65        swfobject.createCSS("#flashContent", "display:block;text-align:left;");
66    </script>
```

Figure 9-6. The update required to index.template.html

Also, you need to change the JavaScript function to match the one you specified to the SWF application.

```
<script>
        function myCallback(item)
        {
                alert( item );
        }
</script>
```

After making all these changes, you can run the example again in Flash Builder 4, and it should look and work exactly the same.

Having shown this connection two questions arise: how many arguments can you send over and how complex can they be? The answer to the first question is as many as you like. As for the second, primitive values (strings, numbers, etc.) all work, as do arrays. Variables of type `Object` can go across as JavaScript associative arrays.

To demonstrate this, we will show one further refinement on the original example. This new code is as follows:

```
<?xml version="1.0" encoding="utf-8"?>
<s:Application xmlns:fx="http://ns.adobe.com/mxml/2009"
               xmlns:s="library://ns.adobe.com/flex/spark"
               xmlns:mx="library://ns.adobe.com/flex/mx"
               minWidth="1024" minHeight="768">

    <fx:Script>
        <![CDATA[
            import mx.collections.ArrayCollection;

            [Bindable]
            private var items:ArrayCollection = ↵
                    new ArrayCollection(["Apples", "Oranges", "Bananas"]);

            private function onDoubleClick(event:Event):void
```

```
            {
                ExternalInterface.call("itemSelected", list.selectedIndex, items.source);
            }

        ]]>
    </fx:Script>

    <s:List id="list" width="300"
            doubleClick="onDoubleClick(event);"
            doubleClickEnabled="true"
            dataProvider="{items}">
    </s:List>

</s:Application>
```

In this case, you send over the index of the selected item and the list of items as an array. Notice that you passed items.source instead of items since JavaScript will not read the ArrayCollection object type. Using the source property will return the array from the ArrayCollection.

The JavaScript code on the other side looks like this:

```
<script>
function itemSelected( index, data )
{
    alert( [ index, data ] );
}
</script>
```

It takes the two arguments, and then puts up an alert with the index and the data.

When you run this from Flash Builder 4 and double-click an item, you should see something like Figure 9-7.

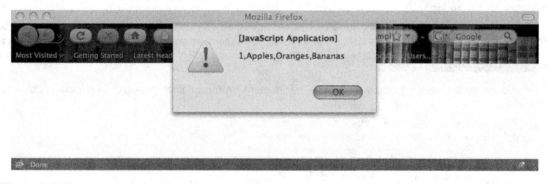

Figure 9-7. The more complex Javascript callback

As you can see, integers strings, and arrays come over just fine.

Calling from JavaScript Into Flex

Now that you know how to call from Flex into JavaScript, you need to learn how to go the other way. To demonstrate, you will allow the JavaScript on the page to dynamically add items to a Flex control using an addItem method that you will export through the ExternalInterface.

Following is the code for this JavaScript-driven Flex application:

```
<?xml version="1.0" encoding="utf-8"?>
<s:Application xmlns:fx="http://ns.adobe.com/mxml/2009"
               xmlns:s="library://ns.adobe.com/flex/spark"
               xmlns:mx="library://ns.adobe.com/flex/mx"
               minWidth="1024" minHeight="768"
               creationComplete="creationCompleteHandler()">
    <fx:Script>
        <![CDATA[
            import mx.collections.ArrayCollection;

            private var itemsList:ArrayCollection= new ArrayCollection();

                    protected function creationCompleteHandler():void
            {
                ExternalInterface.addCallback( "addItem",
                    function(str:String):void {
                        itemsList.addItem(str);
                        list.dataProvider = itemsList;
                    });

                ExternalInterface.call( 'jscallinLoaded' );
            }

        ]]>
    </fx:Script>

    <s:List id="list" width="200" height="250" />

</s:Application>
```

The Flex application is fairly simple. When it starts up, it registers the addItem method as a function that will add an item to an array and then update the dataProvider on the list with the new array.

The Flex application then calls the jscallinLoaded function in the JavaScript code to let it know that the Flash application has been loaded successfully.

The JavaScript code on the page that uses this Flex application is shown in the following code:

```
<script>
    function jscallinLoaded()
    {
        document.getElementById( 'JavaScriptCallingFlexExample' ).
addItem( 'Carrots' );
        document.getElementById( 'JavaScriptCallingFlexExample' ).
addItem( 'Corn' );
```

```
        document.getElementById( 'JavaScriptCallingFlexExample' ).
addItem( 'Peas' );
    }
</script>
```

Note that the element name in the JavaScript code needs to match the SWF / application name so it can retrieve the object. We called the project: JavaScriptCallingFlexExample. When you run this in Flash Builder 4, you should see something like Figure 9-8.

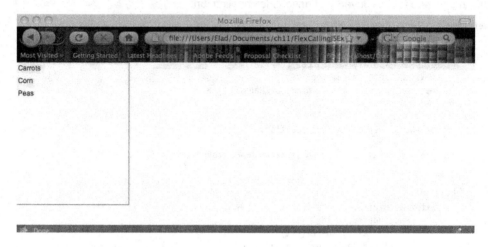

Figure 9-8. The JavaScript-driven Flex application

You might be asking yourself, why call out to JavaScript only to have it call back? Can't the JavaScript call in directly? It could, if the Flex application were loaded. But the loading sequence can vary from browser to browser and between operating systems. We have found that the most predictable way to know that a Flash application has been loaded is for it to call back into the JavaScript layer.

Flex for Widgets

Communicating between JavaScript and Flex is very common when building widgets. However, Flex 1 and 2 should have made building widgets easy, but only up until Flex 3, the file sizes of the Flash applications built by Flex were too large to make for good widgets. Now that we have the ability to cache the framework in the Flash Player using remote shared libraries (RSLs), the size of an individual Flash application can be much smaller. Now, we can truly make widgets and integrate applications fully into the page.

Flex applications built without RSLs are too big to be widgets; 250 kilobytes is too much to download to put an RSS reader on a page. But with RSLs, the application size can decrease to the 60-to-90 kilobyte range. That's very acceptable.

As a real life application example, you will create a widget that communicates between Flex and JavaScript and uses RSL to improve performance. Create a new Flex Project and call it **FlexWidget**.

To get started with RSL, open up the **Project** dialog by selecting the project, right-clicking, and selecting **Properties** from the context menu. Navigate to the **Library Path** section of the **Flex Build Path** tab. This is shown in Figure 9-9.

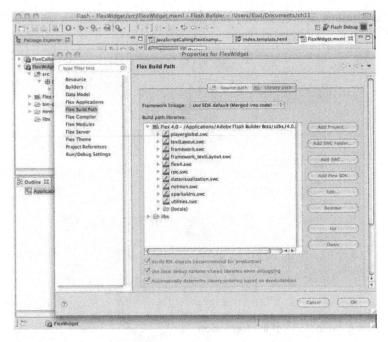

Figure 9-9. The library settings for the project

Next, expand the `framework.swc` library, select **RSL URL,** and click the **Edit** button. This will take you to the dialog shown in Figure 9-10.

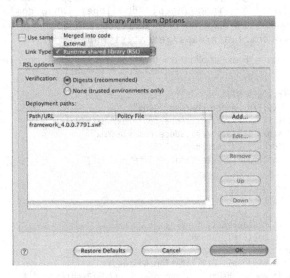

Figure 9-10. The selection of RSL for the framework

From there, select **Runtime Shared Library** and click the **Add** button, which will take you to the dialog, shown in Figure 9-11.

Figure 9-11. Specifying the location of the framework

This dialog allows you to specify the URL where the framework is located on your web site. That means you have to copy this file from the Flash Builder 4 library to your web site in the location you specified.

To experiment with this, we are going to create a little Yahoo! Maps widget using their Flash library. You can download that Flash library from Yahoo (http://developer.yahoo.com/flash/maps/) and install it in your project's lib directory. At the time of writing, you can download the swc directly from here: http://developer.yahoo.com/flash/maps/getLatest.php.

From there, you can create a Flex application that references the library, as shown in the following complete code:

```
<?xml version="1.0" encoding="utf-8"?>
<s:Application xmlns:fx="http://ns.adobe.com/mxml/2009"
               xmlns:s="library://ns.adobe.com/flex/spark"
               xmlns:mx="library://ns.adobe.com/flex/mx"
               minWidth="1024" minHeight="768"
               creationComplete="creationCompletehandler()">

    <fx:Script>
        <![CDATA[

            import mx.events.ResizeEvent;
            import com.yahoo.maps.api.YahooMap;
            import com.yahoo.maps.api.YahooMapEvent;
            import com.yahoo.maps.api.core.location.Address;
            import com.yahoo.maps.webservices.geocoder.GeocoderResult;
            import com.yahoo.maps.webservices.geocoder.events.GeocoderEvent;
```

```
private var yahooMap:YahooMap;
private var location:String = "1 market, san francisco, ca";
private var address:Address = new Address(location);

private function creationCompletehandler():void
{
    ExternalInterface.addCallback( "gotoAddress", function(add:String):void
    {
        address = new Address( add );
        address.addEventListener(GeocoderEvent.GEOCODER_SUCCESS, ↵
            handleGeocodeSuccess);
        address.geocode();
    });

    var appid:String = describeType(this).@name.split("::").join(".");
    yahooMap = new YahooMap();
    yahooMap.addEventListener(YahooMapEvent.MAP_INITIALIZE, handleMapInitialize);
    yahooMap.init(appid, mapContainer.width, mapContainer.height);

    mapContainer.addChild(yahooMap);
    mapContainer.addEventListener(ResizeEvent.RESIZE, handleContainerResize);

    yahooMap.addPanControl();
    yahooMap.addZoomWidget();
    yahooMap.addTypeWidget();
}

private function handleMapInitialize(event:YahooMapEvent):void
{
    address.addEventListener(GeocoderEvent.GEOCODER_SUCCESS, ↵
        handleGeocodeSuccess);
    address.geocode();
}

private function handleGeocodeSuccess(event:GeocoderEvent):void
{
    var result:GeocoderResult = address.geocoderResultSet.firstResult;
    yahooMap.zoomLevel = result.zoomLevel;
    yahooMap.centerLatLon = result.latlon;
    ExternalInterface.call( "mapComplete" );
}

private function handleContainerResize(event:ResizeEvent):void
{
    yahooMap.setSize(mapContainer.width,mapContainer.height);
}

    ]]>
</fx:Script>

<mx:UIComponent id="mapContainer" width="100%" height="100%"/>

</s:Application>
```

There are few important elements in the code. First, create an instance of the YahooMap class and an Address class, which you will be using once you set the Yahoo! map

```
private var yahooMap:YahooMap;
private var location:String = "1 market, san francisco, ca";
private var address:Address = new Address(location);
```

After the application is created, the creationCompletehandler is called, so this is where you add a new external method called gotoAddress. This will allow the JavaScript on the page to navigate the map to any address it wishes. Note that you need to pass the application name, which you extract using the following code:

```
describeType(this).@name.split("::").join(".");
    private function creationCompletehandler():void
    {
        ExternalInterface.addCallback( "gotoAddress", function(add:String):void
        {
            address = new Address( add );
            address.addEventListener(GeocoderEvent.GEOCODER_SUCCESS, ↵
                handleGeocodeSuccess);
            address.geocode();
        });

        var appid:String = describeType(this).@name.split("::").join(".");
        yahooMap = new YahooMap();
        yahooMap.addEventListener(YahooMapEvent.MAP_INITIALIZE, handleMapInitialize);
        yahooMap.init(appid, mapContainer.width, mapContainer.height);

        mapContainer.addChild(yahooMap);
        mapContainer.addEventListener(ResizeEvent.RESIZE, ↵
handleContainerResize);

        yahooMap.addPanControl();
        yahooMap.addZoomWidget();
        yahooMap.addTypeWidget();
    }
```

Once the map was initialized correctly, handleMapInitialize method is called and you can set an event handler and call the geocode() method to start the process.

```
    private function handleMapInitialize(event:YahooMapEvent):void
    {
        address.addEventListener(GeocoderEvent.GEOCODER_SUCCESS, ↵
            handleGeocodeSuccess);
        address.geocode();
    }
```

The second important piece is in handleGeocodeSuccess where the Flex application calls the mapComplete function in the JavaScript code when the map is ready for action.

```
    private function handleGeocodeSuccess(event:GeocoderEvent):void
    {
        var result:GeocoderResult = address.geocoderResultSet.firstResult;
        yahooMap.zoomLevel = result.zoomLevel;
        yahooMap.centerLatLon = result.latlon;
```

```
                ExternalInterface.call( "mapComplete" );
        }
```

Once you receive a resize event, you need to call the setSize() to set the new size.

```
        private function handleContainerResize(event:ResizeEvent):void
        {
                yahooMap.setSize(mapContainer.width,mapContainer.height);
        }


    ]]>
  </fx:Script>
```

Finally, you need to set an empty component to hold the map:

```
  <mx:UIComponent id="mapContainer" width="100%" height="100%"/>
```

Now that you are done creating the application you also create a JavaScript wrapper around this Flex application called MapWidget.js. The code for this is shown in the following:

```
var _gotoLocation = '';

function mapComplete() {
    document.getElementById('MapWidget').gotoAddress( _gotoLocation );
}

function putMapWidget( gotoLocation )
{
    _gotoLocation = gotoLocation;
    AC_FL_RunContent(
            "src", "MapWidget",
            "width", "100%",
            "height", "100%",
            "align", "middle",
            "id", "mapwidget",
            "quality", "high",
            "allowScriptAccess","always",
            "type", "application/x-shockwave-flash",
            "pluginspage", "http://www.adobe.com/go/getflashplayer"
    );
}
```

This script defines a new function called putMapWidget that customers can use to put a mapping widget on their pages. This function takes one parameter, an address. This address is used by the mapComplete function to set the map to the specified address using the exposed gotoAddress method.

You can then replace the entire index.template.html page with the contents shown in the following code:

```
<html lang="en">

    <head>

        <script src="AC_OETags.js" language="javascript"></script>

        <script src="MapWidget.js" language="javascript"></script>

    </head>
```

```
<body>
    <div style="width:200px;height:300px;">
        <script language="JavaScript" type="text/javascript">
            putMapWidget( '357 Riverview Rd., Swarthmore PA, 19081' );
        </script>
    </div>
</body>
</html>
```

This template represents how customers might use the widget on their page. They first include the standard AC_OETags.js JavaScript file and then the MapWidgets.js file. Finally, they invoke the putMapWidget function wherever they want a map.

Figure 9-12 shows the resulting widget page.

Figure 9-12. The mapping widget centered on Swarthmore

From here the customer can scroll around, change mapping modes, zoom in and out, and so on.

What if the customer wants to have a code copy function in the widget, so that anyone who wants the map on his page can click the button and get the JavaScript code that he should use to put the map on their own page?

Most of the code remains the same. Now you need to add a button that the customer can use to get the JavaScript code required to place the widget on any page.

```
<s:Button click="onCopyCode()" label="Copy code to clipboard"  x="12" y="273"/>
```

You need an handler method to add logic when a click event occurs:

```
private function onCopyCode() : void
```

```
{
    var html:String = '';
    html += '<script src="AC_OETags.js" language="javascript"></script>'+"\n";
    html += '<script src="MapWidget.js" language="javascript"></script>'+"\n";
    html += '<script language="JavaScript" type="text/javascript">'+"\n";
    html += 'putMapWidget( "'+location+'" );'+"\n";
    html += '</script>'+"\n";
    System.setClipboard(html);
}
```

When you bring this version up from Flash Builder 4, you see the widget as shown in Figure 9-13.

Figure 9-13. The widget with the code copy button

From there, you can click the copy button and paste the JavaScript code into a TextEdit window. This is shown in Figure 9-14.

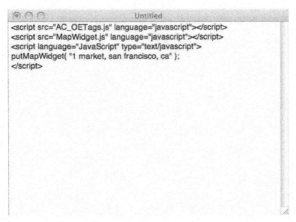

Figure 9-14. The pasted code in a text editor

Not bad. It even has the custom location in the address field. That way the customer will look at whatever you are looking at.

Summary

In this chapter we covered how to create communication between Flex and JavaScript and vice versa. One of the biggest advantages of using Flash and Flex is that you can be rest assured that the application you created will run the same anywhere, because the code deployed is using the Flash Player, which is consistent on devices and different browsers. JavaScript is not as consistent, and differs between browsers so it's important to test your application on different browsers. The ability to create communication between Flex applications and JavaScript opens up some the doors for creating integration and leveraging existing code. As an example of these integrations, we showed you a real-life application using the communication between Flex and JavaScript creating a widget based on Yahoo! map. We also showed you how to leverage Flex RSL to optimize your application size so your widget can be deployed with the minimum size.

Chapter 10

Flex Mashups

by Elad Elrom

In this chapter, we are going to explain one of the most talked-about concepts on the Web today: mashups. What is a mashup? And what is all the buzz about?

The word "mashup" was originally used in the pop and hip hop music industry back in the mid 1990s to describe a song created out of two or more songs mixed together.

An *application mashup* combines at least two data sources to create a new application. For instance, consider mixing Google map with Craigslist real estate results. The result is http://www.housingmaps.com/, as shown in Figure 10-1.

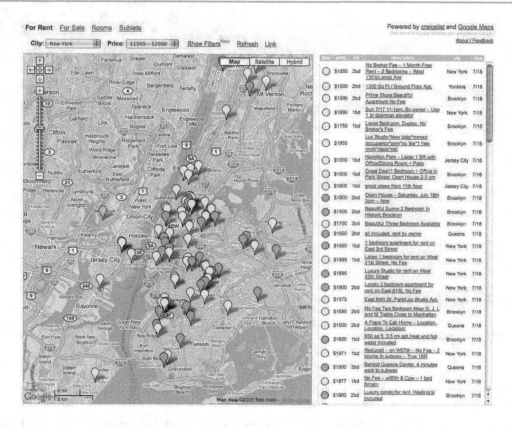

Figure 10-1. Mashup example source: housingmaps.com

As a metaphor for a mashup, take this example from real life: a client hires a detective agency. As a result of the client's request for an investigation, a few detectives are assigned to handle the case. The detectives check all sorts of clues (data sources) found on the Internet, in public records, at the scene itself, etc. All of these clues (data) are processed, filtered, and formed to determine an answer. At that point, the responce is presented to the client with the findings of the investigation (Mashup).

In recent years, the Web has been going through a transformation into what many call **Web 2.0**, a term first used by O'Reilly to describe the transformation of the Web into a sharing and collaborative vehicle. To learn more, visit `http://www.oreillynet.com/pub/a/oreilly/tim/news/2005/09/30/what-is-web-20.html`.

Today, an increasing number of components, web services, data sources, and cloud computing services are available. These services allow developers to create new and exciting applications by simply mixing them together.

> **Cloud computing** is an architecture available on the web which consists of a large network of servers running parallel to each other. Companies such as Amazon (through its EC2) provide cloud computing on a per-usage basis through a web service or RESTful connection. Using cloud servers allows high performance and ensures stability while keeping cost per usage low.

Currently, Flex is not one of the most common technologies used for writing mashups. We believe the reason is that Flex is still relatively new. Additionally, the Flash Player requires remote networks to install a `crossdomain.xml` file. Unfortunately, most services do not upload `crossdomain.xml`, or they upload it with a restricted policy, which adds extra work in order to overcome the security restriction and makes Flex a less common platform to develop mashups (cross-domain will be explained in much more detail later in the chapter). However, the fact that Flex mashups are not so common actually gives you a tremendous opportunity to develop exciting new applications with little effort.

Each mashup should add value to an existing service. Building a Flex Rich Internet Application (RIA) mashup creates an additional value. Not only can you add value by stitching different pieces together, but you can also create an easy-to-use user interface (UI) that will transform an existing data source, such as Craigslist, Google search results, or others, into a cool stateful application that allows the client to view changes without having to refresh his browser.

Now, let's look at an example of a Flex application mashup. In this example, you can submit a location, and the application searches for a product on eBay, Google Merchant Center, and Amazon. It then returns back to the client a list of the available products, as well as a map showing where each product is located.

Here's what is going on behind the scenes. A client submits a request for a product and an address. The Flex application sends the request to Yahoo! Pipes, a mashup platform, which sends requests to all of the services (eBay, Google Merchant Center, and Amazon). The services form a response based on results from the data sources and sends the response back to Yahoo! Pipes. The results are processed and filtered. Yahoo! Pipes then generates a web feed as a response. The Flex application receives the web feed's response, updates the model, and displays the results in a custom `List` component along with a map. Figure 10-2 visually illustrates this process.

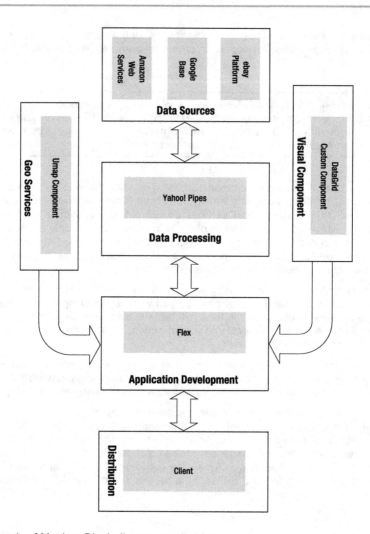

Figure 10-2. Example of Mashup Block diagram application

Accessing Data Sources

The core of building a Flex mashup is accessing data and distributing it into your application. When connecting to services across the web, many technologies are being used such as SOAP, web services, RSS feeds, REST, JSON, Atom, and more. We will cover the different types of data connections that are available in this section. In addition, we will show you how to interconnect the data to create a data object that can be easily used across your application.

Representational State Transfer (REST) is an architecture style used by the Internet. Services that follow REST architecture are described as RESTful.

The Flash Player can connect to different types of remote networks; the connections are made using a Remote Procedure Call (RPC). Using the Flash Player, you have two ways to connect to a remote network. One way is to connect directly to the remote network (see Figure 10-3).

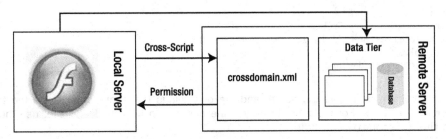

Figure 10-3. Connecting to a remote server through crossdomain.xml

When an RPC is being made, the Flash Player accesses the network and downloads the `crossdomain.xml` policy file. The `crossdomain.xml` file includes a set of permission instructions for connecting the player to the network. After permission is given, the Flash Player creates the connection, and you are able to retrieve data and media.

Otherwise, in the scenario where the `crossdomain.xml` file is not available on the remote network or the policy restricts the Flash Player from accessing the data, you will need to create a proxy interface between your application and the remote network to overcome the `crossdomain.xml` limitation.

The proxy is a server-side script that will be able to access the information and make the information available to the Flash Player (see Figure 10-4). Since the server-side script does not have the same restriction as the Flash Player, it is able to access the file. The Flash Player is able to connect to the proxy since it is located on the same domain.

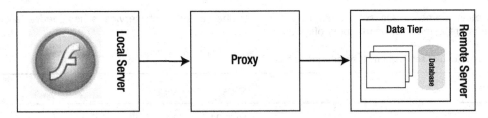

Figure 10-4. Connecting to a remote server through a proxy

The `crossdomain.xml` file is necessary to connect directly to a service on a remote network. It is beneficial to understand how to read and create a `crossdomain.xml` file so you can figure out at an early stage whether you are able to connect directly to a service or need to use a proxy.

Creating the crossdomain.xml Policy File

The Flash Player requires that a `crossdomain.xml` file be uploaded to the root of the server. The file gives instructions to the Flash Player whether to allow a remote SWF to access the server.

Placing the following `crossdomain.xml` file in the root of a server will allow the Flash Player to connect to the server from any domain. In the line of code `allow-access-fromdomain="*"` the star indicates that Flash Player can connect on any domain.

```
<?xml version="1.0 "?>
<!DOCTYPE cross-domain-policy SYSTEM ↵
"http://www.macromedia.com/xml/dtds/cross-domain-policy.dtd">
<cross-domain-policy>
      <allow-access-from domain="*"/>
</cross-domain-policy>
```

The XML file structure is always the same, and the only things that really change are the tags inside `<cross-domain-policy>`. For instance, to restrict the connection to a particular site, use the following tags inside the `crossdomain.xml` node:

```
<allow-access-from domain="www.site1.com"/>
<allow-access-from domain="site2.com"/>
```

Another example is to create a `crossdomain.xml` file that allows a secure server connection. You would use `secure="true"`.

```
<allow-access-from domain="www.site3.com" secure="true" />
```

You can also restrict access to a specific port or ports. For iexample, to allow any remote server to connect to ports 80 and 110, use the following tags:

```
<allow-access-from domain="*" to-ports="21,80"/>
```

You can connect to a lower TCP socket through the Socket and XMLSocket APIs.

Here's an example of a valid socket connection policy:

```
<site-control permitted-cross-domain-policies="master-only"/>
<allow-access-from domain="mysite.com" to-ports="999,8080-8082"/>
```

These ports represent access to different services on the server; each service is assigned to a specific port. Here are some of the ports most often used.

Table 10-1. Popular services and their assigned ports

Service	Port
FTP	Port 21
SSH	Port 22
Telnet	Port 23
SMTP	Port 25

Web	Port 80
Pop 3	Port 110
IMAP	Port 143

You can allow access to every server that ends with a certain name by using an asterisk (*), as shown here:

```
<allow-access-from domain="*.yahoo.com" />
```

You can allow access to a specific IP address:

```
<allow-access-from domain="66.500.0.20" />
```

Since the crossdomain.xml is uploaded to the root directory of the server, such as http://www.WebSite.com/crossdomain.xml, it is easy to find out whether the crossdomain.xml file is installed by navigating to the address of that file.

For example, checking Yahoo! Maps service (http://maps.yahoo.com) reveals a crossdomain.xml file installed when navigating via a browser to http://maps.yahoo.com/crossdomain.xml, as shown in Figure 10-5. Remember that the file can also be written this way: CrossDomain.xml.

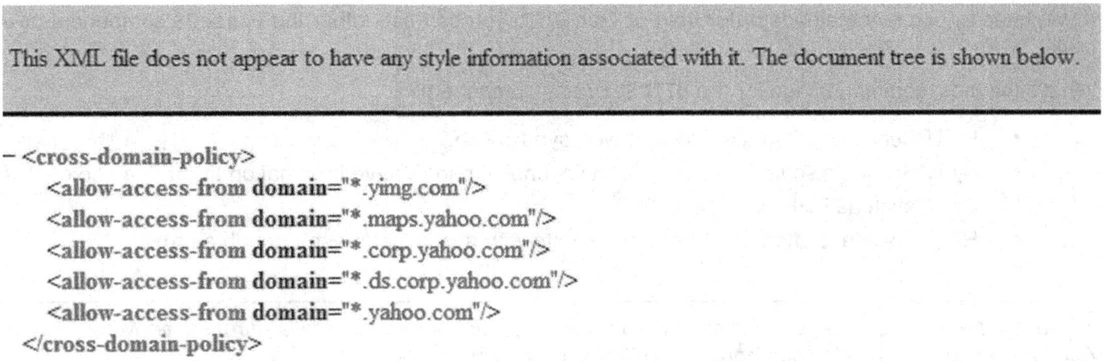

This XML file does not appear to have any style information associated with it. The document tree is shown below.

```
- <cross-domain-policy>
    <allow-access-from domain="*.yimg.com"/>
    <allow-access-from domain="*.maps.yahoo.com"/>
    <allow-access-from domain="*.corp.yahoo.com"/>
    <allow-access-from domain="*.ds.corp.yahoo.com"/>
    <allow-access-from domain="*.yahoo.com"/>
  </cross-domain-policy>
```

Figure 10-5. Connecting to a remote network through crossdomain.xml

Most services you will be using in your Flex mashup that have the crossdomain.xml file installed and unrestricted will allow you to make an RPC. There are three types of RPC components available in Flex: HTTPService, WebService, and RemoteObject. In terms of performance, HTTPService and RemoteObject connections are faster than WebService connections. In small applications with very little data being transferred and few calls, it does not really matter what you choose, but as you increase the number of calls and amount of data, even a mere 100ms difference per call can become noticeable.

The HTTPService component is a powerful method and the most common way to retrieve data. HTTPService allows you to send GET and POST requests. After making the request, you receive a data response. Mashups often use the HTTPService component to access web syndication.

Web syndication is a term used to describe web feeds A link to a web feed can be recognized by the web syndication icon (see Figure 10-6).

Figure 10-6. Web syndication icon

Connecting to a RESTful Data Source

Although Adobe describes the HTTPService component as equivalent to a RESTful service, you can only use the GET and POST methods with this method; you cannot use any other methods such as HEAD, OPTIONS, PUT, TRACE, or DELETE.

If you need to use any methods other than GET or POST, you can use either the BlazeDS component or a proxy.

What's the most common usage for the HTTPService Component?

- HTTPService is often used to load web syndication.
- HTTPService also provides a common connection to retrieve information through a server-side proxy such as PHP, JSP, or ASP.
- HTTPService is often used to communicate with a local database through a proxy.

There are two identical ways to create HTTPService component service calls: through an MXML tag or ActionScript code. Using the component in either way is identical.

We will be using the following XML file, src/assets/xml/employees.xml, in the examples in this chapter:

```
<employees>
        <employee>
                <name>John Do</name>
                <phone>212-222-2222</phone>
                <age>20</age>
                <email>john@youremail.com</email>
        </employee>

                <employee>
                <name>Jane Smith</name>
                <phone>212-333-3333</phone>
```

```
                              <age>21</age>
                              <email>jane@youremail.com</email>
                    </employee>
        </employees>
```

Here is an example of creating a `HTTPService` call using an MXML tag. In Flex 4, you need to markup any custom data classes using `Declarations` tag for cases where you want to reference a component that is not part of the `mx.core`or classes that are not display objects, otherwise you will get a compile time error.

```
<fx:Declarations>
    <s:HTTPService
        url="assets/xml/employees.xml"
        resultFormat="e4x"
        result="resultHandler(event); "
        fault="faultHandler(event); "/>
</fx:Declarations>
```

Using ActionScript 3.0 code, the same `HTTPService` call would look as follows. Notice that the `HTTPService` component has a property called `resultFormat`, which allows you to specify how you would like Flex to format the data response.

```
private var service:HTTPService = new HTTPService();
private function setService():void
{
        service.url = "assets/xml/employees.xml";
        service.resultFormat = "e4x"
        service.addEventListener(ResultEvent.RESULT, resultHandler);
        service.addEventListener(FaultEvent.FAULT, faultHandler);
        service.send();
}
```

After you make a request, the response will be handled either by the `result` or `fault` methods, depending on whether the request was successful or not.

Here's the implementation of the results and fault methods:

```
        private var dataProvider:ArrayCollection = new ArrayCollection();
        private function resultHandler(event:ResultEvent): void
        {
                service.removeEventListener(ResultEvent.RESULT, resultHandler);
                for each (var property:XML in event.result.employees.employee)
                {
                        dataProvider.addItem({name:property.name, phone:property.phone, ⏎
                                email:property.email});
                }
        }

        private function faultHandler(event:FaultEvent): void
        {
                service.removeEventListener(FaultEvent.FAULT, faultHandler);
                Alert.show(event.f ault.message, "Error connecting");
        }
```

`HTTPService` allows you to format the data results you receive. Here are your options:

- *e4x*: Returns XML that can be accessed through `ECMAScript` for XML (e4x) expressions.

- *Flashvars*: returns an object with name-value pairs separated by ampersands.
- *Object*: returns an object parsed as an AS tree.
- *text*: returns a regular string.
- *xml*: returns a `flash.xml.XMLNode` instance.

The format you should be using depends on the results you expect to get from the request. For instance, if the service returns a `success` or `fail` string message, you can just use the `text` result format. However, most services return an XML result, so you will be using either the `xml` or e4x format.

e4x is preferred over regular XML when dealing with XML responses, since you can access the results easily and can perform expressions to filter the results. e4x is a language in its own right, and it has been incorporated into ActionScript 3.0. Many claim e4x to be a simple and easy way to access XML; however, it is not as easy as people make it out to be. To underscore this point, let's take a look at e4x syntax.

We will use the same `employees.xml` file we mentioned before to walk through some examples on how to work with e4x.

The following example demonstrates e4x object style capabilities. The variables `results1` through `results4` are going to give the exact same output, that is, the complete list of employees. The asterisk notation can be used anywhere and gives you powerful control in cases where the node name is different.

> *The two main classes you use in Flex are the XML and XMLList classes. The difference is that XML is part of e4x and is formatted just as the XML object it received, while XMLList is a list of XML nodes. What it means is that XML must always have one single root node and XMLLists can have many nodes at the base depth.*

```
importmx.rpc.events.ResultEvent;

private function resultHandler(event:ResultEvent): void
{
        // results1 - results4 are the same
        var results1:XMLList = xml.employee;
        var results2:XMLList = xml.child("*");
        var results3:XMLList = xml.*;
     var results4:XMLList = xml..employee;
}
```

You can also use the object style to check the amount of items on each node by using the `length` property:

```
var len:int = xml.employee.length();
```

Use XML type to retrieve an item as follows:

```
var firstEmployeeName:String = xml.employee[0].name;
```

The following examples demonstrate using expressions in e4x:

```
var employeeFilter:XMLList = xml.employee.(phone == '212-333-3333');
var ageFilter:XMLList = xml.employee.(age >= 19 || age == 18);
```

In case you need to iterate through the collection, in order to retrieve all the items in the employee node you can use one of one of the following three methods (which return the same results) and you don't need to convert to XMLList first.

```
// iterate through the collection
for each (var item:XML in xml.employee)
{
     trace(item.email);
}

for (var i:int = 0; i < len; i++)
{
     item = xml.employee[i];
     trace(item.email);
}
```

The results in the console window will be:

john@youremail.com
jane@youremail.com
john@youremail.com
jane@youremail.com

The complete working example of using e4x code is below. Create a new Flex project and call it E4XExamples. When testing, place a break point and use Eclipse **variable window** to examine the results:

```
<?xml version="1.0" encoding="utf-8"?>
<s:Application xmlns:fx="http://ns.adobe.com/mxml/2009"
               xmlns:s="library://ns.adobe.com/flex/spark"
               xmlns:mx="library://ns.adobe.com/flex/mx"
               minWidth="1024" minHeight="768"
               initialize="httpService.send();">

    <fx:Script>
        <![CDATA[

            import mx.controls.Alert;
            import mx.rpc.events.FaultEvent;
            import mx.rpc.events.ResultEvent;

            private function resultHandler(event:ResultEvent):void
            {
                httpService.removeEventListener(ResultEvent.RESULT,  ⏎
resultHandler);

                var xml:XML = event.result as XML;

                // results1 - results4 are the same
                var results1:XMLList = xml.employee;
                var results2:XMLList = xml.child("*");
                var results3:XMLList = xml.*;
                var results4:XMLList = xml..employee;

                // length of the employee node
```

```
var len:int = xml.employee.length();

// sort and find items
var firstEmployeeName:String = xml.employee[0].name;
var ageFilter:XMLList = xml.employee.(age >= 19 || age == 18);
var firstEmployee:XML = xml.employee[0];
var findName:XMLList = xml.employee.(name=="John Do");
var employeeFilter:XMLList = xml.employee.(phone == '212-333-3333');

// iterate through the collection
for each (var item:XML in xml.employee)
{
    trace(item.email);
}

for (var i:int = 0; i < len; i++)
{
    item = xml.employee[i];
    trace(item.email);
}
}

private function faultHandler(event:FaultEvent):void
{
    httpService.removeEventListener(FaultEvent.FAULT, faultHandler);
    Alert.show("Error connecting");
}

]]>
</fx:Script>

<fx:Declarations>
    <s:HTTPService id="httpService"
                url="assets/xml/employees.xml"
                resultFormat="e4x"
                result="resultHandler(event);"
                fault="faultHandler(event);"/>
</fx:Declarations>

</s:Application>
```

Flex HTTPService is often used for RESTful services. HTTPService emulates HTTP protocols; however, as mentioned before, it is restricted to GET and POST requests.

Google Merchant Center (fromely known as Google Base) has deprecated SOAP services and is now available through RESTful services. Let's access Google Merchant Center using Flash's HTTPService component.

> Google Merchant Center is an online service that allows you to upload and manage product listings you want to appear in Google Product Search, AdWords, and other Google properties. Once the content is added, it can be accessed through RESTful services.

To view search results from Google Merchant Center, you can send a request with the parameter `bq=keywords`. You will need to pass the variable through the HTTP protocol in the `HTTPService` component. You do so by placing a `request` tag inside the `HTTPService` MXML tag like so:

```
<mx:request>
<bq>digital+camera</bq>
</mx:request>
```

It is recommended that `keywords` be bindable. Attaching a `bindable` variable allows you to reassign different keywords in order to do a new search, with no need to refresh the browser, keepingy our application stateful.

```
<bq>{keywords}</bq>
```

You can pass the variable by sending it directly through the `send` method as follows:

```
httpService.send({bp:digital+camera});
```

You can also invoke the `RESTful` service by attaching the query at the end of the URL as shown here: `http://www.google.com/base/feeds/snippets?bq=digital+camera`.

The results from the query of the feeds are shown in Figure 10-7. Google Merchant Center is using the `Atom` namespace. We will discuss namespaces and `Atom` in more detail in the next section, "Working with Web Feeds and Namespaces," so if you don't understand namespaces now, don't worry.

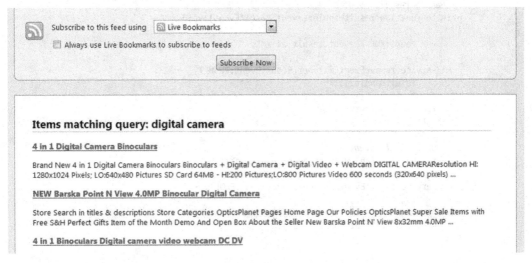

Figure 10-7. Google Merchant Center feeds results

In order to access elements and properties in the XML that was returned from the Google Merchant Center service, you need to define the `Atom` namespace:

```
private namespace atom = "http://www.w3.org/2005/Atom";
use namespace atom;
```

Create a new Flex project and call it GoogleMerchantCenterExample. Here is the complete code of the application for sending a request to Google Merchant Center and receiving a response with the results:

```
<?xml version="1.0" encoding="utf-8"?>
<s:Application xmlns:fx="http://ns.adobe.com/mxml/2009"
               xmlns:s="library://ns.adobe.com/flex/spark"
               xmlns:mx="library://ns.adobe.com/flex/mx"
               minWidth="1024" minHeight="768"
               initialize="service.send()">

    <fx:Script>
        <![CDATA[

            import mx.controls.Alert;
            import mx.rpc.http.HTTPService;
            import mx.rpc.events.ResultEvent;
            import mx.rpc.events.FaultEvent;

            [Bindable]
            private var keywords:String = "digital+camera";

            // Define and use atom namespace.
            private namespace atom = "http://www.w3.org/2005/Atom";
            use namespace atom;

            // Handle results event
            private function resultHandler(event:ResultEvent):void
            {
                var feeds:XML = event.result as XML;

                service.removeEventListener(ResultEvent.RESULT, ⏎
                    resultHandler);

                trace(feeds.entry[0].title);
            }

            // Handle faults event
            private function faultHandler(event:FaultEvent):void
            {
                service.removeEventListener(FaultEvent.FAULT, ⏎
                    faultHandler);

                Alert.show("Error connecting");
            }

        ]]>
    </fx:Script>

    <fx:Declarations>
        <s:HTTPService id="service"
            url="http://www.google.com/base/feeds/snippets"
            resultFormat="e4x"
            result="resultHandler(event);"
            fault="faultHandler(event);">
                <s:request>
                <bq>{keywords}</bq>
```

```
            </s:request>
         </s:HTTPService>
      </fx:Declarations>
```

```
</s:Application>
```

The code makes a call to Google Merchant Center using an HTTPService component to retrieve keywords search results and then parse the title into the console. Notice that you have to use the following code:

```
private namespace atom = "http://www.w3.org/2005/Atom";
use namespace atom;
```

You need to define and use the namespace in order to be able to retrieve the results from the XML.

Connecting to a SOAP Data Source

Another common connection, SOAP, is often used by APIs to send and receive XML messages through HTTP protocols.

SOAP is explained in detail in Chapter 4. Since SOAP is heavy across the wire and requires higher client-side memory and processing, many web services, such as Google, are moving away from SOAP to RESTful services such as web feeds.

Keep in mind that SOAP is still very common and has its own advantages, especially when the communication is done behind proxies or firewalls, or the protocol is utilizing other application layer protocols such as SMTP.

One service that uses SOAP is the Amazon API. Amazon Web Services, which are often used in mashup applications, include the following:

- *Alexa services*: Provides information regarding web pages.
- *Amazon Clouds*: Includes services such as storage, database, and queue services.
- *Amazon Associates*: Allows developers to earn referral fees for every purchase made by your referral.

In the following example, you will be using SOAP to connect to the Amazon Associates service.

To connect to SOAP service, use the <mx:WebService> tag and set the WSDL property.

```
<s:WebService id="AmazonService"
         wsdl="http://webservices.amazon.com/AWSECommerceService/ ↵
AWSECommerceService.wsdl"
         showBusyCursor="true"
         fault="Alert.show(event.fault.faultString)">
```

In this example, you make two calls to two operations (methods). The first operation is to retrieve the list of music based on keywords. You first define the operation:

```
<!-- itemSearch method -->
<s:operation name="ItemSearch" resultFormat="object"
                  fault="faultHandler(event)"
                  result="searchResultHandler(event)">
      <s:request>
            <AWSAccessKeyId>{DEVELOPER_KEY}</AWSAccessKeyId>
            <Shared>
                  <Keywords>beatles</Keywords>
```

```
                    <SearchIndex>Music</SearchIndex>
                    <Count>10</Count>
             </Shared>
       </s:request>
</s:operation>
```

Notice that DEVELOPER_KEY is defined as a static member, so you will be able to assign it to the XML in the operation.

```
[Bindable]
private static var DEVELOPER_KEY:String;
```

In order to get an Amazon access Key ID, apply at:

https://aws-portal.amazon.com/gp/aws/developer/registration/index.html

Once you have your Amazon account, click this URL to generate the developer key:

http://aws-portal.amazon.com/gp/aws/developer/account/index.html?action=access-key

In the second operation you follow the same logic; first, you need to define the operation and the methods that will handle the result. Notice that you are using the same handler to handle the fault response, since you will handle the fault response the same way, by displaying an error message.

```
<s:operation name="ItemLookup" resultFormat="object"
       fault="faultHandler(event)" result="itemResultHandler(event)" >
```

The second XML request will pass the detail of the title found in the first operation; notice the ItemID is bindable so you will be able to pass the asin, which is an Amazon unique primary key needed to retrieve information regarding a product.

```
<s:request>
                   <AWSAccessKeyId>{DEVELOPER_KEY}</AWSAccessKeyId>
                   <Shared>
                            <ItemId>{asin}</ItemId>
                            <ResponseGroup>ItemAttributes,Images</ResponseGroup>
                   </Shared>
</s:request>
```

Create a new Flex project and call it AmazonServices. Below is the complete working code. Notice that you need to replace DEVELOPER_KEY string with your developer key, in order to run this example successfully.

```
<?xml version="1.0" encoding="utf-8"?>
<s:Application xmlns:fx="http://ns.adobe.com/mxml/2009"
                      xmlns:s="library://ns.adobe.com/flex/spark"
                      xmlns:mx="library://ns.adobe.com/flex/mx"
                      minWidth="1024" minHeight="768"
                      initialize="AmazonService.ItemSearch.send();">

    <fx:Script>
       <![CDATA[

           import mx.rpc.events.FaultEvent;

           import mx.controls.Alert;
           import mx.rpc.events.ResultEvent;
```

```
        [Bindable]
        private var asin:String;

        // Replace with Amazon Access Key ID:
        // Apply at: https://aws-portal.amazon.com/gp/aws/ ↵
                    developer/registration/index.html
        // then get AWS access key ID here:
        // http://aws-portal.amazon.com/gp/aws/developer ↵
            /account/index.html?action=access-key
        [Bindable]
        private static var DEVELOPER_KEY:String = "*************";

        // search results handler
        private function searchResultHandler(event:ResultEvent):void
        {
                var object:Object = event.result.Items.Item;
                asin = object[0].ASIN;
                AmazonService.ItemLookup.send();
        }

        // item results handler
        private function itemResultHandler(event:ResultEvent):void
        {
            trace(event.result.Items.Item[0].SmallImage.URL);
        }

        private function faultHandler(event:FaultEvent):void
        {
            Alert.show("Error connecting"+event.fault.faultString);
        }

    ]]>
    </fx:Script>

    <fx:Declarations>
        <s:WebService id="AmazonService"
wsdl="http://webservices.amazon.com/AWSECommerceService/AWSECommerceService.wsdl"
            showBusyCursor="true"
            fault="Alert.show(event.fault.faultString)">

            <!-- itemSearch method -->
            <s:operation name="ItemSearch" resultFormat="object"
                        fault="faultHandler(event)"
                        result="searchResultHandler(event)">
                <s:request>
                    <AWSAccessKeyId>{DEVELOPER_KEY}</AWSAccessKeyId>
                    <Shared>
                        <Keywords>beatles</Keywords>
                        <SearchIndex>Music</SearchIndex>
                        <Count>10</Count>
                    </Shared>
                </s:request>
```

```
        </s:operation>

        <!-- itemLookup method -->
        <s:operation name="ItemLookup" resultFormat="object"
                     fault="faultHandler(event)"
                     result="itemResultHandler(event)">
            <s:request>
                <AWSAccessKeyId>{DEVELOPER_KEY}</AWSAccessKeyId>
                <Shared>
                    <ItemId>{asin}</ItemId>
                    <ResponseGroup>ItemAttributes,Images</ResponseGroup>
                </Shared>
            </s:request>
        </s:operation>

    </s:WebService>
  </fx:Declarations>

</s:Application>
```

Once you compile and run the example you will see the first image icon URL for the first item in the console view.

Connecting to a Data Source Using AMF

Action Message Format (AMF) is a data format created by Macromedia with the release of Flash Player 6. AMF is now open source and part of BlazeDS, available to download here: http://opensource.adobe.com.

> There are many types of AMF connections, but they all share the same basic principles of serializing (encoding) into a binary format and deserializing (decoding) once the data is returned to Flex.

AMF uses code data types such as Byte (8 bit), Int (16 bit), and many others. With the release of ActionScript 3.0, Adobe updated AMF: it is now called AMF3 (the older version now being referred to as AMF0), and it supports more data types.

Working with unformatted binary data has significant advantages: the speed of communication across the wire is much faster, it needs less memory from the client computer, and it reduces processing time over HTTPService or WebService.

Although connecting to AMF services is usually not provided through APIs, you may use it to retrieve data from your own local database or server as part of your data sources to your mashup. Flash provides built-in AMF-based APIs such as the following:

- **RemoteObject**: ActionScript 3.0 API that allows access to Java objects.
- **Socket Connection**: ActionScript 3.0 API that allows connection through sockets.
- **NetConnection**: API used to initiate commands on a remote server and play streaming video.

Additionally, there are many open source and commercial AMF implementations that provide a gateway between the Flash Player and the implementation. Here are some of the popular ones:

- **AMFPHP and SabreAMF**: Allows access to PHP.
- **RubyAMF**: Allows access to Ruby.
- **WebORB and Fluorine**: Allows access to .NET.
- **BlazeDS and LiveCycle**: Allows access to data in real time.

RemoteObject encoding uses AMF and allows you to access Java objects or ColdFusion (which consists of Java objects internally) methods. RemoteObject still connects using the HTTP or HTTPS protocol; however, the data is serialized into a binary format and then deserialized once the data is returned to the Flash Player.

Following is an example of invoking methods on ColdFusion. First, the `RemoteObject` is declared with the destination driver and the source ColdFusion file.

```
<s:RemoteObject
        id="CFService"
        showBusyCursor="true"
        destination="ColdFusion"
        source="cf.R eadFile"
        result="dataHandler(event)"  />
```

To invoke the `RemoteObject` component, you need to call the method inside the ColdFusion file and pass any needed arguments:

```
CFService.getQuery("1");
```

Now let's create the content of `cf/ReadFile.cf`:

```
<cfcomponent>
        <cffunction name="getQuery" access="remote" returntype="query">
        <cfargument name="State" required="true">
                <cfset var qRead="">
                <cfquery name="qRead" datasource="data_source_name"
                            SELECT * FROM 'tableName' WHERE ➥ PrimaryKey=<cfqueryparam
value="#arguments.key#" cfsqltype="CF_SQL_STRING">
                </cfquery>
                <cfreturn qRead>
        </cffunction>
</cfcomponent>
```

The result can be handled with the `dataHandler` method, which casts the object to an `ArrayCollection`.

```
private function dataHandler(event:ResultEvent): void
{
     DataResult = event.result as ArrayCollection;
}
```

Connecting to Data services Through Flash Builder 4 Data Services Plug-ins

In Flash Builder 4 Adobe added a plug-in to manage and connect to data services, which allows you to easily connect to services and attach the data to a UI component. Let's use the same example of connecting to Google Merchant Center to find search results, however, this time you'll do it with very little effort. To get started create a new Flex 4 project and call it **DataServicesExample**.

1. Open the main MXML application **DataServicesExample.mxml** and switch to design view. Drag a `DataGrid` component from Data Controls.

2. Next, in the **Data/Services** window click on **Connect to Data/Services** (see Figure 10-8).

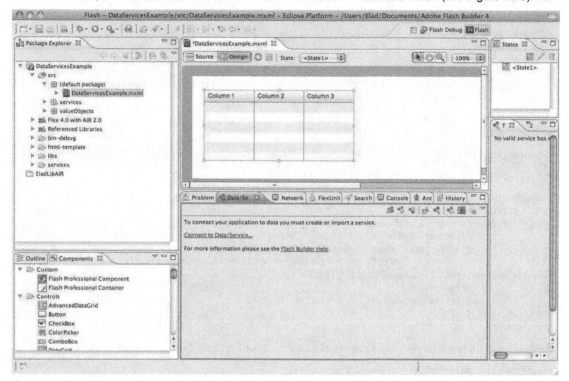

Figure 10-8. Data/Services window

3. Next, you need to set the type of data service you will be setting. Select **HTTPService** and hit **next**. A **new Flex Services** window opens up and allows you to set the properties of the service, as shownin Figure 10-9.

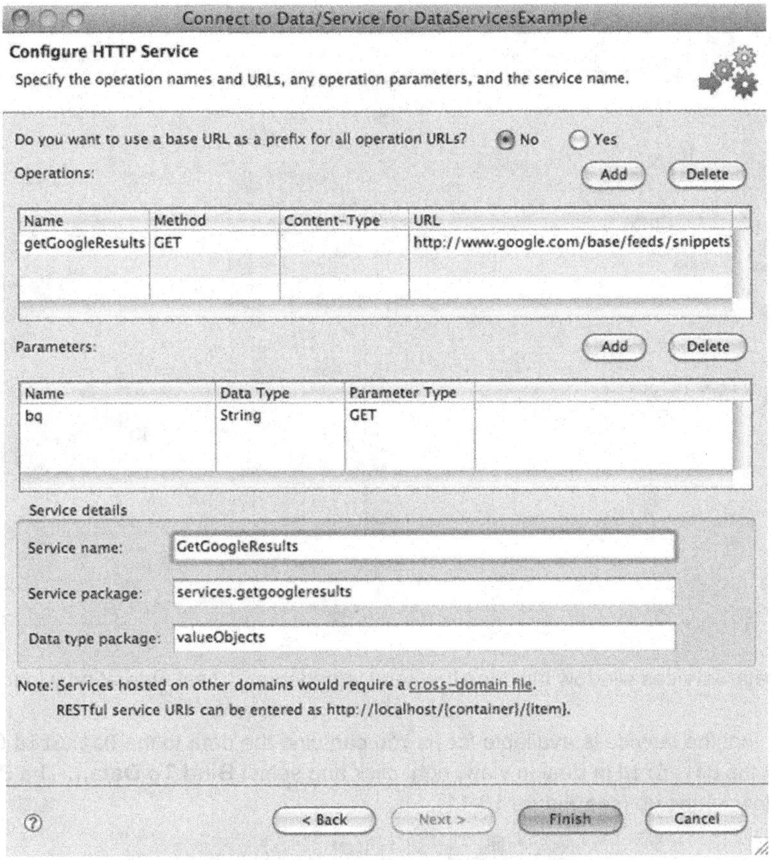

Figure 10-9. Data service properties window

4. You will use the same service you used in the Connecting to RESTful Datasource sub-chapter. Set the following information:

- **URL**: `http://www.google.com/base/feeds/snippets?bq=keyword`

- **Operation**: `getGoogleResults`

- **Service name**: `GetGoogleResults`

5. Click finish when completed. Notice that the service is now available under the **Data?FS?Services** window, you can right click the service and select **Test Operation**. In the **Test Operation** window you can see the results (see Figure 10-10).

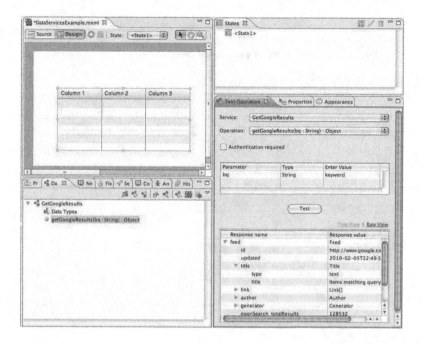

Figure 10-10. Data/Services window includes the service added and Test Operation window.

6. Now that the service is available for us you can bind the data to the DataGrid Component. Click the DataGrid in design view, right click and select **Bind To Data...** The Bind To Data window opens up (see Figure 10-11).

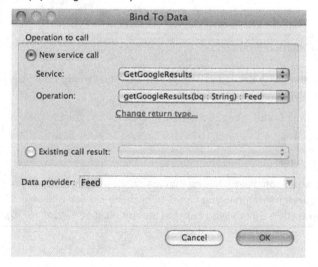

Figure 10-11. Bind To Data window

7. Click the **Configure Return Type**… button to generate all the classes to bind the data. The **Configure Operation Return Type** window opens up. Keep the default: **Auto detects type of data returned by this operation** radio button and click **Next** twice. Then, you can either select the data you will be feeding or leave the default options. Once completed, select **Finish**.

All the code gets generated automatically and includes the services.getgoogleresults package with code to retrieve the results and serialize the results. The application **DataServicesExample.mxml** got changed and includes code to fill the DataGrid, as shown in the following code:

```
<?xml version="1.0" encoding="utf-8"?>
<s:Application xmlns:fx="http://ns.adobe.com/mxml/2009"
               xmlns:s="library://ns.adobe.com/flex/spark"
               xmlns:mx="library://ns.adobe.com/flex/mx"
               minWidth="955" minHeight="600"
               xmlns:getgoogleresults="services.getgoogleresults.*">
    <fx:Script>
        <![CDATA[
            import mx.controls.Alert;
            import mx.events.FlexEvent;

            protected function dataGrid_creationCompleteHandler(event:FlexEvent):void
            {
                getGoogleResultsResult.token = getGoogleResults.getGoogleResults↩
(/*Enter value(s) for */ bq);
            }

        ]]>
    </fx:Script>
    <fx:Declarations>
        <s:CallResponder id="getGoogleResultsResult"/>
        <getgoogleresults:GetGoogleResults id="getGoogleResults"↩
fault="Alert.show(event.fault.faultString + '\n' + event.fault.faultDetail)"↩
showBusyCursor="true"/>
        <!-- Place non-visual elements (e.g., services, value objects) here -->
    </fx:Declarations>
    <mx:DataGrid x="33" y="46" id="dataGrid"↩
creationComplete="dataGrid_creationCompleteHandler(event)"↩
dataProvider="{getGoogleResultsResult.lastResult}">
        <mx:columns>
            <mx:DataGridColumn headerText="id" dataField="id"/>
            <mx:DataGridColumn headerText="updated" dataField="updated"/>
            <mx:DataGridColumn headerText="title" dataField="title"/>
            <mx:DataGridColumn headerText="link" dataField="link"/>
            <mx:DataGridColumn headerText="author" dataField="author"/>
            <mx:DataGridColumn headerText="generator" dataField="generator"/>
            <mx:DataGridColumn headerText="openSearch_totalResults"↩
dataField="openSearch_totalResults"/>
            <mx:DataGridColumn headerText="openSearch_startIndex"↩
dataField="openSearch_startIndex"/>
            <mx:DataGridColumn headerText="openSearch_itemsPerPage"↩
dataField="openSearch_itemsPerPage"/>
            <mx:DataGridColumn headerText="entry" dataField="entry"/>
```

```
        </mx:columns>
    </mx:DataGrid>
</s:Application>
```

Notice that we changed the following code:

```
getGoogleResults.getGoogleResults(/*Enter value(s) for */ bq);
```

To: `getGoogleResults.getGoogleResults("digital+camera");`

You can easily add a TextInput and Button components and allow the user to insert keywords and submit the form to retrieve the results, as well as adjust the results to fit what you need. The Adobe plug-in is a powerful tool and can be used in many cases to speed up development.

Run the application and see results in Figure 10-12.

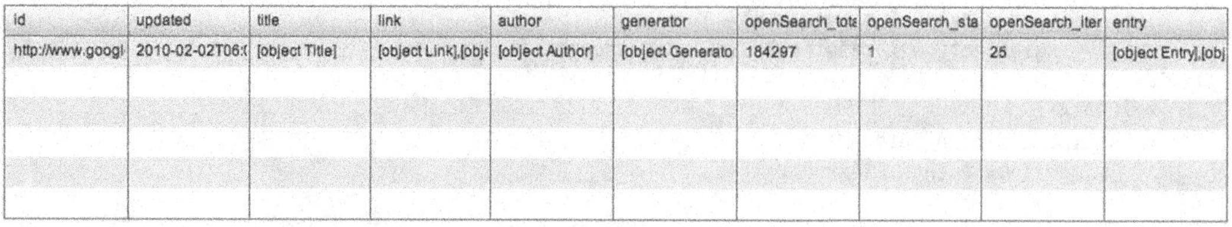

id	updated	title	link	author	generator	openSearch_tota	openSearch_sta	openSearch_iter	entry
http://www.googl	2010-02-02T06:(	[object Title]	[object Link],[obje	[object Author]	[object Generato	184297	1	25	[object Entry],[obj

Figure 10-12. DataGrid showing results retrieved from Google

Working with Web Feeds and Namespaces

Many XML web feeds have elements and attributes that are associated by a namespace. In order to be able to use namespaces, you will need to open the namespaces so you can access and use the elements and attributes on your feeds.

Many different namespace formats exist, and it would be difficult to cover all of them; however, once you master the principles, you will be able to handle any namespace that you come across.

When working with XML files, we recommend installing an open source plug-in for Eclipse called XMLBuddy if it's not already installed. It allows you to work with XML easily and efficiently since it has built-in features such as the following:

- Validating
- Coloring
- Dynamic code assist
- Updated outline (tree) view

To install XMLBuddy, follow these directions:

1. Download the plug-in from `http://www.xmlbuddy.com`.

2. Unzip the plug-in and place it in your Eclipse plug-ins directory: `C:\eclipse\plugins\`, or in Mac, `eclipse>plugins`.

3. Restart Eclipse, and make sure the shortcut has a target argument **–refresh**, in order for Eclipse to recognize the new plug-in.

4. To ensure XMLBuddy was installed correctly, create an XML file: select **File ➤ New ➤ Other ➤ XML ➤ Next**. Enter **NewFile.xml,** and click **Finish**.

With XMLBuddy installed, you can now add elements and attributes as well as namespaces by right-clicking the document.

To use XMLBuddy simple open the document with the XMLBuddy application. Once you right-click on elements you will see the options, as shown in Figure 10-13.

Now that you have XMLBuddy in your toolkit, you are ready to explore some of the most popular namespaces.

SPARQL Namespace

SPARQL is a query language for the Resource Definition Framework (RDF), and it is often used to express SQL queries across various data sources.

RDF is a framework used for describing and interchanging metadata. RDF can be anything with a URI associated to it. For more information visit http://www.w3.org/RDF/.

Here is an example of XML formatted in SPARQL:

```
<?xml version="1.0" encoding="utf-8"?>
<sparql xmlns="http://www.w3.org/2005/sparql-results#">

    <head>
        <variable name="x"/>
        <variable name="hpage"/>
    </head>

    <results>
        <result>
            <binding name="x">
                <bnode>r2</bnode>
            </binding>
            <binding name="hpage">
                <uri>http://work.example.org/bob/</uri>
            </binding>
            <binding name="name">
                <literal xml:lang="en">Bob</literal>
            </binding>
            <binding name="age">
                <literal datatype=
"http://www.w3.org/2001/XMLSchema#integer">
                    30
                </literal>
            </binding>
            <binding name="mbox">
                <uri>mailto:bob@work.example.org</uri>
            </binding>
        </result>
    </results>

</sparql>
```

Define the `SPARQL` namespace and set it to the SPARQL URL. Then, include the `use` statement for that namespace. Without the definition, you do not have access to the contents of the loaded XML document.

```
private namespace sparql="http://www.w3.org/2005/sparql-results#";
use namespace sparql;
```

Once the namespace is defined and is in use, you can access the attributes and elements. Using XMLBuddy and E4X, you can easily set the elements you need (see Figure 10-13).

```
feeds.results.result[0].binding.uri.
```

SPARQL.mxml	X SPARQL.xml ✕	
?-? xml		version="1.0" encoding="utf-8"
ⓔ sparql		
ⓐ xmlns		http://www.w3.org/2005/sparql-results#
ⓔ head		
ⓔ results		
ⓔ result		
ⓔ binding		
ⓔ binding		
ⓐ name		hpage
ⓔ uri		http://work.example.org/bob/
ⓔ binding		
ⓔ binding		
ⓔ binding		

Figure 10-13. SPARQL.xml tree view

Here is the complete code for the example that accesses elements and attributes on the SPARQL XML file:

```
<?xml version="1.0" encoding="utf-8"?>
<s:Application xmlns:fx="http://ns.adobe.com/mxml/2009"
               xmlns:s="library://ns.adobe.com/flex/spark"
               xmlns:mx="library://ns.adobe.com/flex/mx"
               minWidth="1024" minHeight="768"
               initialize="service.send();">

    <fx:Script>
        <![CDATA[
            import mx.controls.Alert;
            import mx.rpc.http.HTTPService;
            import mx.rpc.events.ResultEvent;
            import mx.rpc.events.FaultEvent;

            // Define and use SPARQL namespace.
            private namespace sparql = "http://www.w3.org/2005/sparql-results#";
            use namespace sparql;

            private function resultHandler(event:ResultEvent):void
```

```
            {
                var feeds:XML = event.result as XML;
                trace(feeds.results.result[0].binding.uri);
            }

            private function faultHandler(event:FaultEvent):void
            {
                service.removeEventListener(FaultEvent.FAULT, faultHandler);
                Alert.show(event.fault.message, "Error connecting");
            }
        ]]>
    </fx:Script>

    <fx:Declarations>
        <s:HTTPService id="service"
                       url="assets/xml/SPARQL.xml"
                       resultFormat="e4x"
                       result="resultHandler(event);"
                       fault="faultHandler(event);"/>
    </fx:Declarations>

</s:Application>
```

Atom Namespace

The Atom syndication format is an XML language that is used for web feeds, intended to improve RSS feeds. The primary usage of Atom feeds is syndication of different types of web content, such as that found on weblogs or news sites, to web sites or directly to users. To learn more, visit Atom's official site: http://www.atomenabled.org.

To access Atom attributes, the first step is to define and use Atom's namespace:

```
private namespace atom="http://www.w3.org/2005/Atom";
use namespace atom;
```

Now you can access the elements and attributes of this namespace. For example, let's say you want to access the following XML:

```
<?xml version="1.0" encoding="utf-8"?>
<feed xmlns="http://www.w3.org/2005/Atom">
    <title>Example Feed</title>
    <link href="http://example.org/"/>
    <updated>2003-12-13T18:30:02Z</updated>
    <author>
        <name>John Doe</name>
    </author>
    <id>urn:uuid:60a76c80</id>

    <entry>
        <title>Atom-Powered Robots Run Amok</title>
        <link href="http://example.org/2003/12/13/atom03"/>
        <id>urn:uuid:1225c695</id>
        <updated>2003-12-13T18:30:02Z</updated>
        <summary>Some text.</summary>
```

```
    </entry>
</feed>
```

Again, using e4x and XMLBuddy you can easily access the attribute:feeds.entry[0].title. (see Figure 10-14).

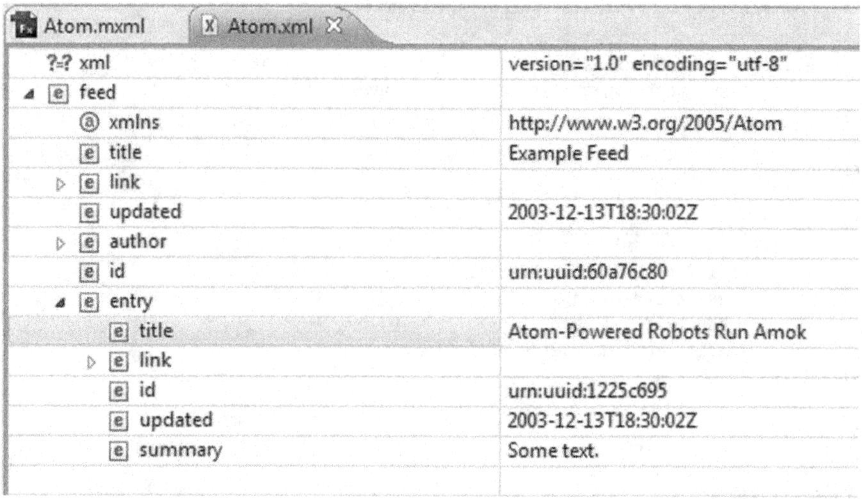

?=? xml	version="1.0" encoding="utf-8"
▲ e feed	
@ xmlns	http://www.w3.org/2005/Atom
e title	Example Feed
▷ e link	
e updated	2003-12-13T18:30:02Z
▷ e author	
e id	urn:uuid:60a76c80
▲ e entry	
e title	Atom-Powered Robots Run Amok
▷ e link	
e id	urn:uuid:1225c695
e updated	2003-12-13T18:30:02Z
e summary	Some text.

(Atom.mxml tab, Atom.xml tab)

Figure 10-14. Atom.xml tree view

Here's the complete code:

```
<?xml version="1.0" encoding="utf-8"?>
<s:Application xmlns:fx="http://ns.adobe.com/mxml/2009"
               xmlns:s="library://ns.adobe.com/flex/spark"
               xmlns:mx="library://ns.adobe.com/flex/mx"
               minWidth="1024" minHeight="768"
               initialize="service.send();">

    <fx:Script>
        <![CDATA[

            import mx.controls.Alert;
            import mx.rpc.http.HTTPService;
            import mx.rpc.events.ResultEvent;
            import mx.rpc.events.FaultEvent;

            // Define and use atom namespace.
            private namespace atom = "http://www.w3.org/2005/Atom";
            use namespace atom;

            private function resultHandler(event:ResultEvent):void
            {
                var feeds:XML = event.result as XML;
                trace(feeds.entry[0].title);
```

```
        }

        private function faultHandler(event:FaultEvent):void
        {
            service.removeEventListener(FaultEvent.FAULT, faultHandler);
            Alert.show(event.fault.message, "Could not load XML");
        }

    ]]>
</fx:Script>

<fx:Declarations>
    <s:HTTPService id="service"
            url="assets/xml/Atom.xml"
            resultFormat="e4x"
            result="resultHandler(event);"
            fault="faultHandler(event);"/>
</fx:Declarations>

</s:Application>
```

Notice how you define the namespace and use it as shown previously:

```
private namespace atom = "http://www.w3.org/2005/Atom";
use namespace atom;
```

Then you use the HTTPService to load the XML and once you receive the result you can retrieve elements.

GeoRSS namespace

GeoRSS is a lightweight format that is often used in feeds to map locations by adding basic geometries such as point, line, and box. To learn more about GeoRSS, visit its official site at http://georss.org/.

Let's look at an example of a GeoRSS XML:

```
<rss version="2.0" xmlns:georss="http://www.georss.org/georss">
<item>
    <georss:point>37.75988 -122.43739</georss:point>
</item>
</rss>
```

To extract the longitude and latitude point values, you first need to set a namespace just as you did before:

```
var georss:Namespace = new Namespace("http://www.georss.org/georss");
```

Then you can pull the xml using e4x standard object type format, as shown in Figure 10-15.

```
var geoResults:S tring = event.result.item.georss::point;
```

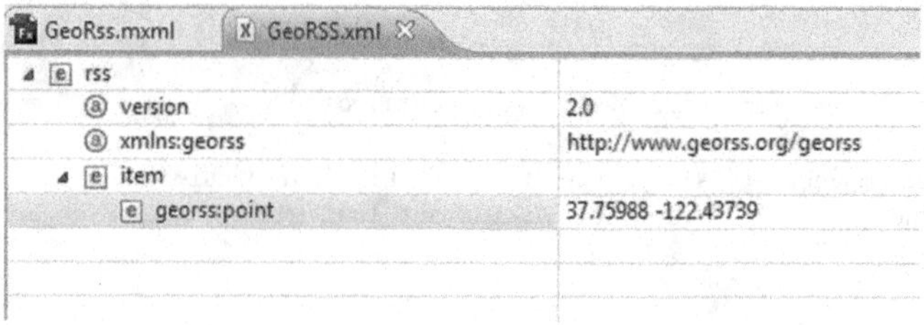

Figure 10-15. GeroRSS.xml tree view

Complete code:

```xml
<?xml version="1.0" encoding="utf-8"?>
<s:Application xmlns:fx="http://ns.adobe.com/mxml/2009"
               xmlns:s="library://ns.adobe.com/flex/spark"
               xmlns:mx="library://ns.adobe.com/flex/mx"
               minWidth="1024" minHeight="768"
               initialize="service.send();">

    <fx:Script>
        <![CDATA[

            import mx.controls.Alert;
            import mx.rpc.http.HTTPService;
            import mx.rpc.events.ResultEvent;
            import mx.rpc.events.FaultEvent;

            private function resultHandler(event:ResultEvent):void
            {
                var georss:Namespace = new Namespace("http://www.georss.org/georss");
                trace(String(event.result.item.georss::point));
            }

            private function faultHandler(event:FaultEvent):void
            {
                service.removeEventListener(FaultEvent.FAULT, faultHandler);
                Alert.show("Error connecting");
            }
        ]]>
    </fx:Script>

    <fx:Declarations>
        <s:HTTPService id="service"
                url="assets/xml/GeoRSS.xml"
                resultFormat="e4x"
                result="resultHandler(event);"
                fault="faultHandler(event);"/>
    </fx:Declarations>

</s:Application>
```

As you can see from the previous example, you make a service call to retrieve the XML and once you retrieve the results You set the name space:

```
var georss:Namespace = new Namespace("http://www.georss.org/georss");
```

Yoou can than access the results.

Creating a Proxy

The lack of `crossdomain.xml` can create a scenario where your Flex application works fine on your local machine but not on your server. The solution for the lack of a `crossdomain.xml` file is to use a proxy to connect to the data source and have Flash connect to the proxy instead of the data source directly. By connecting to a proxy instead of the service, you can access services that don't allow direct access for Flash. Web pages can access other open APIs and expose the data for the Flash player. The reason that using proxy works is that the Flash player allows accessing services from the same domain without the need to install a cross-domain policy.

There are a few ways to use proxies; one is to create a server-side script to connect to the data source.

Following are three open source examples of proxies that can be used for RESTful POST and GET methods, as well as for downloading binary data such as SWF files from a remote server. The proxy scripts will be available for download from the friendsofED site (`www.friendsofed.com`) as part of the example files that accompany this book.

PHP proxy

When using a server with PHP, you can usea lightweight open source PHP proxy script that handles two types of data: RESTful methods of GET and PUT and binary data such as SWF files or images. Keep in mind that PHP supports the CURL method in order for this script to work.

The following example loads XML/text:

```
http://yourserver.com/proxy.php?url= ↵
http://yourserver.com/blog/index.xml
```

This example loads a SWF (binary data) file:

```
http://yourserver.com/proxy.php?url= ↵
http://yourserver.com/files/some.swf& ↵
mimeType=application/x-shockwave-flash
```

Here's the complete code:

```php
<?php
// PHP Proxy
// Responds to both HTTP GET and POST requests
// Author: Abdul Qabiz
// March 31st, 2006

// Get the url of to be proxied
$url = ($_POST['url']) ? $_POST['url'] : $_GET['url'];
$headers = ($_POST['headers'])?$_POST['headers']:$_GET['headers'];
$mimeType =($_POST['mimeType'])?$_POST['mimeType']: ↵
$_GET['mimeType'];
```

```
//Start the Curl session
$session = curl_init($url);

// If it's a POST, put the POST data in the body
if ($_POST['url']) {
    $postvars = '';
    while ($element = current($_POST)) {
        $postvars .= key($_POST).'='.$element.'&';
        next($_POST);
    }
    curl_setopt ($session, CURLOPT_POST, true);
    curl_setopt ($session, CURLOPT_POSTFIELDS, $postvars);
}

// Don't return HTTP headers. Do return the contents of the call
curl_setopt($session,CURLOPT_HEADER,($headers=="true")?true:false);

curl_setopt($session, CURLOPT_FOLLOWLOCATION, true);
//curl_setopt($ch, CURLOPT_TIMEOUT, 4);
curl_setopt($session, CURLOPT_RETURNTRANSFER, true);

// Make the call
$response = curl_exec($session);

if ($mimeType != "")
{
    // The web service returns XML.
    // Set the Content-Type appropriately
    header("Content-Type: ".$mimeType);
}

echo $response;

curl_close($session);

?>
```

You first get the URL using either POST or GET, then you set the curl request and make the call and return the XML.

ASP Proxy

When using a server with ASP technology, you can use a lightweight open source ASP proxy script. This proxy can be used for RESTful services as well as binary data.

Usage:

```
http://yourserver.com/proxy.asp?url=<url_encoded_desitnation_url> ↵
[&mimeType=<mimeType>]
```

Example of using the ASP proxy to download binary data: `http://yourserver.com/proxy.asp?url=http://someserver/1.jpg&mimeType=image/jpg`.

Following is an open source script for a server that supports ASP:

```
<%
set objHttp = Server.CreateObject("Msxml2.ServerXMLHTTP")
strURL = Request("url")"
objHttp.open "GET", strURL, False
objHttp.Send

If objHttp.status = 200 Then
    Response.Expires = 90
    Response.ContentType = Request("mimeType")
    Response.BinaryWrite objHttp.responseBody
    set objHttp = Nothing
End If
%>
```

The ASP example is pretty straightforward. You set the server URL we are accessing and then we paste the content on the page.

JSP Proxy

Using JSP technology is similar to ASP. You can set the following proxy to be used for RESTful services as well as binary data.

The following is an open source script for a server that supports JSP:

```
<%@ page language="java" contentType="text/html; charset=utf-8"
pageEncoding="utf-8"
import="java.io.BufferedReader,
java.io.InputStreamReader,
java.io.IOException,
java.io.InputStream,
java.net.MalformedURLException,
java.net.URL,
java.net.URLConnection"

private String contentURL;
public static final String CONTENT_URL_NAME = "contentURL";

// get the url through the request:
If (contentURL == null) {
    contentURL = (String)request.getAttribute(CONTENT_URL_NAME);

    if (contentURL == null) {
      contentURL=(String)request.getParameter(CONTENT_URL_NAME);
    }
}

if (contentURL == null) {
    throw new ServletException("A content URL must be provided, ←
as a"'" + CONTENT_URL_NAME + ←
"'" request attribute or request parameter.");
    URL url = null;
}

try {
```

```
      // get a connection to the content:
      url = new URL(contentURL);
      URLConnection urlConn = url.openConnection();

      // show the client the content type:
      String contentType = urlConn.getContentType();
      response.setContentType(contentType);

      // get the input stream
      InputStream in = urlConn.getInputStream();
      BufferedReader br = new BufferedReader(↵
new InputStreamReader(in));
      char[] buffer = new char[1024];
      String contentString = "";
      String tmp = br.readLine();

      do
        {
            contentString += tmp + "\n";
            tmp = br.readLine();
        }

      while (tmp != null);
      out.flush();
      out.close();
}

catch (MalformedURLException me)  {
    // on new URL:
    throw new ServletException("URL:'"+contentURL+"' ↵
is malformed.");
}

catch (IOException ioe)  {
    // on open connection:
    throw new ServletException("Exception while ↵
opening '" +
    contentURL + "': " + ioe.getMessage());
}

catch (Exception e) {
    // on reading input:
     throw new ServletException
        ("Exception during proxy request: "+ ↵
e.getMessage());
}

%>
```

The JSP proxy provides you with the XML printed on the page, just as in the other examples.

Utilizing Mashup Platforms As Proxies

You can also utilize a mashup platform to be your proxy when a proxy is needed. Mashup platforms such as Yahoo! Pipes encourage users to create mashups using visual editors. These tools allow users to create a complete application and publish it on their cloud without any programming knowledge at all.

Many of these platforms have a `crossdomain.xml` policy installed already, which allows you to utilize these platforms as your proxy, saving you time and reducing your server resources since you don't need to create a server-side proxy. In addition, these platforms can reduce bandwidth on your server, and they include modules to combine many feeds together, and to filter as well as format results, saving some of the interconnectivity work.

At the time of writing Yahoo! Pipes, is a Flash friendly platform and it has a nonrestrictive (wild card) `crossdomain.xml` policy. To view Yahoo! Pipes' `crossdomain.xml` file, visit `http://pipes.yahooapis.com/crossdomain.xml`.

These services can help you, the Flex developer, create XML feeds that you will be able import into your application, saving you hours of coding; it's also ideal in cases where you are trying to create proof of concept (POC) and need to limit the amount of hours spent on development. As an example, you can create logic by mixing a few feeds together, and then publish the pipe as a service and import it into a Flex application.

Rolex Watches Service

Yahoo! Pipes allows you to create a data source, publish it, and access it in different formats such as RSS or JSON output. As an exercise, let's create a service that will show Rolex watches available for sale in ZIP code 10005 from Google Merchant Center, Craigslist, and Yahoo! Local. You will generate three feeds in Yahoo! Pipes and add a "union" item to combine them into one feed, making the feeds from these three sites ready to import into Flash Builder.

Go to Yahoo! Pipes at `http://pipes.yahoo.com/pipes/` and create an account. Then choose to create a pipe.

First you'll add the data sources using the drag-and-drop toolbar on the left (see Figure 10-16).

1. Drag and drop a **Fetch Feed** module and enter the Craigslist feed URL:
   `http://newyork.craigslist.org/search/sss?query=rolex&format=rss`.

2. Drag and drop a Google Base (that's the old name of Google Merchant Center) module and set the ZIP code in keywords.

3. Drag and drop a **Yahoo! Local** module and set the keyword and ZIP code.

Figure 10-16. Yahoo! Pipes Toolbar

Next, choose **Operators** and then drag and drop a **Union** module in order to combine these three data sources into one feed.

Finally, connect the Yahoo! Pipe **Output** to the **Union** module and test. You should have a pipe that looks like the one in Figure 10-17.

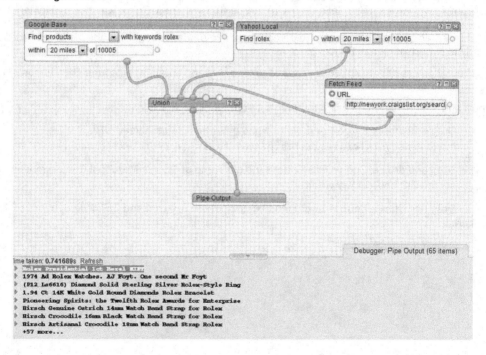

Figure 10-17. Complete Yahoo! pipes

Once the pipe is ready, you can run the pipe and publish it. You can see the results on a map (see Figure 10-18). You have options to access the results in different format. We will show you how to access the results as RSS feeds and JSON.

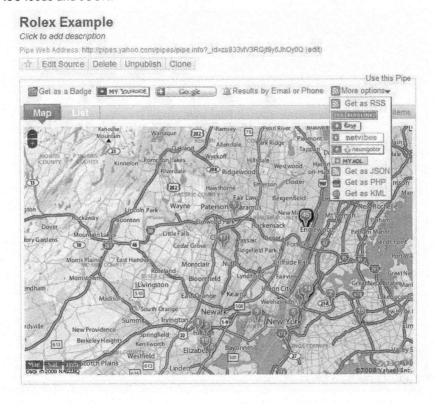

Figure 10-18. Published Yahoo! pipe

You can access the information as RSS feeds using e4x. Choose **More Options,** and then choose **RSS feeds** in the published pipe. You can see the results in Figure 10-19.

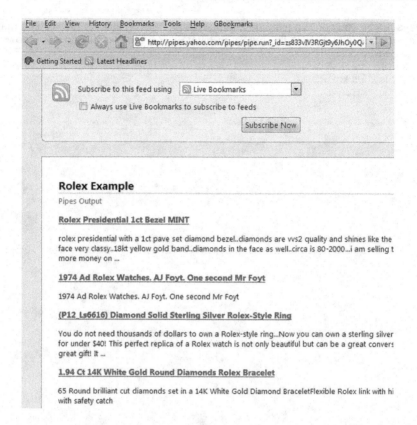

Figure 10-19. Yahoo! pipe RSS feeds

Let's create an application that retrieves the RSS feeds using e4x. Create a new project and call it YahooPipes. Next, create a new MXML application and name it YahooPipesE4X.mxml, as shown in the following code:

```
<?xml version="1.0" encoding="utf-8"?>
<s:Application xmlns:fx="http://ns.adobe.com/mxml/2009"
               xmlns:s="library://ns.adobe.com/flex/spark"
               xmlns:mx="library://ns.adobe.com/flex/mx"
               minWidth="1024" minHeight="768"
               initialize="service.send();">

    <fx:Script>
        <![CDATA[
            import mx.rpc.events.FaultEvent;
            import mx.rpc.events.ResultEvent;

            [Bindable]
            private var urlLocation:String =↩
 "http://pipes.yahoo.com/pipes/pipe.run?_id=zs833vIV3RGjt9y6JhOy0Q&_render=rss";
```

```
            private function handleResults(event:ResultEvent):void
            {
                var list:XML = event.result as XML;
            }


            protected function faultHandler(event:FaultEvent):void
            {
                trace("Error loading URL");
            }

        ]]>
    </fx:Script>

    <fx:Declarations>
        <s:HTTPService id="service"
                        url="{urlLocation}"
                        resultFormat="e4x"
                        result="handleResults(event)"
                        fault="faultHandler(event)"/>
    </fx:Declarations>

</s:Application>
```

Another format you can use to parse the results is JSON. Create a new MXML application and call it JSONExample.mxml. To get started make sure that as3corelib.swc (code.google.com/p/as3corelib/) is added to your **libs** directory before running this script. as3corelib have a class to decode the JSON format.

```
<?xml version="1.0" encoding="utf-8"?>
<s:Application xmlns:fx="http://ns.adobe.com/mxml/2009"
                xmlns:s="library://ns.adobe.com/flex/spark"
                xmlns:mx="library://ns.adobe.com/flex/mx"
                minWidth="1024" minHeight="768"
                initialize="httpService.send();">

    <fx:Script>
        <![CDATA[
            import com.adobe.serialization.json.JSON;

            import mx.rpc.events.FaultEvent;
            import mx.rpc.events.ResultEvent;

            [Bindable]
            private var urlLocation:String =↩
"http://pipes.yahoo.com/pipes/pipe.run?_id=zs833vIV3RGjt9y6JhOyOQ&_render=json";

            private function handleResults(event:ResultEvent):void
            {
                var rawData:String = String(event.result);
                var results:Object = JSON.decode(rawData);
                  var items:Object = results.value.items;
            }

            protected function faultHandler(event:FaultEvent):void
```

```
        {
            trace("Error loading URL");
        }

    ]]>
</fx:Script>

<fx:Declarations>
    <s:HTTPService id="httpService"
            url="{urlLocation}"
            useProxy="false" method="GET"
              resultFormat="text"
            result="handleResults(event)"
              fault="faultHandler(event)">
    </s:HTTPService>
</fx:Declarations>

</s:Application>
```

Place a line break point after the object gets decoded:

```
var items:Object = results.value.items;
```

In the variable window in Eclipse or FlashBuilder, you can view all the items.

Job Search Service

Let's create another Yahoo! pipe In this example, you will create a pipe that allows the user to enter information. It's more complex than the previous example, but it will give you an idea how you can maximize your use of pipes.

You will use some RSS feeds from Indeed.com, a job search service. The RSS service expects three parameters: **q**, **l**, and **radius**.

- **q**: (Stands for query) Allows you to sort results based on keywords.
- **l**: (Stands for location) Accepts an address or a ZIP code.
- **radius**: Accepts a number and represents the distance in miles to retrieve results.

For example, `http://rss.indeed.com/rss?q=flex+developer&l=10005&radius=25` will provide RSS results for Flex developer positions within the ZIP code 10005 and a radius of 25 miles. Please keep in mind that Indeed.com can change their parameters at any time, and you will have to adjust your application accordingly.

We will be using a **URL Builder** module, which allows us to connect an input box module. Let's drag and drop a **URL Builder** module under the **URL** tool. You will place the base URL, `http://rss.indeed.com/rss`, in the **base** input box, and then create three query parameters for each one of the queries: **q**, **l**, and **radius.**

Next, drag and drop a **User Input** module and connect it to the query parameters in the **URL Builder**.

You then add a **Fetch Feed** module and connect it to the **URL Builder** module.

Now, you need to extract and format geographic information. Indeed, RSS has a geo namespace, and you can save work in Flash Builder by using a particular Yahoo! Pipes module: **Location Extractor** analyzes the feeds looking for location and will format in a latitude and longitude subelement.

The last step is to connect **Fetch Feed** to **Pipe Output** (see Figure 10-20), and run and publish the pipe. You can see the final Yahoo! Pipe results in Figure 10-21.

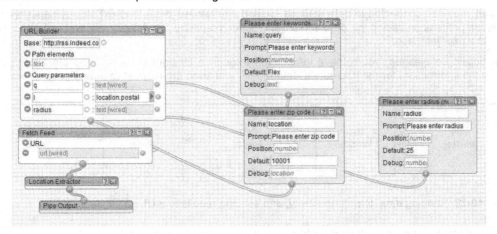

Figure 10-20. Yahoo! pipe RSS diagram

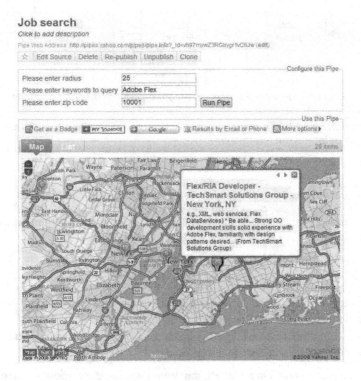

Figure 10-21. Yahoo! pipe published page

Data Interconnectivity

Now that you have connected to data sources to send and retrieve data, the next step is *interconnectivity*. This is the process of placing the data into a data model, preparing the data for display, and attaching the data into a user interface.

When building a mashup, you retrieve information through a UI from the user. You then may need to validate the information, format it, create a data model, and send the request to a data source (see Figure 10-22).

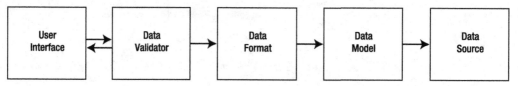

Figure 10-22. Reading data, interconnectivity, and sending results to a UI

Similarly, once you retrieve information from a data source, you may need to validate the information, format it, create a data model, and display the results back in a UI (see Figure 10-23).

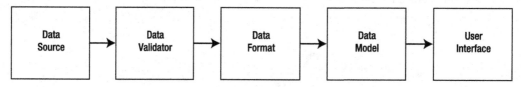

Figure 10-23. Getting information from the user, interconnectivity, and sending results to a data source

Keep in mind that following all these steps is not always necessary, since there may be times when you don't need to validate or format the information.

Data Model

The most popular three ways to deal with data model is either to create a data model using the data model tag in MXML, create a data model object that can be used in MVC (Model, View, controller) enterprise Microarcitecture frameworks, or just place the model into a data provider such as `ArrayCollection` data type or `DataProvider` tag.

A data model is an abstract model to describe the data properties and how to access it.

Advantages of creating data mode object are the follwing:

- A data model object contains properties for storing data and optional helpers' methods for additional functionality.
- Creating a data model allows you to bind a user interface data into a data model or you can bind data from service directly to a data model.

You can define a simple data model in an MXML tag. When you need manipulation, use AS3 Value Object (VO) data model.

Let's create two data models: one is using the MXML tag and the other one as a VO.

Creating Data Model Using the fx:Model and fx:XML Tags

Two helpful tags are the `fx:Model` and the `fx:XML` tag. These tags are compiler tags. See the the following example:

```
<fx:Model id="infoVO">
    <root>
        <fullName>John Doe</fullName>
        <email>john@gmail.com</email>
        <phone>212-222-2222</phone>
        <zip>10001</zip>
    </root>
</fx:Model>
```

MXML is a declarative languge and forming the model is very similar to XML as you can see.

Create a new project and call it DataModel. Take a look at the following two examples, one creates the properties inside the Model tag and one attaches to a source XML file. Run the examples in debug mode to see the results of the trace statements in the console window. The expected results in the console are as follows:

```
infoVO full name property: John Doe
info2VO full name property: John Doe
```

In the DataModel.mxml, write the following complete code:

```
<?xml version="1.0" encoding="utf-8"?>
<s:Application xmlns:fx="http://ns.adobe.com/mxml/2009"
               xmlns:s="library://ns.adobe.com/flex/spark"
               xmlns:mx="library://ns.adobe.com/flex/mx"
               minWidth="1024" minHeight="768"
            creationComplete="creationCompleteHandler(event)">
    <fx:Script>
        <![CDATA[
            import mx.events.FlexEvent;

            protected function creationCompleteHandler(event:FlexEvent):void
            {
                trace("infoVO full name property: "+this.infoVO.fullName);
                trace("info2VO full name property: "+this.info2VO.fullName);
            }

        ]]>
    </fx:Script>

    <fx:Declarations>

        <fx:Model id="infoVO">
            <root>
                <fullName>John Doe</fullName>
                <email>john@gmail.com</email>
                <phone>212-222-2222</phone>
                <zip>10001</zip>
```

```
            </root>
        </fx:Model>

        <fx:Model id="info2VO" source="Info.xml" />

    </fx:Declarations>

</s:Application>
```

Once the creationCompleteHandler method is called, you can access the infoVO model data you created: infoVO.fullName

As for the info2VO class, you will need to create a new XML, call it info.xml, then paste the following content:

```
<?xml version="1.0"?>
<root>
        <fullName>John Doe</fullName>
        <email>john@gmail.com</email>
        <phone>212-222-2222</phone>
        <zip>10001</zip>
</root>
```

We pointed out before that the tags are compiler tags, but what this means is that the mxmlc handles these tags differently than regular tags in MXML. The source can be set to an external source, however the compiler retrieves the information and sets it as an ObjectProxy, which allows the object to be bindable. Additionally, it does direct assignment so there is no service call to retrieve the data as you may expect from an MXML tag, meaning it's strongly typing the data into a class instead of loading it during runtime. Take a look at what the compiler does when you use set info2VO with the source property.

You have two model tags in the code and although one tag calls the xml using the source property and another one does direct assignment, the mxmlc, which will generate the same code for both of these tags. Take a look at what the compiler does when you use set infoVO and info2VO with the source property:

```
private function _DataModel_ObjectProxy2_i() : mx.utils.ObjectProxy
{
        var temp : mx.utils.ObjectProxy = new mx.utils.ObjectProxy();
        temp.fullName = "John Doe";
        temp.email = "john@gmail.com";
        temp.phone = "212-222-2222";
        temp.zip = 10001;
        info2VO = temp;
        return temp;
}

private function _DataModel_ObjectProxy1_i() : mx.utils.ObjectProxy
{
        var temp : mx.utils.ObjectProxy = new mx.utils.ObjectProxy();
        temp.fullName = "John Doe";
        temp.email = "john@gmail.com";
        temp.phone = "212-222-2222";
        temp.zip = 10001;
        infoVO = temp;
        return temp;
}
```

Here's what the mxmlc code generated to create the binding tag:

```
[Bindable(event="propertyChange")]
    public function get info2VO():mx.utils.ObjectProxy
    {
        return this._1945369341info2VO;
    }

    public function set info2VO(value:mx.utils.ObjectProxy):void
    {
        var oldValue:Object = this._1945369341info2VO;
        if (oldValue !== value)
        {
            this._1945369341info2VO = value;
            this.dispatchEvent(mx.events.PropertyChangeEvent.createUpdateEvent(this,↩
"info2VO", oldValue, value));
        }
    }

        /**
         * generated bindable wrapper for property infoVO (public)
         * - generated setter
         * - generated getter
         * - original public var 'infoVO' moved to '_1184171033infoVO'
         */

    [Bindable(event="propertyChange")]
    public function get infoVO():mx.utils.ObjectProxy
    {
        return this._1184171033infoVO;
    }

    public function set infoVO(value:mx.utils.ObjectProxy):void
    {
        var oldValue:Object = this._1184171033infoVO;
        if (oldValue !== value)
        {
            this._1184171033infoVO = value;
            this.dispatchEvent(mx.events.PropertyChangeEvent.createUpdateEvent(this, "infoVO", oldValue,
value));
        }
    }
```

It's good to understand how the mxmlc works which can help you decide what type of model class you want to create.

Creating Data Model Using an Object Class

Here is the same data model as an object class, often used in Flex frameworks. Notice that you set the entire class as Bindable to bind all the properties in the class. The constructor allows you to set all the properties in the VO for easy creation of the class.

```
package vo
{
```

```
[Bindable]
public final class InfoVO
{
    public var fullName:String;
    public var email:String;
    public var phone:uint;
    public var zip:String;

    public function InfoVO(fullName:String, email:String, phone:uint, zip:String)
    {
        this.fullName = fullName;
        this.email = email;
        this.phone = phone;
        this.zip = zip;
    }
}
}
```

Here is how you would set the properties of the VO:

```
public var info:InfoVO = new InfoVO("John Doe", "john@gmail.com", 2122222222, "10005");
```

See the complete code example in the following. Run application in debug mode to see the full name string showing in the console:

```
<?xml version="1.0" encoding="utf-8"?>
<s:Application xmlns:fx="http://ns.adobe.com/mxml/2009"
               xmlns:s="library://ns.adobe.com/flex/spark"
               xmlns:mx="library://ns.adobe.com/flex/mx"
               minWidth="1024" minHeight="768"
               creationComplete="creationCompleteHandler(event)">

    <fx:Script>
        <![CDATA[
            import mx.events.FlexEvent;
            import vo.InfoVO;

            public var info:InfoVO = new InfoVO("John Doe",  ↵
                "john@gmail.com", 2122222222, "10005");

            protected function creationCompleteHandler(event:FlexEvent):void
            {
                trace(info.fullName);
            }

        ]]>
    </fx:Script>

</s:Application>
```

You can also create a collection to hold the information such as XML using the e4x format:

```
<?xml version="1.0" encoding="utf-8"?>
<s:Application xmlns:fx="http://ns.adobe.com/mxml/2009"
               xmlns:s="library://ns.adobe.com/flex/spark"
```

```
            xmlns:mx="library://ns.adobe.com/flex/mx"
            minWidth="1024" minHeight="768"
        creationComplete="creationCompleteHandler(event)">
    <fx:Script>
        <![CDATA[
            import mx.events.FlexEvent;

            protected function creationCompleteHandler(event:FlexEvent):void
            {
                trace(info.fullName);
            }

        ]]>
    </fx:Script>

    <fx:Declarations>
        <fx:XML id="info" format="e4x">
            <root>
                <fullName>John Doe</fullName>
                <email>john@gmail.com</email>
                <phone>212-222-2222</phone>
                <zip>10001</zip>
            </root>
        </fx:XML>
    </fx:Declarations>

</s:Application>
```

So far we talked about the fx:Model and fx:XML tags and how the mxmlc creates an ObjectProxy component: it allows you to bind the data's properties as in the example below. Create a new MXML application and call it SimpleForm.mxml:

```
<?xml version="1.0" encoding="utf-8"?>
<s:Application xmlns:fx="http://ns.adobe.com/mxml/2009"
            xmlns:s="library://ns.adobe.com/flex/spark"
            xmlns:mx="library://ns.adobe.com/flex/mx"
            minWidth="1024" minHeight="768">

    <s:layout>
        <s:BasicLayout/>
    </s:layout>
```

You set the infoVO object using the Model tag. Notice that each property uses the bindable brackets so you will be able to change the Model component as you update the form.

```
    <fx:Declarations>
        <fx:Model id="infoVO">
            <root>
                <fullName>{fullNameTextInput.text}</fullName>
                <email>{emailTextInput.text}</email>
                <phone>{phoneTextInput.text}</phone>
                <zip>{zipTextInput.text}</zip>
            </root>
        </fx:Model>
    </fx:Declarations>
```

You are using a DataGrid to show the results and values of the infoVO object you set. Since the data provider is bindable you can see the information as you change the properties in the VO.

```
<mx:DataGrid x="11" y="164" id="dataGrid"
             dataProvider="{infoVO}">
    <mx:columns>
        <mx:DataGridColumn
            headerText="fullName"
            dataField="fullName"/>
        <mx:DataGridColumn
            headerText="email"
            dataField="email"/>
        <mx:DataGridColumn
            headerText="phone"
            dataField="phone"/>
        <mx:DataGridColumn
            headerText="zip"
            dataField="zip"/>
    </mx:columns>
</mx:DataGrid>
```

The Form tag has all the properties you can change in the infoVO object.

```
<mx:Form>
    <mx:FormItem label="FullName">
        <s:TextInput
            id="fullNameTextInput"/>
    </mx:FormItem>
    <mx:FormItem label="Email">
        <s:TextInput
            id="emailTextInput"/>
    </mx:FormItem>
    <mx:FormItem label="Phone">
        <s:TextInput
            id="phoneTextInput"/>
    </mx:FormItem>
    <mx:FormItem label="Zip">
        <s:TextInput
            id="zipTextInput"/>
    </mx:FormItem>
</mx:Form>
</s:Application>
```

See Figure 10-24 for a screen shot of the application you just created.

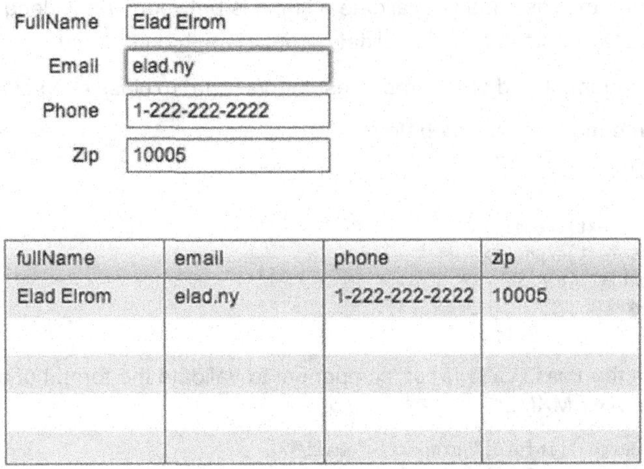

FullName	Elad Elrom
Email	elad.ny
Phone	1-222-222-2222
Zip	10005

fullName	email	phone	zip
Elad Elrom	elad.ny	1-222-222-2222	10005

Figure 10-24. Application containing DataGrid and a simple form to show the Model changing

Data Validation

Data validation is often used as part of building any Flex application in general, but is also an important step to creating a successful Mashup. You will often need to validate UI forms before sending the information through an RPC component.

> *Data validation is the process of ensuring data is evaluated to meet your requirements before sending or displaying the data.*

AS3 has a `Validator` API as part of the framework and allows you to evaluate format from different data types such as:

- `CreditCardValidator` class used to validate credit card length, prefix, and passes card type algorithm.
- `CurrencyValidator` class used to validate currency expression.
- `DateValidator` class used to validate proper dates and format.
- `EmailValidator` class used to validate email address format such as @ sign and other requirements.
- `NumberValidator` class used to ensure a string is a valid number.
- `PhoneNumberValidator` class used to validate that a string is in a valid phone number format.
- `RegExpValidator` class used with a custom `validator` allows you to use a regular expression to validate a field.
- `SocialSecurityValidator` class used to ensure a string is a valid United States Social Security number.

- `StringValidator` class used to validate a string is between certain lengths.
- `ZipCodeValidator` class used to validate proper length and format.

In addition, to verifying the format and other properties, the `Validator`class can set the field as required.

You will be using the same model object as before.

```
<mx:Model id="infoVO">
    <infoVOistration>
        <email>{email.text}</email>
        <phone>{phone.text}</phone>
        <zip>{zip.text}</zip>
    </infoVOistration>
</mx:Model>
```

To create code that uses the `EmailValidator` component to validate the format of a data model, you first need to create the `validator` MXML:

```
<mx:EmailValidator source="{infoVO}" property="email"
    trigger="{submit}" triggerEvent="click" listener="{email}"/>
```

You need to validate more properties upon submitting the form. The `listener` is `bindable` to the UI component and it controls both the border color of the component as well as the `tooltip` error message.

```
<mx:PhoneNumberValidator source="{infoVO}" property="phone"
    trigger="{submit}" triggerEvent="click" listener="{phone}"/>
```

You can see the complete code below:

```
<?xml version="1.0" encoding="utf-8"?>
<s:Application xmlns:fx="http://ns.adobe.com/mxml/2009"
               xmlns:s="library://ns.adobe.com/flex/spark"
               xmlns:mx="library://ns.adobe.com/flex/mx"
               minWidth="1024" minHeight="768">

    <fx:Declarations>

        <fx:Model id="infoVO">
            <infoVOistration>
                <email>{email.text}</email>
                <phone>{phone.text}</phone>
                <zip>{zip.text}</zip>
            </infoVOistration>
        </fx:Model>

        <mx:EmailValidator source="{infoVO}" property="email"
            trigger="{submit}" triggerEvent="click" listener="{email}"/>
        <mx:PhoneNumberValidator source="{infoVO}" property="phone"
            trigger="{submit}" triggerEvent="click" listener="{phone}"/>
        <mx:ZipCodeValidator source="{infoVO}"
            property="zip" trigger="{submit}" triggerEvent="click" listener="{zip}"/>

    </fx:Declarations>

    <!-- Form contains user input controls. -->
    <mx:Form>
```

```
        <mx:FormItem label="Email" required="true">
            <mx:TextInput id="email" width="200"/>
        </mx:FormItem>
        <mx:FormItem label="Phone" required="true">
            <mx:TextInput id="phone" width="200"/>
        </mx:FormItem>
        <mx:FormItem label="Zip" required="true">
            <mx:TextInput id="zip" width="60"/>
        </mx:FormItem>
        <mx:FormItem>

            <s:Button id="submit" label="Validate"/>
        </mx:FormItem>
    </mx:Form>

</s:Application>
```

Creating a validator is an important step in the process and will ensure the user is limited with their choices to enter only values that are expected.

Changing Tool Tip Error Message Color

In case you are not too crazy about the red color of the tool tip, you can change the error message tool tip color easily by setting a style tag and set the errorTip property:

```
<fx:Style>
        .errorTip { borderColor: #00FFCC}
</fx:Style>
```

The final application will look as shown in Figure 10-25.

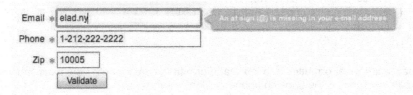

Figure 10-25. Validating form screen shot

Data Format

When sending an RPC request to a service as part of your mashup or when receiving a response from a service, you often need to format some fields before displaying them in a UI or submitting them to a service.

Many services require that you format the date or other fields according to their requirements. In addition, many services will return a result in a format that is common in the native service language and you would need to format the value before displaying the results in a UI.

The data formatting component lets you format data into a customized string.

There are different types of data formatting components such as the following:

- `CurrencyFormatter` class is used for formatting a number, plus adding the currency symbol.
- `DateFormatter` class is used for formatting the date and time in many different combinations.
- `NumberFormatter` class is used for formatting a numeric data.
- `PhoneFormatter` class is used for formatting a phone number.
- `ZipCodeFormatter` class is used for formatting United States and Canadian zip codes.

To format a date, start by declaring a `DateFormatter` component with an MM/DD/YYYY date format. Next `Bind` the formatted version of a Date object, which was returned from a web service to the `text` property of a `TextInput` component. Here is an example:

```
<?xml version="1.0" encoding="utf-8"?>
<s:Application xmlns:fx="http://ns.adobe.com/mxml/2009"
               xmlns:s="library://ns.adobe.com/flex/spark"
               xmlns:mx="library://ns.adobe.com/flex/mx"
               minWidth="1024" minHeight="768">

    <fx:Declarations>
        <mx:PhoneFormatter id="phoneFormatter" areaCode="212"
                           formatString=" ###-####" />
        <mx:DateFormatter id="dateFormatter"
                           formatString="month: MM, day: DD, year: YYYY"/>
    </fx:Declarations>

    <s:VGroup>
            <s:Label text="Enter your Manhattan 7 digit phone number:"/>
            <s:Label id="phone" change="if (phone.text.length == 7) ↵
                  { phone.text = phoneFormatter.format(phone.text) } "/>
            <s: text="Enter date (mm/dd/yyyy):"/>
            <s:Label id="date" change="if (date.text.length == 10) ↵
                  { date.text = dateFormatter.format(date.text); } "/>
    </s:VGroup>

</s:Application>
```

The example uses mx:PhoneFormatter and mx:DateFormatter component. You pass the formatString method and you can then update the Labelcomponent upon change.

Each data formatting component includes event handling for Invalid value and Invalid format. The error message is placed in a public variable called `error`. If an error occurs the formatting component will return an empty string.

See the same example with error message:

```
<?xml version="1.0" encoding="utf-8"?>
<s:Application xmlns:fx="http://ns.adobe.com/mxml/2009" ↵
xmlns:s="library://ns.adobe.com/flex/spark"
xmlns:mx="library://ns.adobe.com/flex/mx"
minWidth="1024" minHeight="768">

    <fx:Declarations>
        <mx:PhoneFormatter id="phoneFormatter" areaCode="212"
                formatString=" ###-####" />
        <mx:DateFormatter id="dateFormatter"
                formatString="month: MM, day: DD, year: YYYY"/>
    </fx:Declarations>

    <s:VGroup>
        <s:Label text="Enter your Manhattan 7 digit phone number:"/>
        <s:TextInput id="phone" change="if (phone.text.length == 7) ↵
{ phone.text = phoneFormatter.format(phone.text); error.text = ↵
 phoneFormatter.error } "/>
        <s:Label text="Enter date (mm/dd/yyyy):"/>
        <s:TextInput id="date" change="if (date.text.length == 10) ↵
{ date.text = dateFormatter.format(date.text); error.text = ↵
dateFormatter.error } "/>
        <s:Label text="Errors:"/>
        <s:TextInput id="error" />
    </s:VGroup>

</s:Application>
```

PhoneFormatter and DateFormatter are similar to the previous example with the mx:PhoneFormatter and mx:DateFormatter component. As you can see, the out of the box Flex components for formatting are easy to use and will fit into most of the applications you build.

Attaching Data to a UI Component

After the data is returned, validated, and formatted, the last part of data interconnection is attaching the data to a UI component. You can use any UI Component, either part of the framework shipped with Flex or a custom component. Most results will be suited to list type components such as:

- `dataGrid/ AdvancedDataGrid`
- `List`
- `TileList`

The commonality to these types of components is that they all accept the ArrayCollection data type as a data feed. Once you retrieve information from RPC, you can format the information and then place it into an ArrayCollection and easily attach it to a component. Once you attach it to a component, you can use a `repeater` or a renderer to style and format the results.

You will create an example to look for product results in Google Merchant Center. The application will look like Figure 10-26.

Figure 10-26. Google Merchant Center search results attached to a UI Component

Create a new Flex application and call it GoogleBaseUI.

Define a Bindable variable to hold the keywords and an ArrayCollection to hold the results.

```
[Bindable]
private var keywords:String = "rolex";
```

```
[Bindable]
private var dataProvider:ArrayCollection = new ArrayCollection();
```

Navigate to Google Merchant Center: http://www.google.com/base/feeds/snippets?bq=[keyword] .

Download a sample XML and place it in Eclipse. You can then view the document structure using XMLBuddy (see Figure 10-27).

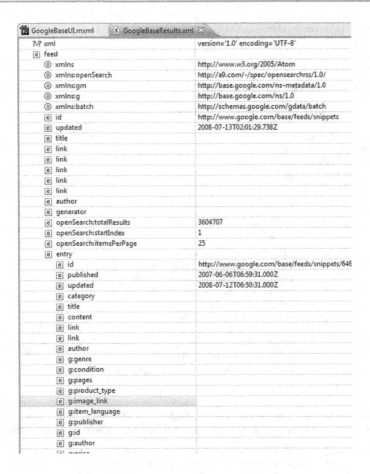

Figure 10-27. Variable window result object.

Looking at the elements tree it appears that each entry has detail nodes under:

```
<g:element>
```

You need to add the namespace to be able to access all the `xmlns:g` namespace elements. Looking at the header of the feeds you can find out the URL that needs to be used to open the `xmlns:g` namespace:

```
http://base.google.com/ns/1.0
```

Define `Atom` and g namespacing:

```
private namespace atom = "http://www.w3.org/2005/Atom";
use namespace atom;
private namespace g = "http://base.google.com/ns/1.0 ";
use namespace g;
```

Create the `HTTPService` component and set the request and response handlers.

```
<s:HTTPService id="service"
```

```
url="http://www.google.com/base/feeds/snippets"
resultFormat="e4x"
result="resultHandler(event); "
fault="faultHandler(event); ">
```

Handle the response for a successful connection:

```
private function resultHandler(event:ResultEvent):void
{
            var title:String;
            var publish:String;
            var content:String;
            var author:String;
            var image:String;
            var price:String;

            for each (var property:XML in event.result.entry)
            {
                        title = property.title;
                        publish = property.published;
                        content = property.content;
                        author = property.author.name;
                        image = property.image_link;
                        price = property.price;

                        dataProvider.addItem({label: title, publish: ↵
                        publish, content: content,
                        author: author, icon: image, price: price});
            }
}
```

Attach the results to a UI component. Notice that the item will be formatted as renderers.TileListItemRenderer, a common practice in dealing with List type component.

```
            <mx:TileList id="CameraSelection" height="250" width="500"
                        itemRenderer="renderers.TileListItemRenderer"
                        maxColumns="5" rowHeight="120" columnWidth="125"
                        dataProvider="{dataProvider}" />
```

Here is the item renderer located here: renderers/TileListItemRenderer. Parameter data is assigned automatically holding the item DataProvider.

```
<?xml version="1.0" encoding="utf-8"?>
<mx:VBox xmlns:mx="http://www.adobe.com/2006/mxml" verticalAlign="middle"
            horizontalAlign="center" horizontalScrollPolicy="off"
            verticalScrollPolicy="off" width="100%" height="100%">

    <mx:Image source="{data.icon}" width="" />
    <mx:Label text="{data.label}" truncateToFit="true" width="100" height="14"/>
    <mx:Label text="{data.price}" truncateToFit="true" width="100" />

</mx:VBox>
```

Complete code is shown below:

```
<?xml version="1.0" encoding="utf-8"?>
```

```
<s:Application xmlns:fx="http://ns.adobe.com/mxml/2009"
               xmlns:s="library://ns.adobe.com/flex/spark"
               xmlns:mx="library://ns.adobe.com/flex/mx"
               minWidth="1024" minHeight="768"
               initialize="service.send();">

    <fx:Script>
        <![CDATA[
            import mx.collections.ArrayCollection;

            import mx.controls.Alert;
            import mx.rpc.http.HTTPService;
            import mx.rpc.events.ResultEvent;
            import mx.rpc.events.FaultEvent;

            [Bindable]
            private var keywords:String = "rolex";

            [Bindable]
            private var dataProvider:ArrayCollection = new ArrayCollection();

            // Define and use atom & g namespace.
            private namespace atom = "http://www.w3.org/2005/Atom";
            use namespace atom;
            private namespace g = "http://base.google.com/ns/1.0";
            use namespace g;

            private function resultHandler(event:ResultEvent):void
            {

                var title:String;
                var publish:String;
                var content:String;
                var author:String;
                var image:String;
                var price:String;

                for each (var property:XML in event.result.entry)
                {
                    title = property.title;
                    publish = property.published;
                    content = property.content;
                    author = property.author.name;
                    image = property.image_link;
                    price = property.price;

                    dataProvider.addItem({label: title, publish: publish, content: content,↩
author: author, icon: image, price: price});
                }
            }

            private function faultHandler(event:FaultEvent):void
            {
```

```
                service.removeEventListener(FaultEvent.FAULT, faultHandler);
                Alert.show("Error connecting");
            }

    ]]>
</fx:Script>

<fx:Declarations>
    <s:HTTPService id="service"
        url="http://www.google.com/base/feeds/snippets"
        resultFormat="e4x"
        result="resultHandler(event);"
        fault="faultHandler(event);">
        <s:request>
            <bq>{keywords}</bq>
        </s:request>
    </s:HTTPService>
</fx:Declarations>

<mx:TileList id="CameraSelection" height="250" width="500"
    itemRenderer="renderers.TileListItemRenderer"
    maxColumns="5" rowHeight="120" columnWidth="125"
    dataProvider="{dataProvider}" />

</s:Application>
```

The example shown demonstrates connection to Google API and retrieving the results as well as displaying them on a TileList. Using a public API makes it easy to create a mashup application quickly. However, there is a caveat, because companies may change their API and your application can stop working.

Mixing Additional Resources

Mashups are not only about mixing data sources. Enormous numbers of open source resources and commercial resources are available for you to mix and integrate, saving you time. These additional resources can be scripts, libraries, skins custom components, and other elements.

Before building your mashup, it is recommended you spend time designing your application and figuring out what components and services are necessary. Then, research to find out if there are any resources you can utilize that will help you and also save you time. There is no need to reinvent the wheel if someone already spent hours creating libraries or classes you can use. Many of these resources are open source, and you can find them in blogs, dedicated web sites, and search engines. In many cases, it would be beneficial to use these open source resources. Once you create your own APIs and components, feel free to share your work with others; that's what open source is all about!

Additional Libraries

Additional libraries consist of classes that add to the Flex framework. These libraries are offered as open source and can be used in accordance with the license agreement provided with them. In the past, Adobe used to host these projects, but many of them have moved to Google Code. Here are some popular libraries:

- *as3youtubelib*: The YouTube library provides an interface to search videos from YouTube.
- *as3flickrlib*: The Flickr library provides classes to access the entire Flickr online photo sharing API.
- *Tweener*: The Tweener library provides classes to help create tweenings and transitions.
- *CoreLib*: The CoreLib library provides classes for working with MD5, SHA 1 hashing, image encoders, JSON serialization, and data APIs.
- *Degrafa*: This framework provides components that can be used as MXML tags to draw shapes.

Custom Components

There are many open source and commercial custom components that can be used as part of your mashup. These components should be used in accordance with their copyright licenses. Adding a prebuilt custom component can quickly enhance your UI. Of course, there are times when you have to write your own custom component. But before doing so, check whether someone already built the exact same component and shared it as open source or with a commercial license.

Here are some Flex component directories you want to visit before starting to code your own components:

- `http://flexbox.mrinalwadhwa.com/`
- `http://flex.org/components/`
- `http://www.afcomponents.com/components/`

Skins and Templates

Part of building a mashup application is manipulating CSS to create your UI. The number of open source skins and templates available keeps increasing. Making a mashup application is all about building an application quickly and mixing existing resources and data sources. Why not take advantage of open source skins and templates already availableHere are two sites that offer free downloading of templates and skins:

- `http://fleksray.org/Flex_skin.html`
- `http://www.scalenine.com`

Some of these skins and templates may not be exactly what you need, but they can provide you with a starting point; and you can adjust the code and make them work with what you need, saving time in design and development. Using these skins and templates can also be a great option while building a POC.

Connections to Popular APIs

There are thousands of different APIs to choose from to use in your mashups. Many of the mashups you will be developing will be based on maps.

Yahoo! Maps API

The Yahoo! Maps SWC works with ActionScript 3.0, so using Yahoo! Maps is relatively easy; however, it doesn't offer full integration as does ASTRA. You will be building a simple application to look for businesses in a particular ZIP code, as shown in Figure 10-28.

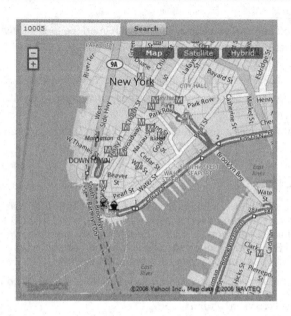

Figure 10-28. Yahoo! Maps mashup

*A **SWC file** is an archive file often used to package Flex components and other assets.*

Create variables to hold the YahooMap component and the geo location.

```
private var yahooMap:YahooMap;
private var location:String = "1 market, san francisco, ca";
private var address:Address = new Address(location);
```

The user interface contains an empty container to hold the YahooMap component, as well as a submit button.

```
<mx:UIComponent id="mapContainer" width="100%" height="100%"/>
```

Once the map application is loaded, you can attach the Map component to the empty container map and controllers on the Map.

```
private function creationCompletehandler():void
{
    var appid:String = describeType(this).@name.split("::").join(".");
    yahooMap = new YahooMap();
    yahooMap.addEventListener(YahooMapEvent.MAP_INITIALIZE, handleMapInitialize);
    yahooMap.init(appid,mapContainer.width,mapContainer.height);

    mapContainer.addChild(yahooMap);
    mapContainer.addEventListener(ResizeEvent.RESIZE, handleContainerResize);

    yahooMap.addPanControl();
```

```
    yahooMap.addZoomWidget();
    yahooMap.addTypeWidget();
}
```

When the map is uploaded, you can resize the map.

```
private function handleContainerResize(event:ResizeEvent):void
{
    yahooMap.setSize(mapContainer.width,mapContainer.height);
}
```

When the map is being handleMapInitialize, you can set the results that will be handled at handlerGeocodeSuccess.

```
private function handleMapInitialize(event:YahooMapEvent):void
{
    address.addEventListener(GeocoderEvent.GEOCODER_SUCCESS, handleGeocodeSuccess);
    address.geocode();
}

private function handleGeocodeSuccess(event:GeocoderEvent):void
{
    var result:GeocoderResult = address.geocoderResultSet.firstResult;
    yahooMap.zoomLevel = result.zoomLevel;
    yahooMap.centerLatLon = result.latlon;
}
```

The complete code is as follows:

```
<?xml version="1.0" encoding="utf-8"?>
<s:Application xmlns:fx="http://ns.adobe.com/mxml/2009"
                      xmlns:s="library://ns.adobe.com/flex/spark"
                      xmlns:mx="library://ns.adobe.com/flex/mx"
                      minWidth="1024" minHeight="768"
                      creationComplete="creationCompletehandler()">

    <fx:Script>
        <![CDATA[

            import mx.events.ResizeEvent;
            import com.yahoo.maps.api.YahooMap;
            import com.yahoo.maps.api.YahooMapEvent;
            import com.yahoo.maps.api.core.location.Address;
            import com.yahoo.maps.webservices.geocoder.GeocoderResult;
            import com.yahoo.maps.webservices.geocoder.events.GeocoderEvent;

            private var yahooMap:YahooMap;
                    private var location:String = "1 market, san francisco, ca";
            private var address:Address = new Address(location);

            private function creationCompletehandler():void
            {
                var appid:String = describeType(this).@name.split("::").join(".");
                yahooMap = new YahooMap();
                yahooMap.addEventListener(YahooMapEvent.MAP_INITIALIZE, handleMapInitialize);
```

```
            yahooMap.init(appid,mapContainer.width,mapContainer.height);

            mapContainer.addChild(yahooMap);
            mapContainer.addEventListener(ResizeEvent.RESIZE, handleContainerResize);

            yahooMap.addPanControl();
            yahooMap.addZoomWidget();
            yahooMap.addTypeWidget();
        }

        private function handleMapInitialize(event:YahooMapEvent):void
        {
            address.addEventListener(GeocoderEvent.GEOCODER_SUCCESS, handleGeocodeSuccess);
            address.geocode();
        }

        private function handleGeocodeSuccess(event:GeocoderEvent):void
        {
            var result:GeocoderResult = address.geocoderResultSet.firstResult;
            yahooMap.zoomLevel = result.zoomLevel;
            yahooMap.centerLatLon = result.latlon;
        }

        private function handleContainerResize(event:ResizeEvent):void
        {
            yahooMap.setSize(mapContainer.width,mapContainer.height);
        }

    ]]>
    </fx:Script>

    <mx:UIComponent id="mapContainer" width="100%" height="100%"/>

</s:Application>
```

Although the Yahoo Map API is a great API for using simple maps, it is limited in functionality. When you require more features, such as creating markers that display information or custom overlays, it is preferable to use the Yahoo ASTRA API.

You can see all the features available here: http://developer.yahoo.com/flash/astra-flash/.

Google Maps API

The Google Maps API lets you embed Google Maps in your Flex application. The API provides the ability for changing the maps and adding content to the map through a variety of services, allowing you to create the same cool Google maps we seen around the web.

To get started download the SDK: http://maps.googleapis.com/maps/flash/release/sdk.zip.

Apply for a Google API token here: http://code.google.com/apis/maps/signup.html.

The application you will be building is based on the Yahoo pipes feed you created to search for Flex jobs.

The complete application screen shot can be seen in Figure 10-29.

Figure 10-29. Google Map job search application

The application will retrieve results from Yahoo Pipes and then format and display these results on Google Maps using a custom image. Create a new Flex application and call it GoogleMapMashup, as shown in the in the following complete application:

```
<?xml version="1.0" encoding="utf-8"?>
<s:Application xmlns:fx="http://ns.adobe.com/mxml/2009"
                  xmlns:s="library://ns.adobe.com/flex/spark"
                  xmlns:mx="library://ns.adobe.com/flex/mx"
                  minWidth="1024" minHeight="768">

    <fx:Script>
        <![CDATA[
            import mx.messaging.AbstractConsumer;
            import com.google.maps.controls.ZoomControl;
            import com.google.maps.controls.PositionControl;
            import com.google.maps.controls.MapTypeControl;
            import mx.controls.Alert;
            import mx.rpc.events.FaultEvent;
            import mx.rpc.events.ResultEvent;
            import com.google.maps.overlays.Marker;
            import com.google.maps.overlays.MarkerOptions;
```

```
import com.google.maps.LatLng;
import com.google.maps.Map;
import com.google.maps.MapEvent;
import com.google.maps.MapType;
```

The Google map allows us to use a custom image for markers. You will be using a purple icon:

```
[Embed(source="blue-dot.png")] private var purpleIcon:Class
```

The onMapReady method will be called once the map is loaded and will add controls:

```
private function onMapReady(event:Object):void
{
    map.addControl(new ZoomControl());
    map.addControl(new PositionControl());
    map.addControl(new MapTypeControl());
}
```

Once the user submits the form you will direct it to the displayResults method, which will use the Yahoo pipes feeds you created and pass the location and keyword information.

```
public function displayResults():void
{
    var pipeURL:String = "http://pipes.yahoo.com/pipes/pipe.run";
    var parameters:Object = new Object;

    parameters._id="vh97mywZ3RGlrygr1vC6Jw"
    parameters._render = "rss"
    parameters.location = location.text;
    parameters.query = keywords.text;

    service.url = pipeURL;
    service.send(parameters);
}
```

The service object will direct to the result handler. To handle the results, you will show the results on the map, so there are few things we would like you to do. You will iterate through the collection and retrieve the longitude, latitude, and title information.

```
protected function service_resultHandler(event:ResultEvent):void
{
    var collection:Object = event.result.rss.channel;
     var len:int = collection.item.length;
    var lat:Number;
    var long:Number;
    var title:String;
    var isDuplicate:Boolean;

    for (var i:int=0; i<len; i++)
    {
        lat = collection.item[i].lat;
        long = collection.item[i].long;
        title = collection.item[i].title;
```

Once you have the longitude and latitude information, you want to ensure there is no duplicate information. The reason you don't want duplicate information is that the markers can overlay each other, so in case there is an overlay you will call the `adjustLatLng` method to adjust a little the longitude, latitude.

```
isDuplicate = isLatLongUsed(lat, long, collection, i);

if (isDuplicate)
{
    lat = adjustLatLng(lat);
    long = adjustLatLng(long);
}

var latLng:LatLng = new LatLng(lat, long);
addMarker(latLng, title);
```

The `setAverageCenter` method will change the map center.

```
setAverageCenter(collection);
        }
    }
```

The isLatLongUsed method will return a flag that indicates weather the results are duplicate or not. You iterate through the collection of results and checking for duplicate.

```
        private function isLatLongUsed(checkAgainstLat:Number, ↵
checkAgainstLong:Number, collection:Object, index:int):Boolean
        {
            var retVal:Boolean = false;
            var lat:Number;
            var long:Number;

            for (var i:int=0; i<index; i++)
            {
                lat = collection.item[i].lat;
                long = collection.item[i].long;

                if (checkAgainstLat == lat && checkAgainstLong == long)
                {
                    retVal = true;
                }
            }

            return retVal;
        }
```

In case you find duplicates, adjust the longitude and latitude so you don't have an overlay of markers. You do that by adding a random number that will shift the icon marker just a little.

```
        private function adjustLatLng(num:Number):Number
        {
            var temp:Array = num.toString().split(".");
            var randomNum:Number = Math.floor(Math.random() * (999 - 0 + 1));
            var newNum:Number = Number( temp[0]+"."+temp[1].toString().substr(0, 3)+↵
String(randomNum) );

            return newNum;
```

```
    }
```

The `setAverageCenter` method will calculate the average longitude and latitude and adjust the map to these coordinates.

```
        private function setAverageCenter(collection:Object):void
        {
            var lat:Number = 0;
            var long:Number = 0;
            var len:int = collection.item.length;

            for (var i:int=0; i<len; i++)
            {
                lat += collection.item[i].lat;
                long += collection.item[i].long;
            }

            lat  = lat/i;
            long = long/i;

            this.map.setCenter(new LatLng(lat, long), 12, MapType.NORMAL_MAP_TYPE);
        }
```

The `service_faultHandler` method shows an alert popup if you cannot connect to the Yahoo pipes feed.

```
        protected function service_faultHandler(event:FaultEvent):void
        {
            Alert.show("Error connecting to Yahoo pipes and retrieve results!");
        }
```

The `addMarker` method will take the longitude, latitude, and title parameters and draw an icon marker on the map.

```
        private function addMarker(latLng:LatLng, title:String):void
        {
            var markerOptions:MarkerOptions = new MarkerOptions();

            markerOptions.icon = new purpleIcon();
            markerOptions.tooltip = title;
            markerOptions.iconAlignment = MarkerOptions.ALIGN_HORIZONTAL_CENTER;
            markerOptions.iconOffset = new Point(1, 1);

            var marker:Marker = new Marker(latLng, markerOptions);
            map.addOverlay(marker);
        }

    ]]>
</fx:Script>
```

The UI consists of a search text input, submit button and the Google map component.

```
    <s:VGroup>

        <s:HGroup>
            <s:TextInput id="location" x="21" y="10" width="46" text="10005" maxChars="5"↵
```

```
restrict="0-9"/>
            <s:TextInput id="keywords" x="75" y="10" width="118" text="Adobe Flex"/>
            <s:Button id="findhouse" x="201" y="10" label="Look for Jobs"↵
click="displayResults()" />
        </s:HGroup>

        <maps:Map xmlns:maps="com.google.maps.*" id="map"
                mapevent_mapready="onMapReady(event)"
                width="400" height="400"
                key="** PLACE YOUR GOOGLE MAP DEVELOPER KEY ** "/>

    </s:VGroup>
```

Lastly, you have the service tag that you will be using to retrieve the Yahoo Pipe feed.

```
<fx:Declarations>
    <mx:HTTPService id="service"
                    result="service_resultHandler(event)"
                    fault="service_faultHandler(event)" />
</fx:Declarations>

</s:Application>
```

The application you built uses two data sources to create the Mashup. As you can see, the integration of the application was relatively easy and you created a whole application with very little coding.

UMap

Another choice for displaying results on a map is UMap, which stands for Universal Mapping. UMAP integrates with Yahoo Maps, OpenStreetMap and Microsoft Virtual Earth map data to display map results. Additionally, UMap has an API to create routes and set them on the map.

Download the swc from here: http://www.afcomponents.com/components/umap_as3/.

Create a new application and call it UMapExample, as shown in the following code:

```
<?xml version="1.0" encoding="utf-8"?>
<s:Application xmlns:fx="http://ns.adobe.com/mxml/2009"
                xmlns:s="library://ns.adobe.com/flex/spark"
                xmlns:mx="library://ns.adobe.com/flex/mx"
                width="600" height="400"
                creationComplete="onCreationComplete(event)">

        <fx:Script>
            <![CDATA[

            import mx.controls.scrollClasses.ScrollBar;
            import com.afcomponents.umap.styles.MarkerStyle;
            import com.afcomponents.umap.styles.Style;
            import com.afcomponents.umap.overlays.Marker;
            import com.afcomponents.umap.types.LatLngBounds;
            import mx.collections.ArrayCollection;
            import com.afcomponents.umap.display.InfoWindow;
            import com.afcomponents.umap.types.LatLng;
            import mx.core.UIComponent;
```

```
import com.afcomponents.umap.gui.*;
import com.afcomponents.umap.core.UMap;
import com.afcomponents.umap.types.LatLng;
import com.afcomponents.umap.styles.InfoWindowStyle;
import com.afcomponents.umap.styles.TextStyle;
import com.afcomponents.umap.display.InfoWindow;
import com.afcomponents.umap.types.Size;
import com.afcomponents.umap.styles.DropShadowStyle;

private var map:UMap;

private var myWindow:InfoWindow;
private var infoWindowOpenFlag:Boolean = false;
public var mapReadyFlag:Boolean = false;

public function onCreationComplete(event:Event):void
{
    var ref:UIComponent = new UIComponent();
    map = new UMap();
    map.setSize(this.width-15, this.height-30);
    ref.addChild(map);
    mapCanvas.addChild(ref);
    ref.focusManager.deactivate();
    map.addControl( new MapTypeControl() );
    map.addControl(new ZoomControl());
    map.addControl(new PositionControl());
    mapReadyFlag = true;
}

public function setCenter(latLng:LatLng):void
{
    map.setCenter(latLng);
}

public function zoomMap(times:int):void
{
    for (var i:int=0; i<times; i++)
    map.zoomIn();
}

public function openInfo(latLng:LatLng, title:String, description:String):void
{

    if (infoWindowOpenFlag)
        map.closeInfoWindow();

    // define info window style
    var infoStyle:InfoWindowStyle = new InfoWindowStyle();
    infoStyle.fill = "rgb";
    infoStyle.fillRGB = 0x000000;
    infoStyle.fillAlpha = .65;
    infoStyle.strokeRGB = 0xFF66CC;
    infoStyle.strokeAlpha = .6;
```

```
        infoStyle.closeRGB = 0x6699FF;
        infoStyle.closeAlpha = .6;
        infoStyle.radius = 3;

        //Sets Scroll Bar in Info Window
        InfoWindow.setScrollBarClass(ScrollBar);
        infoStyle.scroll = true;
        infoStyle.maxSize = new Size(300, 150);

        //Style Title in Info Window
        var infoTitleStyle:TextStyle = new TextStyle();
        infoTitleStyle.textFormat.bold = true;
        infoTitleStyle.textFormat.color = 0xFFFFFF;
        infoTitleStyle.textFormat.font = "verdana";
        infoTitleStyle.textFormat.size = 14;
        infoStyle.titleStyle = infoTitleStyle;

        //Turn on HTML, use a style sheet to style content text
        infoStyle.contentStyle.html = true;
        infoStyle.contentStyle.styleSheet = new StyleSheet();
        infoStyle.contentStyle.styleSheet.setStyle("html",
        {fontFamily:"arial", fontSize:12, color:"#CCCCCC"});

        //Style Drop Shadow
        var shadowStyle:DropShadowStyle =
        new DropShadowStyle();
        shadowStyle.blurX = 5;
        shadowStyle.blurY = 5;
        shadowStyle.alpha = .5;
        shadowStyle.angle = 20;
        shadowStyle.color = 0xFF6699;
        shadowStyle.distance = .5;
        infoStyle.shadowStyle = shadowStyle;

        //Define the Parameters of our Info Window
        var param:Object = new Object();
        param.title = title;
        param.content = description;
        param.position = latLng;
        param.autoClose = false;
        map.openInfoWindow(param, infoStyle);
        infoWindowOpenFlag = true;
}

public function setMarkersLocations(dp:ArrayCollection):void
{
        // create new MarkerStyle
        var style:MarkerStyle = new MarkerStyle();

        style.fill = "rgb";
        style.fillAlpha = 0.9;
        style.strokeRGB = 0x0;
        style.strokeAlpha = 1.0;
```

```
            var pos:LatLng;
            var geoArray:Array;
            var bounds:LatLngBounds = map.getBoundsLatLng();
            var marker:Marker;

            // create Markers
            for (var i:int = 0; i < dp.length; i++)
            {
                style.fillRGB = Math.random() * 0xFFFFFF;
                geoArray = new Array();
                geoArray = String(dp.getItemAt(i).geo).split(" ");

                //trace(geoArray[0]+","+geoArray[1]);
                pos = new LatLng(geoArray[0], geoArray[1]);
                marker = new Marker({autoInfo: false, draggable:false});

                marker.index = String.fromCharCode(65 + i);
                marker.position = pos;
                marker.setStyle(style);
                map.addOverlay(marker);
            }
        }

        ]]>
    </fx:Script>

    <mx:Canvas id="mapCanvas"
            backgroundColor="#352D69"
            x="20" y="30"
            horizontalScrollPolicy="off"
            verticalScrollPolicy="off"/>


</s:Application>
```

Once you compile the application, you can see the results in Figure 10-30.

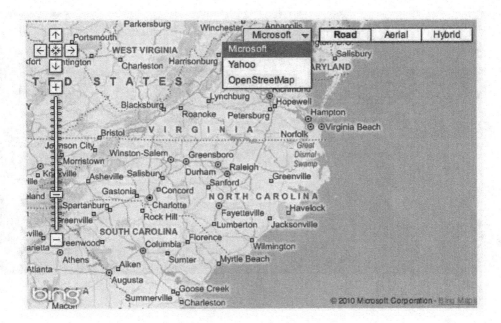

Figure 10-30. UMap with menu to choose the map provider

As seen from the previous example, using UMap you can provide the user with the ability to switch to the three popular maps and it's easy to use and integrate.

Flickr

A common integration in mashups is photos. Flickr is an online photo management and sharing application. Flickr is a good choice for mashups since it has the `crossdomain.xml` policy file installed on its remote server. You will be using an open source library that was developed by Adobe and can handle all the integration with Flickr.

You will create a Flickr mashup that allows you to search by tags or user names. It then displays the results in two components, and images can be dragged to a wish list. Once an image is dragged, the component will reorganize itself, as shown in Figure 10-31.

Figure 10-31. Flickr mashup

To access Flickr, you will be using an adobe open source API. The script below connects to Flickr and retrieves results.

```
<?xml version="1.0" encoding="utf-8"?>
<s:Application xmlns:fx="http://ns.adobe.com/mxml/2009"
               xmlns:s="library://ns.adobe.com/flex/spark"
               xmlns:mx="library://ns.adobe.com/flex/mx"
               minWidth="1024" minHeight="768"
               initialize="initApp(); searchFlikr('flower');">


    <fx:Script>
        <![CDATA[
            import com.adobe.flickr.SearchCriteria;
            import mx.collections.ArrayCollection;
            import mx.controls.Alert;
            import com.adobe.flickr.events.FlickrEvent;
            import com.adobe.flickr.Flickr;

            private var flickr:Flickr = new Flickr();

            private function initApp() : void
            {
                flickr.addEventListener( FlickrEvent.SEARCH_COMPLETE_EVENT, ↵
searchCompleteEventHandler );
                flickr.addEventListener( FlickrEvent.CONNECTION_FAILED_EVENT, ↵
                    function(event:FlickrEvent):void ↵
                        { Alert.show( event.failMsg, "Connection Failure" ) } );
                flickr.addEventListener( FlickrEvent.PHOTO_INFO_EVENT, ↵
photoInfoEventHandler );
```

```
            }

            private function searchFlikr(tags:String):void
            {
                var numPerPage:Number = 50;
                var searchCriteria:SearchCriteria = new SearchCriteria();
                searchCriteria.tags = tags;
                flickr.photoSearch(numPerPage,searchCriteria);
            }

            private function searchCompleteEventHandler( event:FlickrEvent ) : void
            {
                var data:Object = event.data;
                var dp:ArrayCollection = (data.photo as ArrayCollection);
                flickr.getPhotoInfo( dp.getItemAt(0).id, dp.getItemAt(0).secret );
            }

            private function photoInfoEventHandler(event:FlickrEvent):void
            {
                var result:Object = event.data;
            }

        ]]>
    </fx:Script>

</s:Application>
```

The next step is you are going to take a custom open source component that was built by Ely Greenfield. You can download the component from here:

`http://demo.quietlyscheming.com/DragTile/DragDrop.html`

This component is an animated `DragTile` component in which the container re-organizes itself once you drag and drop an item.

```
package qs.event
{
    import flash.events.Event;

    public class DragTitleEvent extends Event
    {
        //Define static constant
        public static const SELECTED_IMAGE_CHANGED:String = ↵
            "selectedImageChanged";

        // Define public variable to hold the state of the enable property
        public var selectedImage:String;

        public function DragTitleEvent(type:String, selectedImage:String)
        {
            super(type);
            this.selectedImage = selectedImage;
        }
    }
```

}

You will be adding a custom event to dragDrop(e:DragEvent) at qs.controls.DragTile after dispatchEvent(newEvent("change")); so you can display the image that was dragged in a larger format.

```
this.dispatchEvent( new DragTitleEvent( DragTitleEvent.SELECTED_IMAGE_CHANGED,↵
 this.dataProvider[_dragTargetIdx] ) );
```

Here is the complete code:

```
<?xml version="1.0" encoding="utf-8"?>
<s:Application xmlns:fx="http://ns.adobe.com/mxml/2009"
                          xmlns:s="library://ns.adobe.com/flex/spark"
                          xmlns:mx="library://ns.adobe.com/flex/mx"
                          xmlns:f="flash.filters.*"
                          xmlns:qs="qs.controls.*"
                          backgroundColor="#343434" initialize="initApp()">

    <fx:Script>
        <![CDATA[

            import qs.event.DragTitleEvent;
            import mx.events.DragEvent;
            import com.adobe.flickr.SearchCriteria;
            import mx.collections.ArrayCollection;
            import mx.controls.Alert;
            import com.adobe.flickr.events.FlickrEvent;
            import com.adobe.flickr.Flickr;

            [Bindable]
            public var images:Array;
            [Bindable]
            public var targetData:Array = [];

            protected var flickr:Flickr = new Flickr();
            protected var searchCriteria:SearchCriteria = new SearchCriteria();

            private function initApp() : void
            {
                flickr.addEventListener( FlickrEvent.USER_INFO_EVENT, handleUserInfo );
                flickr.addEventListener( FlickrEvent.SEARCH_COMPLETE_EVENT,↵
searchCompleteEventHandler );
                flickr.addEventListener( FlickrEvent.CONNECTION_FAILED_EVENT,↵
function(event:FlickrEvent):void { Alert.show( event.failMsg, "Connection Failure" ) } );
                cmp.addEventListener(DragTitleEvent.SELECTED_IMAGE_CHANGED,↵
selectedImageChangedEventHandler);
                cmp2.addEventListener(DragTitleEvent.SELECTED_IMAGE_CHANGED,↵
selectedImageChangedEventHandler);
            }

            private function searchFlikrTags():void
            {
                var numPerPage:Number = 50;
                flickr.photoSearch(numPerPage,searchCriteria);
```

```
        }

        private function searchCompleteEventHandler(event:FlickrEvent):void
        {
            var data:Object = event.data;
            var ac:ArrayCollection = (data.photo as ArrayCollection);
            var len:int = ac.length;
            var imageURL:String;
            var images:Array = [];
            var list:Array = [];

            for (var i:int = 0; i<len; i++)
            {
                imageURL = "http://static.flickr.com/"+ac.getItemAt(i)↩
.server+"/"+ac.getItemAt(i).id+"_"+ac.getItemAt(i).secret+"_s.jpg";
                list.push(imageURL);
            }

            for(var j:int=0;j<3;j++)
            {
                images = images.concat(list);
            }

            this.images = images;
            cmp.dataProvider = images;
        }

        private function startSearchFlikr():void
        {
            searchCriteria.tags = tagsTextInput.text;
            searchCriteria.userName = userTextInput.text;

            if (userTextInput.text != "")
            {
                flickr.findByUsername(userTextInput.text);
                return;
            }

            searchFlikrTags();
        }

        private function handleUserInfo(event:FlickrEvent):void
        {
            searchCriteria.nsid = event.data.nsid;
            searchFlikrTags();
        }

        private function selectedImageChangedEventHandler(event:DragTitleEvent):void
        {
            var imgURL:String = event.selectedImage;
            image.source = imgURL.replace("_s", "");
            trace(imgURL);
        }
```

```
        ]]>
    </fx:Script>

    <fx:Style>
        @namespace mx "library://ns.adobe.com/flex/mx";

        .insetBox {
            paddingBottom: 30;
            paddingLeft: 30;
            paddingRight: 30;
            paddingTop: 30;
        }
    }

    </fx:Style>

    <mx:VBox height="100%" backgroundColor="#565656" width="400"
            horizontalAlign="right" styleName="insetBox">

        <mx:Canvas width="100%" height="61" horizontalScrollPolicy="off"↵
verticalScrollPolicy="off">
            <mx:Label text="User name: " x="132.5" y="4"/>
            <mx:TextInput id="tagsTextInput" x="10" y="28" width="100" color="black"/>
            <mx:Label text="Tags: " x="10" y="4"/>
            <mx:TextInput id="userTextInput" y="28" x="127.5" width="102" color="black"/>
            <mx:Button label="submit" x="237.5" y="28" width="81.5"↵
click="{startSearchFlikr()}"/>
        </mx:Canvas>
        <mx:Image id="image" width="300" />
    </mx:VBox>

    <s:Group width="600" height="100%" x="400" y="0">
        <mx:VRule height="100%" />

        <mx:VBox width="100%" horizontalGap="20" height="100%" styleName="insetBox"↵
clipContent="true">

            <mx:VBox width="100%" horizontalGap="0" height="100%" borderColor="#FFFFFF"↵
borderStyle="solid">
                <qs:DragTile id="cmp" width="100%" height="100%"
                        dragEnter="event.target.allowDrag(event);"
                        dragOver='event.target.showDragFeedback(event,event.shiftKey?↵
"copy":"move")'>
                    <qs:itemRenderer>
                        <fx:Component id="imageRenderer">
                            <qs:BitmapTile />
                        </fx:Component>
                    </qs:itemRenderer>
                </qs:DragTile>
            </mx:VBox>

            <mx:VBox width="100%" horizontalGap="0" height="150" borderColor="#FFFFFF"↵
borderStyle="solid">
```

```
                <qs:DragTile id="cmp2" width="100%" height="100%" dataProvider="{targetData}"
                        dragEnter="event.target.allowDrag(event);"
                        dragOver='event.target.showDragFeedback(event,event.shiftKey?↵
"copy":"move");'>
                    <qs:itemRenderer>
                        <fx:Component>
                            <qs:BitmapTile />
                        </fx:Component>
                    </qs:itemRenderer>
                </qs:DragTile>
            </mx:VBox>

        </mx:VBox>
    </s:Group>

</s:Application>
```

The example is a great demonstration of how you hacked together a mashup application that allows the user to search through the Flikr API and provide a good user experience built on top of separate components.

Creating Your Own Flex Mashup

Now that you know about data accessinterconnectivity, and mixing additional scripts, you are ready to create your own Flex mashup. But, where do you start?

I suggest splitting the process of creating mashups into four steps:

1. ***Pick a subject***: Picking a subject is the base for every Flex mashup. Your subject should add value, although Flex has an advantage as a starting point, because the Flex stateful user interface already adds value. Many times you will add a service or data source to an existing application so the subject is already known. A good place to start is to get familiar with all the available APIs, and a good resource to find all the APIs that are available is http://www.programmableweb.com/apis.

2. ***Choose services***: Now that you know the subject of your mashup application, the next step is to decide which service or services you will use. Many times you have available more than one API that provides the same or similar functionality, so you need to decide which one to use or whether to combine a few together.

3. I personally prefer using services that are part of a cloud. You can rely on a service that sits on a cloud server's infrastructure rather than a small web site hosted by a shared hosting plan. The following companies have a massive network of servers: Google, Yahoo!, Amazon, and Salesforce.

4. Once you select all the APIs and services you will be using in your mashup, sign up for or download the APIs needed. Many APIs provide a key or a unique ID number. Some APIs are being sold on a license basis or given away as open source. Once you select the APIs you will be using, spend some time checking out the manuals, the reliability of service, and the performance.

5. For example, you may find a few services that offer the same functionality, but one may have a better performance because it is based on REST rather than SOAP. Although you will be able to switch and change your application later, it is better to check the service or API before you get started.

6. **Design**: Follow the same patterns you use when developing any Flex application such as creating a UML diagram, design document, or any other process you use. In addition to your regular process, it is recommended you figure out the design of the services you will be using. By this, we mean you create a block diagram covering all the services, APIs, and any other additional resources you will be using up front.

7. Microsoft Visio is a good tool to create block diagrams, but feel free to use any other software you are comfortable with. To create a block diagram in MS Visio, follow these instructions:

   Choose **File** on the top menu, point to **New**, select the General folder, and choose **Block Diagram**.
   Drag shapes onto the drawing page.
   Right-click a shape, and then select Fill to change the default color.
   Double-click a shape to add text.
   Ctrl-click corners to resize the drawing page.
   For an example of a Visio 2007 block diagram, see Figure 10-2 earlier in the chapter.

8. **Start coding**: Once your block diagram and any other support documents such as UML diagram, wire frames, and design documents are ready, you can start coding.

We recommend creating a connection to any API or services following best practices such as using loosely coupled components, so you can reuse a component and publish it as open source for the benefit of others.

Summary

In this chapter, we covered all the basics you need to know in order to build a successful mashup. As the web is undergoing transformation into sharing and collaboration, and an increasing number of services are available, developers can now create new and exciting applications by simply mixing these services together.

You learned how to read and create the crossdomain.xml file policy and how to overcome restricted or lack of crossdomain.xml policy by creating a proxy. You also saw how to utilize mashup frameworks to act as your proxies, reducing resources on your server. You learned how to deal with different types of namespaces that you can encounter using web feeds. You then explored some of the best practices of interconnectivity involving such factors as valuators, format, data model, and attaching data to a UI. You also explored how to utilize the Web and the enormous amount of resources available today, such as APIs, libraries, custom components, and skins.

To help you get started, we showed you how to build some exciting mashups using some of the most popular APIs such as Yahoo!, Amazon, Flickr, and UMap, as well as giving you tips and tricks on how to start building your own mashup application.

Mashup applications include some of the most visited and interesting sites available on the Web today. Flex mashups offer a Flex stateful paradigm where you can keep changing your application, without refreshing your browser, giving additional value for every mashup application.

Have fun creating exciting mashup applications!

Chapter 11

Flash Security

by Elad Elrom

Flash has become very popular among developers as it is available on many devices, thanks to the Open Screen Project. In fact, some people estimate that there are as many as two million Flash developers as of 2010. Unfortunately, just as with any mainstream technology, it is a big, inviting target for attackers to try to exploit.

This chapter will explain some of the most important security threats to Flash and Flex applications, and give you advice on how to avoid them. Security is a huge topic. In this chapter we'll focus on specific vulnerabilities, showing examples of how an attacker can abuse Flash or Flex applications, and pointing out ways to help prevent these attacks. The purpose of these examples is to raise your awareness, so you'll take security into consideration when building your applications.

Part 1: Cross-Domain Scripting

Cross-domain scripting vulnerabilities are among the most serious threats to Flash/Flex applications.

An application may be hosted on a server where the cross-domain policy allows loading a remote SWF, which gives unintended access to the loader's domain and data. If the loading SWF loads the remote SWF into its security domain, the remote SWF could gain access to the parent SWF's data, modify properties, and even send that information back to an attacker. Moreover, attackers can download a SWF, decompile and change it, and host it back somewhere else, pretending it is the original application.

Decompiling and Modifying a SWF File

The concept of downloading Flash applications, decompiling them, modifying them, and then recompiling them is one of the oldest and most used cross-domain scripting techniques out there. Hackers use programs such as the Sothink SWF Decompiler, which allow them to modify the SWF. And many people may not be aware yet, but these programs are now capable of decompiling Flex 3 projects as well Flash applications. Let's take a look at a simple example. Create this simple Flex 3 application:

```
<?xml version="1.0" encoding="utf-8"?>
<mx:Application xmlns:mx="http://www.adobe.com/2006/mxml"
                layout="absolute" minWidth="1024" minHeight="768">

    <mx:Label x="23" y="31" text="Hello World"/>

</mx:Application>
```

Compile the application. Now we can import the SWF file and use Sothink to decompile it back into a Flex 3 project as shown in Figure 11-1.

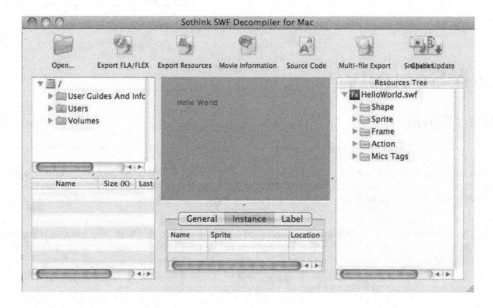

Figure 11-1. Decompiling a Flex 3 project

After the project is restored, you can import the project back into Flash Builder and change it.

```
<?xml version="1.0" encoding="UTF-8"?>
<mx:Application layout="absolute" xmlns:mx="http://www.adobe.com/2006/mxml">
    <mx:Script><![CDATA[
        import mx.events.*;
        import mx.controls.*;
        import mx.core.*;
        import mx.styles.*;
    ]]></mx:Script>

    <mx:Label text="Hello World" x="23" y="31"/>
```

```
</mx:Application>
```

This example is harmless since we only modified a label; however, as you can imagine, hackers can do much more than just modify a label once they have access to the complete application code. For instance, they can steal the source code, republish the application on a fake URL, send e-mails out to users, and take credit card information or other important information. This type of attack is known as *phishing*.

> *A phishing attack is when a hacker tries to obtain users' sensitive information by impersonating a trustworthy entity.*

Hacking a client SWF is a common method for cheating at games (modifying speed, going through walls etc.). To avoid these types of attacks, you should validate important actions against a server.

For the next example, I went to a Flash template site, used a web proxy to extract the SWF URL, and downloaded the SWF file to my desktop. See Figure 11-2.

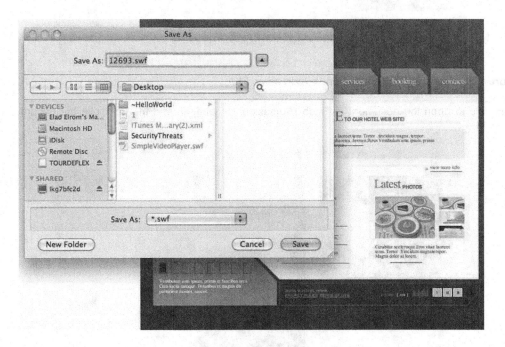

Figure 11-2. Extracting the SWFURL and downloading the SWF file

I then imported the file into a decompiler and exported it as an FLA, as shown in Figure 11-3.

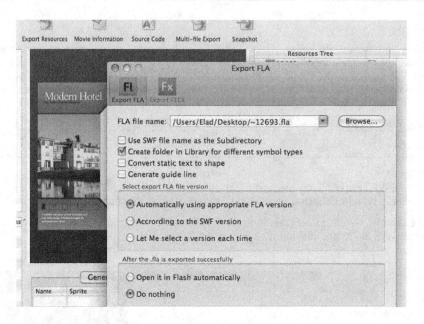

Figure 11-3. Import into decompiler and export as an FLA.

I was able to open the document in Flash Professional, modify it, and then compile the document. See Figure 11-4.

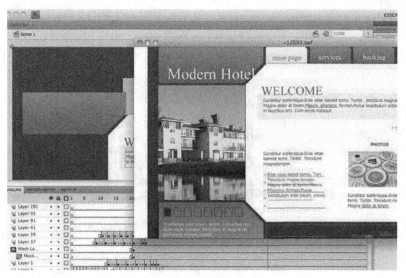

Figure 11-4. Using Flash Professional to modify and compile a document

Loading a SWF File into Another Project

Another known attack is loading a SWF file belonging to a Flex project and then having the accessing application make changes to the accessed application. In the example below, the accessing application gains access to another application, and I can then change the text property on a label and even use a login service method.

Create a new project. Call it **CrossScriptingFlex**, and paste the following code:

```
<?xml version="1.0" encoding="utf-8"?>
<s:Application xmlns:fx="http://ns.adobe.com/mxml/2009"
                xmlns:s="library://ns.adobe.com/flex/spark"
                xmlns:mx="library://ns.adobe.com/flex/mx" minWidth="1024" minHeight="768"
                initialize="initializeHandler()">
    <fx:Script>
        <![CDATA[
            import mx.controls.Alert;
            import mx.core.IFlexModuleFactory;
            import mx.events.FlexEvent;

            // define variables
            private var loader:Loader;
            private var content:*;

            // load swf
            private function initializeHandler():void
            {
                loader = new Loader();
                loader.contentLoaderInfo.addEventListener↵
(SecurityErrorEvent.SECURITY_ERROR, securityErrorHandler);
                loader.contentLoaderInfo.addEventListener↵
(Event.COMPLETE, loadContent_onComplete);
                loader.contentLoaderInfo.addEventListener↵
(IOErrorEvent.IO_ERROR, ioErrorHandler);
                loader.load(new URLRequest("main.swf"));

                component.addChild(loader);
            }

            // Event Handler

            private function loadContent_onComplete(event:Event):void
            {
                content = event.target.content;

            var onContentApplicationComplete:Function = function(event:Event):void
            {
                // content loaded successfully
            }

            content.addEventListener↵
(FlexEvent.APPLICATION_COMPLETE, onContentApplicationComplete);
                }
```

```
            private function ioErrorHandler(event:IOErrorEvent):void
            {
                    loader.contentLoaderInfo.removeEventListener↵
(IOErrorEvent.IO_ERROR, ioErrorHandler);
                    Alert.show(event.text);
            }

            private function securityErrorHandler(event:SecurityErrorEvent):void
            {
                    loader.contentLoaderInfo.removeEventListener↵
(SecurityErrorEvent.SECURITY_ERROR, securityErrorHandler);
                    Alert.show(event.text);
            }

            // methods to access loaded swf

            private function changeTextOnSWF(str:String):void
            {
                    this.content.document.label.text = str;
            }

            private function login():void
            {
                    this.content.document.signupUtil.signup();
            }

        ]]>
    </fx:Script>

    <mx:UIComponent id="component" width="400" height="400" x="0" y="100" />

    <s:Button label="Change text on loaded SWF"
              click="changeTextOnSWF('Hello again!')"  x="84" y="0"/>

    <s:Button label="Login"
              click="login()" />

</s:Application>
```

The accessed application will hold a label field and an instance of a class that enables the user to log in. Create a Flex application in FlashBuilder 4, and call it **AccessedApplication**.

```
<?xml version="1.0" encoding="utf-8"?>
<s:Application xmlns:fx="http://ns.adobe.com/mxml/2009"
               xmlns:s="library://ns.adobe.com/flex/spark"
               xmlns:mx="library://ns.adobe.com/flex/mx"
               minWidth="1024" minHeight="768">
    <fx:Script>
        <![CDATA[

            import utils.CallSignupService;

            public var signupUtil:CallSignupService = new CallSignupService();
```

```
        ]]>
    </fx:Script>

    <s:Label id="label" text="Hello!"  x="8" y="9"/>

</s:Application>
```

Here's the class that allows the user to sign into the application. This is just an experiment in which we didn't implement a service call; however, it gives you the idea.

```
package utils
{
    import mx.controls.Alert;

    public class CallSignupService
    {
        public function CallSignupService()
        {
        }

        public function signup():void
        {
            // method to signup to using a service
            Alert.show("User login!");
        }
    }
}
```

Copy the SWF from the accessed application (main.swf), and place it in the "bin-debug" folder of the accessing application. Run the accessing application. Figure 11-5 shows the result.

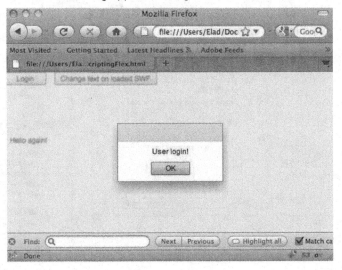

Figure 11-5. Accessing the application shown in the browser

Right now we are loading the accessed application from the same domain. However, if you place the accessed application and the accessing application in two separate domains and create a domain policy that allows accessing the domain from any domain, as in this example below, it will work.

```
<?xml version="1.0"?>
<!DOCTYPE cross-domain-policy SYSTEM "http://www.adobe.com/xml/dtds/cross-domain-policy.dtd">
<cross-domain-policy>
    <allow-access-from domain="*"/>
</cross-domain-policy>
```

Figuring Out the Application Source Code

In this example, of course we have access to the source code. Normally, attackers don't have direct access to the source code, but as we'll see, they can find the source code in two ways.

Once the content is loaded, you can actually place a break point and see all the methods you have access to, as Figure 11-6 shows.

document	main (@240b6851)
▶ [inherited]	
▶ _102727412label	spark.components.Label (@3cc510b1)
▶ label	spark.components.Label (@3cc510b1)
▶ signupUtil	utils.CallSignupService (@3cc09551)

Figure 11-6. Variables window showing loaded content object

Additionally, using decompiling software, the attacker can decompile the accessed application and browse through the classes (as we showed previously). See Figure 11-7.

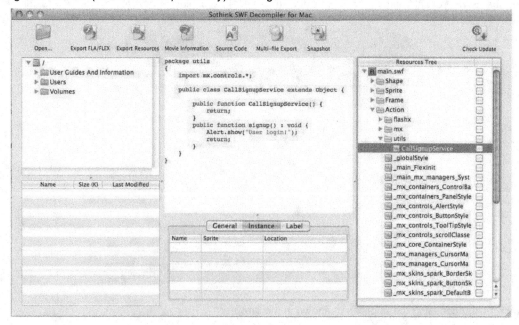

Figure 11-7. Decompiling the accessed application

Accessing Another Domain Through the Accessed Application

As in the application we showed you previously, an attacker could load a SWF from one domain that has access to another domain and then make unauthorized service calls.

For instance, let's say that DomainA allows access to DomainB, as you can see in this cross-domain policy:

```
<?xml version="1.0"?> <!DOCTYPE cross-domain-policy    SYSTEM
 "http://www.macromedia.com/xml/dtds/cross-domain-policy.dtd">
<cross-domain-policy>
     <allow-access-from domain="domainB" secure="false" />
</cross-domain-policy>
```

In the following example, the accessed application holds a service class.

```
<?xml version="1.0" encoding="utf-8"?>
<s:Application xmlns:fx="http://ns.adobe.com/mxml/2009"
                    xmlns:s="library://ns.adobe.com/flex/spark"
                    xmlns:mx="library://ns.adobe.com/flex/mx"
                    minWidth="1024" minHeight="768">
     <fx:Script>
          <![CDATA[
               import mx.controls.Alert;
               import mx.rpc.events.FaultEvent;
               import mx.rpc.events.ResultEvent;

               protected function service_faultHandler(event:FaultEvent):void
               {
                    Alert.show("fault error: "+event.fault.faultDetail);
               }

               protected function service_resultHandler(event:ResultEvent):void
               {
                    Alert.show(event.result.toString());
               }

          ]]>
     </fx:Script>

     <fx:Declarations>
          <s:HTTPService id="service"
                    url="domainB"
                    resultFormat="text"
                    fault="service_faultHandler(event)"
                    result="service_resultHandler(event)" />
     </fx:Declarations>

</s:Application>
```

The accessing application can load the SWF and access the service class to make an illegal call, and then it can retrieve the data. For instance, let's assume that a site allows a certain authorized domain to make service calls, but the API is not public. If the authorized domain holds a SWF that can be accessed, you can use that SWF to gain access to the API and make unauthorized service calls. The following code shows how:

```
<?xml version="1.0" encoding="utf-8"?>
<s:Application xmlns:fx="http://ns.adobe.com/mxml/2009"
               xmlns:s="library://ns.adobe.com/flex/spark"
               xmlns:mx="library://ns.adobe.com/flex/mx"
               minWidth="1024" minHeight="768"
               initialize="initializeHandler()">
    <fx:Script>
        <![CDATA[
            import mx.controls.Alert;
            import mx.events.FlexEvent;
            import mx.rpc.events.FaultEvent;
            import mx.rpc.events.ResultEvent;

            // define variables
            private var loader:Loader;
            private var content:*;

            // load swf
            private function initializeHandler():void
            {
                loader = new Loader();
                loader.contentLoaderInfo.addEventListener↩
(SecurityErrorEvent.SECURITY_ERROR, securityErrorHandler);
                loader.contentLoaderInfo.addEventListener↩
(Event.COMPLETE, loadContent_onComplete);
                loader.contentLoaderInfo.addEventListener↩
(IOErrorEvent.IO_ERROR, ioErrorHandler);
                loader.load(new URLRequest("main.swf"));

                component.addChild(loader);
            }

            // Event Handler

            private function loadContent_onComplete(event:Event):void
            {
                content = event.target.content;

                var onContentApplicationComplete:↩
Function = function(event:Event):void
                {
                    // content loaded successfully
                }

                content.addEventListener↩
(FlexEvent.APPLICATION_COMPLETE, onContentApplicationComplete);
            }

            private function ioErrorHandler(event:IOErrorEvent):void
            {
                loader.contentLoaderInfo.removeEventListener↩
(IOErrorEvent.IO_ERROR, ioErrorHandler);
                Alert.show(event.text);
```

```
                    }

                    private function securityErrorHandler(event:SecurityErrorEvent):void
                    {
                            loader.contentLoaderInfo.removeEventListener↵
(SecurityErrorEvent.SECURITY_ERROR, securityErrorHandler);
                            Alert.show(event.text);
                    }

                    // methods to access loaded swf

                    private function callServiceCall():void
                    {
                            this.content.document.service.send();
                    }

            ]]>
        </fx:Script>

        <mx:UIComponent id="component" width="400" height="400" x="0" y="100" />

        <s:Button label="Call accessed application service"
                    click="callServiceCall()" x="84" y="0"/>

    </s:Application>
```

How to Avoid Cross-Domain Scripting Attacks

Bad enough in themselves, cross-domain attacks can also expose a SWF to other threats, such as spoofing, script injection into the browser, malicious data injection, DNS rebinding, and insufficient authorization restrictions.

You can decrease the chances of an attack by setting a restricted cross-domain policy that limits the domains that can access the application, and by loading all the content from one remote source instead of from many remote sources that use the same security domain policy. For more information, see http://www.adobe.com/devnet/articles/crossdomain_policy_file_spec.html.

Additionally, you can use code obfuscation software such as secureSWF from Kindisoft (www.kindisoft.com/), which helps to protect your ActionScript from Flash decompilers. By protecting your SWFs and preventing attackers from decompiling your application, you can make it much harder for attackers to perform some of the cross-scripting tricks I've shown you in this chapter.

Part 2: Cross-Site Scripting (XSS) Vulnerability

Cross-Site Scripting (XSS) is a vulnerability that allows attackers to inject client-side script into a web page. XSS is the cause of many of the attacks we see on the Web today. Attackers find some kind of creative way to inject script into web pages, which can then expose the user to many security risks. For instance, attackers can do the following:

- **Account theft:** Attackers can grab cookie information, which can lead to account hijacking since many cookies hold account information.

- **Changing content on a page:** Attackers can mislead the user into entering information on a phony site, store incorrect content, or read the user's cookies.

The idea is to involve more than one site, which is where the name (cross-site) comes from. The second site injects a script into the first site and can then do anything it wants with the page.

Vulnerability in Flex Applications

Flash Player is not directly vulnerable to cross-scripting since the byte code gets compiled through the Virtual Machine (VM). However, Flash is often used on a page that includes other scripts, and your application may interact with other web page elements. That can open a security hole since web pages generate content dynamically without filtering the results first. Attackers can exploit your application and create XSS.

Cross-Site Scripting Attack on a Web Page from Flex

In this example, the user enters her name and the information is passed to a JavaScript function. Take a look.

```
<?xml version="1.0" encoding="utf-8"?>
<s:Application xmlns:fx="http://ns.adobe.com/mxml/2009"
               xmlns:s="library://ns.adobe.com/flex/spark"
               xmlns:mx="library://ns.adobe.com/flex/mx"
               minWidth="1024" minHeight="768">
    <fx:Script>
        <![CDATA[

            protected function clickHandler(name:String):void
            {
                ExternalInterface.call('submitInfo', name);
            }

        ]]>
    </fx:Script>

    <mx:Form x="10" y="10" width="286" height="115">
        <mx:FormItem label="First Name: ">
            <s:TextInput id="firstNameTextInput"/>
        </mx:FormItem>
        <mx:FormItem>
            <s:Button label="Submit" click="clickHandler(firstNameTextInput.text)"/>
        </mx:FormItem>
    </mx:Form>

</s:Application>
```

Add the JavaScript function to `index.template.html` in the header tag. The `index.template.html` is used by FlashBuilder to generate your HTML page, so adding this script will ensure you always have the script once you clean your project.

```
<script type="text/javascript">
    function submitInfo(name) {
        document.write(name);
```

```
    }
</script>
```

Compile the example and take a look at Figure 11-8, which shows the application.

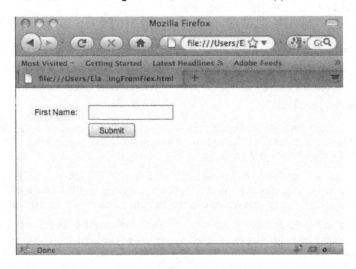

Figure 11-8. Application with a text box and a submit button to call a JavaScript function

After the user submits the form, the name displays on the web page as intended. However, take a look in Figure 11-9 at what happens if the user inserts the following code instead of a name:

```
<script>alert('Test')</script>
```

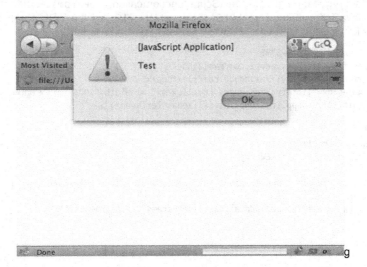

Figure 11-9. The browser showing the JavaScript method called

As you can see, we inserted JavaScript code, which was passed to the HTML page and executed by the browser. Displaying an alert box is pretty harmless, but having the ability to add the script tag lets the attacker inject a script, such as:

```
<script src="http://www...malicious-script.js"></script>
```

Or a redirect:

```
<script type="text/javascript">window.location = "http://www.google.com/"</script>
```

A malicious script can do anything it wants with a web page that allows executing the JavaScript code.

Malicious Data Injection

In cases where a web page has permission to read from and write to another web page, an attacker can abuse this and rewrite the web page or redirect users from the web page to a phishing site. This type of attack is known as malicious data injection, or script injection.

The attacker can inject data and create a cross-site scripting (XSS) attack with coding in ActionScript, using APIs such as `ExternalInterface`, `navigateToURL` or `getURL`. The attacker can then redirect the URL and even post JavaScript code that would capture the user's cookies with personal information.

Let's say we need a script to retrieve a parameter that was passed through the URL into my Flex application. As you know, you can pass variables using `FlashVar` and then use the following syntax in Flex 4 to read the parameter:

```
FlexGlobals.topLevelApplication.parameters.name
```

However, if you want to pass the parameters through the URL, you need to call the SWF directly like so:

```
MyApp.swf?name=Elad
```

The code allows me to read the parameter from the URL—without calling the SWF directly.

Here's how it works. I register a callback JavaScript function called `getParams`. When the user clicks on a button, I call the JavaScript method `getURLString`, which retrieves the URL parameter and passes it back to the callback.

```
<?xml version="1.0" encoding="utf-8"?>
<s:Application xmlns:fx="http://ns.adobe.com/mxml/2009"
               xmlns:s="library://ns.adobe.com/flex/spark"
               xmlns:mx="library://ns.adobe.com/flex/mx" minWidth="1024" minHeight="768"
               initialize="application1_initializeHandler(event)">
    <fx:Script>
        <![CDATA[
            import mx.controls.Alert;
            import mx.events.FlexEvent;

            protected function application1_initializeHandler(event:FlexEvent):void
            {
                ExternalInterface.addCallback("getParams", getParamCallBack);
            }

            protected function clickHandler():void
            {
                ExternalInterface.call('getURLString');
            }
```

```
        public function getParamCallBack(name:String):void
        {
            Alert.show(name);
        }

    ]]>
  </fx:Script>

  <s:Button label="Get name from URL string" click="clickHandler()"/>

</s:Application>
```

Take a look at the following JavaScript code, which includes the two methods getURLString and sendInfoToFlexApp. Once the Flex application calls getURLString, the URL parameter is retrieved. The sendInfoToFlexApp method then checks the type of navigator (Explorer or other) to access the Flex application element and sends the information to the callback method in Flex and calls an element on the page.

Note: instead of using the application name, I am using ${application} since this code is placed inside of html-template/index.template.html, which will replace the token with the application name when I compile.

```
<script language="JavaScript" type="text/javascript">

    function getURLString() {
        var name = decodeURIComponent(window.location.search.substring(6)) || "";
        sendInfoToFlexApp('${application}').getParams(name);

        document.write(name);
    }

    function sendInfoToFlexApp(appName) {
            if (navigator.appName.indexOf ("Microsoft") !=-1) {
              return window[appName];
            } else {
              return document[appName];
            }
    }

</script>
```

Compile and run the application. Don't forget to pass a parameter in the URL:

```
App.html?name=Elad
```

See Figure 11-10.

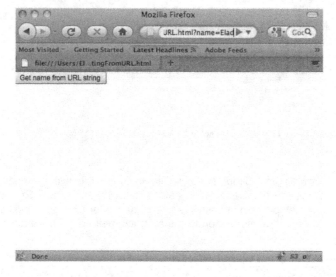

Figure 11-10. Browser showing application to retrieve name from URL string

Once you click the button, the URL parameter is retrieved, and Flex opens an alert popup to display the name, as Figure 11-11 shows.

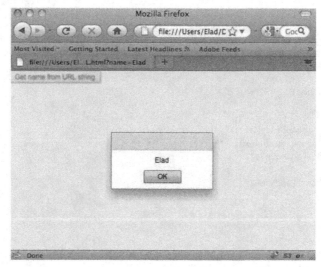

Figure 11-11. Browser showing alert with parameter passed

Although this looks pretty harmless and commonplace, take a look at what happens when instead of passing `?name=Elad`

I pass the parameter

```
?name=%3Cscript%3Ealert('Elad')%3C/script%3E
```

See Figure 11-12.

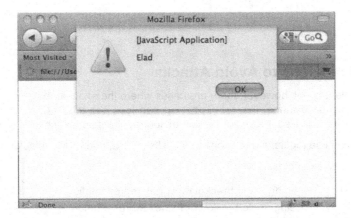

Figure 11-12. Browser showing JavaScript script passed from application

---

Note: This same type of cross-site scripting vulnerability is found in Flex 3's History Management handled by `historyFrame.html`. The vulnerability occurs in code used by the History Management feature. If you use this feature, you need to upgrade to at least the Flex 3.0.2 SDK Update, or just replace the HTML files from Flex 3.02.

How to Avoid Cross-Scripting Attacks

The way to avoid most cross-scripting attacks is to sufficiently sanitize user-supplied data. What this means is that you should apply the same best practices as in an old-fashioned web application, and filter any data a user enters to ensure that the user entry is in the proper format and contains only expected data; you should restrict the data using `maxChars`, `Validator,` or `RegExpValidator`.

To avoid this type of vulnerability, you can add a piece of code to your Flex/Flash application that will strip HTML tags, tag attributes, values, JavaScript, CSS, HTML and URL. There are two approaches. You can take the whitelist or blacklist approach in regards to validating the data. Whitelist is preferred, however whitelisting isn't always possible so blacklisting can be used.

Find HTML tags

In this example, you can adjust the `clickHandler` method and escape HTML and script tags. When you set the split method, you can be more specific and point to particular HTML elements or just look for a character:

```
protected function clickHandler(name:String):void
{
    if (ExternalInterface.available)
    {
        name = name.split("&").join("&amp;");
        name = name.split("'").join("&#039;");
```

```
        name = name.split("\"").join("&quot;");
        name = name.split("<").join("&lt;");
        name = name.split(">").join("&gt;");
        ExternalInterface.call("submitInfo", name);
    }
}
```

Use Regular Expressions to Avoid Attacks

The previous example is great; however, there are cases where the attacker may try to camouflage strings with hex equivalents. For instance, the `<script>` tag can look like this: `%3C%73%63%72%69%70%74%3E`. Additionally, the attacker can also abuse conversion of special characters such as < to %3C and > to %3E.

In these cases you can use regular expressions to find URL, CSS, and HTML attacks.

Here are some common examples:

- `((\%3C)|<)` - Opening angle bracket or its hex representation
- `((\%3E)|>)` - Closing angle bracket or its hex representation
- `((\%2F)|\/)*` - Forward slash for a closing tag or its hex representation
- `[a-z0-9\%]+` - Alphanumeric string inside the tag, or the hex representation

Note that checking for an opening angle bracket will also secure you from cross-site scripting using the `<img src=>` technique.

Take a look at the following example:

```
<s:Application xmlns:fx="http://ns.adobe.com/mxml/2009"
            xmlns:s="library://ns.adobe.com/flex/spark"
            xmlns:mx="library://ns.adobe.com/flex/mx"
            minWidth="1024" minHeight="768">
    <fx:Script>
        <![CDATA[
            import mx.validators.Validator;

            protected function clickHandler(name:String):void
            {
                if ( validate().length )
                {
                    ExternalInterface.call('submitInfo', name);
                }
            }

            public function validate():Array
            {
                validator.expression = "((\%3C)|<)";
                var invalidResults:Array = Validator.validateAll([validator]);

                return invalidResults;
            }
        ]]>
    </fx:Script>

    <mx:Form x="10" y="10" width="286" height="115">
```

```
<mx:FormItem label="First Name: ">
    <s:TextInput id="firstNameTextInput"/>
</mx:FormItem>
<mx:FormItem>
    <s:Button label="Submit" click="clickHandler(firstNameTextInput.text)"/>
</mx:FormItem>
</mx:Form>

<fx:Declarations>
    <mx:RegExpValidator id="validator" source="{firstNameTextInput}"
                        property="text" />
</fx:Declarations>

</s:Application>
```

We am using the `RegExpValidator` component and passing the regular expression "((\%3C)|<)". If there is no match, you get "field is invalid."

You can insert all the regular expressions and see if you get zero results, which means that the expression was present.

To read more about using regular expressions to check for cross-site scripting attacks, see the Symantec article:

`http://www.symantec.com/connect/articles/detection-sql-injection-and-cross-site-scripting-attacks`

Update Flash Player and SDK Often

Adobe works constantly to fight attackers. For instance, during the upgrade to Flex SDK 3.4, Adobe solved an issue regarding ticket CVE-2009-1879, which took care of a cross-site scripting vulnerability in the `index.template.html` in SDK 3.3. When the installed Flash version was older than a specified `requiredMajorVersion` value, it had allowed remote attackers to inject arbitrary web script or HTML via the query string.

Spoofing Attacks

In some cases a remotely loaded SWF can try to overlay controls on a loading SWF. If the attempt is successful, the SWF can potentially hijack control from the loading SWF, or carry out clickjacking—tricking a user into clicking on something that seems harmless, but isn't. Setting masks on Loaders can avoid this type of attack by limiting the SWF to a certain area on the display object.

Summary

In this chapter, we touched just the tip of the security iceberg. In Part 1, we covered decompiling and modifying a SWF file and loading the Flash app SWF file into another project. We showed how attackers can figure out the application source code and access other domains through the accessed application. We then showed how to avoid cross-domain scripting attacks.

In the second part we looked at the cross-site scripting (XSS) vulnerability by showing vulnerability in Flex applications. We continued by describing a cross-scripting attack on a web page from Flex and from a

URL. We pointed out the Flex History Management vulnerability, which Adobe has closed, and ways to avoid Cross-Scripting attack. Lastly, we covered spoofing attacks. After reading this chapter, you should have more awareness of some of the things you need to consider when publishing your application.

Links

Adobe Security Topic Center:

http://www.adobe.com/devnet/security/

White paper: Adobe Flash Player 10 security:

http://www.adobe.com/devnet/flashplayer/articles/flash_player10_security_wp.html

Check OWASP Flash Security Project that includes numerous resources on security

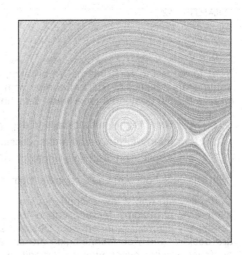

Chapter 12

Migrating Web 1.0 Interfaces to RIA

by Shashank Tiwari

Many enterprises and organizations are heavily invested in legacy web technologies, ranging from first-generation applets to recent HTML-based and Ajax powered user interfaces. Therefore, even if the organizations have a compelling need to adopt today's rich and engaging platforms, writing off all that investment and starting from scratch is not an option for them. Often, the preferred course is to reuse as much as possible and add bits of the newer technologies incrementally, thus gaining some benefits without disrupting existing systems that continue to work effectively.

A few purists argue against such reuse, but the possibilities of substantial and quick benefits from incremental adoption are immense, and it would be imprudent for you to ignore them. Moreover, your development team members may not be ready to discard their faithful old technologies and tools completely and move on with the newer options. For now, let us leave the purists aside and find solutions to the quest of adopting RIA gradually, while keeping parts of the legacy intact.

While the benefits of incremental adoption are talked about, the argument isn't that creating RIA from scratch is a bad idea. The viewpoint is that reality may not allow you to start from scratch in many cases, especially when the potential costs of change are high and the return on the investment is not entirely understood upfront. This chapter will help further the cause of incremental RIA adoption and will provide a path to achieving success in this pursuit.

The chapter starts by talking about minor refactoring and restructuring to plug in RIA on top of existing systems and moves on to providing ideas for substantial replacements of existing modules, where necessary.

Weighing Up the StatusQuo

Let's first survey the current landscape and understand the starting context.

Your target is the Rich Internet Application (RIA), so your starting point could be any platform that has some characteristics of RIA or benefits from the features that RIA supports. This raises obvious question: what is RIA? A comprehensive literal definition is easy enough to give. RIA is

- Rich: Highly interactive and engaging, desktop-like in a traditional sense
- Internet: Networked and accessible worldwide and across devices
- Application: An implementation of a required (business) solution

With this definition, you could consider both desktop and web applications as your starting point.

Currently, with only a few exceptions, the desktop and web technologies are disparate and are viewed as alternative paradigms for application deployment and distribution. Also, they are seen as satisfying completely different requirements. Desktop applications are suitable where high performance "fat clients" are desired, and web technologies are suitable where the application needs to be accessible to a large audience and flexible enough to be modified easily to keep up with changing requirements.

Desktop applications are usually built using C, C++, Java, or the Microsoft alternatives (including C# .NET). They usually implement the two-tier client-server communication model. They often make use of native calls to the operating system and its hardware drivers. Although sometimes viewed as legacies, they thrive as heavy-duty office and enterprise applications. In the last few years, desktop applications have started leveraging the Internet and often connect to networks using the Internet protocols. Instant messaging clients and soft-phones are examples of such applications.

Web applications, on the other hand, are built using a number of different technologies, programming paradigms, programming languages, and frameworks. However, they could be classified under two categories:

- HTML-based web applications
- Virtual machine (VM) based web applications

HTML–based web applications have user interfaces that are interpreted and rendered within the browser. This means the output is HTML markup, with JavaScript elements. These user interfaces are generated mostly on the server and only sometimes have large client-centric manipulations. JSP and PHP applications fall in this category.

VM-based web applications live and run within a virtual machine. The virtual machines themselves are housed within the browser, but applications existing in a virtual machine don't interact with the browser directly. The virtual machines exist as plug-ins in the browser, and interpret code in a browser-independent manner. Applications built using Java applets, Flex, and Silverlight are VM-based web applications.

RIA is Flex-based, so migrating to RIA implies moving from any of these web technologies to Flex. Desktop applications also have a few features in common with RIA. So porting them over to Flex and AIR is also a possibility, though that topic is out of scope for this chapter. The focus here is on web applications only.

The next couple of sections dig deeper into web applications, the source applications that you intend to port over to Flex.

HTML Web Technologies

As mentioned, HTML technologies can be further classified as server centric or client centric. We will illustrate HTML technologies using this classification.

Server-centric Approaches

A large number of web user interfaces leverage server-side platforms to generate HTML outputs. Sometimes they supplement these HTML outputs with dynamic JavaScript (which manipulates the HTML Document Object Model at run time) based decorations that add richer functionality. The server-side platforms are varied and diverse, but they are often written in Java, PHP, ColdFusion, Python, or Ruby. Irrespective of the programming languages and framework used to generate the user interface, these server-side options generate HTML and JavaScript outputs. Figure 12-1 shows this in a diagram.

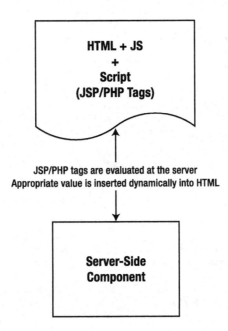

Figure 12-1. HTML generation in typical server-centric web applications

Let's first see some simple JSP and PHP applications so you can understand how they work. Later, you will morph these simple applications to work with Flex. If you don't use either of these technologies, you will still find the discussion useful. The idea of these examples is not to teach you to write web applications using any of these server-side technologies, but to show how they can be migrated from their current forms to a new form that includes a Flex user interface. You will be able to apply what you learn to your own server-centric web environment, which may be Ruby, Python, Perl, ColdFusion, or anything else.

The simple JSP example displays a list of stock prices in an HTML table. The example is crude because it uses direct database connection and includes all the code together. In a real-life situation, you will distribute the code into three separate tiers: database, middle tier (with database access and business logic), and web layer. The code for this example is as follows:

```
<%@ page import="java.sql.*"%>
<%@ page import="java.util.*"%>
<%
List stockList = new ArrayList();
```

```
Class.forName("sun.jdbc.odbc.JdbcOdbcDriver");
Connection conn =
DriverManager.getConnection↵
(//pass the connection credentials);
Statement stmt = conn.createStatement();
ResultSet rs =
stmt.executeQuery↵
("select id,symbol, name, price from Stocks");
while(rs.next()){
Map stock = new HashMap();
stock.put("id",rs.getInt(1));
stock.put("Symbol",rs.getString(2));
stock.put("name",rs.getString(3));
stock.put("price",rs.getString(4));
stockList.add(stock);
}
rs.close();
stmt.close();
conn.close();
%>
<html><head>
<title>Stocks</title>
</head>
<body>
<h1>Stocks</h1>
<table border="1">
<%
for(int i=0;i<stockList.size();i++){
Map stock = (Map)stockList.get(i);
%>
<tr>
<td align="right"><%=stock.get("id")%></td>
<td><%=emp.get("symbol")%></td>
<td><%=emp.get("name")%></td>
<td><%=emp.get("price")%></td>
</tr>
<%
}
%>
</table>
</body></html>
```

In this simple example, you bind the result set of your database queries to an HTML table. This is a typical case where data is dynamically accessed and presented as HTML. Later in this chapter, you will see how XML could be generated (instead of HTML) and consumed in a Flex interface.

The next example, a PHP web application, is another that is trivial from a real-life point of view. It shows a simple form that has a button to submit the input data. All the code is in a single file that mixes HTML with PHP script. Here is what the code looks like:

```
<html>
<head>
<title>Login Form</title>
```

```
</head>
<body>
<form method="post" action="<?php echo $PHP_SELF;?>">
User Name:<input type="text"
size="12"
maxlength="36"
name="username">:<br />
Password:<input type="text"
size="12"
maxlength="15"
name="password">:<br />
Role::<br />
Administrator:<input type="radio" value="Admin" name="role">:<br />
Super User:<input type="radio" value="SuperUser" name="role">:<br />
Regular User:<input type="radio"
value="RegularUser"
name="role">:<br />
Please choose your preferences::<br />
Remember Password:<input type="checkbox"
value="RememberPassword"
name="preferences[]">:<br />
Expire session only on logout:<input type="checkbox"
value="ExpireOnLogout"
name="preferences[]">:<br />
<textarea
rows="5"
cols="20"
name="quote"
wrap="physical">
Leave a message for the administrator if required
</textarea>:<br />
Select your department:<br />
<select name="department">
<option value="InformationSystems">Information Systems</option>
<option value="Sales">Sales</option>
<option value="Operations">Operations</option></select>:<br />
</body>
</html>
```

In this PHP example, there isn't much server-side data access. The example has user interface components. These are plain HTML elements with PHP code that adds the processing conveniences and the additional rendering and validation features. When porting such applications to Flex, you would use only the data access and business logic parts and discard the user interface elements. Figure 12-2 shows a screenshot of the PHP example.

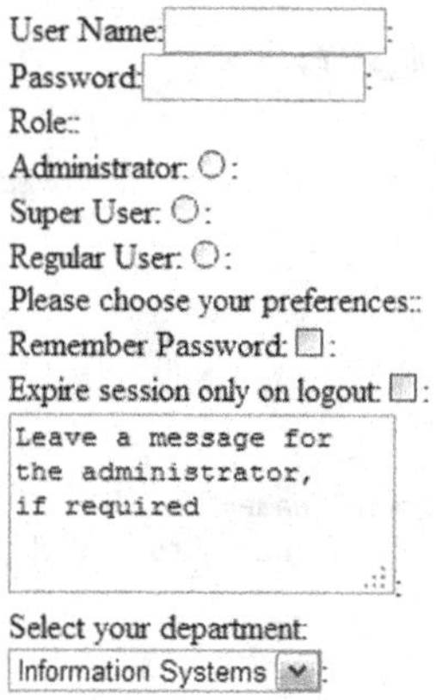

User Name: [_____] :
Password: [_____] :
Role::
Administrator: ⦿ :
Super User: ⦿ :
Regular User: ⦿ :
Please choose your preferences::
Remember Password: ☐ :
Expire session only on logout: ☐ :

```
Leave a message for
the administrator,
if required
```

Select your department:
[Information Systems ▾] :

Figure 12-2. The simple PHP example

Although web applications are almost always more complicated than these two examples, they are often built using similar concepts. A little later we will inspect these, and a few other examples, to see how to modify them and convert them to Flex applications.

Client-centric Alternatives

Although server-side HTML technologies are popular and widespread, rich JavaScript-based client-centric manipulations are now commonly becoming part of web applications. This client-centric asynchronous interaction approach is popularly known as Ajax. With Ajax, JavaScript and DHTML are becoming more than mere animation decorations. In some cases, Ajax clients are able to provide some of the rich functionality that VM-based options provide. From a Flex perspective, interacting with JavaScript is easy. (You can read Chapter 9 to understand how to connect JavaScript and Flex). When replacing JavaScript user interfaces with Flex alternatives, the same remoting infrastructure can be reused, but often the user interface components themselves overlap with what Flex provides and need to be completely discarded. I will discuss a few bits of this in the context of your solutions later in this chapter.

Next, let's take a quick look at the VM-based web applications.

Virtual Machines in the Browsers

Unlike HTML-based web applications, VM-based web applications run in a managed VM environment. A managed VM environment provides a uniform run-time platform across browsers and keeps the code shielded from the difficulties arising due to browser differences. Applets have existed since the mid1990s and so has Flash, whereas Silverlight is only a little over a couple of years old. Flex applications run on Flash and are VM-based RIA frameworks; most often migrating from another VM environment to Flex implies recreating the entire UI. The only portions that are reused are the services that the UI interacts with.

In practice, almost all popular HTML-based web applications, whether built for consumers or enterprises, use frameworks under the hood. In complex scenarios, frameworks manage all the basic plumbing. The next section lists a few of these frameworks.

Frameworks behind the scenes

There are innumerable numbers of frameworks out there to build web applications. Every language has a few popular ones.

Popular web frameworks written in PHP include the following:

- symfony: http://www.symfony-project.org/
- CakePHP: http://cakephp.org/
- ZEND: http://framework.zend.com

Then there are full-stack, pluggable, module-based frameworks like Drupal (http://drupal.org/), which are especially popular for content management.

Ruby has an extremely popular web framework offering in Rails (http://www.rubyonrails.org/). Python has a framework similar to Rails called Django (http://www.djangoproject.com/). Groovy's Grails (http://grails.org/) is a web framework that falls in the same category as Rails and Django.

Some newer languages like Scala (http://www.scala-lang.org/) also offer web frameworks; Scala's answer to agile web frameworks is called Lift (http://liftweb.net/index.php/Main_Page).

Java has uncountable web frameworks. Apache Struts (http://struts.apache.org/) historically has been the most popular of them all. Newer web frameworks include JBoss Seam (http://seamframework.org/), Spring MVC and Web Flow (http://www.springframework.org/), Tapestry (http://tapestry.apache.org/), Wicket (http://wicket.apache.org/), Struts 2 (http://struts.apache.org/2.x/index.html), and Stripes (http://www.stripesframework.org/display/stripes/Home). There are many other frameworks apart from the ones just listed. Most frameworks have their own unique proposition. Some enable Ajax, some simplify and enhance Java Server Faces (JSF), a few provide deeper integration with the server side, and a few offer a set of user interface components.

We could fill up a lot of pages listing web frameworks. What you need to understand here is how to migrate applications built using these frameworks to leverage Flex. Because each framework has its own complexity, there is no universal porting strategy that will work for all.

Therefore, we will pick two important frameworks from this list and see how applications built using them can be refactored to use Flex. The two frameworks of choice are

- Apache Struts
- Ruby on Rails

Discussions about migrating applications built using these two frameworks are included in the sections where we talk about migration strategies. The specific section that deals with porting framework applications is entitled "Strategies to Port Framework-Based Applications."

Coverage of only two frameworks is not comprehensive, but what you will learn in their context will help you create your own strategy for your framework, outside this list.

Now let's start with some recommendations and recipes for migration.

Migration Strategies

This chapter does not provide an exhaustive list of migration strategies and techniques. It only analyzes a few very important ones. Most of the recommendations apply to HTML–based web applications, and don't necessarily hold good for applications that run in browser plug-ins.

Generating XML

As a first step, you need to explore replacing the HTML in web applications with a Flex user interface and reusing everything up to the point where HTML generation starts. Most often the embedded script tags in HTML, which are interpreted on the server, are dynamically replaced with HTML elements. These embedded script tags could be JSP or PHP tags. This is how dynamic data is incorporated, while the output remains plain HTML.

Although Flex applications can be made to consume HTML as text—and possibly you could write a parser to glean the data from it—this technique is both inefficient and ugly. An elegant modification would be to generate XML instead of HTML. Then you could apply an XSLT (http://www.w3.org/TR/xslt) stylesheet to transform the XML output to an XHTML output. That way you still generate HTML (or more accurately XHTML) while creating XML as an intermediate output. Flex applications can consume the intermediate XML. So an old application gets refactored to work simultaneously with both HTML and Flex. Figure 12-3 summarizes this technique in a diagram.

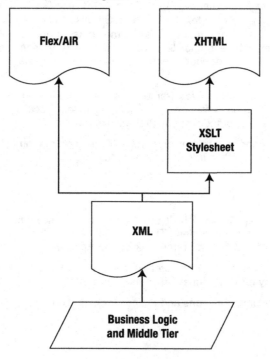

Figure 12-3. Generate XML. Consume XML in Flex and transform it to XHTML using an XSLT stylesheet.

Let's take the earlier JSP example and make it generate XML. Here is the modified code:

```
<?xml version="1.0" encoding="ISO-8859-1"?>
<%@ page contentType="text/xml;charset=ISO-8859-1" %>
<%@ page import="java.sql.*"%>
<%@ page import="java.util.*"%>
<%
List stockList = new ArrayList();
Class.forName("sun.jdbc.odbc.JdbcOdbcDriver");
Connection conn =
DriverManager.getConnection↵
(//pass the connection credentials);
Statement stmt = conn.createStatement();
ResultSet rs =
stmt.executeQuery↵
("select id,symbol, name, price from Stocks");
while(rs.next()){
Map stock = new HashMap();
stock.put("id",rs.getInt(1));
stock.put("Symbol",rs.getString(2));
stock.put("name",rs.getString(3));
stock.put("price",rs.getString(4));
stockList.add(stock);
}
rs.close();
stmt.close();
conn.close();
%>
<%
for(int i=0;i<stockList.size();i++){
Map stock = (Map)stockList.get(i);
%>
<Stocks>
<stock><%=stock.get("id")%></stock>
<symbol><%=emp.get("symbol")%></symbol>
<name><%=emp.get("name")%></name>
<price><%=emp.get("price")%></price>
</Stocks>
<%
}
%>
```

The HTML elements are taken out and XML tags, including the XML declaration tag, are introduced into the code. This JSP creates XML. An XSLT stylesheet can be applied to the XML to generate XHTML. I won't go into how that happens, because it's not relevant to your purpose here.

Assuming this JSP is accessible via a URL, say `http://localhost:8080/generateXML.jsp`, it can be consumed in Flex using the `HTTPService` component. Flex has rich capabilities for XML parsing. Its XML capabilities can be utilized to bind the data effectively to the desired interfaces. The `HTTPService` code in MXML could be as follows:

```
<s:HTTPService
id="xmlFromJSP"
url="http://localhost:8080/generateXML.jsp"
```

```
useProxy="false"
method="GET"
resultFormat="e4x" />
```

This code assumes no usage of a server-side proxy and the presence of required security definitions in a `crossdomain.xml` file. The cross-domain policy file is discussed in Part 2 of this book.

The trick of generating XML instead of HTML is very simple and straightforward, but it does have its limitations. Such a transformation assumes that you still keep all the logic and state in the server. But that is not the best way of using Flex, which is capable of managing state and interaction logic on the client. This capability is a big driver for rich and engaging experiences. In the next case, you'll see how a server-side service orientation could be an improvement over plain XML data access.

Service-Orienting Legacy Applications

Existing web applications could be restructured according to the business functions they accomplish. Each function would be encapsulated in an independent service. Service outcomes could be controlled using passed-in parameters. In short, an application could be reengineered using Service-Oriented Architecture (SOA) concepts.

Although it all sounds fairly logical and simple, converting traditional web applications to service-oriented forms is neither easy nor quick. Also, migrating applications implies smoothly converting over from one form to the other, without seriously affecting the users. This can be a challenging requirement.

A few modern web applications already include service-oriented features. Such applications are great candidates for migration to Flex. The next few paragraphs examine such a case and scrutinize the details of the migration.

I will take the Google Weather application as an example. You may already have seen Google Weather. If not, then browse to www.google.com and type "weather for <your city>" to access the application. The response set of this search returns the weather conditions for <your city> for the next four days. The information is displayed using a combination of text and images and shows up as the top most result for your search. Thus this application is rendered as HTML and accessible via the web browser. However, an alternative way to access and interact with this application is the Google Weather REST API, which I use with my Flex application.

The Google Weather REST API provides a clean service oriented access to the application and neatly separates application access and data from the HTML rendering aspects. This API is accessible using the standard HTTP mechanisms. It returns the expected results in XML format. Flex applications are capable of communicating with HTTP services and can easily handle XML data, therefore using the Google Weather REST API with Flex is easy and effortless. Let's see how.

The Google Weather web application is shown in Figure 12-4.

Figure 12-4. HTML based Google Weather

The new Flex interface is shown in Figure 12-5 The Flex interface is a simple rendering of the Google Weather data. The interface could be very interactive and dynamic, but for the moment let'skeep it simple. The entire source code for the Flex interface is provided a little later in this section.

The most interesting part in this example is how you hook into the services and consume the data. You use the Flex `HTTPService` components to do that because the services are exposed as RESTful web services via HTTP `GET` calls. For example, if you had to get the weather data for New York, NY, you would invoke the following HTTP request `http://www.google.com/ig/api?weather=new+york,ny`. This is a simple HTTP GET request, where the only parameter is the place, which can be specified as city, state, or zip code.

This URL, when invoked using the `HTTPService` components, is as follows:

```
<s:HTTPService id="googleWeatherAPI"
                  url="http://www.google.com/ig/api?"
                  resultFormat="e4x"
                  result="googleWeatherAPI_resultHandler(event)"
                  fault="googleWeatherAPI_faultHandler(event)"/>
```

The place information is made available via a user input and added to the HTTP request as a parameter.

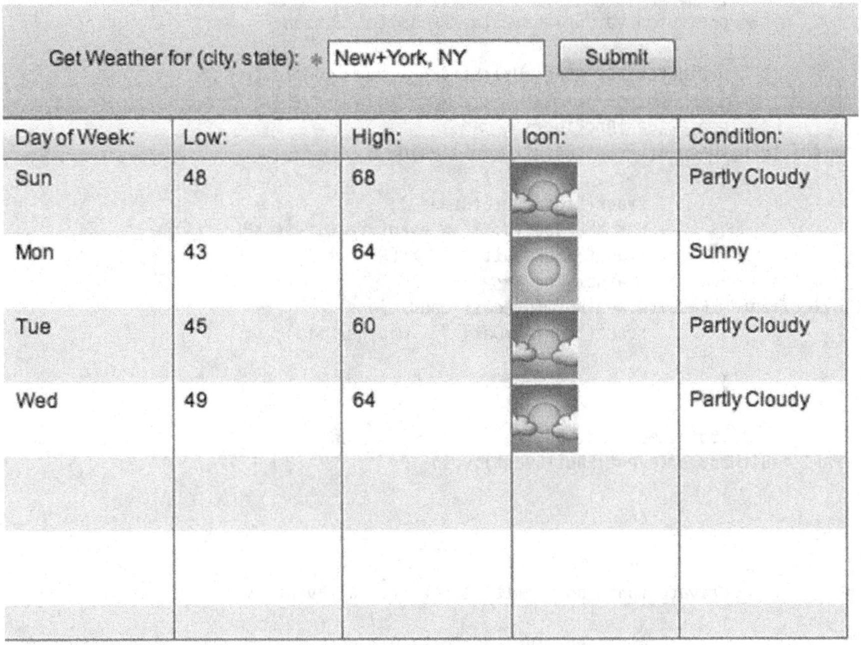

Get Weather for (city, state): New+York, NY	Submit			
Day of Week:	Low:	High:	Icon:	Condition:
Sun	48	68		Partly Cloudy
Mon	43	64		Sunny
Tue	45	60		Partly Cloudy
Wed	49	64		Partly Cloudy

Figure 12-5. Flex interface for the Google Weather API based sample application

`googleWeatherAPI_resultHandler(event)` is the method that is invoked on return of a successful result set. That function is responsible for transforming the data you receive into a form that binds to a DataGrid.

The entire Flex application that provides the new front end to the Google Weather API based application is in a single MXML file and is as follows:

```
<?xml version="1.0" encoding="utf-8"?>
<s:Application xmlns:fx="http://ns.adobe.com/mxml/2009"
                      xmlns:s="library://ns.adobe.com/flex/spark"
                      xmlns:mx="library://ns.adobe.com/flex/mx"
                      minWidth="955"
                      minHeight="600">
        <fx:Script>
                <![CDATA[
                        import mx.collections.XMLListCollection;
                        import mx.controls.Alert;
                        import mx.events.ValidationResultEvent;
                        import mx.rpc.events.FaultEvent;
                        import mx.rpc.events.ResultEvent;
                        import mx.utils.StringUtil;

                        [Bindable]
                        protected var weatherData:XMLListCollection;

                        protected var googleUrl:String = "www.google.com";

                        protected function↵
  googleWeatherAPI_resultHandler(event:ResultEvent):void
                                {
                                        trace("result returned");
                                        var XMLResults:XML = event.result as XML;
                                        trace("XMLResults " + XMLResults);
                                        weatherData =↵
 new XMLListCollection(XMLResults.weather.forecast_conditions);
                                        trace("weatherData " + weatherData);

                                }

                        protected function↵
 googleWeatherAPI_faultHandler(event:FaultEvent):void
                                {
                                        //
                                }

                        private function submit_click(evt:MouseEvent):void
                                {
                                        var result:ValidationResultEvent = stringValidator.validate();
                                        var params:Object = {};

                                        switch (result.type) {
                                                case ValidationResultEvent.INVALID:
                                                        Alert.show(result.message, result.type);
                                                        break;
                                                case ValidationResultEvent.VALID:
                                                        params["weather"] =↵
```

```
StringUtil.trim(cityAndState.text);
                                       googleWeatherAPI.send(params);
                                       break;
                        }

                }
        ]]>
    </fx:Script>
    <fx:Declarations>
        <!-- Place non-visual elements (e.g., services, value objects) here -->
        <s:HTTPService id="googleWeatherAPI"
                            url="http://www.google.com/ig/api?"
                            resultFormat="e4x"
                            result="googleWeatherAPI_resultHandler(event)"
                            fault="googleWeatherAPI_faultHandler(event)"/>
        <mx:StringValidator id="stringValidator"
                                        source="{cityAndState}"
                                        property="text"
                                        minLength="2"
                                        maxLength="{cityAndState.maxChars}" />
    </fx:Declarations>
    <s:controlBarContent>
        <mx:Form>
                <mx:FormItem label="Get Weather for (city, state):"
                                required="true"
                                direction="horizontal">
                    <s:TextInput id="cityAndState"
                                        maxChars="50"/>
                    <s:Button label="Submit"
                                click="submit_click(event);"/>
                </mx:FormItem>
        </mx:Form>
    </s:controlBarContent>

    <mx:DataGrid id="weatherDataGrid" dataProvider="{weatherData}">
        <mx:columns>
            <mx:DataGridColumn id="day_of_week_column"
                                        dataField="day_of_week.@data"
                                        headerText="Day of Week:" />
            <mx:DataGridColumn id="low_column"
                                        dataField="low.@data"
                                        headerText="Low:" />
            <mx:DataGridColumn id="high_column"
                                        dataField="high.@data"
                                        headerText="High:" />
            <mx:DataGridColumn id="icon_column"
                                        headerText="Icon:" >
                <mx:itemRenderer>
                    <fx:Component>
                        <s:MXDataGridItemRenderer>
                            <mx:Image↵
source="http://www.google.com{data.icon.@data}" height="40" width="40"/>
                        </s:MXDataGridItemRenderer>
```

```
                                  </fx:Component>
                                </mx:itemRenderer>
                          </mx:DataGridColumn>
                    <mx:DataGridColumn id="condition_column"
                                            dataField="condition.@data"
                                            headerText="Condition:" />
              </mx:columns>
        </mx:DataGrid>

</s:Application>
```

The preceding code is fairly straightforward and self-explanatory. This was a good example of a service-oriented legacy web application that can be easily transformed to become rich and interactive. The modifications were deliberately kept simple. Advanced behavior and better interaction can be added to the Flex version of this user interface.

Resolving State Management Complexity

In the previous couple of cases, you read data. In real-life situations you will also create, update, and delete data. The moment such manipulations come into play, you need to decide where you want to hold the data state and where you wish to manipulate the data. In Flex applications, the recommendation is to hold the state at the client and manipulate the data right there before it's committed.

The legacy web applications are of two types, HTML-based and VM-based. HTML-based applications typically perform state maintenance on the server. These applications keep a conversation going between a client and the server using some shared token, most often a session. VM-based applications hold state on the client.

When talking migration or porting, we are primarily talking about moving HTML web technologies over to Flex, because moving VM-based technologies is closer to starting from scratch in most cases.

So the big question to answer when remastering HTML web applications is this: where should you keep the state? The right answer in a new project is to keep state on the client and leverage the rich, interactive, and engaging model. However, this may imply completely trashing the current infrastructure and rendering it useless when migrating over (i.e., when not starting from scratch).

In general, it's advisable to put some effort into getting rid of session management and the complications around it, and abstract the create, read, delete, and update (CRUD) operations into services. Keep the services fine-grained to allow flexibility but also have coarse-grained aggregations of these services. For most read calls, use the coarse-grained calls. Maintain application state on the client and be sure to switch off auto-commits to avoid excessive back-and-forth traffic. Demarcate your CRUD, especially create, update, and delete operations, using transactions, as you do in traditional client-server operations. On every transaction milestone, invoke the fine-grained service calls to complete the operation. For example, you may be manipulating a related set of rows in a data grid and may want to commit the changes only after all the modifications to the related set of rows are made and not when each constituent change occurs.

Flex has server-side remoting counterparts. Such server-side software is available for Java, PHP, Python, .NET, and Ruby. These server-side frameworks leverage HTTP endpoints as gateways and have the capability to create and maintain sessions between the Flex client and the server side. In some cases, it may be useful to use this facility.

A related problem that needs to be tackled is that of the frequency of round-trips from the client to the server and back.

Optimizing the Frequency of Round-trips

In traditional client-server applications, the number of calls between the client and the server is drastically reduced. The client is thick, so it holds the data and the logic and interacts with the server only to share the updates or save the commits back to the database.

In web applications, this problem is not as straightforward. The immediacy of the web, combined with the concurrency requirements of such applications, pose the age-old complications around dirty and phantom reads. Let's take a small diversion and recap what these problems are.

The problems of dirty and phantom reads are defined under the larger umbrella of isolation and concurrency. Typically, isolation levels are defined under the following four categories:

- Read uncommitted: One transaction may see uncommitted changes made by another transaction. Dirty reads may occur in this case.
- Read committed: Data records retrieved by one transaction are not protected from being modified by another transaction. Nonrepeatable reads may occur.
- Repeatable read: All retrieved data cannot be changed by another process because it is locked by the transaction that retrieves it. Phantom reads can occur though as range locks are not established. In other words, the where clause of a select statement may have candidate rows that have newly appeared since the select was made, but these new rows will not show up.
- Serializable: Everything is isolated and no transactional problems occur.

The question is which isolation level is best when creating a Flex interface with a legacy server side? A naïve recommendation is to use the serializable level to avoid all problems, but this is usually not practical, as the impact on performance and scalability would be unacceptable. What then is the right level?

Also, is it advisable to lock pessimistically every time, or to use optimistic locking in most cases? Pessimistic locking means you expect conflicts to occur often and so lock every time you initiate an operation. Optimistic locking means you lock only in exceptional cases, because you don't expect conflicts to occur often.

As with state management, the choice is neither universal nor easy. In most cases, optimistic locking and maintaining repeatable reads is advisable. Setting up explicit transactional boundaries to avoid unnecessary round-trips is a good idea, too.

Next, we consider a completely different scenario. This is a case where the application is database driven, and the screens act as windows to the underlying tables.

Generating Database-driven Applications

Database-driven applications are built using all types of web development technologies. With either HTML or VM technologies, if the application is largely database driven, it may be beneficial to recreate the application when building it using Flex. Flash Builder 4 has a nifty little feature for generating database-driven applications that you could try. In this case, reinvention is faster and better than incremental adoption.

We will create a Flex, PHP, and MySQL database application to delve deeper into how the database creation utility in Flash Builder 4 can be leveraged. Our PHP application is auto-generated using the database definition.

The example was built on a Mac, so chose to download and use the ready to go MAMP distribution. You can grab a copy of this free PHP, MySQL and Apache pre-configured bundle for Mac from `http://sourceforge.net/projects/mamp/`. If you aren't on a Mac, you could grab an analogous distribution for your platform. Alternatively, you can install and configure the individual pieces of software.

Be sure the Flash Builder 4 plugin is installed in your Eclipse setup. If you would like also go ahead and install PDT, the Eclipse plug-in for PHP development. The PDT update site is `http://download.eclipse.org/tools/pdt/updates/site.xml`. The steps for adding plugin(s) to Eclipse are not shown or explained here. It's assumed you know how to do it. If not, then please consult the Eclipse documentation for help.

As a first step, let's create the database table(s) for the application. We are using a MAMP installation so the MySQL client in this bundle can be accessed via the phpMyAdmin application or the command line. We prefer the command line, so open a terminal window and access the MySQL client as follows:

```
/Applications/MAMP/Library/bin/mysql -uroot -p
```

The default password for the database "root" user is "root". You can always open up the MAMP start page at http://localhost:8888/MAMP/?language=English and verify the credentials if you have changed the defaults and don't recall the values.

Once logged in, create a database called "flex4" and change to it, using: "use flex4". Then create a table called "books" as follows:

```
CREATE TABLE books (
    title VARCHAR(100),
    author VARCHAR(100),
    publisher VARCHAR(30),
    topic VARCHAR(20),
    comment VARCHAR(100),
    price FLOAT
);
```

Once the database table is created, its time to create a Flex project that supports a PHP application server. Figures 12-6 and 12-7 show snapshots of the New Flex Project Creation Wizard. We call our project **DatabaseDrivenSampleApplication**. Figure 12-7 shows how the web root and root URL for the PHP application are specified. It's possible to validate this configuration before moving forward. Validation can be done with a single click of the button labeled **Validate Configuration**. Errors will be thrown if the web server configurations are not correct.

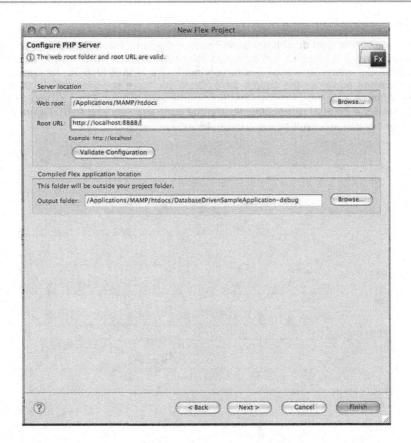

Figure 12-7. New Flex Project Creation Wizard, second screen

This newly created Flex project will be the target for the database-driven application. To invoke the wizard to create an application from a database, you choose **Data ➤ Connect to PHP,** as shown in Figure 16-8.

Figure 12-8. Choose Connect to PHP from the Data menu

On the next screen, your wizard brings you to the page that lets you configure a PHP service. This allows you to choose a PHP service class that can be configured as a service endpoint and be bound to a Flex application. In this example, you don't have a PHP class yet so use Flash Builder's help to create it. Click on "click here to generate a sample". On selection the next screen is as shown in Figure 12-9. On this screen, we provide the database credentials to connect to the MAMP MySQL database and specify the books table we created earlier as the source table. Once you have specified the database, you can test the connection. After clicking the button to test the connection, you would be prompted the first time to download and install the Zend AMF remoting library that connects Flex and PHP. Figure 12-10 shows the message that prompts you to download the Zend AMF library.

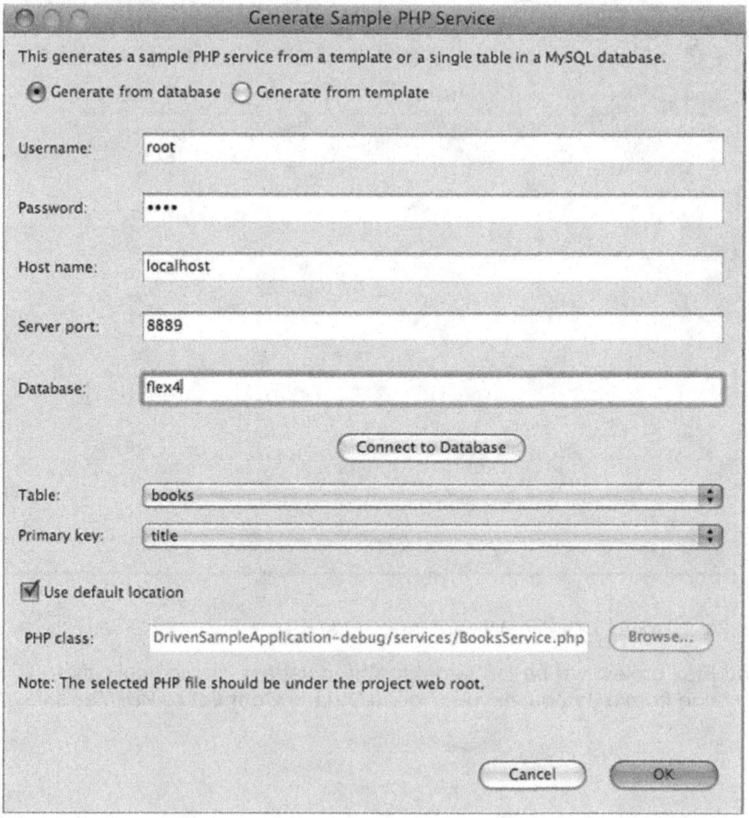

Figure 12-9. Database credentials passed to the wizard

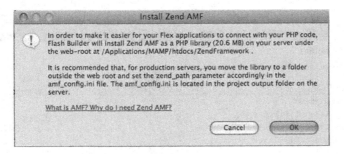

Figure 12-10. Message asking to download Zend AMF

At this stage you can click "Generate from database" and Flash Builder would generate the PHP classes for you. Figure 12-11 shows what the wizard screen appears like. It shows the path to the generated classes and mentions the service name, package name and data type package. Figure 14612 shows the list of service operations available through the generated classes.

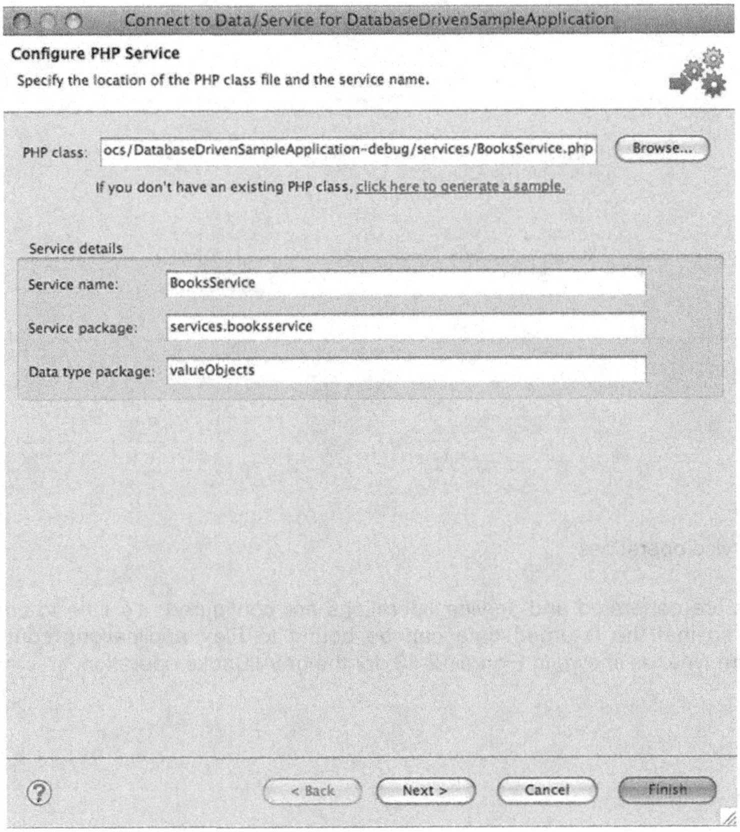

Figure 12-11. Generated PHP classes

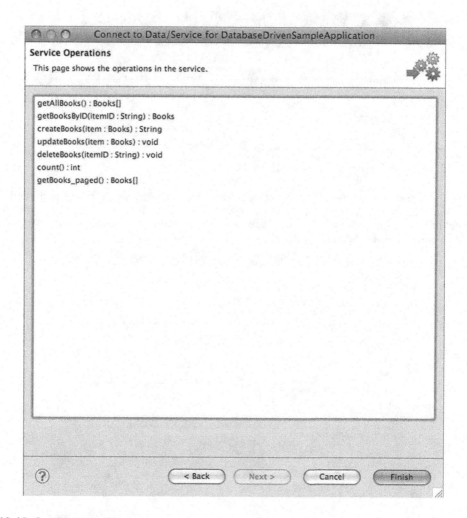

Figure 12-12. Service operations

Once the classes are generated and service operations are configured, it's time to configure the return type of services so that the returned data can be bound to Flex applications controls. For starters, configure the return type, as shown in Figure 12-13, for the getAllBooks operation.

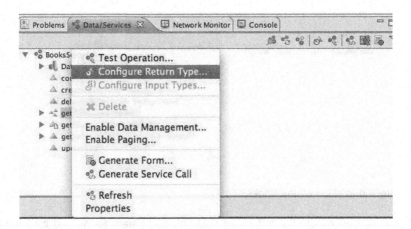

Figure 12-13. Configure return type

Then change to the design view of the Flex application and drop in a DataGrid control. Now you can bind the DataGrid and the service operation. Figure 12-14 shows how the getAllBooks operation can be bound to the DataGrid.

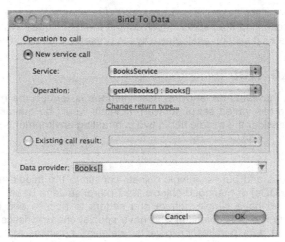

Figure 12-14. Bind to Data

Once the operation is bound to the DataGrid, the columns of the DataGrid are configured based on the operation return type. Figure 12-15 shows how the DataGrid bound to getAllBooks appears.

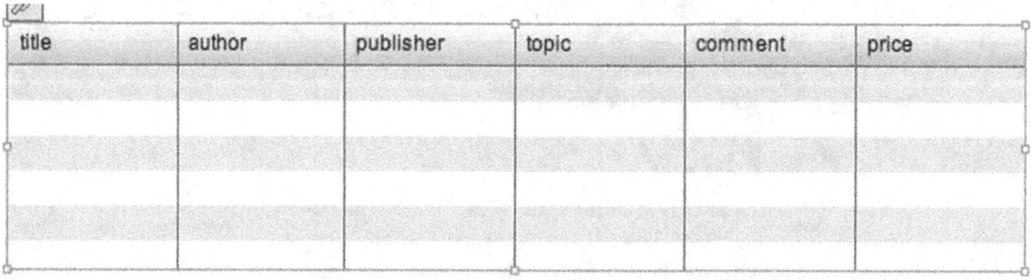

title	author	publisher	topic	comment	price

Figure 12-15. DataGrid to show all the books

To manage CRUD operations on the underlying data you can create forms and bind the operations as required. While you could continue to keep building the example application, let's stop at this time as the essential ideas around Flash Builder 4's database based application generation capabilities have been illustrated.

The preceding paragraphs showed how easy it is to generate Flex applications based on database tables. So it's always prudent to create applications from scratch when the primary purpose is to create a user interface for a table data.

Continuing the quest of presenting the aspects involved and the techniques available to migrate from Web 1.0 applications to RIA, the next section evaluates ways to preserve the middle tier.

Reusing the Middle Tier

Everything lying between the database and the user interface is termed the middle tier. So choosing a single strategy to preserve this varied set of software artifacts would be overambitious. To make it more specific, let's separately consider the middle tier in two contrasting environments: Java EE and PHP.

Java EE Middle Tier

In Java EE, the data access and business logic objects constitute the middle tier. These objects can be Plain Old Java Objects (POJOs) or managed objects like Enterprise Java Beans (EJBs) and Spring beans. POJOs run in the JVM and have simple getters and setters to access and manipulate their member variables. Managed objects live in a container and have special characteristics depending on their type. For example, EJBs can be data persistence objects, stateless business logic components, or stateful business logic entities. Spring beans, objects that live within the Spring Framework, can have dependencies injected into them at initialization.

The Flex and Java EE environments can be integrated in many ways. (Chapters 7 and 8 give details of how Flex and Java can be integrated.) Both POJOs and managed objects can be invoked and accessed via the Remote Procedure Call (RPC) mechanism.

Therefore, when migrating, you could reuse your middle-tier Java EE objects and access and invoke them from your new Flex interface.

Next, let's quickly review a typical PHP middle tier.

PHP Middle Tier

PHP objects and scripts are less governed by specification than Java EE objects. Therefore, the form in which a PHP middle tier exists could be quite varied. It could be within a container, like the Zend engine, or it could live as objects on a PHP-enabled web server. The PHP code may be procedural or object oriented.

Flex to PHP remoting options like the AMFPHP remoting library can be used to facilitate RPCs. However, there is one possible obstacle to direct usage of the middle-tier methods. Not all PHP applications cleanly demarcate between presentation logic and behavior, so directly consuming the data returned by PHP methods in Flex may require additional parsing on the Flex side. In such situations, you may benefit from following the preceding advice on making PHP generate XML or service-orienting the existing application.

Strategies to Port Framework-based Applications

As mentioned earlier, we pick two frameworks, Apache Struts and Ruby on Rails, and port them over to use a Flex user interface. If you are planning to port applications of either of these two types, then this section will give you a starting point in your endeavor. If your framework is not one of these two, then you will still benefit indirectly, as the examples will give you some insight into the migration options at your disposal.

Let's rework an Apache Struts 1.x application to include a Flex user interface.

Apache Struts 1.x and Flex

First, take a look at Figure 12-16, which pictorially describes Apache Struts. Requests to an Apache Struts–powered web application are intercepted by its front controller. The front controller routes requests to appropriate action classes. The framework configuration and the request URL to action mapping are accessed from the `struts-config.xml` file and the action mapping class instance. Action classes access the middle-tier objects and the underlying data and then forward the output to a JSP. Alternatively, Apache Tiles can be used to construct the views.

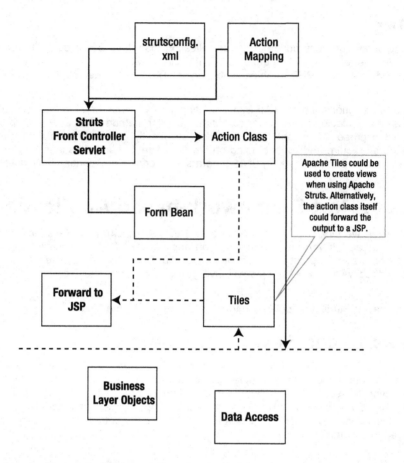

Figure 12-16. Apache Struts—its front controller, action classes, action mapping, configuration, and form bean

The preceding description is true for Apache Struts 1.x. Apache Struts 2.0 is a drastic overhaul of the framework and is out of the scope of the current discussion.

A possible migration path from Apache Struts 1.x to Flex is to replace the View part of the Apache Struts Model-View-Controller (MVC) structure. (In order to migrate smoothly, you need to make the following modifications:

- Create a new Flex user interface.
- Invoke Apache Struts actions based on requests from Flex.
- Forward the output to a JSP that does not display the data but forwards the data in a format that can be consumed by the Flex interface.
- Forward the error messages to a JSP that does not display the error messages but forwards the data in a format that can be consumed by the Flex interface.

The Model and Controller parts can be kept as they are.

Data can be exchanged between the Flex user interface and the Apache Struts application either in a text-based format like XML or in an object format streamed over the binary Action Message Format (AMF) protocol. When using XML, the Flex `HTTPService` object can be used to invoke the Apache Struts action URLs. For example, a current Apache Struts action may be accessed using a URL string as follows: `http://hostname:port/SomeAction.do`. Such a URL can be invoked using the Flex `HTTPService` object as well.

When using object streams and AMF, you need to write a component on the Apache Struts side that can marshal and unmarshal between the AS3 and Java objects.

Although you can write all the artifacts required to migrate an Apache Struts 1.x application to Flex, you can also leverage open source implementations that already do part or all of this job. One such package to look at is FxStruts. FxStruts is an open source set of components and libraries that facilitates the migration from Apache Struts 1.x to Flex. FxStruts is hosted on Google Code and can be accessed at `http://code.google.com/p/fxstruts`.

FxStruts implements the JSPs and tag libraries that route output and error messages to a Flex user interface. It also implements a Flex component that extends the `HTTPService` component and enables HTTP requests that send and receive data over the binary AMF protocol. A component to marshal and unmarshal between AS3 and Java is also included in the package. The distribution comes as a couple of JAR files and a Flex SWC library file. The JAR files are deployed with the Apache Struts application, and the SWC file is referenced from within the Flex project.

Apache Struts provides a tag library to include in the JSPs. These tag libraries implement the features that write the output and the error messages as well. For example, the `bean:write` tag facilitates the writing of Java objects to display elements on the JSP. FxStruts implements a tag library that uses a similar nomenclature and includes an `fx:write` tag that behind the scenes facilitates the writing of a JavaBean to a Flex interface, on the way converting the Java object to AS3 and turning it into a format that the Flex interface understands.

FxStruts comes with documentation and includes a sample application. I suggest that you refer to the documentation available online from Google Code to learn the details. Although the fundamental concepts illustrated are explained, the details are intentionally left out because duplicating publicly available information in this book would be redundant.

The information given so far will get you ready to refactor your Apache Struts 1.x application to utilize a Flex interface. This knowledge will also help you improvise on the techniques to successfully migrate Apache Struts applications that use Apache Tiles to generate views.

Next, we look at using Ruby on Rails and Flex together.

Ruby on Rails and Flex

Rails is an agile web application development framework that is built using the dynamic Ruby language. If you don't know Ruby, then you may want to start by downloading and installing it from `http://ruby-lang.org`. Exhaustive documentation on Ruby and Rails is available from the following online resources:

- Extracts from *Programming Ruby: The Pragmatic Programmer's Guide*: `http://www.rubycentral.com/book`
- *Why's (poignant) Guide to Ruby* (free book): `http://www.poignantguide.net/ruby`
- Ruby on Rails Wiki: `http://wiki.rubyonrails.com/rails`

- Rails API: http://api.rubyonrails.org

Here, I assume you know the basics of both Ruby and Rails.

For the purpose of adding a Flex interface to a Ruby on Rails application, let's revisit the example application presented in the section "Generating database-driven applications." That example application showed how a Flex interface facilitated CRUD operations on a table that maintained a list of books. Ruby on Rails is very capable of generating CRUD applications based on database tables, and so the example fits in well to demonstrate how Rails and Flex can be combined effectively.

The Rails framework provides an MVC implementation, in which the model, view, and controller classes are generated based on the configuration and the underlying database. When you use Flex and Rails together, you keep the model and the controller within Rails and create a Flex view to work with the Rails model and controller.

If you worked through the example earlier, you have the MySQL table called books within the saventech database. If not, create the table and populate it with data as instructed earlier in the chapter.

Now go to the directory where you would like to create your Rails application and enter **rails book_list** on the command-line interface. This will create a rails project called "book_list" for you. Remember that the command-line interface will vary according to your operating system. (Moreover, I am assuming that you have Rails installed and configured.)

At this stage, the Rails framework generates the essential artifacts, which will be used to generate the model, view, and controller. Now get inside the project directory, book_list, and enter the command to generate the model and the controller.

To create the model, you enter the following command:

```
ruby script/generate model book
```

Similarly, to create the controller, you enter the following command:

```
ruby script/generate controller books
```

So far the model and controller classes are generated to support CRUD operations on the books table.

The database credentials can be specified in the database configuration file, called database.yml, that resides in the Rails project folder. This will help the Rails application connect to the database.

By default, a Rails application will not generate the view output in a format that a Flex application can use. As in the case of Apache Struts, we can do one of the following:

- Exchange data in XML format and use the standard Flex HTTPService component to call the Ruby methods.
- Exchange data in object format streamed over the binary AMF protocol and use a custom component on the Flex side to facilitate the HTTP-based calls.

XML data exchange is simpler, and you will choose that for your current example. The only required modification is to output the data from the controller in XML format. On the other hand, using object-based data exchange requires us to implement a component that can marshal and unmarshal between Ruby and AS3 objects on both ends of the wire. Also, it's necessary to extend the HTTPService component to make HTTP requests and consume object streams over AMF.

To make the controller return XML data for all the CRUD operations, we only need to modify the generated `books_controller.rb` Ruby source file. You will find this file in the `book_list/app/controllers` folder.

Add the following code to the `books_controller.rb` file:

```ruby
def create
    @book = Book.new(params[:book])
    @book.save
    render :xml => @book.to_xml
end

def list
    @books = Book.find :all
    render :xml => @books.to_xml
end

def update
    @book = Book.find(params[:book])
    @book.update_attributes(params[:book])
    render :xml => @book.to_xml
end

def delete
    @book = Book.find(params[:id])
    @book.destroy
    render :xml => @book.to_xml
end
```

The methods `create`, `list`, `update`, and `delete` map to the CRUD features create, read, update, and delete, respectively. A Rails application exposes these methods over REST-style HTTP GET URLs. Assuming you set this Rails application with the default web server, WEBrick, and used the default port 3000 on a host called "hostname," the following URLs would be chosen for these operations:

- Create: http://hostname:3000/books/create
- Read: http://hostname:3000/books/list
- Update: http://hostname:3000/books/update
- Delete: http://hostname:3000/books/delete

These URL requests can be made to the server from a Flex interface using the HTTPService component. I will not show the Flex interface here.

This completes our brief example of migrating a regular Ruby on Rails application to a Flex user interface.

On the basis of the two examples we have shown, you should now be able to refactor applications built using other frameworks as well. In all cases, remember to keep the model and controller within the framework, and use Flex as the view.

Summary

This chapter surveyed a few topics that arise when you migrate a legacy HTML-based web application to RIA. First, you learned about possible migration candidates. Then you saw the challenges and benefits of different techniques that come into play. You also looked at a couple of framework-based applications refactored to utilize a Flex interface.

A few things to keep in mind:

- Migrating a VM-based web application to Flex implies rewriting it.
- HTML-based web applications can be refactored to use a Flex interface.
- There are many ways to make a web application talk to a Flex interface. XML and object-based data exchange are the most common options.
- Most web applications are built using a framework. Migrating a framework-based application to Flex can be thought of as using Flex as the view within the framework's MVC structure.

Adopting RIA gradually can be beneficial, because you have many ways to follow an incremental adoption path.

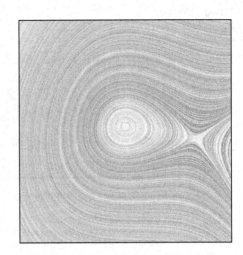

Chapter 13

Working with Web 2.0 APIs

by Elad Elrom

Web 2.0 is a huge change from Web 1.0 for two main reasons: the emphasis on community and the emphasis on services. Successful sites like YouTube, Twitter, Salesforce, and others emphasize both of these. They use the Web to build communities around content and then use services to distribute the content outside of the walls of their sites.

In this chapter, you will use Flex in combination with these sites and services to learn how to connect and interact with them at the API level.

Twitter API for Flex and AIR Apps

The first example we will show you an AIR/Flex application that allows the customer to update their Twitter (http://twitter.com) status. To get started, you will need a free account on Twitter, so open one in case you don't have one already.

Twitter changed their cross-domain policy and they are not allowing anyone to access their site via cross-domain requests because of a security hole that was found. You can see Twitter cross-domain policy at http://twitter.com/crossdomain.xml. At the time of writing, you can only access Twitter API in Flash originating from twitter.com (see Figure 13-1).

```
<allow-http-request-headers-from domain="*.twitter.com" headers="*" secure="true"/>
```

The Twitter API will only work for Adobe Integrated Runtime (AIR) applications so to create a Twitter web client you will have to use a proxy. We will show you both ways.

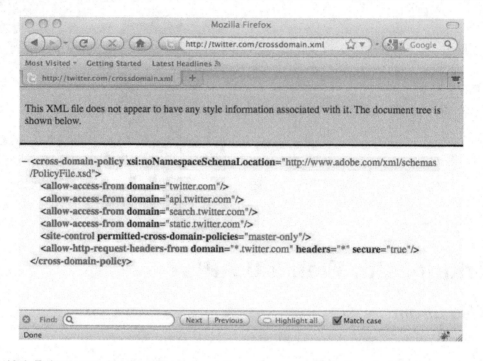

Figure 13-1. Twitter cross-domain policy

Twitter API Using an AIR Application

First, download the Twitter Flex library from here: `http://code.google.com/p/twitterscript/`.

Next, create `TwitterAIRExample` AIR application and paste the library you downloaded from Google code and the following code.

```
<?xml version="1.0" encoding="utf-8"?>
<s:WindowedApplication xmlns:fx="http://ns.adobe.com/mxml/2009"
                 xmlns:s="library://ns.adobe.com/flex/spark"
                 xmlns:mx="library://ns.adobe.com/flex/mx"
                 creationComplete="creationCompleteHandler(event)">
    <fx:Script>
        <![CDATA[
            import twitter.api.Twitter;
            import mx.events.FlexEvent;

            private var twitterapi:Twitter = new Twitter();

            protected function creationCompleteHandler(event:FlexEvent):void
            {
                twitterapi.setAuthenticationCredentials( "Your-User-Name", "Your-Password" );
                twitterapi.setStatus("Updated my status from an AIR app");
            }
```

```
        ]]>
    </fx:Script>

</s:WindowedApplication>
```

Compare your code with ours: http://code.google.com/p/advancedflex4/ under Chapter 13. The code does authentication of the twitter's user credentials and then sets a new status on the account.

Twitter API Using Flex Application

As mentioned before, since the cross-domain policy requires that the calls originate from Twitter.com you need to use a proxy to access Twitter. You will be using a PHP proxy. To do this, you first need to download the Twitter Flex library created by Austin Marshall (http://youxylo.com/projects/twitter/).

After downloading the Twitter library, create a new Flex project and call it TwitterFlexExample and add the ActionScript source for the library you previously downloaded to it. You then need to modify the endpoint.php script with your login and password:

```
curl_setopt($ch,CURLOPT_USERPWD,"user:password");
```

curl is a command line tool for transferring data with URL syntax. In your case, you use it to pass the user name and password information.

After you change the file, save it under the following location in your project: TwitterFlexExample/assets/php.

To test the application, install a local server by using Mamp (http://www.mamp.info/en/index.html) for Mac OS or you can use XAMPP (http://www.apachefriends.org/en/xampp.html) or WAMP (http://www.wampserver.com/) for PC.

Use the following code to create the Twitter Flex application:

```
<?xml version="1.0" encoding="utf-8"?>
<s:Application xmlns:fx="http://ns.adobe.com/mxml/2009"
                    xmlns:s="library://ns.adobe.com/flex/spark"
               xmlns:mx="library://ns.adobe.com/flex/mx"
               minWidth="1024" minHeight="768"
               creationComplete="creationCompleteHandler(event)">

    <fx:Script>
        <![CDATA[
            import twitter.api.Twitter;
            import mx.events.FlexEvent;

            private var twitterapi:Twitter = new Twitter();

            protected function creationCompleteHandler(event:FlexEvent):void
            {
                twitterapi.setProxy( ↵
"http://localhost:8888/TwitterFlexExample/assets/php/endpoint.php" );
                twitterapi.setAuth( "Your-User-Name", "Your-Password" );

                // -- make sure to update endpoint.php in order for this script to run --
                // curl_setopt($ch,CURLOPT_USERPWD,"user:password");
```

435

```
                    twitterapi.setStatus( "Playing around" );
            }


        ]]>
    </fx:Script>


</s:Application>
```

Once the creationCompleteHandler method is called, you call the twitter API and set the proxy, and then you can set the status of the user. Remember to change the setting so the project is deployed on the local server, by right-clicking the project and selecting the project. From the context menu, select **Properties ➤ Flex Build Path** then set the localhost location (see Figure 13-2).

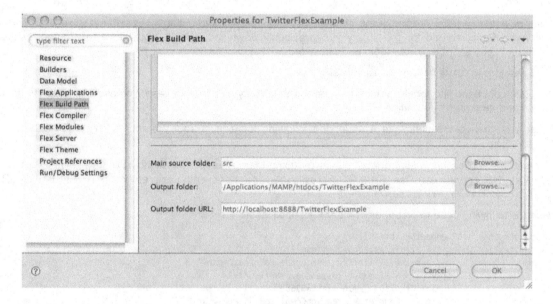

Figure 13-2. Properties window for project TwitterFlexExample

The Flex API for Twitter is really easy to use. You just give it your authentication details and the location of the proxy, and then set your status to whatever you choose. In this case, you can easily update the user's status. In the following script, an input box and a button are added so the user can update their status.

```
<?xml version="1.0" encoding="utf-8"?>
<s:Application xmlns:fx="http://ns.adobe.com/mxml/2009"
                xmlns:s="library://ns.adobe.com/flex/spark"
                xmlns:mx="library://ns.adobe.com/flex/mx"
                minWidth="1024" minHeight="768"
                        width="349" height="43"
                creationComplete="creationCompleteHandler(event)">


    <fx:Script>
        <![CDATA[
```

```
        import twitter.api.Twitter;
        import mx.events.FlexEvent;

        private var twitterapi:Twitter = new Twitter();

        protected function creationCompleteHandler(event:FlexEvent):void
        {
            twitterapi.setProxy( ↩
"http://localhost:8888/TwitterFlexExample/assets/php/endpoint.php" );
            twitterapi.setAuth( "Your-User-Name", "Your-Password" );

            // -- make sure to update endpoint.php in order for this script to run --
            // curl_setopt($ch,CURLOPT_USERPWD,"user:password");

        }

    private function updateStatus(newStatus:String):void
    {
        twitterapi.setStatus( newStatus );
    }

    ]]>
</fx:Script>

    <s:TextInput id="textInput" width="200" height="21" x="10" y="10"/>
    <s:Button label="Update my status" x="220" y="10"
                    click="updateStatus(textInput.text)"/>

</s:Application>
```

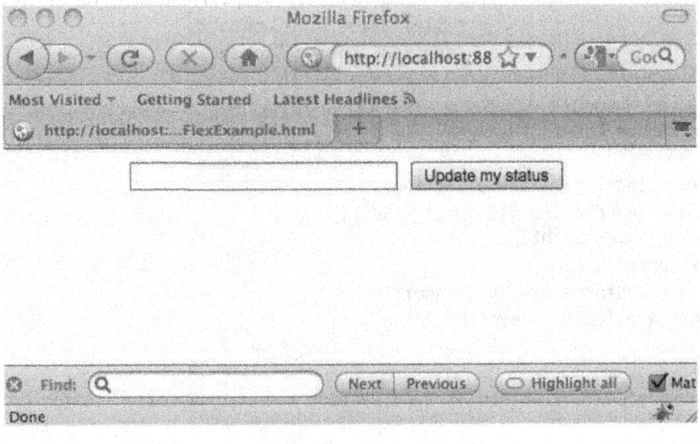

Figure 13-3. The simple Twitter Updater interface

The new updated code includes a text input and an update button. Once you click the update button, the updateStatus method is called.

Once you click the **Update my status** button, you can go to the Twitter site and see for yourself that the status has been updated.

But you could put any user interface you want on it. You could set the status using a set of preloaded buttons or read the status from a local application.

Integrating with Salesforce

Salesforce (http://salesforce.com) might not be sexy, but it's definitely Web 2.0. Sales and service people can collaborate around their customer bases, using not only the standard Salesforce applications, but also additional web applications built on the AppExchange protocol (http://www.salesforce.com/developer/). Salesforce excels at putting its services in the hands of engineers as well. Both of these are hallmarks of a good Web 2.0 application.

To demonstrate Salesforce's Flex API, you will first create an application that shows the contact details of the customers in my Salesforce development database. To get started, you need to sign up for a free Salesforce developer account. You can sign for an account here:

http://www.developerforce.com/events/regular/registration.php

Once you have that, you can download the Flex Salesforce developer API (http://code.google.com/p/force-flex/) and install either the source or SWC libraries (force-air.swc and force-flex.swc) in your project.

The code for the contact-viewing application is shown here:

```
<?xml version="1.0" encoding="utf-8"?>
<s:WindowedApplication xmlns:fx="http://ns.adobe.com/mxml/2009"
                         xmlns:s="library://ns.adobe.com/flex/spark"
                         xmlns:mx="library://ns.adobe.com/flex/mx"
                         xmlns:salesforce="http://www.salesforce.com/"
                         title="Salesforce contacts"
                         creationComplete="login()">
    <fx:Script>
        <![CDATA[
            import mx.managers.CursorManager;

            import mx.collections.ArrayCollection;
            import com.salesforce.results.QueryResult;
            import mx.utils.ObjectUtil;
            import mx.controls.Alert;
            import com.salesforce.AsyncResponder;
            import com.salesforce.objects.LoginRequest;

            [Bindable]
            private var accountCollection:ArrayCollection = new ArrayCollection();

            protected function login():void
            {
                var loginRequest:LoginRequest = new LoginRequest();

                loginRequest.server_url = parameters.server_url;
                loginRequest.session_id = parameters.session_id;
```

```
            // password must consist of your password plus the token
            // If your password = "mypassword"
            // And your security token = "XXXXXXXXXX"
            // You must enter "mypasswordXXXXXXXXXX" in place of your password
            // to get a token login into your account: Setup (from top) -> Reset your security token
            loginRequest.username = "Your-email";
            loginRequest.password = "Your-Password-And-Security-token";

            loginRequest.callback = new AsyncResponder( loginSuccessfullHandler, loginFailedHandler );
            connection.login( loginRequest );

            // show busy cursor while retrieving results
            CursorManager.setBusyCursor();
        }

        private function loginFailedHandler( fault:Object ):void
        {
            Alert.show(ObjectUtil.toString(fault));
        }

        private function loginSuccessfullHandler( loginRequest:Object ):void
        {
            connection.query("Select FirstName, LastName, Phone, Email,↵
Title From Contact",
                    new AsyncResponder(
                        function(queryResult:QueryResult):void
                        {
                            if (queryResult.size > 0)
                            {
                                accountCollection = queryResult.records;

                                // remove busy cursor
                                CursorManager.removeBusyCursor();
                            }
                        },
                    loginFailedHandler) );
        }

    ]]>
    </fx:Script>

    <fx:Declarations>
        <salesforce:Connection id="connection"
                            serverUrl="https://www.salesforce.com/services/Soap/u/9.0" />
    </fx:Declarations>

    <mx:DataGrid dataProvider="{accountCollection}"
             left="10" right="10" top="10" bottom="10">
        <mx:columns>
            <mx:DataGridColumn dataField="FirstName"/>
            <mx:DataGridColumn dataField="LastName"/>
            <mx:DataGridColumn dataField="Phone"/>
            <mx:DataGridColumn dataField="Email"/>
```

```
                <mx:DataGridColumn dataField="Title"/>
        </mx:columns>
    </mx:DataGrid>

</s:WindowedApplication>
```

You can download the application from the book's SVN or www.friendsofed.com under ch15/ForceAIRExample-step1.

Much like the Twitter application, the code first creates a connection to the service by providing your login credentials. However, in the case of Salesforce, you will need to add your secret key to the end of your password to get the service to respond to your requests. If you don't know your secret key, just request a new password and Salesforce will send you an e-mail with your new secret key and instructions on how to use it.

Once a connection has been established, the application will run a query for all of the contacts against the Salesforce database. Salesforce's API is a lot like SQL. When the query result is returned, the application sets the `dataProvider` on a `DataGrid` control to show the contacts.

In order to view your contacts, you must have contacts under your Salesforce account. I have imported my contacts to Salesforce and run the application (see Figure 13-4).

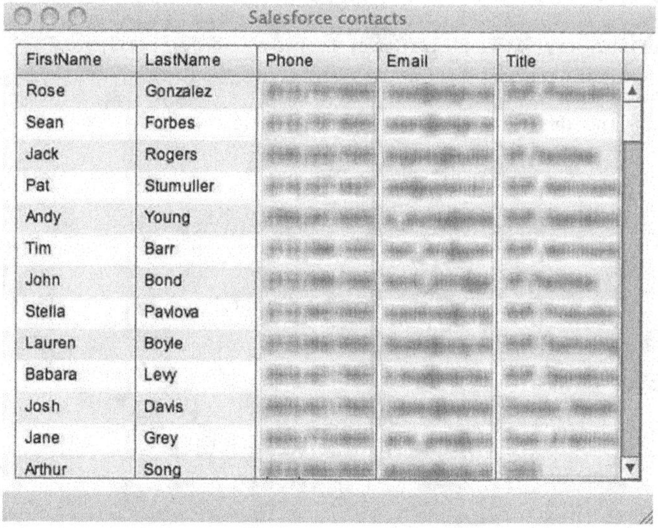

Figure 13-4. Salesforce AIR application with Elad Elrom contacts

If that works, you know you can connect to the Salesforce database properly. If not, you will likely need to check your password, add the secret key value, or add your current IP address to the list of secure addresses in your Salesforce accounts administration page.

When that's all working, the next step is to write data to Salesforce. In this case, you will allow the user to add a contact from a VCard file. That means adding a menu item and parsing the contents of the VCard file, which you can do using the VCard parser in the AS3 Core Library at http://as3corelib.googlecode.com. After downloading the AS3 Core Library, remember to add the as3corelib.swc folder to your project lib.

Here's the new code for the Salesforce Contacts application:

```
<?xml version="1.0" encoding="utf-8"?>
<s:WindowedApplication xmlns:fx="http://ns.adobe.com/mxml/2009"
                       xmlns:s="library://ns.adobe.com/flex/spark"
                       xmlns:mx="library://ns.adobe.com/flex/mx"
                       xmlns:salesforce="http://www.salesforce.com/"
                       title="Salesforce contacts"
                       creationComplete="login();
                       createFileMenu()">
    <fx:Script>
        <![CDATA[
            import flash.events.Event;
            import com.salesforce.objects.SObject;
            import com.adobe.fileformats.vcard.Email;
            import com.adobe.fileformats.vcard.VCardParser;
            import com.adobe.fileformats.vcard.VCard;
            import com.adobe.fileformats.vcard.Phone;
            import flash.display.NativeMenuItem;
            import mx.managers.CursorManager;

            import mx.collections.ArrayCollection;
            import com.salesforce.results.QueryResult;
            import mx.utils.ObjectUtil;
            import mx.controls.Alert;
            import com.salesforce.AsyncResponder;
            import com.salesforce.objects.LoginRequest;

            [Bindable]
            private var accountCollection:ArrayCollection = new ArrayCollection();

            private function createFileMenu() : void
            {
                if( NativeApplication.supportsMenu )
                {
                    var fileMenu:NativeMenuItem =
        NativeApplication.nativeApplication.menu.getItemAt(1);
                    fileMenu.submenu.addItemAt(new NativeMenuItem("-",true),0);

                    var openDirectory:NativeMenuItem = new NativeMenuItem
        ( "Import Contact..." );
                    fileMenu.submenu.addItemAt(openDirectory,0);

                    openDirectory.addEventListener(Event.SELECT, onImportContact);
                }
            }

            protected function login():void
            {
                var loginRequest:LoginRequest = new LoginRequest();
```

```
            loginRequest.server_url = parameters.server_url;
            loginRequest.session_id = parameters.session_id;

            // password must consist of your password plus the token
            // If your password = "mypassword"
            // And your security token = "XXXXXXXXXX"
            // You must enter "mypasswordXXXXXXXXXX" in place of your password
            // to get a token login into your account: Setup (from top) ->⏎
Reset your security token
            loginRequest.username = "Your-email";
            loginRequest.password = "Your-Password-And-Security-token";

            loginRequest.callback = new AsyncResponder( readAllContacts,⏎
loginFailedHandler );
            connection.login( loginRequest );

            // show busy cursor while retrieving results
            CursorManager.setBusyCursor();
        }

        private function loginFailedHandler( fault:Object ):void
        {
            Alert.show(ObjectUtil.toString(fault));
        }

        private function readAllContacts( loginRequest:Object ):void
        {
            connection.query("SELECT FirstName, LastName, Phone, Email,⏎
Title FROM Contact",
                new AsyncResponder(
                    function(queryResult:QueryResult):void
                    {
                        if (queryResult.size > 0)
                        {
                            accountCollection = queryResult.records;

                            // remove busy cursor
                            CursorManager.removeBusyCursor();
                        }
                    },
                loginFailedHandler) );
        }

        private function onImportContact( event:Event ) : void
        {
            var f:File = File.desktopDirectory;
            f.addEventListener(Event.SELECT, fileSelected);
            f.browseForOpen( "Import Contact" );
        }

        private function fileSelected( event:Event ) : void
        {
            var fs:FileStream = new FileStream();
```

```
            fs.open( event.target as File, FileMode.READ );
            var contents:String = fs.readUTFBytes( fs.bytesAvailable );
            fs.close();

            var ncon:SObject = new SObject( "contact" );
            for each( var line:String in contents.split( /\n/ ) ) {
                var nameFound:Array = line.match( /^N:(.*);/ );
                if ( nameFound != null && nameFound.length > 1 ) {
                    var nameElems:Array = nameFound[1].split( /;/ );
                    ncon.LastName = nameElems[0];
                    ncon.FirstName = nameElems[1];
                    break;
                }
            }

            var vcp:Array = VCardParser.parse( contents );
            var vcard:VCard = vcp[0] as VCard;
            for each ( var email:Email in vcard.emails ) {
                if ( email.type == 'work' )
                    ncon.Email = email.address;
            }
            for each ( var phone:Phone in vcard.phones ) {
                if ( phone.type == 'work' )
                    ncon.Phone = phone.number;
            }

            connection.create( [ ncon ],
                new AsyncResponder( function( result:Object ) : void {

                    // display alert
                    Alert.show(ncon.FirstName+" "+ncon.LastName+" was added↵
to your contacts");

                    // update contacts
                    readAllContacts(null);
                } ) );
        }

    ]]>
</fx:Script>

<fx:Declarations>
    <salesforce:Connection id="connection"
                           serverUrl="https://www.salesforce.com/services/Soap/u/9.0" />
</fx:Declarations>

<mx:DataGrid dataProvider="{accountCollection}"
        left="10" right="10" top="10" bottom="10">
    <mx:columns>
        <mx:DataGridColumn dataField="FirstName"/>
        <mx:DataGridColumn dataField="LastName"/>
        <mx:DataGridColumn dataField="Phone"/>
        <mx:DataGridColumn dataField="Email"/>
```

```
            <mx:DataGridColumn dataField="Title"/>
        </mx:columns>
    </mx:DataGrid>

</s:WindowedApplication>
```

Let's take a closer look at the code. After the creation complete event is called, the method creates the Salesforce connection and authenticates the user. At the same time you call the method and can now add a method menu item to the File menu.

```
        private function createFileMenu() : void
        {
            if( NativeApplication.supportsMenu )
            {
                var fileMenu:NativeMenuItem =↵
 NativeApplication.nativeApplication.menu.getItemAt(1);
                fileMenu.submenu.addItemAt(new NativeMenuItem("-",true),0);

                var openDirectory:NativeMenuItem = new NativeMenuItem↵
( "Import Contact..." );
                fileMenu.submenu.addItemAt(openDirectory,0);

                openDirectory.addEventListener(Event.SELECT, onImportContact);
            }
        }
```

When the customer selects the menu item, the application runs the `browseForOpen` method on the desktop directory to get the file.

```
        private function onImportContact( event:Event ) : void
        {
            var f:File = File.desktopDirectory;
            f.addEventListener(Event.SELECT, fileSelected);
            f.browseForOpen( "Import Contact" );
        }
```

The fileSelected method then parses the file that the customer has selected using a combination of a regular expression to get the first and last name, and the VCard parser to get the e-mail addresses and phone numbers. From there, the application creates a new contact object and adds it to the database using the create method on the Salesforce connection. Notice that you are using the regexp ^N:(.*); to find the Name location.

```
        private function fileSelected( event:Event ) : void
        {
            var fs:FileStream = new FileStream();
            fs.open( event.target as File, FileMode.READ );
            var contents:String = fs.readUTFBytes( fs.bytesAvailable );
            fs.close();

            var ncon:SObject = new SObject( "contact" );
            for each( var line:String in contents.split( /\n/ ) ) {
                var nameFound:Array = line.match( /^N:(.*);/ );
                if ( nameFound != null && nameFound.length > 1 ) {
                    var nameElems:Array = nameFound[1].split( /;/ );
                    ncon.LastName = nameElems[0];
```

```
                ncon.FirstName = nameElems[1];
                break;
            }
        }

        var vcp:Array = VCardParser.parse( contents );
        var vcard:VCard = vcp[0] as VCard;
        for each ( var email:Email in vcard.emails ) {
            if ( email.type == 'work' )
                ncon.Email = email.address;
        }
        for each ( var phone:Phone in vcard.phones ) {
            if ( phone.type == 'work' )
                ncon.Phone = phone.number;
        }
```

When Salesforce responds that the contact has been created, the application once again queries the contact table in Salesforce and updates the DataGrid with the new records as well as displaying an alert with the new contact first and last name.

```
        connection.create( [ ncon ],
            new AsyncResponder( function( result:Object ) : void {

                // display alert
                Alert.show(ncon.FirstName+" "+ncon.LastName+"↵
was added to your contacts");

                // update contacts
                readAllContacts(null);
        } ) );
    }
```

When you compile this in Flash Builder 4 and select the **Import Contact** menu item, you see something like Figure 13-5.

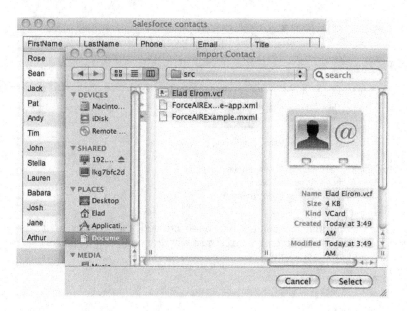

Figure 13-5. Adding a VCard to the Salesforce account

I then select the Elad Elrom contact file and click **Select**. This launches the file parser, which then creates a contact in the Salesforce database. The result is shown in Figure 13-6.

Figure 13-6. The updated Salesforce contacts

You can get access to every element of your Salesforce application through this extensive Flex API. Salesforce, the company, has entered into a strategic partnership with Adobe around Flex, so it is committed to the resulting Flex/Salesforce API. You can download the complete application from the book's SVN or `www.friendsofed.com` under: `ch15/ForceAIRExample-step2`.

Using Amazon S3 for File Sharing

An important part of collaboration is sharing resources like documents, images, and other files. To make that easy, Amazon has created a set of services for Web 2.0 applications, including one called S3, which is a distributed storage service. For a small monthly fee, you can store any type of data you want on S3 and access it from anywhere.

To get started, you need to sign up for the S3 service. You do that by going to the Amazon Web Services site (`http://www.amazonaws.com`), creating an Amazon account (if you don't have one already), and adding the S3 service to it. This is shown in Figure 13-7.

Figure 13-7. Setting up the S3 service on Amazon

From here, you will get a public key and a secret key to the S3 service. You will need both of these to read and write data to S3. At the time of writing, the keys can be found here:

Amazon Web Services Home ➤ Account ➤ Your Account ➤ Security Credentials ➤ Account Identifiers.

As an example, you are going to build a drag-and-drop repository for images, where the images themselves are hosted on S3. To create it easily, you are going to use the excellent Amazon Web API for Flex library (`http://code.google.com/p/as3awss3lib/`). This library also requires the AS3 Crypto library (`http://crypto.hurlant.com/`) and the AS3 Core Library (`http://code.google.com/p/as3corelib/`). At the time of writing, there is no zip archive available for the Amazon Web API for Flex library, so you will need to check the code out using subversion.

To start, you have created a new AIR application and added the necessary AS3 libraries to the project under the **lib** directory for as3 Core lib and Crypto as well as copying the as3awss3lib classes under the **src** folder. See Figure 13-8.

Figure 13-8. Folder structure and import libraries for Amazon project

Amazon S3 Firefox Organizer plug-in is a useful tool to view your S3 bucket and be able to add files (`https://addons.mozilla.org/en-US/firefox/addon/3247`). You can then input your credentials and create a bucket that can be used to load your files into. The Amazon cloud is shared by all users, so the bucket has to be unique across the entire S3 service. You can set your bucket's access to be public or private as well as add access to users. We created a bucket and called it `EladElromImages`.

> *Buckets in Amazon S3 are unique and only one person (or company) can own a bucket and you own the bucket until the account is closed. You can create a uniquely named bucket. The bucket can be organized and you can name the objects within the bucket in any way you like.*

Using the Firefox plugin you can add a folder to sync. Select **Synchronize Folders** from the top menu and add an existing folder from your desktop, as shown in Figure 13-9.

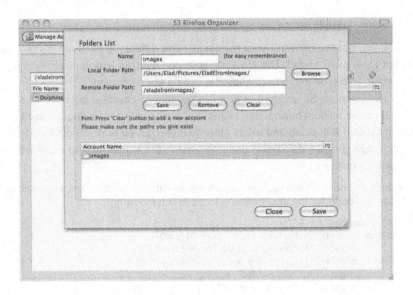

Figure 13-9. S3 Firefox organizer plug-in

Once the folder is set, you can sync between your desktop and Amazon S3. Click **Synchronize Folders ➤ Folder Name ➤ Put to S3**. You sync a folder that has an image and you can see the image loaded to S3, as shown in Figure 13-10.

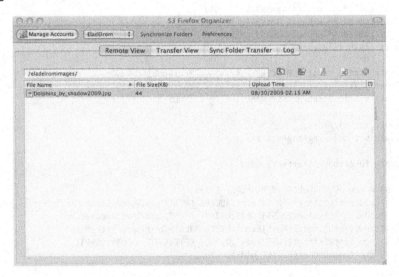

Figure 13-10. S3 Firefox organizer plugin remote view

The following are some possible errors:

- In case you get the following error message: "The difference between the request time and the current time is too large." The clock on your computer is wrong. You need to make sure the time, date, timezone and daylight savings setting are all correct.
- You must have an S3 account in order to be able to create a bucket and add files. You can sign up for an account here: http://aws.amazon.com/s3/. Pricing is based on usage.
- Path must end with slash and exists otherwise you get an error: "SignatureDoesNotMatch: The request signature we calculated does not match the signature you provided. Check your key and signing method."

Now that you understand how S3 works, you can create an application that lets you sync between S3 and your local machine. The code for the application is listed in the following:

```
<?xml version="1.0" encoding="utf-8"?>
<s:WindowedApplication xmlns:fx="http://ns.adobe.com/mxml/2009"
                       xmlns:s="library://ns.adobe.com/flex/spark"
                       xmlns:mx="library://ns.adobe.com/flex/mx"
                       height="600" width="800"
                       creationComplete="onStartup()"
                       title="S3 Image Store"
                       nativeDragEnter="onNativeDragEnter(event);"
                       nativeDragDrop="onNativeDrop(event);">
    <fx:Script>
        <![CDATA[

            import com.adobe.webapis.awss3.S3Object;
            import com.adobe.webapis.awss3.AWSS3Event;
            import com.adobe.webapis.awss3.AWSS3;
            import flash.filesystem.*;

            private static const PUBLIC_KEY:String = "Your-public-key";
            private static const SECRET_KEY:String = "Your-secret-key";
            private static const BUCKET_NAME:String = "Your-bucket";

            private var s3:AWSS3;
            private var uplodingImages:Array = [];

            private function onStartup():void
            {
                s3 = new AWSS3(PUBLIC_KEY,SECRET_KEY);
                s3.addEventListener(AWSS3Event.BUCKET_CREATED,onBucketCreatedReturn);
                s3.addEventListener(AWSS3Event.OBJECT_SAVED,onObjectSavedReturn);
                s3.addEventListener(AWSS3Event.LIST_OBJECTS,onObjectListReturn);
                s3.addEventListener(AWSS3Event.OBJECT_RETRIEVED,onObjectGet);
                s3.createNewBucket(BUCKET_NAME);

                s3images.dataProvider =↵
    File.applicationStorageDirectory.getDirectoryListing();
            }

            private function onObjectGet( event:AWSS3Event ):void
```

```
        {
            var s3obj:S3Object = event.data as S3Object;

            if ( File.applicationStorageDirectory.exists == false )
                File.applicationStorageDirectory.createDirectory();


            var f:File = new File( File.applicationStorageDirectory.nativePath↵
                        + File.separator + s3obj.key );
            var fs:FileStream = new FileStream();
            fs.open( f, FileMode.WRITE );
            fs.writeBytes( s3obj.bytes, 0, s3obj.size );
            fs.close();

            s3images.dataProvider =↵
File.applicationStorageDirectory.getDirectoryListing();
        }

        private function onObjectSavedReturn( event:AWSS3Event ):void
        {
            s3.listObjects(BUCKET_NAME);
            s3images.dataProvider = File.applicationStorageDirectory.↵
                    getDirectoryListing();
            uploadImage();
        }

        private function onObjectListReturn( event:AWSS3Event ):void
        {
            for each ( var s3obj:S3Object in event.data )
            {
                var f:File = new File( File.applicationStorageDirectory.nativePath +
                        File.separator + s3obj.key );
                if ( f.exists == false )
                    s3.getObject(BUCKET_NAME,s3obj.key);
            }
        }

        private function onBucketCreatedReturn( event:AWSS3Event ):void
        {
            s3.listObjects(BUCKET_NAME);
        }

        private function uploadImage():void
        {
            if ( uplodingImages.length > 0 )
            {
                var f:File = uplodingImages.pop();
                s3.saveObject(BUCKET_NAME,f.name,'image/jpeg',f);
                s3upload.dataProvider = uplodingImages;
            }
        }

        private function onNativeDragEnter( event:NativeDragEvent ):void
```

```
        {
            if(event.clipboard.hasFormat(ClipboardFormats.FILE_LIST_FORMAT))
            {
                var files:Array =↵
event.clipboard.getData(ClipboardFormats.FILE_LIST_FORMAT) as Array;
                if( files.length > 0 ) NativeDragManager.acceptDragDrop(this);
            }
        }

        private function onNativeDrop( event:NativeDragEvent ):void
        {
            for each ( var f:File in event.clipboard.getData(
                ClipboardFormats.FILE_LIST_FORMAT) as Array )
            uplodingImages.push(f);
            s3upload.dataProvider = uplodingImages;
            uploadImage();
        }
    ]]>
</fx:Script>

<mx:VDividedBox width="100%" height="100%">
    <mx:Panel title="S3 Images" width="100%" height="60%">
        <mx:TileList id="s3images" width="100%" height="100%" >
            <mx:itemRenderer>
                <fx:Component>
                    <mx:HBox paddingBottom="5" paddingLeft="5" paddingRight="5"
                            paddingTop="5">
                        <mx:Image source="{data.url}" height="150" width="150"
                                horizontalAlign="center" verticalAlign="middle" />
                    </mx:HBox>
                </fx:Component>
            </mx:itemRenderer>
        </mx:TileList>
    </mx:Panel>
    <mx:Panel title="Uploading Files" width="100%" height="40%">
        <mx:TileList id="s3upload" width="100%" height="100%">
            <mx:itemRenderer>
                <fx:Component>
                    <mx:HBox paddingBottom="5" paddingLeft="5" paddingRight="5"
                            paddingTop="5">
                        <mx:Image source="{data.url}" height="150" width="150"
                                horizontalAlign="center" verticalAlign="middle" />
                    </mx:HBox>
                </fx:Component>
            </mx:itemRenderer>
        </mx:TileList>
    </mx:Panel>
</mx:VDividedBox>

</s:WindowedApplication>
```

It may look complex, but it really isn't. The code starts in the `onStartup` method, which connects to S3. It then creates the bucket for the images if there isn't one already.

From there, the application gets the contents of the bucket by calling listObjects on the S3 connection. That method calls back to onObjectListReturn, which in turn calls getObject for any file that has not been previously downloaded. The getObject method calls back to onObjectGet, which stores the image locally for fast access. Each time the local store is updated, the dataProvider is set on the list of images in the user interface, which is updated to show the thumbnails of the local images.

To facilitate the drag and drop, you include two event handlers, onNativeDragEnter and onNativeDrop. The onNativeDragEnter method is called whenever a customer drags something over the window. The code checks to see whether it's a list of image files, and if so, it says it can handle the drop. The onNativeDrop method is called if the customer does indeed drop the files onto the application. It uses the uploadImage method to add the images to S3 one by one. In case you set a bucket that doesn't exist, it will create one for you.

When you compile and run this application in Flash Builder 4 and drag an image onto it, you will see something like Figure 13-11.

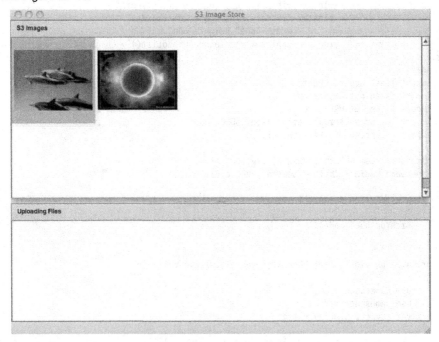

Figure 13-11. The shared S3 image store application

Anyone that uses this application can then add their files to a central repository of images. Since all of the files are downloaded locally, you can all share all of the files as a community.

Of course, you can use this code to manage any type of files, not just images. You can download the complete code from www.friendsofed.com or the book's SVN here: ch15/AmazonS3.

Hacking YouTube

If there is one service that typifies Web 2.0, it's YouTube. Something that has always frustrated about YouTube is that it's bound to the online nature of the network. There is no offline access mode. To fix that, I built a small AIR application that uses YouTube's feeds to find videos and then downloads and caches the videos for later playback offline.

This application requires the AS3 Core Library (http://code.google.com/p/as3corelib/). This library provides a JSON interpreter that's used to parse the video details from YouTube's HTML page. With these details, the code can get direct access to the raw FLV file that contains the video.

The code for this application is shown in the following:

```
<?xml version="1.0" encoding="utf-8"?>
<s:WindowedApplication xmlns:fx="http://ns.adobe.com/mxml/2009"
                       xmlns:s="library://ns.adobe.com/flex/spark"
                       xmlns:mx="library://ns.adobe.com/flex/mx"
                            width="800" height="600"
                       creationComplete="updateLocalVideoList()">
    <fx:Script>
        <![CDATA[
            import flash.events.Event;
            import flash.net.URLStream;
            import flash.net.URLRequest;
            import com.adobe.serialization.json.JSONDecoder;
            import mx.rpc.events.ResultEvent;

            namespace atom = "http://www.w3.org/2005/Atom";
            namespace media = "http://search.yahoo.com/mrss/";

            private function onSearch(  ):void
            {
                srchYoutube.send();
            }

            private function onSearchResult( event:ResultEvent ):void
            {
                use namespace atom;
                use namespace media;
                var movieList:Array = [];

                for each( var entry:XML in event.result..entry ) {
                    var group:XML = entry.group[0];
                    movieList.push( {
                    id:group.player.@url.toString(),
                    description:entry.content.toString(),
                    thumbnail:group.thumbnail[0].@url.toString() } );
                }

                srchFound.dataProvider = movieList;
            }

            private function onThumbComplete( movieData:Object, event:Event ):void
```

```
        {
            var stream:URLStream = event.target as URLStream;
            var movieID:String = movieData.id.split( /=/ )[1];

            var byteLength:int = stream.bytesAvailable;
            var bytes:ByteArray = new ByteArray();
            stream.readBytes( bytes, 0, byteLength );
            stream.close();

            if ( File.applicationStorageDirectory.exists == false )
            File.applicationStorageDirectory.createDirectory();

            var f:File = new File( File.applicationStorageDirectory.nativePath↵
+ File.separator + movieID + '.jpg' );
            var fs:FileStream = new FileStream();
            fs.open( f, FileMode.WRITE );
            fs.writeBytes( bytes, 0, byteLength );
            fs.close();

            updateLocalVideoList();
        }

        private function onVideoComplete( movieData:Object, event:Event ):void
        {
            var stream:URLStream = event.target as URLStream;
            var movieID:String = movieData.id.split( /=/ )[1];

            var byteLength:int = stream.bytesAvailable;
            var bytes:ByteArray = new ByteArray();
            stream.readBytes( bytes, 0, byteLength );
            stream.close();

            if ( File.applicationStorageDirectory.exists == false )
            File.applicationStorageDirectory.createDirectory();

            var f:File = new File( File.applicationStorageDirectory.nativePath↵
+ File.separator + movieID + '.flv' );
            var fs:FileStream = new FileStream();
            fs.open( f, FileMode.WRITE );
            fs.writeBytes( bytes, 0, byteLength );
            fs.close();

            updateLocalVideoList();
        }

        private function onHTMLReturn( movieData:Object, event:ResultEvent ):void
        {
            var youTubeHTML:String = event.result.toString();

            var found:Array = youTubeHTML.match( /var swfArgs =(.*?);/ );
            var argsJS:JSONDecoder = new JSONDecoder( found[1] );
            var args:Object = argsJS.getValue();
```

```
            var thumbReq:URLRequest = new URLRequest( movieData.thumbnail );
            var thumbLoader:URLStream = new URLStream();
            thumbLoader.addEventListener(Event.COMPLETE, function ( event:Event↩
): void { onThumbComplete( movieData, event ); } );
            thumbLoader.load( thumbReq );

            var id:String = String(movieData.id).split("?v=")[1];
            var tmpURL:String = "http://localhost:8888/getVideoId.php?id="+id;

            var flvReq:URLRequest = new URLRequest( tmpURL );
            var flvLoader:URLStream = new URLStream();

            flvLoader.addEventListener(Event.COMPLETE, function ( event:Event ↩
):void { onVideoComplete( movieData, event ); } );
            flvLoader.load( flvReq );
        }

        private function downloadVideo():void
        {
            var htmlGet:HTTPService = new HTTPService();

            htmlGet.resultFormat = 'text';
            htmlGet.url = srchFound.selectedItem.id;
            htmlGet.addEventListener(ResultEvent.RESULT,
                function(event:ResultEvent ):void { onHTMLReturn↩
( srchFound.selectedItem, event ); } );

            htmlGet.send();
        }

        private function playVideo():void
        {
            movieDisplay.source = localList.selectedItem.movie.url;
            movieDisplay.play();
        }

        private function updateLocalVideoList():void
        {
            var fileNames:Object = new Object();

            for each ( var file:File in↩
  File.applicationStorageDirectory.getDirectoryListing() )
            {
                var fName:String = file.name.split( /[.]/ )[0];
                fileNames[ fName ] = true;
            }

            var movieList:Array = [];

            for( var fileKey:String in fileNames )
            {
                var thumb:File = new File(↩ File.applicationStorageDirectory.nativePath +↩
  File.separator + fileKey + '.jpg' );
```

```
                    var movie:File = new File(↩ File.applicationStorageDirectory.nativePath +↩
File.separator + fileKey + '.flv' );

                if ( thumb.exists && movie.exists )
                    movieList.push( { thumbnail: thumb, movie: movie } );
            }

            localList.dataProvider = movieList;
        }
    ]]>
</fx:Script>


<fx:Declarations>
    <mx:HTTPService id="srchYoutube"
                    url="http://gdata.youtube.com/feeds/api/videos/?vq=↩
{escape(txtSearch.text)}&amp;orderby=updated"
                    resultFormat="e4x" result="onSearchResult( event );" />
</fx:Declarations>


<mx:HDividedBox width="100%" height="100%">

    <mx:Panel width="40%" title="Search" height="100%"
            paddingBottom="5" paddingLeft="5" paddingRight="5" paddingTop="5">
        <mx:HBox width="100%">
            <mx:TextInput id="txtSearch" text="lady gaga" width="100%" />
            <mx:Button label="Search" click="onSearch()" />
        </mx:HBox>
        <mx:TileList id="srchFound" width="100%" height="100%"
                    doubleClickEnabled="true"
                    doubleClick="downloadVideo()">
            <mx:itemRenderer>
                <fx:Component>
                    <mx:HBox paddingBottom="5" paddingLeft="5" paddingRight="5"
                            paddingTop="5">
                        <mx:Image source="{data.thumbnail}"
                                    toolTip="{data.description}"
                                    height="100" width="130">
                        </mx:Image>
                    </mx:HBox>
                </fx:Component>
            </mx:itemRenderer>
        </mx:TileList>
    </mx:Panel>
    <mx:Panel width="60%" height="100%" title="Offline Videos"
            paddingBottom="5" paddingLeft="5" paddingRight="5" paddingTop="5">
        <mx:HorizontalList id="localList" width="100%"
                        doubleClickEnabled="true"
                        doubleClick="playVideo()">
            <mx:itemRenderer>
                <fx:Component>
                    <mx:HBox paddingBottom="5" paddingLeft="5" paddingRight="5"
                            paddingTop="5">
                        <mx:Image source="{data.thumbnail.url}" height="100"↩ width="130">
```

```
                    </mx:Image>
                </mx:HBox>
            </fx:Component>
        </mx:itemRenderer>
    </mx:HorizontalList>
    <mx:HBox width="100%" height="100%" verticalAlign="middle"
            horizontalAlign="center">
        <mx:VideoDisplay id="movieDisplay" width="400" height="300" />
    </mx:HBox>
</mx:Panel>

</mx:HDividedBox>
```

```
</s:WindowedApplication>
```

If you notice from the script, you are calling a php proxy to extract the FLV video from YouTube. At the time of writing, the proxy works. However, YouTube is changing often and the script may stop working. In case this happened, you will have to find a new PHP proxy to replace this one. Place the proxy on your local server or web server.

```php
<?php
    $id = trim($_REQUEST['id']);

    $url = "http://www.youtube.com/watch?v=" . $id;

    $url = $url . "&fmt=18"; //Gets the movie in High Quality, uncomment this↵
line to get it in normal quality

    $ch = curl_init();

    curl_setopt($ch, CURLOPT_URL, $url);
    curl_setopt($ch, CURLOPT_HEADER, false);
    curl_setopt($ch, CURLOPT_RETURNTRANSFER, true);

    $info = curl_exec($ch);

    if (!preg_match('#var swfArgs = (\{.*?\})#is', $info, $matches))
    {
        echo "Check the YouTube URL : {$url} <br/>\n";
        die("Couldnt detect swfArgs");
    }

    if (function_exists(json_decode)) # >= PHP 5.2.0
    {
        $swfArgs = json_decode($matches[1]);
        $video_id = $swfArgs->video_id;
        $t = $swfArgs->t;
    }
    else
    {
        preg_match('#"video_id":.*?"(.*?)"#is', $matches[1], $submatches);
        $video_id = $submatches[1];

        preg_match('#"t":.*?"(.*?)"#is', $matches[1], $submatches);
```

```
        $t = $submatches[1];
    }

    curl_close($ch);

    $fullPath = "http://www.youtube.com/get_video.php?video_id=" . $video_id . "&t=↵
" . $t; // construct the path to retrieve the video from

    $headers = get_headers($fullPath); // get all headers from the url

    foreach($headers as $header){ //search the headers for the location url of↵ youtube video
        if(preg_match("/Location:/i",$header)){
            $location = $header;
        }
    }

    header($location); // go to the location specified in the header and get the↵ video
?>
```

Much like the user interface shown in Figure 13-12, the code for this application is really broken into two parts. The first is the search portion, on the left of the display, which uses YouTube's feed system to run searches for video and to present thumbnails. The right side of the display shows the current videos that are stored locally and starts playback if the customer double-clicks a video.

Figure 13-12. The offline YouTube viewer

The search code starts with the onSearch method, which sends a request to the YouTube search service. The XML returned from the service is parsed in the onSearchResult method. That method sets the dataProvider on the List object to show the thumbnails of the videos that were found.

The download starts when the user double-clicks an item in the search list. From there, the downloadVideo method is called. This method gets the HTML page for the requested video and finds the JavaScript portion that contains the details necessary for the PHP proxy request. This information is parsed out in the onHTMLReturn method.

The onHTMLReturn method makes a request for the thumbnail and the video, which are both stored in the local directory. Once the downloads are complete, the updateVideoList is called. That method looks at the local directory to see what videos are available and updates the list of thumbnails on the right-hand panel of the display.

When the user double-clicks a local video, the VideoDisplay object is given the URL of the local file and playback begins.

Summary

Flash and Flex are already key components of successful Web 2.0 applications. The ability to view video, reliably connect to services, and work across platforms even on the desktop is indispensable to Web 2.0 developers. Hopefully, this chapter has given you a taste of the kinds of things that Flex can be used for in this context. I can't wait to see where you take it from here.

Chapter 14

Facilitating Audio and Video

by Elad Elrom

Video and audio are the key elements in rich, compelling experiences across platforms: Web, desktop, and mobile. They are used everywhere—in news, blogs, music videos, web TV, social media, live Internet radio, amateur productions, and movie promotions.

In particular, video has become one of the critical components of the Web experience and, according to Comcast in August 2008, Flash is used 86 percent of the time when online videos are viewed in the U.S. Flash Player has supported video playback across multiple platforms since version 6.

Creating a video and audio player is a simple process; however, constraints such as bandwidth differences can complicate matters. It's not easy to cover all of the issues in one chapter, but we'll tell you enough so you'll understand your options, and we'll give you practical examples you can use. We'll show you how to build an audio and video player that uses progressive download as well as streaming. And we'll demonstrate how to play audio and video files using the Open Source Media Framework (OSMF).

Supported Video and Audio Formats

Video and audio files that are to be deployed on platforms with constraints and limitations—such as the Web and mobile devices—need to be compressed.

The compression is done by a *codec* (enCOder/DECoder) algorithm. Codecs, as their name implies, are programs that compress and decompress data. There are audio codecs as well as video codecs. Compression has two purposes: reducing the file size to speed up transmission, and reducing the data storage space needed on the destination device.

Most codecs are *lossy*. Lossy compression (or data lossiness) means that some of the data is lost during compression and can't be recovered during subsequent decompression.

Lossless codecs preserve all original data and are therefore a 100-percent faithful transcription of the original data set when uncompressed. Lossless compression is not well-suited to the web or mobile devices.

A codec can be either a physical device or a software process that, on the encoding side, manages the compression of raw digital audio or video data into files of reduced size. This optimizes both download and playback performance. On the decoding side, the process is reversed, with the codec uncompressing the file to produce a high quality *facsimile* of the original content. Because the object of compression is to reduce the overall file size and bandwidth requirements for a given segment of video, it is typically necessary to "throw away" some of the data during the compression process. This means that when the codec reproduces content, it will have incrementally lower production values than the original.

At this point, we depart from the domain of science and cross over into craft and art. To create an acceptable result, compression algorithms must strike a complex balance between the visual quality of the video and the amount of data necessary to render it. For multimedia content, the key measure of codec performance is the **bit rate**. In the context of transmitting multimedia data over the Internet or mobile carrier connections, bit rate quantifies the number of bits required per increment of playback time that allows the viewer to see smooth, uninterrupted content. For streaming video, this degree of playback quality is also called **goodput**. Goodput is the effective transmission rate that supports what the user actually sees on her device. In other words, it is the amount of data transferred after deducting factors like Internet, network, and datalink-layer protocol overhead; network congestion; and retransmission of data that was corrupted or lost in transit. The ability to empirically measure the performance of various codecs is key because they have different strengths and, therefore, different applications.

Essentially, codecs are optimization tools, and they are many and diverse, often with thriving application genres based on them. The choice of a particular codec is driven by what rendering or transmission characteristics are the focus of optimization; what codecs a developer can reasonably assume to be present on the target platforms; and what post-processing tools the developer has available for converting raw data into a video file format. It is unsurprising that there's a great deal of competition among the developers of codec technology, because achieving a big advance in compression without corresponding loss of quality would have tremendous commercial value. On the other hand, if all codec technologies were secret, a crippling fragmentation in the industry would result from dozens of incompatible proprietary file formats for encoded video. This problem is neatly solved by an extensive, widely embraced standards-making process for video encoding.

Video codec designs are precisely specified by the Motion Picture Experts Group (MPEG), an international body that includes 350 members representing media industries, universities, and research institutions. MPEG is chartered by the International Standards Organization (ISO) and is tasked with publishing standards documents that detail how various codecs work. What is interesting about this is that MPEG's published specifications assume that the compression of video files is *asymmetrical*. In this sense, asymmetrical means that *compressing* data is far more complex and difficult than *decompressing* it. As a standards making group, MPEG is exclusively interested in creating a framework for interoperability among various vendors' codecs and products. *This effectively means that only the decoding process needs to be enshrined in a public standard.* The encoding process is not constrained by a published MPEG standard. As long as the compressed video files can be decoded as described in the MPEG spec, innovators are encouraged to design new and better encoders, achieving advances in optimizations, while secure in the knowledge they will reap the accompanying economic benefits. As encoder technology moves forward, the deployed decoder technology will continue to work, because the decoder side has no knowledge of encoder implementation and can't be broken by encoder evolution.

Since there is a great deal at stake, the exact strategies of popular encoder designs are usually not public (There are exceptions, such as Ogg Theora; http://www.theora.org/), but the general nature of recent advances is an open secret. Most codecs have transitioned from logic that compresses video data frame-by-frame to an object-based model where the encoder detects regions of frames that don't change rapidly and caches those semi-static portions. This is a tremendous advantage for bandwidth-constrained scenarios like mobile video because it prevents transmission of redundant data.

Decoding the results of various encoders can differ dramatically from one encoder implementation to another in terms of both transmission speed and the quality of the video rendering. Moreover, there can be significant trade-offs in video codecs' decoder runtime performance and resource utilization. It is a subtle point, but an important one: Codec standards enable interoperability, *but they do not imply uniformity of performance or quality across mobile devices.* This potentially complicates life for content designers and developers because you need to know what codec is going to play your content back in order to ensure that video files provide acceptable playback performance. Desktop and laptop computers generally have a variety of codecs available, and the absence of a single one is rarely an issue for content developers. In any case, a desktop video app can request the user download a needed codec if it's not already present. This is not so with mobile devices.

Let's go over some of the most popular audio and video formats.

FLV

FLV is the most popular video format available on the Internet, with some of the best web sites engaging their viewers with Flash-based videos. This video format is available for Flash Player and can be used on mobile phones through the Flash Lite 3 player.

An FLV file encodes synchronized audio and video streams. The audio and video data within FLV files is encoded in the same way as audio and video within SWF files. SWF files published for Flash Player 6 can exchange audio, video, and data over RTMP connections with Adobe Flash Media Server as well.

It is estimated that a one-minute video consumes 2–3MB of RAM, while a five-minute video consumes an average of 3–4MB. Longer videos play without requiring a linear increase in memory. This is true for progressive, streaming, local, and remote videos.

F4V and F4P

The F4V format is newer, supported in Flash Player 9.0.115 and later. You'll often see F4V and F4P attached as the same format; the two are simply Adobe's wrapper for the H.264 video. The reason there's even a need for a wrapper is to overcome the limitations of the H.264 format, which doesn't support features such as alpha channel or cue points. F4V maintains the dimensions and frame rate of the source and eliminates black borders. F4P is the protected video format.

FLV and F4V have an open specification, which you'll find at

```
http://www.adobe.com/devnet/flv/pdf/video_file_format_spec_v10.pdf
```

MPEG-4

MPEG-4 Part 14, also known as MP4, is a collection of audio and video encoding methods. MPEG-4 is the standard compression format of many software companies, such as Apple and Microsoft. It is a container that allows you to combine audio and video, as well as other streams, into a single file. The MPEG-4 video codec and H.264 are the included standards for video coding and compression. H.264 is the evolutionary step that improves the quality and efficiency of the format. The format is available for Flash Player 9 and above.

H.264

H.264, also known as MPEG-4 Part 10, is the next-generation video-compression technology in the MPEG-4 standard. H.264 delivers excellent video quality across the entire bandwidth spectrum from 3G to high-definition video players. This format is preferred because it produces incredible video quality with the smallest amount of video data. This means you see crisp, clear video in much smaller files, saving you bandwidth and storage costs over previous generations of video codecs. The format is available for Flash Player 9 and later and Flash Lite 3.1.

MP3

Part of the MPEG-1 standard, also known as MPEG-1 Audio Layer 3, MP3 is a patented digital audio encoding format. It is a popular audio format and the standard for lossy data compression of digital audio files.

Flash Player 6.0r40 and later support MP3, and audio in Flash video files is usually encoded as MP3. MP3 also supports ID3 metadata containers, which allow the passing of data about music files.

Advanced Audio CodingSupported by Flash Player 9 Update 3 and later, Advanced Audio Coding (AAC) was designed to be the successor to the MP3 format. AAC is a high-efficiency (HE), high-fidelity (HiFi), low-bandwidth audio codec; it is a lossy compression and encoding standard for digital audio. AAC is a higher-quality format than MP3 and generally achieves better sound quality at similar bit rates. The format is often packaged in a video format container.

MOV

Available from Flash Player 9 Update 3 and later, you can play MOV and MP4 containers using MPEG-4 codecs. They are mostly interchangeable in a QuickTime-only environment; however, since MP4 is an international standard, it has more support. This is especially true on hardware devices such as the Sony PSP and various DVD players. On the software side, most DirectShow/Video for Windows codec packs include an MP4 parser but not one for MOV.

3GP and 3GPP

3GP (the 3GPP file format) is a simplified version of the MPEG-4 format. It is designed to optimize video content for mobile devices, and built specifically to accommodate low bandwidths and little storage. 3GP is based on MPEG-4 and H.263 video and AAC or AMR audio. It is a supported by many mobile devices. The file extension is either .3gp for GSM-based phones or .3g2 for CDMA-based phones.

F4A and F4B

Flash Player 9 and above support F4A and F4B audio. The format is nothing more than an MP4 audio file; F4A refers an audio file while F4B stands for an audio book. The reason the format exists is to bridge and avoid compatibility issues between different platforms such as Adobe Flash Player, QuickTime, iPod, and so forth.

M4V and M4A

Flash Player 9 Update 3 and above support M4V and M4A. While MP4 is the official extension, Apple introduced M4V and M4A formats, which are the standard file formats for videos and audio for iTunes, iPod, and PlayStation portables.

M4V and M4A file formats are identical to MP4 and can be renamed to MP4. M4V stands for video while M4A is the audio layer of MP4 movies.

Note that M4V files contain DRM and the purchasing user's information. You can use Requiem (`http://undrm.info/remove-DRM-protection/Requiem-freeware-Mac-and-PC-DRM-remover-for-iTunes-files.htm`) to remove the DRM.

Why did Apple create this format? The different file extension allows associating the file type with iTunes, so when you double-click the file, iTunes opens if it's installed. M4V files are often used for movies, TV episodes, and music videos.

Encoding Video for Flash Applications

Encoding videos for compression is a challenge as the compression process needs to maintain the video quality and bit rate, while decreasing the file size. And there are other factors to consider, such as seeking, encoding, and decoding algorithms, as well as resistance to data loss and errors.

> The bitrate (in the context of video files) means the number of bits that are processed or transferred per second. The unit is bps or bit/s (bits per second).

The software that handles the compression of video files is called a video codec. The goal is to deliver faster videos for web, desktop, and mobile applications. The key is to find that delicate balance between compression, bitrate, quality, and data lossiness, which is fundamental to a good user experience, while taking into account hardware characteristics and limited bandwidth. Additionally, there are cases, such as on some mobile devices, where users pay a per-increment charge for data they download, so there is an immediate disincentive if applications overuse bandwidth.

Out of the box, Flash 10 supports dynamic bitrate switching using the `play2` method in NetStream. The key to bitrate switching is to have a variety of profiles so you can switch to a different video file if the user's bandwidth decreases.

You can create many different bitrate profiles and later, when you have checked the user's bandwidth, decide which profile to use. Many online video file storage services offer the ability to load a video file and encode the files to the different bitrate sizes automatically.

Here are some common video and audio bitrate profiles.

Video quality:

- **Lowest** (minimum needed to see moving images): 16 Kbps
- **Medium** (video conferencing): 128–384 Kbps
- **VCD:** 1.25 Mbps
- **DVD:** 5 Mbps

- **HD TV:** 15 Mbps
- **HD DVD:** 36 Mbps
- **Blue-ray Disc:** 54 Mbps

Audio quality:

- **Lowest** (telephone): 8 Kbps
- **Low** (AM): 32 Kbps
- **Medium** (FM): 96 Kbps
- **Standard Bitrate:** 128–160 Kbps
- **Digital Audio Broadcasting (DAB):** 192 Kbps
- **High** (VBR to highest MP3): 224–320 Kbps
- **Speech** (minimum necessary for recognizable speech): 800 Kbps
- **Lossless audio:** 500–1,411 Kbps
- **Highest** (PCM sound format of Compact Disc Digital Audio): 1,411.2 Kbps

For example, delivering a compelling video and audio experience to mobile devices requires placing the highest priority on compression, which means lossy data compression (sometimes very lossy).

On the other hand, delivering video or audio on the desktop can use lossless data compression and high quality since the user has more resources and the files can be installed locally.

For best results, always begin the encoding process with raw files because repetitive compression can destroy the integrity of video imagery.

Compressing a Video File Using the Adobe Media Encoder

If your needs are simple and you are looking for an inexpensive solution, you can use the Adobe Media Encoder (AME) to compress video and create video files for use in your application. AME is included in Flash CS4 and several other Adobe products. AME integrates well with other elements of the Adobe toolset and has an extensive collection of predefined settings (presets) for importing the most common formats. This is of particular value because, for encoding video, there are a surprising number of user-defined parameters to customize and optimize codec output.

Adobe Media Encoder (AME) replaces the Flash Video Encoder that used to be bundled with Flash Professional. AME offers more than just an encoder and includes features such as video manipulation, H.264 encoding, integration with other Creative Suite (CS) products such as Premier Pro and After Effects, cue points, two-pass variable bitrate encoding with the ON2VP6 codec, and the ability to load directly to the server.

AME has useful productivity features, including the ability to queue many files and then run them through the encoding process at night or some other convenient time. For files that are more than trivial in terms of window size or length, encoding can be an extremely lengthy process, so queuing is definitely an efficient option. Furthermore, you can add prebuilt components that embed playback and volume controls in the FLV file, providing content interactivity right out of the box. In addition to compressing raw video, AME converts common video file formats to FLV, including QuickTime Movie, AVI, MPEG, Digital Video (.dv), and Windows Media.

Let's look at an example of working with AME. First we need a video file. You can use any video file you have in your library, or download free footage from sites like http://stockfootageforfree.com.

Once you have the raw video file, open AME, which you'll find at:

- PC: C:/Program Files/Adobe/Adobe Media Encoder CS5
- Mac: Applications/Adobe Media Encoder CS5

1. Use the **Add...** button to add a video, as shown in Figure 14-1. Use the **Duplicate** button to create identical profiles of the same video so you can change the decoding options.

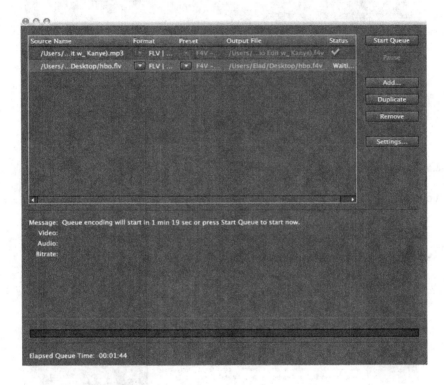

Figure 14-1. Adding an Adobe Media Encoder file

2. You can configure different settings for different files that can be used with streaming. To change the bitrate settings, select **Edit ➤ Export Settings**. See Figure 14-2.

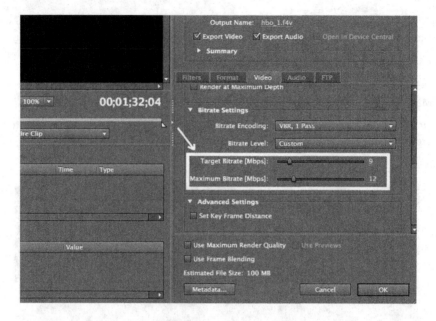

Figure 14-2. Adobe Media Encoder bitrate settings

You can set cue points, frame size, audio, and other options, as well as a profile, as you can see in Figure 14-3.

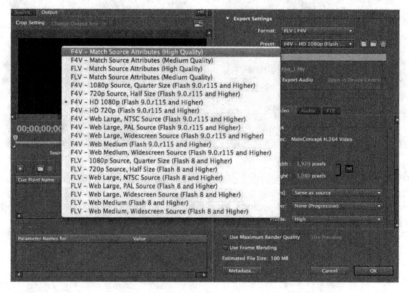

Figure 14-3. Adobe Media Encoder profile drop-down menu

For audio files, you can set the **Export Video** check box to false and choose the format as well as other settings, such as the codec, channels, and bitrate. See Figure 14-4.

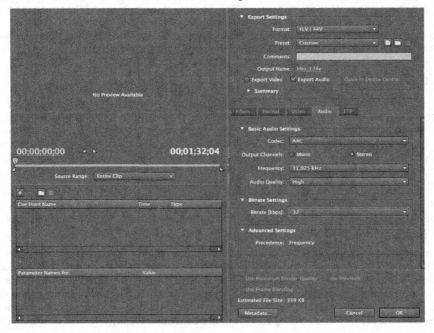

Figure 14-4. Adobe Media Encoder audio settings

Although AME allows some manipulation of video files—for example, cropping and selecting subsets of a given video clip for encoding—if you need full-featured audio and video editing, it will not be your only tool. Fortunately, there are a variety of professional-quality tools available with a broad range of capabilities and pricing. While some tools offer complete video and audio production with effects, transitions, additions of callouts, and so forth, others are simpler with just basic editing and converting abilities.

These tools optimize and edit video and audio files:

- **Adobe's Premiere Pro CS5**: Captures, edits, and delivers digital video online, on air, on disc, or on device. Premium toolset, but costly. Adobe Premiere Elements is a lighter, less costly version for consumers.
- **Apple QuickTime Pro**: Edits video clips using cut, copy and paste; merges separate audio and video tracks; crops and rotates video; saves and exports to codecs supported by QuickTime; includes presets for exporting video to a iPod, Apple TV, and iPhone; Inexpensive, ($29.99) but heavily biased toward Apple technologies.
- **Windows Movie Maker**: Modest video editing, but it's a free tool bundled with Windows operating systems.
- **Adobe SoundBooth**: Creates and edits audio files; let's you customize music, add sound effects in a familiar environment and work on multiple files at once.

Streaming vs. Progressive Download

There are two main ways to deliver your video through a web server: streaming and progressive download. The key difference is that with streaming, no file is downloaded to the user, while with progressive download, the file is physically stored on the user's machine. It is important to understand the implications of each so you can successfully select the appropriate server to use.

Progressive Download

Let us say you want to deliver a video file to a user. You can either upload the file to a server and link a video component to the URL of the file, or you can place the file on a media server for streaming. When you place the video on a regular server, such as your website hosting company, and use the URL to link the video component to the video, the file starts downloading as soon as the user clicks. The file seems to be streaming, since it starts playing before the entire file has been downloaded. The Flash interface is designed to start the video playback as soon as there is enough data. The limitation is that you can't fast forward (seek) to a part in the video file that has not downloaded yet.

The file is downloaded to a temporary location on the user's system, so there's no need to download the file again to replay the video. However, downloading the file to the user's machine does add more overhead compared with streaming.

With progressive download, the file is downloaded using an HTTP connection, which uses the **Transport Control Protocol** (TCP) to manage the transfer of data packets over the network. TCP is built to handle large file sizes by allowing the client (browser) to resend packets in case data gets lost. Once the download is complete, you can rest assured that the integrity of the file is the same as the original. The downside is that TCP is not designed for real-time streaming and does not concern itself with how long it takes to download the file or with ensuring that the video continues to play.

Streaming

Streaming servers (such as Adobe Flash Media Server, Wowza or Red5) are designed to deliver video. They are software placed on a server that allows using a persistent connection with the server. The server transfers the data to play the video at a defined transfer rate. It is aware of the bandwidth and is able to communicate with the device playing the video. Since the media server is aware of conditions such as bandwidth, it can adjust accordingly to changes and offer the ability to create Action Script Communication File (.asc extension), which can take into account the information.

The video file is not stored on the user's computer and a part will get discarded once it is not needed anymore. This non-caching feature of streaming ensures a smoother playback experience for the end user. Streaming offers services for both users and content owners to monitor video playing, enhanced seeking (so you don't have to wait until the entire video is downloaded), video search, and more.

The media server, unlike TCP, does not try to resend missing packets. If frames get dropped, the server just keeps sending data (though it allows the tracking down of dropped frames), since users generally prefer to see a small glitch in a media file rather than have the file stop file until the missing data arrives. Some media servers (such as FMS) use multicast for delivery of live webcam streams, which allows more than one client to connect to a single stream, as well as a two-way communication channel (client to user and user to client), which actually allows clients to communicate with each other. This type of technology minimizes the bandwidth necessary for delivery of video, allowing a large number of connections at the same time.

HTTP Video Streaming

A new popular solution is HTTP video streaming, which is sometimes called PHP streaming since PHP is mostly used for this solution. The idea is to overcome the limitations of progressive download and offer streaming without the need to upload software to a server that's usually expensive and complicated to install. This is accomplished by using a small server-side script.Progressive download doesn't allow seeking to a location that hasn't yet been downloaded; HTTP streaming handles seeking differently. When a seek operation is performed, the application makes a request to the server-side script to play the file starting from a certain position. The script then starts the video from the offset given.

Selecting the Right Type of Server

To know whether you need a web server or a media server, you need to understand what each offers. Table 14-1 shows the relative advantages of each, so you can select the most appropriate type of server for a given purpose. Keep in mind that media servers offer HTTP connections. It is also important to know that the cost for a media smedia server is high.

Table 14-1. The Relative Advantages of Media and Web Servers

Parameter	Media Server	Web Server
* Short video	-	+
Allow user to copy video	-	+
Ensure data integrity	-	+
Long video	+	-
Interactivity	+	-
Social features	+	-
Live WebCam	+	-
Advanced user's features	+	-
Cost	-	+

Note that mobile devices may lose network connections and packets of data often, so while it's generally preferable to deploy short videos on a web server, at times it may be better to stream short videos.

Creating a Music Player

Now let's create a custom music player generic enough to be used with any application, and then use it to play music files.

You can download the complete code for the Music Player API from http://github.com/EladElrom/
eladlib/blob/master/EladLibFlex/src/PlayerExample.mxml which includes the code and an example of a
working music player.

IPlayer

A good place to start is the interface. The music player interface, IPlayer, is the contract the music player
will obey. It includes methods the music player needs, such as pausing the music player or playing a track.

```
package com.elad.framework.musicplayer
{

public interface IPlayer
    {
        function playTrack(songUrl:String, songLenght:Number=0):void
        function pauseTrack():void
        function stopTrack():void
        function fastforward(timeInSeconds:Number=2):void
        function rewind(timeInSeconds:Number=2):void
        function setVolume(vol:Number):void

    }

}
```

AbstractPlayer

The music player's abstract class AbstractPlayer, just like any other abstract class, should not be
instantiated. The abstract class is the parent class from which the music player is derived. The class
includes methods that any subclass will need; as well as incomplete methods, which will be left
unimplemented.

> Although AS3 doesn't really support "real" Abstract, developers should resist instantiating Abstract classes
> or use one of the available hacks (such as creating a singleton) to ensure the abstract class doesn't get
> instantiated. These solutions are hack-ish, but they get the job done

```
package com.elad.framework.musicplayer
{

    import flash.events.EventDispatcher;
    import flash.media.Sound;
    import flash.media.SoundChannel;
    import flash.media.SoundTransform;
    import flash.utils.Timer;

    public class AbstractPlayer extends EventDispatcher
    {
```

The Sound class lets us load and play an external file, while SoundChannel allows us to assign a song to
a sound channel.

```
        protected var sound:Sound;
        protected var channel:SoundChannel;
```

We'll use a timer to keep track of the sound position and `fileBytesTotal` to keep track of the bytes loaded.

```
protected var soundPosition:Timer = null;
protected var fileBytesTotal:Number;
```

`isDownloadCompleted` is a flag indicates whether the download of the file has completed.

```
protected var isDownloadCompleted:Boolean = false;
```

Once the file is downloaded, the variable `pausePosition` will hold the pause position

```
protected var pausePosition:Number;
```

The `isPause` flag indicates whether the track is in pause mode.

```
protected var isPause:Boolean = false;
```

The `isPlaying` flag indicates whether the track is currently playing.

```
protected var isPlaying:Boolean = false;
```

The `_songPosition` variable holds the play position in seconds. Note that we will be using the underscore to indicate that the variable is private and has a setter and getter.

```
private var _songPosition:Number;
```

The variable `_ songLength` holds the total song length in seconds.

```
private var _songLength:Number;
```

The variable `_songURL` holds the song we will be streaming.

```
private var _songURL:String;
```

Setters and getters are defined below:

```
public function get songPosition():Number
{
        return _songPosition;
}

public function set songPosition(val:Number):void
{
        _songPosition = val;
}

public function get songLength():Number
{
        return _songLength;
}

public function set songLength(val:Number):void
{
        _songLength = val;
}

public function get songURL():String
{
```

```
            return _songURL;
    }

    public function set songURL(val:String):void
    {
            _songURL = val;
    }

      public function AbstractPlayer()
      {
      }
```

The playTrack method will be used to play a track based on a given URL. This method handles cases where the user clicks on the play button after the track is already playing, as well as cases where the track was paused. The music file doesn't provide the length of the song right away. This changes during the progress of the music file, so you can pass information regarding the length of the song; otherwise, you can take it from the PlayProgressEvent. Two parameters are provided: the songUrl, which is the location of the music file and the songLength. Downloading music file does not provide the length of the song right away, but after a portion of the song has been downloaded.

```
    public function playTrack(songUrl:String, songLength:Number=0):void
    {
            // needs to implement
    }
```

We need to be able to pause a playing song. This is achieved by stopping the soundPosition timer and the channel. We also need to set the isPause flag and keep track of our position so we can resume playing from the same position where we stopped.

```
    public function pauseTrack():void
    {
            soundPosition.stop();
            channel.stop();

              isPause = true;
            pausePosition = channel.position;
    }
```

The stopTrack method is used to completely stop a playing song. We first verify that the song is really playing by checking soundPosition, since the timer get implemented only after the song is playing via

```
soundPosition = new Timer(50);
```

stopTrack lets us stop the timer and the channel, as well as call the resetPlayer, which handles the logic to reset the player.

```
    public function stopTrack():void
    {
            if (soundPosition != null)
            {
                    soundPosition.stop();
                    channel.stop();
                    resetPlayer();
            }
    }
```

The `setTrackPosition` method is used to change the position of the track and it generates the seek capability. The `newPosition` position is provided in milliseconds. We then verify that we are not trying to seek the song to a position that is not available.

```
public function setTrackPosition(newPosition:Number):void
{
        soundPosition.stop();
        channel.stop();

        var currentPosition:Number = channel.position/1000;
        var position:Number

        if (newPosition<currentPosition)
        {
                position = newPosition*1000;
        }
        else
        {
                position = Math.min(sound.length, newPosition*1000);
        }

        channel = sound.play(position);
        soundPosition.start();
}
```

The method placeholder below will be used to remove all listeners and empty objects once a track stops. This method will be implemented in the `Player` class.

```
protected function resetPlayer():void
{
    // need to implement
}
```

The `fastforward` method fast-forwards a track. The parameter `timeInSeconds` represents the fast-forward time we want to seek. The default is two seconds.

```
public function fastforward(timeInSeconds:Number=2):void
{
        var currentPosition:Number = channel.position/1000;
        setTrackPosition(timeInSeconds+currentPosition);
}
```

The `rewind` method rewinds a track to a certain position. `timeInSeconds` is the time we want to rewind. The default is two seconds.

```
public function rewind(timeInSeconds:Number=2):void
{
        var currentPosition:Number = channel.position/1000;
        setTrackPosition(currentPosition-timeInSeconds);
}
```

The `setVolume` method adds the capability to adjust the sound volume. The `vol` parameter is the volume in percentage. The expected values are between 0-1.

```
public function setVolume(vol:Number):void
{
```

```
                var transform:SoundTransform = new SoundTransform(vol);
                channel.soundTransform = transform;
        }
    }
}
```

Player Class

After completing the abstract class we can create an implementation of the abstract class that will complete the unimplemented methods and add capabilities such as event metadata. The Player class will extend AbstractPlayer and implement IPlayer.

```
package com.elad.framework.musicplayer
{
```

Dispatched while downloading a music file in progress:

```
        [Event(name="downloadProgress", type="com.elad.framework.musicplayer.events.DownloadEvent")]
```

Dispatched when music file was downloaded successfully:

```
        [Event(name="downloadCompleted", type="com.elad.framework.musicplayer.events.DownloadEvent")]
```

Dispatched when there is an error playing a track:

```
        [Event(name="playerError", type="com.elad.framework.musicplayer.events.PlayerEvent")]
```

Dispatched when track playing is completed

```
        [Event(name="trackCompleted", type="com.elad.framework.musicplayer.events.PlayerEvent")]
```

Dispatched while track progress playing

```
        [Event(name="playerProgress", type="com.elad.framework.musicplayer.events.PlayProgressEvent")]
```

Dispatched when data information is available regarding a track

```
        [Event(name="id3", type="com.elad.framework.musicplayer.events.Id3Event")]

    public class Player extends AbstractPlayer implements IPlayer
    {
```

Default constructor

```
        public function Player()
        {
        }
```

playTrack is a method used to play a track based on a given URL. The method handles cases where the user clicks a play button after a song is already playing and cases where the track is paused..

```
        override public function playTrack(songUrl:String, songLenght:Number=0):void
        {
            if (isPause)
            {
                replay();
                return;
            }
```

```
        if (isPlaying)
        {
                return;
        }

        songURL = songUrl;
        songLength = Number((songLenght/1000).toFixed(2));

    var request:URLRequest = new URLRequest(songUrl);
    sound = new Sound();

    sound.addEventListener(Event.COMPLETE, downloadCompleteHandler);
    sound.addEventListener(IOErrorEvent.IO_ERROR, ioErrorHandler);
    sound.addEventListener(ProgressEvent.PROGRESS, downloadProgressHandler);
    sound.load(request);

    channel = sound.play();
    channel.addEventListener(Event.SOUND_COMPLETE, trackCompleteHandler);

    soundPosition = new Timer(50);
    soundPosition.addEventListener(TimerEvent.TIMER, positionTimerHandler);
    soundPosition.start();
    isPlaying = true;
}
```

resetPlayer is used to remove all listener and empty objects once the track has stopped. It implements the class from the abstract class.

```
    override protected function resetPlayer():void
    {
        this.isPause = false;
        this.isPlaying = false;

        sound.removeEventListener(Event.COMPLETE, downloadCompleteHandler);
        sound.removeEventListener(IOErrorEvent.IO_ERROR, ioErrorHandler);
        sound.removeEventListener(ProgressEvent.PROGRESS, downloadProgressHandler);
        channel.removeEventListener(Event.SOUND_COMPLETE, trackCompleteHandler);
        soundPosition.removeEventListener(TimerEvent.TIMER, positionTimerHandler);

        sound = null;
                channel = null;
        soundPosition = null;
    }
```

The replay method is used internally to resume playing after the pause method was used. We use the pause position, which was captured when the user paused a song, and we start the timer and set the pause flag to off.

```
    private function replay():void
    {
            channel = sound.play(pausePosition);
            soundPosition.start();
```

```
        isPause = false;
    }
```

`formatTimeInSecondsToString` is a static method used to convert a time in seconds to the format 0:00. We are using a static method since we may need to use this method for other reasons outside the scope of this class. The method belongs to the class and not to an instance of the class.

```
    public static function formatTimeInSecondsToString(time:Number):String
    {
        var retVal:String = "";

        var timeString:String = (time/60).toFixed(2);
        var timeArray:Array = timeString.split(".");

        if (timeArray[1] == 60)
        {
            timeArray[0] += 1;
            timeArray[1] -= 60;
        }

        var minutes:String = (timeArray[0].toString().length < 2) ? "0"+timeArray[0].toString() :
timeArray[0].toString();
        var seconds:String = (timeArray[1].toString().length < 2) ? "0"+timeArray[1].toString() :
timeArray[1].toString();

        retVal = minutes+":"+seconds;

        return retVal;
    }
```

The `positionTimerHandler` event handler is used once the track position has changed. It updates the song length since the song length changes as the song is being downloaded, and it sends the `PlayProgressEvent` event once the track position changes. `PlayProgressEvent` event is a custom event we created.

```
    private function positionTimerHandler(event:TimerEvent):void
    {
        songPosition = Number((channel.position/1000).toFixed(2));
        var totalPosition:Number = Number((this.sound.length/1000).toFixed(2));

        if (songLength < totalPosition && isDownloadCompleted == false)
        {
            songLength = totalPosition;
        }

        if (songLength > 0 && songPosition > 0)
        {
            // end of song
            if (Math.round(songLength) == Math.round(songPosition))
            {
                soundPosition.removeEventListener(TimerEvent.TIMER, ↵
positionTimerHandler);
                trackCompleteHandler(null);
            }
```

```
              else
              {
                      this.dispatchEvent( new PlayProgressEvent(songPosition,↵
songLength) );
              }
          }
      }
```

The downloadComplete handler gets called once the song has completed downloading. We clear our listeners so we won't have memory leaks, update the song's total length, and dispatch the DownloadEvent custom event to notify us that the song download has completed.

```
      private function downloadCompleteHandler(event:Event):void
      {
          sound.removeEventListener(Event.COMPLETE, downloadCompleteHandler);
          sound.removeEventListener(ProgressEvent.PROGRESS, downloadProgressHandler);

          // set the lenght of the track to the total position to ensure that the↵
length was entered correctly.
          isDownloadCompleted = true;
          var totalPosition:Number = Number((event.currentTarget.↵
length/1000).toFixed(2));
          songLength = totalPosition;

          this.dispatchEvent(new DownloadEvent(DownloadEvent.DOWNLOAD_COMPLETED,↵
fileBytesTotal, fileBytesTotal));
      }
```

The ID3 information gets redispatched:

```
      private function id3Handler(event:Id3Event):void
      {
          this.dispatchEvent(event);
      }
```

The method to handle IO network errors will dispatch the PlayerEvent custom event to notify of the error.

```
      private function ioErrorHandler(event:Event):void
      {
          sound.removeEventListener(IOErrorEvent.IO_ERROR, ioErrorHandler);
          this.dispatchEvent(new PlayerEvent(PlayerEvent.PLAYER_ERROR, "Error loading↵
music file, please check cross domain policy and that file exists."+event.toString()));
          resetPlayer();
      }
```

ProgressHandler will capture the ID3 information if available and dispatch the DownloadEvent custom event.

```
      private function downloadProgressHandler(event:ProgressEvent):void
      {
          this.dispatchEvent(new DownloadEvent(DownloadEvent.DOWNLOAD_PROGRESS,↵
event.bytesLoaded, event.bytesTotal));
          fileBytesTotal = event.bytesTotal;

          // check if ID3 information is avaliable, needed since id3 event doesn't↵
always work correctly.
```

```
            if (this.sound.id3.album != null || this.sound.id3.artist != null ||
↵ this.sound.id3.songName != null || this.sound.id3.genere != null)
            {
                    var evt:Id3Event = new Id3Event(this.sound.id3);
                    id3Handler(evt);
            }
        }
```

trackCompleteHandler is called once the song completes. It calls the method resetPlayer to clean up the event listeners and timer and dispatch the custom complete event

```
        private function trackCompleteHandler(event:Event):void
        {
            channel.removeEventListener(Event.SOUND_COMPLETE, trackCompleteHandler);
            resetPlayer();
            this.dispatchEvent(new PlayerEvent(PlayerEvent.TRACK_COMPLETED));
        }


    }
}
```

The Player class uses four custom events that hold the constants of the event types and the variables we need to pass such as taking a look at one of the custom events.

```
public static const PLAYER_PROGRESS:String = "playerProgress";
```

stands for the event type. Then we capture the playPosition, and total variables.

```
public var playPosition:Number;
public var total:Number;
```

Here is the complete code:

```
package com.elad.framework.musicplayer.events
{
    import flash.events.Event;

    public class PlayProgressEvent extends Event
    {
        public static const PLAYER_PROGRESS:String = "playerProgress";

        public var playPosition:Number;
        public var total:Number;

        public function PlayProgressEvent(playPosition:Number, total:Number)
        {
            this.playPosition = playPosition;
            this.total = total;
            super(PLAYER_PROGRESS);
        }
    }
}
```

Music Player GUI

We can now create a simple GUI to implement the API and play music to test our API.

```
<?xml version="1.0" encoding="utf-8"?>
<s:Application xmlns:fx="http://ns.adobe.com/mxml/2009"
               xmlns:s="library://ns.adobe.com/flex/spark"
               xmlns:mx="library://ns.adobe.com/flex/mx"
               minWidth="1024" minHeight="768">

<fx:Script>
        <![CDATA[
```

Now we set an instance of the Player and store the song URL:

```
        private var player:Player = new Player();
        private var songUrl:String;
```

The playSong method will be called when we want to play a song. To do this, we set all the custom events we defined in the Player class and call the playTrack method on the Player class.

```
        private function playSong():void
        {
                player.addEventListener(PlayProgressEvent.PLAYER_PROGRESS,↵
onPlayerProgress);
                player.addEventListener(DownloadEvent.DOWNLOAD_PROGRESS,↵
onDownloadProgress);
                player.addEventListener(PlayerEvent.PLAYER_ERROR, onPlayerError);
                player.addEventListener(Id3Event.ID3, onTrackDataInformation);
                player.playTrack(songUrl);  // songLenght
        }
```

The onTrackDataInformation method will display ID3 information once it's available.

```
        private function onTrackDataInformation(event:Id3Event):void
        {
                songInfoText.text = event.id3.artist+" - "+event.id3.album;
        }
```

The onPlayerProgress method will show the progress of the download as the song is loaded, and set a slider to move as the progress continues.

```
        private function onPlayerProgress(event:PlayProgressEvent):void
        {
                songSlider.value = event.playPosition;
                currentTimeText.text = Player.formatTimeInSecondsToString↵
(event.playPosition);
                totalTimeText.text = Player.formatTimeInSecondsToString(event.total);
                songSlider.maximum = event.total;
        }
```

The onPlayerError event handler will be called if we get an error due to network or other player errors.

```
        private function onPlayerError(event:PlayerEvent):void
        {
                throw new Error(event.message);
```

```
            }
```

The `dragStartHandler` method will handle changes in the slider. It will stop tracking the progress of the song so we can move the slider thumb without the event changing the location of the thumb. Otherwise, it will return to the same location when we start to drag the slider.

```
        protected function dragStartHandler(event:TrackBaseEvent):void
        {
                player.removeEventListener(PlayProgressEvent.PLAYER_PROGRESS,↵
onPlayerProgress);
        }
```

Once the user drops the slider, we call `dragDropHandler` as we need to change the song position to the position the user selected and add back the progress event so the thumb will move as the song plays.

```
        protected function dragDropHandler(event:TrackBaseEvent):void
        {
                player.setTrackPosition(songSlider.value);
                player.addEventListener(PlayProgressEvent.PLAYER_PROGRESS,↵
onPlayerProgress);
        }
```

`onDownloadProgress` will handle the progress of the song download and display the results on a progress bar.

```
        private function onDownloadProgress(event:DownloadEvent):void
        {
                progressBar.setProgress(event.bytesLoaded, event.bytesTotal);
        }
```

The `dragVolumeHandler` method handles the slider for the volume and calls `setVolume` to change the volume to the new values.

```
        protected function dragVolumeHandler(event:TrackBaseEvent):void
        {
                player.setVolume(volumeSlider.value);
        }
    ]]>
</mx:Script>
```

Now that we are done creating the logic, we can create the presentation. We'll display song information, such as the artist name and the song name:

```
<s:Label id="songInfoText" x="10" y="5" text="Artist - song name" />
```

The slider will allow us to do a seek within the song.

```
<s:HSlider id="songSlider" y="25" x="10" width="400" minimum="0"
                liveDragging="true"
                thumbDrag="dragStartHandler(event)"
                thumbRelease="dragDropHandler(event)"/>
```

The progress bar will display the progress of the file as it downloads.

```
    <mx:ProgressBar id="progressBar" y="45" x="15" width="390" height="1" minimum="0"↵
maximum="100" labelWidth="0"
        direction="right" mode="manual" />
```

```
<s:Label y="45" x="420" text="Track Loader"/>
```

We need some text fields to display the current time the song is playing and the total time or the song length.

```
<s:HGroup y="30" x="420" gap="0">
        <s:Label id="currentTimeText" text="00:00"/>
        <s:Label text="/"/>
        <s:Label id="totalTimeText" text="00:00"/>
</s:HGroup>
```

We add buttons to play, stop, pause, fast forward and rewind:

```
<s:HGroup y="60" x="10" gap="12">
        <s:Button id="playButton" label="play" click="playSong();" enabled="false" />
        <s:Button label="pause" click="player.pauseTrack()" />
        <s:Button label="stop" click="songSlider.value=0; currentTimeText.text =↵
'00:00'; player.stopTrack()" />
        <s:Button label="fastforward" click="player.fastforward();" />
        <s:Button label="rewind" click="player.rewind();" />
</s:HGroup>
```

The form will allow us to paste the URL of a song. We can provide a URL from the Internet or from our local library.

```
<mx:FormItem y="90">
        <mx:FormItem label="Music Url:" />
        <s:HGroup>
            <s:TextInput id="textInput" width="200" height="20"↵
text="http://www.themagicofdc.com/multimedia/mp3/WonderfulWorld.mp3"/>
            <s:Button label="Submit" click="this.songUrl=textInput.text; playSong();↵
playButton.enabled=true" />
        </s:HGroup>
</mx:FormItem>
```

Lastly, the volume slider allows us to change the volume value.

```
<s:HSlider id="volumeSlider"
                x="120" y="90"
                width="100" value="1"
                minimum="0" maximum="1"
                liveDragging="true"
                thumbDrag="dragVolumeHandler(event)" />

</s:Application>
```

Compile and run the application, and you can test the functionality. Figure 14-5 shows what the player will look like.

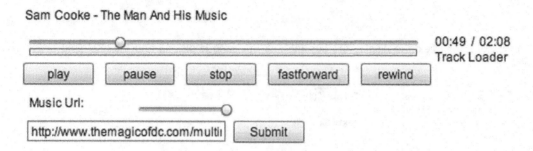

Sam Cooke - The Man And His Music

00:49 / 02:08
Track Loader

| play | pause | stop | fastforward | rewind |

Music Url:

http://www.themagicofdc.com/multi   Submit

Figure 14-5. A generic music player application

Creating a Video Player for Flash 10

To create a simple, custom video player for Flash 10, we'll use Flash Builder 4.

Open Flash Builder 4 or Eclipse with the Flex plug-in. Select **File ➤ New ➤ Flex Project**. Set the project name to **VideoPlayerExample,** and use the Flex 4 SDK in **Flex SDK version**. Select **Finish** to create the project.

Paste the following code into the **VideoPlayerExample.mxml** file.

```
<?xml version="1.0" encoding="utf-8"?>
<s:Application xmlns:fx="http://ns.adobe.com/mxml/2009"
                       xmlns:s="library://ns.adobe.com/flex/spark"
                       xmlns:mx="library://ns.adobe.com/flex/mx"
                       minWidth="1024" minHeight="768"
                       creationComplete="creationCompleteHandler(event)">

    <fx:Script>

        <![CDATA[
            import mx.events.FlexEvent;

            import utils.CustomStreamClient;

            private var videoURL:String = "http://foreversideways.simplespider.co.uk/↵
flv/cm_snowmonte.flv";
            private var connection:NetConnection;
            private var netStream:NetStream;

            protected function creationCompleteHandler(event:FlexEvent):void
            {
                connection = new NetConnection();
                connection.addEventListener(NetStatusEvent.NET_STATUS, netStatusHandler);
                connection.addEventListener(SecurityErrorEvent.SECURITY_ERROR,↵
    securityErrorHandler);
                connection.connect(null);
            }

            private function setNetStream():void
```

```
{
    netStream = new NetStream(connection);
    netStream.addEventListener(NetStatusEvent.NET_STATUS, netStatusHandler);
    netStream.addEventListener(IOErrorEvent.IO_ERROR, onNetworkError);
    netStream.client = new CustomStreamClient();

    var video:Video = new Video();
    video.attachNetStream(netStream);

    netStream.play(videoURL);
    netStream.seek(0.01);
    netStream.pause();

    component.addChild(video);
}

private function netStatusHandler(event:NetStatusEvent):void
{
    switch (event.info.code)
    {
        case "NetConnection.Connect.Success":
        {
            playButton.enabled = true;
            this.setNetStream();
            break;
        }
        case "NetStream.Play.StreamNotFound":
        {
            trace("StreamNotFound: " + videoURL);
            break;
        }
        case "NetStream.Buffer.Full":
        {
            trace("bufferLength:"+netStream.bufferLength);
            break;
        }
        case "NetStream.Buffer.Flush":
        {
            trace(event.info.code);
            break;
        }
        case "NetStream.Seek.Notify":
        {
            trace(event.info.code);
            break;
        }
        case "NetStream.Buffer.Empty":
        {
            trace(event.info.code);
            break;
        }
    }
}
```

```
        private function securityErrorHandler(event:SecurityErrorEvent):void
        {
            trace( "securityError: " + event.toString() );
        }

        private function onNetworkError(event:IOErrorEvent):void
        {
            trace( "NetworkError: " + event.toString() );
        }


    ]]>
    </fx:Script>

    <s:VGroup>

        <mx:UIComponent id="component" width="200" height="240" />

        <s:Button id="playButton" label="Play"
                    click="netStream.resume()"
                    enabled="false" />
    </s:VGroup>

</s:Application>
```

Once you compile and run this application, you'll be able to view the video playback. Let's examine the code.

The application starts by setting the creation complete event to call `creationCompleteHandler` method.

```
<?xml version="1.0" encoding="utf-8"?>
<s:Application xmlns:fx="http://ns.adobe.com/mxml/2009"
                xmlns:s="library://ns.adobe.com/flex/spark"
                xmlns:mx="library://ns.adobe.com/flex/mx"
                minWidth="1024" minHeight="768"
                creationComplete="creationCompleteHandler(event)">

    <fx:Script>

        <![CDATA[
```

We set global parameters that we will use in our application, such as the video URL location, the `NetConnection` and `NetStream`.

```
                    private var videoURL:String =↵
 "http://foreversideways.simplespider.co.uk/flv/cm_snowmonte.flv";
                    private var connection:NetConnection;
                    private var netStream:NetStream;
```

`creationCompleteHandler` is called once the component finishes the tasks of processing, measuring, layout, and drawing. At this point, we create the net connection and set event listeners for the messages to know when the connection is ready, as well as error messages due to security restrictions.

```
        protected function creationCompleteHandler(event:FlexEvent):void
        {
```

```
            connection = new NetConnection();
            connection.addEventListener(NetStatusEvent.NET_STATUS, netStatusHandler);
            connection.addEventListener(SecurityErrorEvent.SECURITY_ERROR,←
securityErrorHandler);
            connection.connect(null);
        }
```

The netStatusHandler method will handle messages coming from the NetConnection object. We are using a switch to handle the different messages. We won't go into detail regarding these common messages now; the names of the event constants are self-explanatory. Later in this chapter we'll discuss what these messages mean.

```
        private function netStatusHandler(event:NetStatusEvent):void
        {
            switch (event.info.code)
            {
```

Once the connection is established correctly, we call the setNetStream method. When the connection is established, we call the method to set the net stream, and the user is able to play the video. We set the playButton-enabled property to true so the user can click the play button and view the video.

```
            case "NetConnection.Connect.Success":
            {
                playButton.enabled = true;
                this.setNetStream();
                break;
            }
            case "NetStream.Play.StreamNotFound":
            {
                trace("StreamNotFound: " + videoURL);
                break;
            }
            case "NetStream.Buffer.Full":
            {
                trace("bufferLength:"+netStream.bufferLength);
                break;
            }
            case "NetStream.Buffer.Flush":
            {
                trace(event.info.code);
                break;
            }
            case "NetStream.Seek.Notify":
            {
                trace(event.info.code);
                break;
            }
            case "NetStream.Buffer.Empty":
            {
                trace(event.info.code);
                break;
            }
        }
    }
```

The securityErrorHandler handler will let us know whether there are any security restrictions that block us from creating the connection.

```
private function securityErrorHandler(event:SecurityErrorEvent):void
{
    trace( "securityError: " + event.toString() );
}
```

The setNetStream method is called once we established a connection. We can now create a new net stream and use the connection we established to listen to events and network errors. For the video we set a new Video component.

```
private function setNetStream():void
{
    netStream = new NetStream(connection);
    netStream.addEventListener(NetStatusEvent.NET_STATUS, netStatusHandler);
    netStream.addEventListener(IOErrorEvent.IO_ERROR, onNetworkError);
```

We can specify a client property. The property allows us to direct all the calls back to the client we define.

```
    netStream.client = new CustomStreamClient();

    var video:Video = new Video();
    video.attachNetStream(netStream);
```

When we're ready, we will play the video, seek to the 0.01 seconds point, and pause the video. The reason we do this is to display the first frame of the video and wait for user interaction to play the video.

```
    netStream.play(videoURL);
    netStream.seek(0.01);
    netStream.pause();
```

We also add the video component we set in this method to a placeholder we defined.

```
    component.addChild(video);
}
```

Here is the handler for I/O network errors:

```
private function onNetworkError(event:IOErrorEvent):void
{
    trace( "NetworkError: " + event.toString() );
}


    ]]>
</fx:Script>
```

We set a component as a placeholder so we can add the video object we are creating. The playButton button will allow us to play the video. Notice that we start the button as enabled="false" so the user won't be able to play the video before the video component is ready for playback.

```
<s:VGroup>

    <mx:UIComponent id="component" width="200" height="240" />

    <s:Button id="playButton" label="Play"
                    click="netStream.resume()"
```

```
                          enabled="false" />
        </s:VGroup>

</s:Application>
```

Video Player for Flash 10

In Flash 10, Adobe has added a component for Flex Gumbo called the `FxVideoDisplay` class, which is in addition to the `VideoDisplay` component in Flex. The main benefits are that the new video player component supports skinning, progressive download, multi-bitrate, and streaming of video right out of the box.

The MXML code to create the `FxVideoDisplay` component looks like this:

```
<FxVideoDisplay id="videoDisplay" />
```

To create a video player, you create the component and set the video file like so:

```
<?xml version="1.0" encoding="utf-8"?>
<s:Application xmlns:fx="http://ns.adobe.com/mxml/2009"
               xmlns:s="library://ns.adobe.com/flex/spark"
               xmlns:mx="library://ns.adobe.com/flex/mx"
               minWidth="1024" minHeight="768">

    <s:VideoPlayer id="player"
source="some_video_file.flv" />

</s:Application>
```

Once you compile and run the application, you can see the result, as in Figure 14-6.

Figure 14-6. Flash 10 progressive download application deployed in a browser

Out of the box, the component includes a toolbar for common operations, such as pause, stop, mute, fullscreen, volume, and seek. To skin the component, do the following, **File ➤ New ➤ MXML Skin**. The wizard opens up and you can set the host component as `VideoPlayer`, as well as the package and name, as in Figure 14-7.

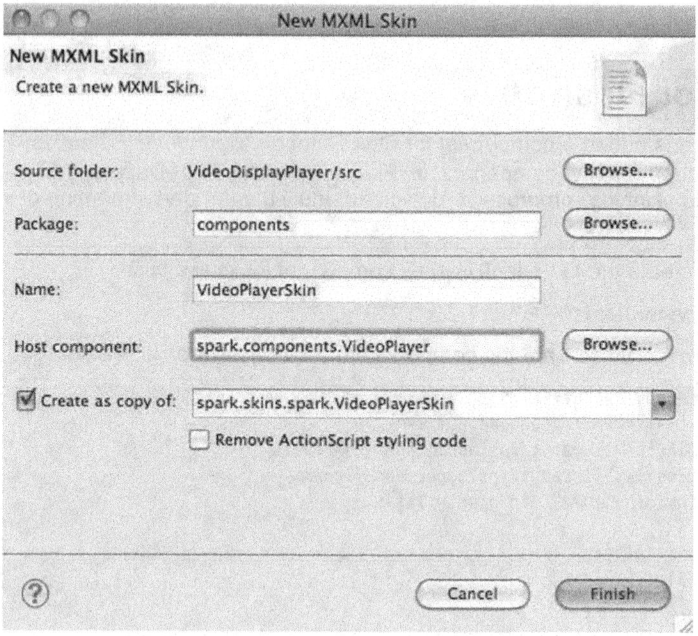

Figure 14-7. New MXML Skin wizard

Once you have the skin, you can pick the subcomponents, re-skin them by pointing to skins other than the default ones, and reposition elements.

Embed a Video File in Flash 10

So far we created video player with Flex. However, the asset was loaded at run time as an external file, and you had to provide the video file with your application or point to a separate URL. Flex allows embedding assets into your applications. When using the embed tag, the assets are compiled into the SWF file of your Flex application, and you don't need to provide the image with the application. Once the application is loaded, the video asset will be available automatically. The content of the SWF file can be created in Flash Professional.

Unfortunately, Flex does not support embedding video file as it does with images or SWFs, and until it does, we have to use the approach of creating a SWF and embedding the SWF into our application. Let's take a look.

```
<?xml version="1.0" encoding="utf-8"?>
<s:Application xmlns:fx="http://ns.adobe.com/mxml/2009"
               xmlns:s="library://ns.adobe.com/flex/spark"
               xmlns:mx="library://ns.adobe.com/flex/mx"
               minWidth="955" minHeight="600">

    <fx:Script>
```

```
            <![CDATA[

            import mx.events.VideoEvent;
            import mx.events.FlexEvent;

            [Embed(source="assets/videofile.swf")]
            [Bindable]
            public var videoFile:Class;

            ]]>
        </fx:Script>

        <mx:SWFLoader source="{videoFile}" />

</s:Application>
```

We will be using the SWFLoader component to load our SWFs. We created a class to hold the asset and used the bindable tag, so once the asset is loaded we'll be able to attach it automatically to the component source property.

There is another simpler way to embed an asset. You can replace the code with the following MXML tag:

```
<mx:SWFLoader source="@Embed('assets/videofile.swf')" />
```

To create the SWF, open Flash Professional CS5 and create a new project. Next, choose **Flash ➤ Import ➤ Import Video**.

As Figure 14-8 shows, there are four options to import a video:

- Load external video with playback component
- Embed FLV in SWF and play in timeline
- Import as mobile device video bundled in SWF
- Already deployed to a web server, Flash Video Streaming Service, or Flash Media Server

The option to **load an external video with playback component** loads the video during runtime as an external file. The options to **Embed FLV in SWF and play in timeline** and **Import as mobile device video bundled in SWF** allow embedding video files in the FLA document.

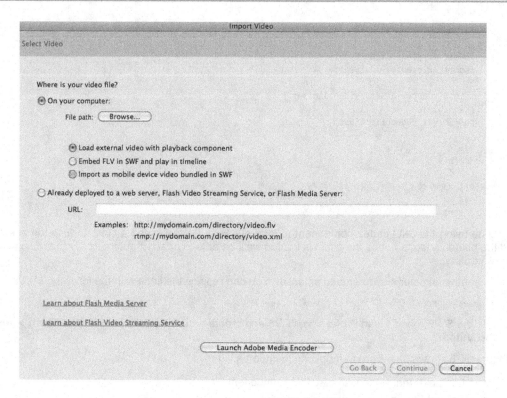

Figure 14-8. Flash Professional CS4 stage, including video componenent with bundled source

> *Please note that the option to **Import as mobile device video bundled in SWF** can be used with Flash Lite 2.0 or higher. What it does is create an embedded copy of the video file within our SWF, and we don't need to point to any external link to have the video playback.*

Select **On your computer** ➤ **Browse**. Import as mobile device video bundled in SWF. Select **Continue** and click **Finish**.

In older versions of Flash Professional you had to drag and drop the video component to the stage, set the name to **video** in the properties, and add a script to play the video, `video.play();`

In Flash Professional CS5, these steps have been done for you automatically so you can just compile the project and the SWF is ready.

Adobe Open Screen Media Framework

The video player ecosystem is complex. We've already pointed out the complexity of creating a video player; however, it does not end there. There are other elements, such as advertisement elements, social network elements, reporting, content management, DRM etc, which make a video player a complex composition. Adobe recently released a new framework called Adobe Open Screen Media Framework (OSMF, formerly known as Strobe) that is aimed at solving these issues.

OSMF is an open source AS3 media framework that supports the workflow around video playback and monetization. Video players have different features set. The skins are different, as are the integration and architecture workflows. They essentially do the same thing and can be created using the OSMF framework. The framework is focuses on the quality of the video player and addresses the common challenges.

The foundation of the framework is Qos (quality of service), which is based on the Open Video Player (OVP) initiative and provides a quick start for playing videos (smallest buffer size needed to start the video), efficient connection logic, and switching bitrates dynamically (recall the metric monitor service in OVP).

With the framework you can:

- Create a component user interface for integration of audio, videos, and images.
- Use the plug-in architecture to integrate CDN, ad partners, publishers, analytics, social networks, and developers.

The framework by itself is not powerful. Its power comes from having partners embrace the framework—CDNs, publishers, ad analytics, social networks, and developers. The pluggable components can allow publishers to easily switch and test performance and service across different services. The framework offers many advantages:

- **Reduces the barrier of entry for new publishers:** With a framework to integrate the different pieces of the video player, new publishers can get started quickly and with fewer resources, and can scale up as requirements increase.

- **Provides a flexible framework:** OSMF provides an easy way to extend each component and allows these components to act as building blocks that can be extensible and compositable (meaning you can apply a multimedia mode, such as image or video operations, to the data your object represents).

- **Leverages existing code:** The OSMF framework uses the Flash Player from Open Video Player (OVP). No need to have duplication of efforts to solve basic problems.

- **Drives standards and allows custom workflows:** Many of the elements that connect to a video player are not standard yet, and Adobe OSMF will help standardize these components as well as allow them to be configured.

- **No runtimes or framework dependency:** The framework is based on Flash 10 AS3 and is not dependent on any framework such as the Flex SDK, Cairngorm, or others. With that said, some integrated elements may be created using a framework, but these are loosely coupled and can be replaced if needed.

- **Partners can focus:** There are two partners: publishers and CDNs. CDNs can focus on services and integration, and publishers can focus on user experience.

- **Integrates with existing Adobe tools:** Adobe OSMF will be integrated with other Adobe Suite tools and services such as Catalyst, Illustrator, FMS 3.5, and FMRMS.

- **Optimizes performance:** With the ability to separate the core framework and each element as a separate SWC, you can increase performance by keeping the file size to a minimum and remove components not used.

The Adobe OSMF framework consists of the following building blocks:

MediaPlayer: The MediaPlayer class represents the controller class for media playback. You can play any type of media (video, audio, images, SWFs, etc.). Instead of using DisplayObject, use MediaPlayerSprite. To use the media, you can employ the following methods: play(), pause(), seek(), as well as the following properties: volume, autoRewind, loop. The events for the media are: seekingChange, volumeChange, complete.

MediaElements and Traits: The MediaElement class represents a unified media presentation (video, image, or a grouping of media that's shown together). It takes a resource (URL, array of dynamic streams, etc.). You can then present/play the media using one or more MediaTraitBase. MediaTraitBase represents an intrinsic capability of a piece of media (ability to play, ability to seek, audio, etc.). This class is dynamic in nature, can come and go over the life of the media Trait APIs; it is also media-type-agnostic. Keep in mind that not all traits apply to all media types. For instance, AudioElement doesn't have DisplayObjectTrait, and ImageElement doesn't have PlayTrait.

> *Rule of thumb—A trait represents a media capability or characteristic. A trait can't apply to every piece of media and must be something that a player developer might act upon, such as LoadTrait, PlayTrait, SeekTrait, DisplayObjectTrait.*

As an example, take a look at the VideoElement traits in Figure 14-9.

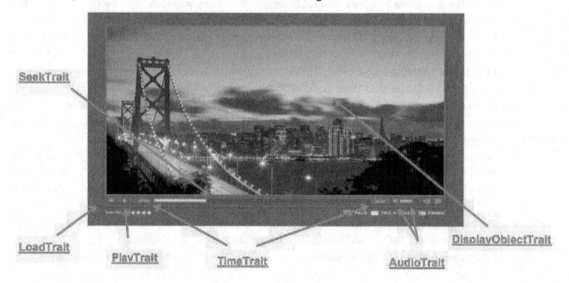

Figure 14-9. VideoElement traits

Media Elements: The `ParallelElement` class represents a set of `MediaElements` that are presented in parallel. It is a media composition whose elements are presented in parallel. The `SerialElement` class represents a set of `MediaElements` that are presented one after the other. These classes used together create two composite `MediaElements` that can represent complex, "tree-like" media experiences.

To better understand how this works, take a look at Figure 14-10.

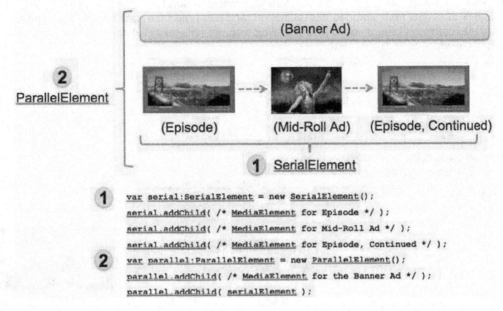

Figure 14-10. Creating both parallel and serial elements

As you can see, we have three related `MediaElements`: (Episode), (Mid-Roll Ad), and (Episode, Continued). Together they create a media experience and are grouped as `serialElement`. Once you create the `serialElement`, you can add that group to a `parallelElement` with other `serialElements`.

Composite Elements: A composite `MediaElement` is a `MediaElement` that exposes composite traits. Composite traits aggregate multiple traits of the same type. For instance, you can take two VideoElements and create a `SerialElement`, and then have access to both `playTrait` properties from each `VideoElement`. Together these `playTraits` are a `CompositePlayTrait`.

Proxy Elements: The `ProxyElement` class wraps up (proxies) with another `MediaElement`. These classes expose the same API. The class signature is as follow:

```
public function ProxyElement(wrappedElement:MediaElement)
```

By default, all methods, properties, and events are passed through subclasses and can change. This can be used to modify the behavior of another `MediaElement`. Clients think they're working with a `VideoElement` when they're actually working with a `ProxyElement` that wraps a `VideoElement`. This is incredibly useful for plug-ins.

Here are two examples of using `ProxyElement`:

- **User Analytics:** `ProxyElement` listens for changes to the wrapped MediaElement and reports them to a server.
- **Seamless Video Switching:** `ProxyElement` wraps up two `VideoElements`, and switches from one to the other without rebuffering.

Take a look at the example in Figure 14-10. Here we created an `AnalyticsProxyElement` element. The proxy listens to events from wrapped `MediaElement` and can report the data back to the Omniture API. The `AnalyticsProxyElement` does this by wrapping an `UnseekableProxyElement` that prevents seeking of the wrapped `MediaElement`.

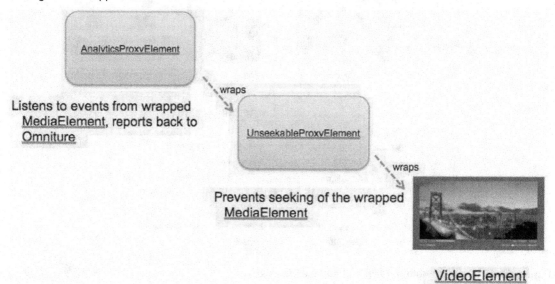

Figure 14-11. An example of a ProxyElement

Plug-ins: The real challenge is third-party integration. There are many third-party vendors that make a player, such as CDNs, ad servers/networks, analytics providers, "social" providers, and many others.

To allow integration between the player and the vendors, OSMF created player/plug-in contract, which declares what the plug-in capabilities are.

Plug-ins don't have free rein over the player, meaning that the players can load plug-ins, but players don't integrate with custom plug-in APIs directly. The way it works is that OSMF acts as the broker between the player and the plug-in.

There are different plug-in types:

- **Media plug-ins** declare new media types. Examples are video plug-ins and image plug-in.
- **Loader plug-ins** declare new ways of "loading" media. An example is the Akamai plug-in for connection authentication.
- **Proxy plug-ins** declare ways to modify (or listen to) the behavior of media. Examples are: a plug-in that prevents seeking on all videos, or the Omniture reporting plug-in.

- **Reference plug-ins** declare the range of media they'd like to reference. An example might be a plug-in that creates an overlay ad SWF that can pause the main video when displayed.

For info about creating plug-ins, check ASDOC PluginInfo:

```
http://help.adobe.com/en_US/FlashPlatform/reference/actionscript/3/org/osmf/media/⤸
PluginInfo.html
```

Metadata: There are two types of metadata: Resource-level and MediaElement.

Resource-level metadata was created to address the challenge of figuring out what, for example, "http://example.com/myvideo" represents. The `MediaResourceBase.addMetadataValue` method can be used to further qualify a resource with "static" data (e.g., MIME type). For instance, we can assign the "`video/x-flv`" MIME type to a resource with a URL so we can know it's a video.

MediaElement metadata was created to address the challenge of representing custom information about what's playing. The `MediaElement.addMetadata` method can be used to model metadata during playback.

For instance, let's say we have dynamically generated "ad" rather than "episode" metadata. We want to be able to know that so we can have the UI update the chrome during ad breaks.

The OSMF code is available at www.osmf.org. To read more see the resources listed in this page: `http://forums.adobe.com/message/2392184#2392184`

Hello World Example

Let's take a look at a simple implementation of the framework provided by Adobe. We created this example using OSMF build 0.9. The example creates a video player that plays a video using progressive download as an ActionSctipt 3.0 project:

```
package
{
    import flash.display.Sprite;

    import org.osmf.display.MediaPlayerSprite;
    import org.osmf.media.URLResource;
    import org.osmf.net.NetLoader;
    import org.osmf.utils.URL;
    import org.osmf.video.VideoElement;

    /**
     * The simplest OSMF application possible.
     *
     * The metadata sets the SWF size to match that of the video.
     **/
    [SWF(width="640", height="352")]
    public class OSMFHelloWorld extends Sprite
    {
        public function OSMFHelloWorld()
        {
            // Create the Sprite class that holds our MediaPlayer.
            var sprite:MediaPlayerSprite = new MediaPlayerSprite();
            addChild(sprite);
```

```
        // Set the MediaElement on the MediaPlayer.  Because
        // autoPlay defaults to true, playback begins immediately.
        sprite.mediaElement = new VideoElement
            ( new NetLoader
                , new URLResource(new URL(REMOTE_PROGRESSIVE))
            );
    }

    private static const REMOTE_PROGRESSIVE:String
    = "http://mediapm.edgesuite.net/OSMF/content/test/AFaerysTale_sylviaApostol⏎
_640_500_short.flv";
    }
}
```

Our next (minimalist) example loads an image using Flex 4. We create a sprite that contains a MediaPlayer to manage the display and control of the MediaElements we'll be using. We then create and set the MediaElement (in our case ImageElement) with a resource and path. Lastly, we add the sprite to the UIComponent.

```
<s:Application xmlns:fx="http://ns.adobe.com/mxml/2009"
                        xmlns:s="library://ns.adobe.com/flex/spark"
                        xmlns:mx="library://ns.adobe.com/flex/mx"
                        minWidth="1024" minHeight="768"
                        creationComplete="creationCompleteHandler()">

    <fx:Script>
        <![CDATA[
                import org.osmf.elements.ImageElement;
                import org.osmf.elements.VideoElement;
                import org.osmf.media.MediaPlayerSprite;
                import org.osmf.media.URLResource;

                //path of media to be displayed: Image
                private static const MEDIA_PATH:String =
"http://mediapm.edgesuite.net/strobe/content/test/train.jpg";

                protected function creationCompleteHandler():void
                {
                    //sprite that contains a MediaPlayer to manage display and control of
MediaElements
                    var playerSprite:MediaPlayerSprite = new MediaPlayerSprite();

                    //creates and sets the MediaElement (ImageElement) with a resource and
path
                    playerSprite.media = new ImageElement( new URLResource( MEDIA_PATH )
);

                    //Adds the sprite to the UIComponent defined in MXML
                    mediaHolder.addChild( playerSprite );
                }

        ]]>
    </fx:Script>
```

```
          <mx:UIComponent id="mediaHolder" />
```

```
</s:Application>
```

Here's another minimalist example that creates a progressive download video player using OSMF and Flex 4. Just as in the image example, we create a sprite that contains a MediaPlayer to manage the display and control of the MediaElements we will be using. We then create and set the MediaElement (in our case VideoElement) with a resource and path. Lastly, we add the sprite to the UIComponent.

```
<s:Application xmlns:fx="http://ns.adobe.com/mxml/2009"
                    xmlns:s="library://ns.adobe.com/flex/spark"
                    xmlns:mx="library://ns.adobe.com/flex/mx"
                    minWidth="955" minHeight="600"
                    creationComplete="creationCompleteHandler()">

     <fx:Script>
          <![CDATA[
                import mx.core.UIComponent;

                import org.osmf.elements.VideoElement;
                import org.osmf.media.MediaPlayerSprite;
                import org.osmf.media.URLResource;

                //path of media to be displayed: Progressive Video
                private static const MEDIA_PATH:String =
"http://mediapm.edgesuite.net/strobe/content/test/AFaerysTale_sylviaApostol_640_500_short.flv";

                protected function creationCompleteHandler():void
                {
                    //sprite that contains a MediaPlayer to manage display and control of
MediaElements
                    var playerSprite:MediaPlayerSprite = new MediaPlayerSprite();

                    //creates and sets the MediaElement (VideoElement) with a resource and
path
                    playerSprite.media = new VideoElement( new URLResource( MEDIA_PATH )
);

                    //Adds the sprite to the UIComponent defined in MXML
                    var component:UIComponent = new UIComponent();
                    component.addChild( playerSprite );
                    mediaHolder.addElement( component );
                }

          ]]>
     </fx:Script>

     <s:Group id="mediaHolder" />

</s:Application>
```

If we want to serve an audio file via progressive download, we can just use AudioElement instead of VideoElement.

Here is a minimalist example of streaming a video using OSMF and Flex 4. The URL points to a streaming server. The OVP player will be able to recognize that and provide streaming instead of progressive download.

```
<s:Application xmlns:fx="http://ns.adobe.com/mxml/2009"
                         xmlns:s="library://ns.adobe.com/flex/spark"
                         xmlns:mx="library://ns.adobe.com/flex/mx"
                         minWidth="1024" minHeight="768"
                         creationComplete="creationCompleteHandler()">

        <fx:Script>
                <![CDATA[
                        import org.osmf.elements.ImageElement;
                        import org.osmf.elements.VideoElement;
                        import org.osmf.media.MediaPlayerSprite;
                        import org.osmf.media.URLResource;

                        //URI of connection/media to be displayed: RTMP - Streaming Video
                        private static const MEDIA_PATH:String =
"rtmp://cp67126.edgefcs.net/ondemand/mediapm/strobe/content/test/SpaceAloneHD_sounas_640_500_short";

                        protected function creationCompleteHandler():void
                        {
                                //sprite that contains a MediaPlayer to manage display and control of
MediaElements
                                var playerSprite:MediaPlayerSprite = new MediaPlayerSprite();

                                //creates and sets the MediaElement (VideoElement) with a resource and
path
                                playerSprite.media = new VideoElement( new URLResource( MEDIA_PATH )
);

                                //Adds the sprite to the UIComponent defined in MXML
                                mediaHolder.addChild( playerSprite );
                        }

                ]]>
        </fx:Script>

        <mx:UIComponent id="mediaHolder" />

</s:Application>
```

Here's an example of dynamic streaming using FMS server. We set the host URL for the steaming server and then we can add the profile files for the videos. The dynamic switching will be handled automatically by the OVP player based on the user's bandwidth.

```
<s:Application xmlns:fx="http://ns.adobe.com/mxml/2009"
                         xmlns:s="library://ns.adobe.com/flex/spark"
                         xmlns:mx="library://ns.adobe.com/flex/mx"
                         minWidth="1024" minHeight="768"
                         creationComplete="creationCompleteHandler()">

        <fx:Script>
```

```
                <![CDATA[
                        import org.osmf.elements.VideoElement;
                        import org.osmf.media.MediaPlayerSprite;
                        import org.osmf.net.DynamicStreamingItem;
                        import org.osmf.net.DynamicStreamingResource;

                        //URI of host RTMP/E connection for streaming server
                        private static const HOST:String = "rtmp://cp67126.edgefcs.net/ondemand";

                        protected function creationCompleteHandler():void
                        {
                                //sprite that contains a MediaPlayer to manage display and control of
MediaElements
                                var playerSprite:MediaPlayerSprite = new MediaPlayerSprite();

                                //Resource containing the pointers, bitrate, width, and height of each
DynamicStreamingItem to be in the set
                                var dsr:DynamicStreamingResource = new DynamicStreamingResource( HOST
);
                                dsr.streamItems.push( new DynamicStreamingItem(
"mp4:mediapm/ovp/content/demo/video/elephants_dream/elephants_dream_768x428_24.0fps_408kbps.mp4", 408,
768, 428) );
                                dsr.streamItems.push( new DynamicStreamingItem(
"mp4:mediapm/ovp/content/demo/video/elephants_dream/elephants_dream_768x428_24.0fps_608kbps.mp4", 608,
768, 428) );
                                dsr.streamItems.push( new DynamicStreamingItem(
"mp4:mediapm/ovp/content/demo/video/elephants_dream/elephants_dream_1024x522_24.0fps_908kbps.mp4", 908,
1024, 522) );
                                dsr.streamItems.push( new DynamicStreamingItem(
"mp4:mediapm/ovp/content/demo/video/elephants_dream/elephants_dream_1024x522_24.0fps_1308kbps.mp4", 1308,
1024, 522) );
                                dsr.streamItems.push( new DynamicStreamingItem(
"mp4:mediapm/ovp/content/demo/video/elephants_dream/elephants_dream_1280x720_24.0fps_1708kbps.mp4", 1708,
1280, 720) );

                                //Creates the MediaElement (VideoElement) adding the
DynamicStreamingResource to it, and setting to as the mediaElement on the MediaPlayerSprite
                                playerSprite.media = new VideoElement( dsr );

                                //Adds the sprite to the UIComponent defined in MXML
                                mediaHolder.addChild( playerSprite );
                        }

                ]]>
        </fx:Script>

        <mx:UIComponent id="mediaHolder" />

</s:Application>
```

Last example (more advanced) shows you how to create a streaming video player and listen to events to recognize once the video is ready to play, as well as access properties in the video player and the net stream:

```
<s:Application xmlns:fx="http://ns.adobe.com/mxml/2009"
                         xmlns:s="library://ns.adobe.com/flex/spark"
                         xmlns:mx="library://ns.adobe.com/flex/mx"
                         minWidth="1024" minHeight="768">

        <fx:Script>
               <![CDATA[
                       import org.osmf.elements.VideoElement;
                       import org.osmf.events.DisplayObjectEvent;
                       import org.osmf.events.MediaPlayerCapabilityChangeEvent;
                       import org.osmf.media.MediaPlayer;
                       import org.osmf.media.URLResource;

                       private var playerContainer:Sprite = new Sprite;
                       private var mediaPlayer:MediaPlayer = new MediaPlayer();

                       private function playVideoURL(url:String):void
                       {
                               mediaPlayer.addEventListener(
MediaPlayerCapabilityChangeEvent.CAN_PLAY_CHANGE, onVideoLoadedAndReady );
                               mediaPlayer.addEventListener( DisplayObjectEvent.MEDIA_SIZE_CHANGE,
onDimensionChange );

                               var videoElement:VideoElement = new VideoElement(  new URLResource(
url ) );

                               mediaPlayer.media = videoElement;
                               mediaHolder.addChild( playerContainer );
                       }

                       private function
onVideoLoadedAndReady(event:MediaPlayerCapabilityChangeEvent):void
                       {
                               if (event.enabled  && mediaPlayer.canPlay)
                                       mediaPlayer.play()
                       }

                       private function onDimensionChange( event:DisplayObjectEvent ):void
                       {
                               mediaPlayer.displayObject.width = event.newWidth;
                               mediaPlayer.displayObject.height = event.newHeight;

                               mediaHolder.addChild( mediaPlayer.displayObject );
                       }

                 ]]>
        </fx:Script>

        <s:Rect top="0" width="660" height="365"
                       x="0" y="0">
               <s:fill>
                       <s:SolidColor color="#000000"/>
               </s:fill>
```

```
            </s:Rect>

            <mx:UIComponent id="mediaHolder" />

            <s:TextInput id="mediaPath" width="400"  x="48" y="330"
text="rtmp://cp67126.edgefcs.net/ondemand/mediapm/strobe/content/test/SpaceAloneHD_sounas_640_500_short"/>
            <s:Button x="456" y="331" label="Play" click="playVideoURL(mediaPath.text)"/>
            <s:Button x="534" y="331" label="Pause" click="mediaPlayer.pause()"/>

</s:Application>
```

The toolkit and documentation are available for download at:

`www.OpenSourceMediaFramework.com`

You can find more information at the OSMF developer forums:

`http://forums.adobe.com/community/opensource/osmf/developers`

and at the OSMF User Group:

`http://groups.adobe.com/groups/7af970e6e4/summary`

Summary

In this chapter we introduced you to video and audio using the Flash platform. We covered the supported video and audio formats such as FLV and MPEG-4. We then looked at encoding video for Flash applications by compressing video files using the Adobe Media Encoder. We examined the difference between streaming and progressive download, and looked at creating custom music and video players. We showed you how to create a simple video player using the Flex 4 component out of the box, and how to embed a video file in Flash Player 10. Finally, we covered Adobe Open Screen Media Framework (OSMF).

Chapter 15

Using 3D in Flex

by Charlie Schulze

In one chapter it would be impossible to learn everything about 3D in Flex, but this chapter gives you enough knowledge to get started. There are several APIs at your disposal if you want to work with 3D in Flex. The API covered in this chapter will be Papervision.

The goal of this chapter is not to teach you 3D but rather teach you how you can use the Papervision API in your Flex projects. Getting started is a relatively painless process.

Before You Begin

First download the Papervision source or swc. For the examples in this chapter we will use the Papervision3D_2.0.883.swc file (`http://papervision3d.googlecode.com/files/Papervision3D_2.0.883.swc`).

In the following examples we will extend BasicView, which is included with Papervision3D. There is one important difference between Papervision's BasicView in Flex, and Flash. Since a Papervision BasicView extends Sprite and not UIComponent, you cannot add it to your application with a simple addChild or addElement. An easy way to get around this is to create a wrapper for adding it to the application, as you'll see shortly.

Creating 3D Objects

One of the most basic things you can do in Papervision is add a primitive object to your scene. Examples of primitive objects are a cone, plane, sphere, cylinder, and so on. Let's start with using BasicView and adding a sphere.

First create an ActionScript file called SphereExample and have it extend BasicView - org.papervision3d.view.basicView.

```
package
{
    import org.papervision3d.objects.primitives.Sphere;
    import org.papervision3d.view.BasicView;

    public class SphereExample extends BasicView
    {
        private var sphere:Sphere;
        public function SphereExample()
        {
            super();

            sphere = new Sphere();
            scene.addChild(sphere);
            startRendering();
        }
    }
}
```

We start this class by extending BasicView to bypass all the setup work. The BasicView class automatically sets up our camera, renderer, and scene and adds the hooks to allow us to start and stop rendering our file. Since we are extending the BasicView class, we need to be sure to call super() in the constructor. Otherwise, our BasicView will be of very little use to us. Our next line of code inside our constructor creates a sphere that is a primitive object of Papervision. Finally, we add our sphere to the scene and then call startRendering().

There are two ways to render your scene.

You can use singleRender(), which does exactly what it sounds like. It will render the scene only once. Using singleRender() is fine if you want a snapshot of what is happening or plan on continually calling it as needed from a Tween engine, such as TweenLite.

Calling startRendering() starts a frame loop to constantly render your 3D. This is great if you know you're always going to have objects in your scene animating. Since 3D in Flash is a processor intensive action you would want to call stopRendering() as much as possible when the constant render is not needed.

Now that we have our class that extends BasicView, it's time to add it to our Flex application. Here is our application code.

```
<?xml version="1.0" encoding="utf-8"?>
<s:Application xmlns:fx="http://ns.adobe.com/mxml/2009"
             xmlns:s="library://ns.adobe.com/flex/spark"
             xmlns:mx="library://ns.adobe.com/flex/mx" minWidth="1024" minHeight="768"
```

```
                applicationComplete="applicationComplete()">
     <fx:Script>

         <![CDATA[
         import mx.core.UIComponent;

         private function applicationComplete():void
         {
             var sphereExample:SphereExample = new SphereExample();

             var pv3DWrapper:UIComponent = new UIComponent();
             pv3DWrapper.addChild( sphereExample );
             addElement( pv3DWrapper );
         }
         ]]>
     </fx:Script>
</s:Application>
```

Once our application is ready, we call applicationComplete() and create an instance of our SphereExample. Then, as stated earlier, we need to create a wrapper for our SphereExample.

```
var sphereExample:SphereExample = new SphereExample();

var pv3DWrapper:UIComponent = new UIComponent();
pv3DWrapper.addChild( sphereExample );
addElement( pv3DWrapper );
```

After adding our SphereExample to our wrapper, we add the wrapper UIComponent to our application. Here is the result:

Figure 15-1. A simple sphere created using Papervision 3D

Exciting, I know.

Working with Materials

In Papervision you have objects (planes, cubes, cones, 3D Models, etc.) and then you have the textures or materials that you add to these objects. Think of materials as picking out a new car and being able to choose your paint color or pin-stripes. When working with materials we are essentially working on the same principle. We have our object, such as a sphere (car), and a material, a colorMaterial (paint). Then we just need to apply the material to the object.

Let's start by adding a material to our sphere.

```
var colorMat:ColorMaterial = new ColorMaterial(0xFF0000);
sphere = new Sphere(colorMat);

//We could also apply the material this way
sphere.material = colorMat;
```

In the first line of code we create a new ColorMaterial and pass in the color we want to use. Next, we add that color to our sphere. We can do this one of two ways. We can pass it into the constructor when we create our sphere, or we can apply it afterward via the material property of our Sphere object.

Experiment using the different materials that Papervision has to offer, including bitmap and shading materials.

Animating Objects

Let's add a little animation to our example. The only thing we need to do is go back to our SphereExample.as class, override the onRenderTick method, and add some simple math to our code.

```
override protected function onRenderTick(event:Event=null) : void
{
    super.onRenderTick(event);
    sphere.rotationY += 10;
}
```

First we need to make sure that we have properly imported our Event class.

```
import flash.events.Event;
```

Then be sure to call super on the onRenderTick method or we will not see anything on the screen. Next we add 10 to the y rotation of the sphere object. You should see your sphere rotating on its *y* axis. If you still have a material applied to your sphere, remove it, so you can better see the rotation animation.

Here is the full SphereExample.as code:

```
package
{
    import flash.events.Event;

    import org.papervision3d.objects.primitives.Sphere;
    import org.papervision3d.view.BasicView;

    public class SphereExample extends BasicView
    {
        private var sphere:Sphere;

        public function SphereExample()
        {
            super();
            sphere = new Sphere();
            scene.addChild(sphere);
            startRendering();
        }
```

```
    override protected function onRenderTick(event:Event=null) : void
    {
        super.onRenderTick(event);
        sphere.rotationY += 10;
    }
  }
}
```

As you can see from this example, you could quickly connect some interactivity with the Flex components, adding a few buttons and controlling the position of elements.

```
<s:HGroup>
    <s:Button id="zoomInBtn" label="Zoom In" mouseDown="zoomIn()"/>
    <s:Button id="zoomOutBtn" label="Zoom Out" mouseDown="zoomOut()"/>
</s:HGroup>
```

Then back in our Script block we could add the code to control the Papervision.

```
private function zoomIn():void
{
    sphereExample.zoomIn();
}

private function zoomOut():void
{
    sphereExample.zoomOut();
}
```

Here is what we add inside our SphereExample.as class.

First, outside of your constructor, declare your zoomAmount variable; then add the zoomIn and zoomOut methods.

```
private var zoomAmount:Number = 0;

public function zoomIn():void
{
    zoomAmount = -10;
}

public function zoomOut():void
{
    zoomAmount = 10;
}
```

Inside our onRenderTick method we will now add this one line of code:

```
sphere.z += zoomAmount;
```

What we have done here is add some simple interactivity between Flex and Papervision. This is some very basic movement that you can do with any Papervision object.

Creating a Papervision Coverflow Utilizing ArrayCollection

Before we begin this coverflow example, please download the AS3 version TweenLite from http://blog.greensock.com/tweenlite/.

To start, create a new Flex project and call it FlexCoverflow. Next, place the TweenLite src file in your libs folder so we can have full access to those classes.

We need to start by creating a new ActionScript class that extends BasicView.

```
package
{
    import org.papervision3d.view.BasicView;

    public class PapervisionView extends BasicView
    {
        public function PapervisionView()
        {
            super();
        }
    }
}
```

Next, we need to add some variables that we'll be using in our coverflow application.

```
private var planes:Array = [];
private var colorBlocks:Array = [];
private var colorCollection:ArrayCollection = new ArrayCollection();
private var numberOfPlanes:Number = 5;
private var currentPlaneIndex:Number = 0;
private var planeAngle:Number = 35;
private var distanceApart:Number = 140;
```

We first create an array to store our planes, then one to store our movieClips that will be used as our plane materials. Next we create an arrayCollection, which we will use to store the colors we are using to tint our movieClips. Feel free to adjust the numberOfPlanes variable to add more items to your coverflow. We will be updating and using currentPlaneIndex so we always know which plane is the frontmost item in our coverflow. Finally, we create the planeAngle and distanceApart to set the angle and distance between our planes to the left or right of the centermost plane. We'll be working with those a little later.

```
public function start() : void
{
    //Activate our Tint Plugin
    TweenPlugin.activate([TintPlugin]);

    //Set viewport.interactive to true
    viewport.interactive = true;

    //Create the arrayCollection that holds our material colors
    createColorCollection();
    createChildren();
```

```
        startRendering();
        animate();
}
```

To get our application started, we first need to activate our TintPlugin. This plug-in will be used to tint our movieClips from one color to another. Next, we need to make sure that our viewport has interactive events enabled. The way we do this is by setting viewport.interactive to true. With this we will be able to use things like InteractiveScene3DEvent.OBJECT_PRESS to interact with our 3D items. Next we call methods to create our arrayCollection and the objects we'll use in our coverflow. Then we call startRendering, which will begin rendering our Papervision objects. Finally, we call animate, which will place our items.

Let's first discuss the creation of our arrayCollection, which is little more than a holder for our movieClips tint color.

```
private function createColorCollection():void
{
    for(var i:int = 0;i<numberOfPlanes;i++)
    {
        colorCollection.addItem({color:0x000000});
    }
    colorCollection.addEventListener(CollectionEvent.COLLECTION_CHANGE,onCollectionChange);
}
```

After we add all our colors, we set an event listener on the collection so when we want to update any single item we have a way for our application to react.

Next, let's look into the creation of our 3D objects.

```
private function createChildren() : void
{
    for (var planeIndex:int = 0; planeIndex < colorCollection.length; planeIndex++)
    {
        createPlaneWithMaterial(planeIndex);
    }
}

private function createPlaneWithMaterial(atIndex:int):void
{
    //Create MovieClip for Movie Material;
    var colorBlock:MovieClip = new MovieClip()
    colorBlock.graphics.beginFill(0);
    colorBlock.graphics.drawRect(0,0,200,400);
    colorBlock.graphics.endFill();

    //Create MovieMaterial
    var movieMat:MovieMaterial = new MovieMaterial(colorBlock);
    movieMat.interactive = true;
    movieMat.animated = true;

    //Apply Tint to movieClip used in Material
    applyTint(colorBlock,atIndex);

    //Create the plane
```

```
    var plane:Plane = new Plane(movieMat, 200, 400,4,4);

    //Add listener for plane click
    plane.addEventListener(InteractiveScene3DEvent.OBJECT_PRESS, onPlaneClick,false,0,true);
    plane.id = atIndex;

    //Push items into arrays for later
    planes.push(plane);
    colorBlocks.push(colorBlock);

    //Add our plane to our PV3D scene
    scene.addChild(plane);
}
```

Inside createChildren we loop through the number of items in our colorCollection and call createPlaneWithMaterial. Inside the createPlaneWithMaterial function we start off by creating a movieClip that we'll use inside our Papervision MovieMaterial. We are simply drawing a box and filling it with black. Next, we create our MovieMaterial, passing in the colorBlock movieClip we just created. Next, we need to set the movieMat.interactive to true so that we can use our OBJECT_PRESS event. We also need to set movieMat.animated to true—if we did not do this, Papervision would assume that the material never needs to update from its original snapshot. Setting animated to true is what allows us to fade it from one color to another. We then apply the tint to the colorBlock. We'll learn more about the applyTint function shortly.

Next, we move to creating our Papervision Plane. We pass in our MovieMaterial, setting the width and height, and then segment width and segment height. The default for the segment width and height is 0. The greater this number is, the better our materials will look when rendered, but it comes with a performance hit.

After creating our plane we want to be able to interact with it. Luckily, Papervision gives us access to these objects via the InteractiveScene3DEvent. We then set the ID of our plane so that we can identify it later.

After we push our planes and colorBlocks to arrays, we need to make sure our planes get added to our scene. The scene was already created for us in our BasicView.

Let's now take a closer look at our onCollectionChange and applyTint functions.

```
private function onCollectionChange(evt:CollectionEvent):void
{
    var colorBlock:MovieClip = colorBlocks[evt.location];
    applyTint(colorBlock,evt.location);
}
```

Whenever we update an item in our arrayCollection we find out which one of the items was updated and then call applyTint.

```
private function applyTint(colorBlock:MovieClip,val:int):void
{
    var color:int = ColorUtil.adjustBrightness(colorCollection[val].color,val * 20);
    TweenLite.to(colorBlock, 1, {tint:[color]});
}
```

The applyTint method simply gets the color from the arrayCollection, and we use TweenLite to tint the color of the entire movieClip from its current color to the new color. You could simply use the color in the colorCollection. Since in this example we will be using one color for all the items in our ArrayCollection, we adjust the brightness to give a contrast from one to the next.

Now we get to the meat of our coverflow—the animation.

```
private function onPlaneClick(evt:InteractiveScene3DEvent):void
{
    currentPlaneIndex = evt.target.id;
    animate();
}

private function animate():void
{
    for (var planeIndex:int = 0; planeIndex < planes.length; planeIndex++)
    {
        var plane:Plane = planes[planeIndex];

        //Each if statement will adjust these numbers as needed
        var planeX:Number;
        var planeZ:Number;

        //Place  & Animate Center Item
        if (planeIndex == currentPlaneIndex)
        {
            planeZ               = -200
            planeX               = 0;
            TweenLite.to(plane, 1, { rotationY:0,x:planeX,z:planeZ,ease:Quint.easeInOut } );
        }

        //Place & Animate Right Items
        if(planeIndex > currentPlaneIndex)
        {
            planeZ = 0
            planeX = (planeIndex - currentPlaneIndex + 1) * distanceApart;
            TweenLite.to(plane, 1, {↩
rotationY:planeAngle,x:planeX,z:planeZ,ease:Quint.easeInOut } );
        }

        //Place & Animate Left Items
        if (planeIndex < currentPlaneIndex)
        {
            planeZ = 0
            planeX = (currentPlaneIndex - planeIndex + 1) * -distanceApart;
            TweenLite.to(plane, 1,↩
{ rotationY:-planeAngle,x:planeX,z:planeZ,ease:Quint.easeInOut } );
        }
    }
}
```

Each time we select a plane we call the animate loop and adjust the currentPlaneIndex to the item selected. Every time we call animate we loop through the planes in our planes array. First, we get which plane we are working with, then create three variables that we will use in each of our if statements. In our first if statement, we are trying to determine if the plane is the frontmost plane. If it is, we set its z location to -200. This will actually bring it closer to the camera. Then we set the x to 0, which in Papervision terms is the center of the view. Finally, we set the rotationY to 0 so the plane appears to lay flat.

In the next two if statements we decide if the plane is to the left or the right of the frontmost plane. When we are working with the items on the right, the x location of our plane is set like this:

```
planeX = (planeIndex - currentPlaneIndex + 1) * distanceApart;
```

This is just a little simple math. We subtract the currentPlaneIndex from planeIndex but add 1. The reason we add 1 is just to add a little spacing between the frontmost item and this plane. We then multiply this by our distanceApart number we created earlier.

Finally we tween the properties of the plane, setting the planeX, planyY, planeZ, and rotationY. For our rotationY property we use the planeAngle number from earlier.

```
TweenLite.to(plane, 1, { rotationY:planeAngle,x:planeX,z:planeZ,ease:Quint.easeInOut } );
```

In our if statement where we are placing the items on the left, our math is almost identical, with a few important changes.

```
planeX = (currentPlaneIndex - planeIndex + 1) * -distanceApart;
TweenLite.to(plane, 1, { rotationY:-planeAngle,x:planeX,z:planeZ,ease:Quint.easeInOut } ) ;
```

Notice that now the math for our planeX is a little bit different. We are now subtracting planeIndex from our currentPlane index, and instead of multiplying by distanceApart we are multiplying by negative - distanceApart. Then for our tween the rotationY is also set to negative -planeAngle.

Finally, for this class we need a public method to update the colors of our planes.

```
public function changeMaterialColor(color:int):void
{
    for(var i:int = 0;i<colorCollection.length;i++)
    {
        colorCollection.setItemAt({color:color},i);
    }
}
```

We call changeMaterialColor, passing in any color value. This updates our arrayCollection, which dispatches an event that there was a change, thereby changing the tint of our movieClips in our materials.

Let's now connect this to Flex.

```
<?xml version="1.0" encoding="utf-8"?>
<s:Application xmlns:fx="http://ns.adobe.com/mxml/2009"
               xmlns:s="library://ns.adobe.com/flex/spark"
               xmlns:mx="library://ns.adobe.com/flex/mx" minWidth="1024" minHeight="768"
               frameRate="32"
               applicationComplete="applicationComplete()">

    <fx:Script>
        <![CDATA[
            import mx.core.UIComponent;

            private var coverflow:Coverflow;
            private var pv3dWrapper:UIComponent;
```

```
            private function applicationComplete():void
            {
                pv3dWrapper = new UIComponent();
                coverflow = new Coverflow();

                pv3dWrapper.addChild(coverflow);
                addElement(pv3dWrapper);

                coverflow.start();
            }

            private function colorPickerChanged():void
            {
                coverflow.changeMaterialColor(colorPicker.selectedColor)
            }
        ]]>
    </fx:Script>
    <s:HGroup paddingLeft="10" paddingTop="10">
        <s:Label text="Change Color"/>
        <mx:ColorPicker id="colorPicker" change="colorPickerChanged()"/>
    </s:HGroup>
</s:Application>
```

We first create our UIComponent to act as our wrapper so we can add it to our Flex application. Then we create an instance of our coverflow and call start(). Here we have also added a ColorPicker and label to the application. When we select a color from our color picker, it calls the colorPickerChanged function, which then calls changeMaterialColor inside our coverflow instance passing in the selected color. You'll notice each panel fading from one color to the next. Now we're done.

Here is the full source code for Coverflow.as.

```
package
{
    import com.greensock.TweenLite;
    import com.greensock.easing.Quint;
    import com.greensock.plugins.TintPlugin;
    import com.greensock.plugins.TweenPlugin;

    import flash.display.MovieClip;

    import mx.collections.ArrayCollection;
    import mx.events.CollectionEvent;
    import mx.utils.ColorUtil;

    import org.papervision3d.events.InteractiveScene3DEvent;
    import org.papervision3d.materials.MovieMaterial;
    import org.papervision3d.objects.primitives.Plane;
    import org.papervision3d.view.BasicView;

    public class Coverflow extends BasicView
    {
```

```
private var planes:Array = [];
private var colorBlocks:Array = [];
private var colorCollection:ArrayCollection = new ArrayCollection();
private var numberOfPlanes:Number = 5;
private var currentPlaneIndex:Number = 0;
private var planeAngle:Number = 35;
private var distanceApart:Number = 140;

public function start() : void
{
    //Activate our Tint Plugin
    TweenPlugin.activate([TintPlugin]);

    //Set viewport.interactive to true
    viewport.interactive = true;

    //Create the arrayCollection that holds our material colors
    createColorCollection();
    createChildren();
    startRendering();
    animate();
}

private function createColorCollection():void
{
    for(var i:int = 0;i<numberOfPlanes;i++)
    {
        //Adding just a generic starter color
        colorCollection.addItem({color:0x000000});
    }
    colorCollection.addEventListener
(CollectionEvent.COLLECTION_CHANGE,onCollectionChange);
}

private function createChildren() : void
{
    for (var planeIndex:int = 0; planeIndex < colorCollection.length; planeIndex++)
    {
        createPlaneWithMaterial(planeIndex);
    }
}

private function createPlaneWithMaterial(atIndex:int):void
{
    //Create MovieClip for Movie Material;
    var colorBlock:MovieClip = new MovieClip()
    colorBlock.graphics.beginFill(0);
    colorBlock.graphics.drawRect(0,0,200,400);
    colorBlock.graphics.endFill();

    //Create MovieMaterial
```

```
        var movieMat:MovieMaterial = new MovieMaterial(colorBlock);
        movieMat.interactive = true;
        movieMat.animated = true;

        //Apply Tint to movieClip used in Material
        applyTint(colorBlock,atIndex);

        //Create the plane
        var plane:Plane = new Plane(movieMat, 200, 400,4,4);

        //Add listener for plany click
        plane.addEventListener(InteractiveScene3DEvent.OBJECT_PRESS,↩
onPlaneClick,false,0,true);
        plane.id = atIndex;

        //Push items into arrays for later
        planes.push(plane);
        colorBlocks.push(colorBlock);

        //Add our plane to our PV3D scene
        scene.addChild(plane);
    }

    public function changeMaterialColor(color:int):void
    {
        for(var i:int = 0;i<colorCollection.length;i++)
        {
            colorCollection.setItemAt({color:color},i);
        }
    }

    //When the collection changes we need to update our items
    private function onCollectionChange(evt:CollectionEvent):void
    {
        var colorBlock:MovieClip = colorBlocks[evt.location];
        applyTint(colorBlock,evt.location);
    }

        //Use TweenLite to fade movieclip from one color to another
    private function applyTint(colorBlock:MovieClip,val:int):void
    {
        var color:int = ColorUtil.adjustBrightness(colorCollection[val].color,val * 20);
        TweenLite.to(colorBlock, 1, {tint:[color]});
    }

    //When a plane is clicked we need to go to that item
    private function onPlaneClick(evt:InteractiveScene3DEvent):void
    {
        currentPlaneIndex = evt.target.id;
        animate();
    }
```

```
        //Animate the coverflow left / right based off of currentPlaneIndexs
        private function animate():void
        {
            for (var planeIndex:int = 0; planeIndex < planes.length; planeIndex++)
            {
                var plane:Plane = planes[planeIndex];

                //Each if statement will adjust these numbers as needed
                var planeX:Number;
                var planeZ:Number;

                //Place  & Animate Center Item
                if (planeIndex == currentPlaneIndex)
                {
                    planeZ = -200
                    planeX = 0;
                    TweenLite.to(plane, 1,↵
{ rotationY:0,x:planeX,z:planeZ,ease:Quint.easeInOut } )
                }

                //Place & Animate Right Items
                if(planeIndex > currentPlaneIndex)
                {
                    planeZ = 0
                    planeX = (planeIndex - currentPlaneIndex + 1) *↵
distanceApart;
                    TweenLite.to(plane, 1,↵
{ rotationY:planeAngle,x:planeX,z:planeZ,ease:Quint.easeInOut } )
                }

                //Place & Animate Left Items
                if (planeIndex < currentPlaneIndex)
                {
                    planeZ = 0
                    planeX = (currentPlaneIndex - planeIndex + 1) *↵
-distanceApart;
                    TweenLite.to(plane, 1,↵
{ rotationY:-planeAngle,x:planeX,z:planeZ,ease:Quint.easeInOut } )
                }
            }
        }
}
```

Once you test your project, you'll see a beautiful Papervision coverflow where you can use the color picker to change the colors of the 3D planes.

Change Color

Figure 15-2. A fully working coverflow in Flex

Some ways that you could expand upon this would be to add left and right buttons or a scrollbar for alternative navigation. You could also change the materials to accept text data, images, etc. We've created the base—it's up to you to build upon what has been created.

Summary

In this chapter, we've just scratched the surface of the capability of Papervision. With very little work you can create amazing interactive experiences. The quickest way to learn is to just practice. The need to know Papervision will increase more and more as companies become aware of its possibilities. You can find tons of tutorials online, most of which relate only to Flash, but, as you have seen, we can quickly add them to our Flex project.

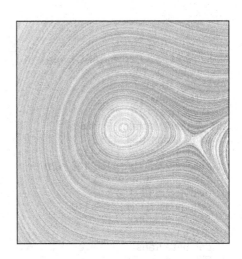

Index